Sharia Transformations

Sharia Transformations

Cultural Politics and the Rebranding
of an Islamic Judiciary

———

Michael G. Peletz

UNIVERSITY OF CALIFORNIA PRESS

University of California Press
Oakland, California

Library of Congress Cataloging-in-Publication Data

Names: Peletz, Michael G., author.
Title: Sharia transformations : cultural politics and the rebranding of an
    Islamic judiciary / Michael G. Peletz.
Description: Oakland, California : University of California Press, [2020] |
    Includes bibliographical references and index.
Identifiers: LCCN 2019042710 | ISBN 9780520339910 (cloth) |
    ISBN 9780520339927 (paperback) | ISBN 9780520974470 (ebook)
Subjects: LCSH: Islamic law—Malaysia. | Islam—Social aspects—Malaysia. |
    Islam and politics—Malaysia. | Islamic ethics—Malaysia. | Islamic law. |
    Islam and politics.
Classification: LCC KPG469.5 .P47 2020 | DDC 349.595—dc23
LC record available at https://lccn.loc.gov/2019042710

Manufactured in the United States of America

28 27 26 25 24 23 22 21 20
10 9 8 7 6 5 4 3 2 1

For Susan
And for Zachary and Alexander

CONTENTS

ILLUSTRATIONS

MAPS

TABLE

FIGURES

ACKNOWLEDGMENTS

This book draws on ethnographic research and archival study spanning four decades, during which time I have incurred innumerable debts. To all of the Malaysians and others I have thanked in previous publications, I would like to reiterate my heartfelt gratitude for the many kinds of assistance that made this project possible. The residents of the village that I refer to as Bogang, who welcomed me into their community in 1978–80 and 1987–88, deserve special mention for their hospitality, generosity, and willingness to share their knowledge, experiences, and quotidian life with me. Bogang is a pseudonym, as are the names of most living people (other than public figures) I discuss in the pages that follow. I utilize this convention in accordance with established anthropological practice, so as to protect the anonymity of those who shared their thoughts and views with me. My adoptive parents, who passed away some years ago, would have preferred that I use their real names, and were hurt that I did not do so. I wish that I had discussed the relevant issues with them in greater detail, in terms that would have made sense to them. For posterity, I want to identify them by their full names—Hajah Rahmah binti Haji Tahir and Haji Kassim bin Haji Bulat—and to use this occasion to again underscore my enduring gratitude for the deep kinship they extended to me, my wife, and my son Zachary.

Others in Malaysia to whom I offer thanks include Mano Maniam, former Executive Director of the Malaysian-American Commission on Educational Exchange (MACEE) and Shamsul A.B., of Universiti Kebangsaan Malaysia (Malaysian National University), both of whom have been marvelous friends, mentors, guides, and dining partners extraordinaire since we first met more than thirty years ago. Tan beng hui, an academic-activist whose work has focused on women and sexuality rights, has also been a valued friend and has kindly shared her expertise on some of the themes addressed in this book. The executive directors of the progressive Muslim feminist organization Sisters in Islam (SIS) have discussed their important work with me over the years and have offered feedback on the projects I have pursued in the *sharia* courts; for this I would especially like to thank Zainah Anwar, Norani Othman, Ratna Osman, and Rozana Isa.

At the University of Malaya (UM) I am indebted to Dean Azirah Binti Hashim for inviting me to join the Humanities and Ethics Research Cluster as Visiting Professor in July 2012. I am also grateful to Ahmad Hidayat Buang, Raihanah Binti Haji Abdullah, and Siti Zubaidah Binti Ismail for welcoming me in September-October 2013 as Visiting Professor in the Department of *Syariah* and Law at the Academy of Islamic Studies, and inviting me to participate in the UM research project on Islamic Law in Practice. Najibah Binti Najat provided much appreciated research assistance during that time. Thanks also to Hariz Shah, my research assistant in July 2018, for his help navigating not only religious and other state bureaucracies but also Kuala Lumpur's challenging roadways and traffic.

Judges and others in Malaysia's *sharia* judiciary deserve special recognition as well. Dato' Haji Mohamad Shakir bin Haji Abdul Hamid, Chief *Syariah* Judge of Penang and former Chief Registrar at the *Jabatan Kehakiman Syariah Malaysia* (JKSM; Malaysian Department of *Syariah* Judiciary) in Putrajaya, was incredibly generous with his time, providing voluminous quantitative data and other material relevant to the myriad questions I put to him, particularly in 2010–13. His successor at the JKSM, Hajah Noor Hadina Binti Ahmad Zabidi, was also quite helpful, as were *sharia* judges and their staff in Rembau, Negeri Sembilan, particularly Mohd. Abu Hassan Bin Abdullah and Wan Mohamad Helmi Bin Masran. The many registrars, prosecutors, mediation officers, lawyers, journalists, activists, artists, academics, and others in Kuala Lumpur, Selangor, Negeri Sembilan, Penang, and elsewhere who kindly gave of their time and shared their perspectives and expertise with me also helped make this a better book.

A variety of institutions and agencies have contributed financial support for my research and writing over the years. I would like to renew my thanks to the organizations that made my earlier research possible and register my gratitude to those that followed. Listed more or less chronologically, these institutions and agencies include the National Science Foundation, the University of Michigan (the Center for South and Southeast Asian Studies and the Rackham School of Graduate Studies), the Fulbright Scholar Program, the Wenner-Gren Foundation for Anthropological Research, the Social Science Research Council, Colgate University, the National Humanities Center, the Pacific Basin Research Center, the Erasmus Institute at the University of Notre Dame, the Institute for Advanced Study in Princeton, Emory University, the University of Malaya, the Koninklijk Instituut voor Taal-, Land- en Volkenkunde (KITLV), and the Rockefeller Foundation's Bellagio Center.

I have also had the good fortune of being the recipient of four separate fellowships from the National Endowment for the Humanities since the early 1990s. The completion of this book was made possible by the award of a residential fellowship from the Bill and Carol Fox Center for Humanistic Inquiry at Emory University (2018–19). For that gift I thank Walter Melion, Keith Anthony, Amy Erbil, and Colette Barlow, who run the Center with consummate professionalism and good humor.

Reem Abdalla, my undergraduate research assistant at Emory, was extremely conscientious and helpful in tracking down sources, following up my other queries and requests, and assisting me in preparing this book for publication. Another Emory undergraduate, Ikmal Adian Mohd Adil, merits mention and thanks as well both because of the extensive work he did for me at Emory and because he accompanied me to and took voluminous notes on many dozens of hearings and interviews in Malaysia's *sharia* courts and their civil counterparts in 2012.

A number of friends and colleagues have read early versions of parts of the manuscript and offered their wisdom and advice. In this connection I want to acknowledge my deep gratitude to Michael Gilsenan, former Director of the Hagop Kevorkian Center for Near Eastern Studies at New York University, who convened annual workshops on the study of Islamic Law and Society at the Kevorkian Center during the period 2010–16. I participated in six of those workshops, and in five of them I shared work in progress (early versions of portions of chapters 2–6). Michael assembled a vibrant group of specialists from diverse fields (anthropology, history, rhetoric, Islamic Studies, and international relations, among others), thus ensuring expansive and rewarding interdisciplinary dialogue. Attendees included Hussein Agrama, Fahad Bishara, Jonathan Brown, Guy Burak, Morgan Clarke, Matthew Erie, Samira Esmeir, Daragh Grant, Iza Hussin, Darryl Li, Jessica Marglin, Mark Massoud, Brinkley Messick, Tamir Moustafa, and Intisar Rabb, many of whom offered valuable feedback on early formulations of material in this book.

Jim Hoesterey read the penultimate draft of the manuscript and kindly offered critical suggestions and other comments. So too did two anonymous reviewers for UC Press who later authorized the press to share their identities with me: Robert Hefner and Lawrence Rosen. Susan Peletz read portions of the manuscript and offered many sensible suggestions based on her early career as a journalist. Individuals who commented on early versions of material in specific chapters are thanked in the acknowledgments preceding the notes to those chapters.

At the University of California Press, I am grateful to Reed Malcolm for his strong interest in the project and his assistance and guidance throughout the publication process. Archna Patel and Kate Hoffman also shared their expertise to make this a better book, as did Catherine Osborne and David Robertson, who undertook the copyediting and index, respectively. Thanks also to the publishers who granted permission to include material adapted from previous publications (Peletz 2013, 2015, 2016, 2018); and to Ellen Walker, who provided various kinds of assistance and support during the first two periods of fieldwork and also drew the maps and inspired the book's cover.

Friends, family, and fellow travelers who have provided inspiration and camaraderie over many years include Peter Balakian, Robert Hefner, Jim Hoesterey, Robert Hogan, Carla Jones, Bruce Knauft, Michael Lambek, Tamara Loos, David Nugent, Aihwa Ong, Sherry Ortner, Andrew Rotter, Patricia Sloane-White, Nancy Smith-Hefner, Amanda Whiting, and the late Aram Yengoyan. My siblings, Nan and Steve Peletz, have inspired me in countless ways and have always been there for me; I am exceedingly grateful for that enduring solidarity.

I wish that I had been able to show this book to my father, Cyril M. Peletz (1919–2018), who passed away before it went into production; it would have brightened his day. I dedicate the book to my wife, Susan, and my children, Zachary and Alexander; their gifts of love, support, and irreverent humor have greatly enriched my life.

ABBREVIATIONS AND ACRONYMS

ADR	Alternative dispute resolution
ABIM	Angkatan Belia Islam Malaysia (Malaysian Islamic Youth Movement)
IC	Identity Card
IIUM	International Islamic University of Malaysia
ISA	Internal Security Act
ISO	International Organization for Standardization
JAIS	Jabatan Agama Islam Negeri Selangor (Selangor Department of Islamic Religion)
JAKIM	Jabatan Kemajuan Islam Malaysia (Malaysian Department of Islamic Development)
JAWI	Jabatan Agama Islam Wilayah Persekutuan (Federal Territory Department of Islamic Religion)
JKSM	Jabatan Kehakiman Syariah Malaysia (Malaysian Department of *Syariah* Judiciary)
KLCC	Kuala Lumpur City Centre
KPI	Key performance indicator
MSC	Multi-Media Super Corridor
NDP	New Development Policy (1991–2001)
NEP	New Economic Policy (1971–90)
NGO	Non-governmental organization
OKB	*Orang kaya baru* (new rich people)
OWC	Obedient Wives Club
PAS	Parti Islam Se-Malaysia (Pan-Malaysian Islamic Party)
PC	Polygamy Club

PGSM   Persatuan Peguam Syarie Malaysia (Malaysian *Syarie* Lawyers
        Association)
RELA   Ikatan Relawan Rakyat Malaysia (The Malaysian People's Volunteer
        League)
RM   Ringgit Malaysia, the Malaysian unit of currency
SIS   Sisters in Islam
SO   *Sulh* officer
TQM   Total quality management
UKM   Univeristi Kebangsaan Malaysia (National University of Malaysia)
UM   Universiti Malaya (University of Malaya)
UMNO   United Malays National Organization
USIM   Universiti Sains Islam Malaysia (Islamic Science University of
        Malaysia)

NOTE ON SPELLING, TERMINOLOGY, AND CURRENCY

I spell most Malay terms, including those of Arabic origin, in accordance with the conventions of standard Malay as set out in Hajah Noresah bt. Baharom's (ed.) *Kamus Dewan*, 4th edition, 2015. The main exceptions involve citations of published material and designations of formal organizations that follow other guidelines, as well as references to *sharia* (variably rendered *syariah, syarak, shariah*, etc. in Malay), a term I use interchangeably with Islamic law. Official spelling conventions are not always followed in contemporary Malaysia; earlier practices still prevail in some cases, especially with regard to the rendering of people's names and titles, as well as aspects of Islamic law and religion. In the Malay language, a noun typically has the same form regardless of whether or not the context implies that its number is singular or plural. As is common scholarly practice, I adhere to this convention in citing Malay-language terms, except when quoting published material that conforms to other standards. Finally, following established usage, Malays and certain ethnic Chinese Malaysians are typically designated by that part of their name which appears first in the word order (unless they follow other practices), since this is the name by which they are known to most people in both formal and informal contexts; for example, Prime Minister Mahathir Mohamad (r. 1981–2003, 2018–present) is referred to as Prime Minister Mahathir, never as Prime Minister Mohamad. Bibliographic entries are consistent with these practices (i.e., Malay and a few Chinese Malaysian entries are alphabetized according to first name). In-text citations provide the full name (e.g., Mahathir Mohamad 2011). Readers who are not familiar with the Malay language may find it useful to consult the Glossary of Frequently Used Malay Terms.

Virtually all ethnic Malays are Muslims, following the Shafi'i legal tradition of Sunni Islam, and around 85 percent of the nation's Muslims are Malay (the others are mostly of Indonesian or South Asian ancestry); hence I commonly use the terms "Malay" and "Muslim" (and "non-Malay" and "non-Muslim") interchangeably when discussing the Malaysian context.

Malaysian currency is denominated in *ringgit*. One *ringgit* (RM$1) was equivalent in value to approximately US$0.46 at the time of my 1978–80 fieldwork and US$0.39 when I returned to the field in 1987–88. Subsequent years witnessed sharp fluctuations in the strength of the *ringgit*, which was pegged to the U.S. dollar from 1998 to 2005. At the time of my 2010–13 research the value of a *ringgit* ranged between US$0.31 and US$0.34. As of this writing (April 2019) it is worth approximately US$0.24.

GLOSSARY OF FREQUENTLY USED MALAY TERMS

Includes foreign (e.g., Arabic-origin) terms that are in common usage in Malaysia's Islamic courts or among Malays generally.

akal	Reason, rationality.
alim	Religious scholar, man of learning (pl. = *ulama*).
asal	Origins, social origins.
aurat	Parts of the body that must be clothed or covered.
baju Melayu	Malay (male) traditional costume with matching pants and shirt.
dakwah	To invite or call or answer the invitation or call; missionary work; Islamic resurgence.
edah	The one-hundred-day period following a divorce or a husband's death during which time a woman may not remarry and is normally entitled to support from her husband or his estate.
encik	Sir; Mr.
fasakh	Divorce by judicial proceedings; judicial rescission or voiding of marriage contract; annulment.
fatwa	Authoritative legal opinion or ruling by a *mufti* or other Islamic scholar.
fiqh	Islamic jurisprudence.
hadith	Written accounts of the sayings and deeds of the Prophet Muhammad.
haji	A man who has made the pilgrimage (*haj*) to Mecca (feminine = *hajah*).

hakim	Judge (civil or Islamic).
halal	Acceptable or permitted in Islam.
haram	Forbidden in Islam.
harta sepencarian	Conjugal earnings.
hudud	Laws bearing on various criminal offenses and some of the more severe penalties for their transgression, as specified in the Quran.
ijtihad	Judicial creativity.
ikrar	Oath, vow, pledge.
kadi	Judge or magistrate in an Islamic court.
khalwat	Illicit proximity.
khuluk	See *tebus talak.*
lafaz	Pronunciation, utterance, recitation (especially of standardized divorce formula).
liwat	Sodomy.
mufti	Juriconsult.
nafkah	Material maintenance and support that a man is normally required to provide his wife and children.
nafkah anak	Mandatory child support.
nafkah edah	Normally mandatory material maintenance and support for a divorcee through her *edah* period (usually three months and ten days).
nafsu	Passion, lust.
nasihat	Advice.
nusyuz	Spousal, especially wifely, disobedience.
puan	Madam; Mrs.
rujuk	Reconcile; reconciliation.
sharia	Islamic law.
songkok	Fez-like cap worn by Muslim males.
sulh	Mediation.
sumpah	An oath; to take an oath, to swear.
Surah	Chapter of the Quran.
taklik	Conditions attached to a marriage contract which, if broken, entitle a woman to divorce.
talak	Divorce of a wife through repudiation; pronouncement of divorce formula.
tebus talak	A type of divorce in which the wife compensates her husband for agreeing to release her (also known as *khuluk*).

telekung	Prayer cloak worn by Muslim females.
tudung	Headscarf worn by Malay/Muslim females; *hijab*.
ulama	Religious scholars; men of learning (sing. = *alim*).
ummah	Community of (Muslim) believers.
zina	Illicit sexual intercourse; fornication; adultery.

Introduction

Sharia, Cultural Politics, Anthropology

Few symbols in today's world are as laden and fraught as *sharia,* an Arabic-origin term referring to the straight path, the path God revealed for humans, the norms and rules guiding Muslims on that path, and Islamic law and normativity as enshrined in sacred texts or formal statutes. A number of historical and other factors help explain the heightened centrality of the term *sharia* in contemporary global discourse and the intensity of the emotions and imagery it evokes. One has to do with the emergence in recent decades of violent fringe groups such as Boko Haram in Nigeria and the Islamic State (ISIS) in Syria and Iraq. These groups seek the instantiation of *sharia* as the law of the land, much like the Taliban in Afghanistan and the global network known as al-Qaeda, all of which continue to wage armed struggle against military forces from a number of allied nations.

Another relevant factor is the rise in the new millennium of Muslim terrorist cells in Europe and elsewhere whose disaffected members sometimes claim allegiance to ISIS and do, in any event, exercise a disproportionate influence on Westerners' understandings of and attitudes towards the world's 1.8 billion Muslims, the religion of Islam, and *sharia* in particular. It is largely because of the outsized influence of such groups and networks that politicians and journalists in the West have sometimes seized on *sharia* as a preeminent threat to their own liberal-democratic societies. Some have argued that even its limited accommodation in the form of state recognition of "*sharia* councils" formed to help manage marital disputes and other conflicts in Muslim communities in Western nations, typically through mediation, negotiation, and compromise, is an exceedingly dangerous, slippery slope that must be avoided at all costs. And a number of them have sponsored legislation to that end. This despite the fact that such councils as have been

1

established in the United States and United Kingdom, for example, typically lack formal powers of adjudication (Bowen 2012). Arguably more relevant is that most Western constitutions already categorically prohibit the prioritizing of religious laws over their ostensibly secular counterparts, thus rendering the proposed legislation altogether redundant and unnecessary (Emon 2016; Broyde 2017). It would appear that "anti-*sharia* activists" operating in Western contexts are more concerned to stoke and rally fear than to achieve meaningful legislative change.

The widespread Western view that the existence of *sharia* is a dilemma that needs to be resolved, ideally by its elimination, is sharply at odds with most Muslim perspectives on *sharia*, though this should not be taken as support for the largely discredited "clash of civilizations" thesis. Muslims typically view *sharia* as a repertoire of sacred resources bequeathed to them by God for the management or solution of problems, and a guide for life's uncertainties, precarities, and rewards, not a problem in need of resolution. And for many (perhaps most) of them a key challenge, at once spiritual, ethical, and sometimes political, is how to safeguard its majesty and ideally revive it in the face of strong historical and contemporary pressures arrayed against it. Relevant in this context is that in most Muslim-majority countries, the jurisdiction, power, and prestige of courts involved in the implementation of *sharia* have long been seriously constrained in relation to the systems of civil courts established by colonizers and other modernizing elites throughout the Muslim world during the high period of European colonial rule from 1870 to 1930. Indeed, present-day *sharia* courts are commonly confined to matters of Islamic "family law" and other personal status law; this is often all that remains of an historically male-dominated religious community's "collective right to religious liberty and their sovereignty over a domain in which they are understood to have jurisdiction" (Mahmood 2012, 56). Campaigns by political and religious elites and "ordinary Muslims" (defined as those who are not in the forefront of political or religious movements) to expand the jurisdiction of the *sharia* are thus part of efforts, increasingly common throughout the Global South and the West alike, to reclaim the glory and majesty of a real or imagined past along with the cultural authenticity and political sovereignty imaginatively associated with it.

Sometimes complicating such endeavors are the views of eminent scholars of *sharia*. Some of these scholars argue that current instantiations of *sharia* in Muslim-majority nations' formal legal arenas bear no resemblance to the *sharia* of classical and other pre-modern times (An-Na'im 2008; Hallaq 2009, 2013); and that present-day attempts to create modern states whose constitutions and other institutions of governance are grounded in *sharia* are deeply misguided, if not potentially disastrous, judging from the experiences of places like Sudan (Massoud 2013). These, more generally, are some of the other reasons why *sharia* is a powerful, polyvalent symbol of past, present, and future, one that will likely galvanize the emotions of diverse groups—in diverse ways—for some time to come.

Clearly relevant as well is the florescence of Islamic piety and religiosity that we have seen since the early 1970s among ordinary Muslims, a trend that has gone hand-in-hand with diverse manifestations of a resurgent or revitalized Islam in public and private arenas alike. Certain forms of this Islam are oriented primarily toward cultivating more meaningful relationships with God through the refinement of techniques of prayer and worship and the development of various other technologies of the self that are keyed to ethical self-fashioning. Some of these are not particularly socially or politically engaged (Mahmood 2005; Hirschkind 2009; Hoesterey 2016). Others highlight one or another dimension of such engagement (Deeb 2006; Wickham 2013). Some of the latter are strongly activist; still others are occasionally (though not commonly) militant, and sometimes—though this is quite rare in a statistical sense when one considers the entire global population of Muslims—violent. The evidence thus adduced comes from most parts of the Muslim world. Scholars of comparative religion rightfully point out, however, that we see generally similar dynamics in predominantly Christian contexts, as well as among Jews, Hindus, Sikhs, and Buddhists (Casanova 1994; Juergensmeyer 2003; Luhrmann 2012), thus offering a vital corrective to the idea of modern "Muslim exceptionalism." As with capitalist markets, modern states, and civil society, public religions may be here to stay. This despite their much-heralded demise in most of the literature bearing on modernization produced during the twentieth century, which posited both the decline of religious beliefs and practices and their relegation to marginalized private domains as a key signifier if not the *sine qua non* for joining the ranks of the modern (Asad 2003).

Many scholars have conceptualized these dynamics as manifestations of processes involving the deprivatization of religion or the desecularization of public life. Others, assuming they are dealing with Muslim-majority nations in which *sharia* has gained currency, refer to the Islamization or *sharia*tization of legal systems, state structures, or national cultures (e.g., Hamayotsu 2002; Kepel 2002; Fealy 2005; Shaikh 2007; Salim 2008; Lee 2010; Liow 2009; Ricklefs 2012). Academic growth-industries, think tanks, and media circuses have sprung up in the wake of these processes. I would argue, though, that in many instances both the processes and their entailments are poorly understood. This is particularly so when one ranges beyond the conventional area foci of Islamic studies—the Middle East and North Africa—and engages data from Southeast Asian nations such as Malaysia, a religiously and ethnically diverse Muslim-majority country that in recent decades has experienced stunning rates of urbanization, educational attainment, and sustained economic growth that are probably second to none in the Muslim world. The Malaysian case is of further significance because in the 1980s and 1990s the nation's political and religious elites enjoyed a reputation in much of the world for representing the best of Islam and modernity, if not "*the* 'shining light' of moderate Islam" (Shamsul A. B. 2001, 4709; emphasis added), and also offered their formula for national development as a model for the entire Global South (Hilley 2001). The questions thus become: How are processes of Islamization playing out in Malaysia? What types of discourses and dynamics characterize the operations of the *sharia* judiciary, which is an important player in a wide array of legal, political, and religious arenas? And what comparative-historical and theoretical insights can this material help generate?

One of the main arguments I develop in this book has to do with the heuristic value, in the Malaysian setting and elsewhere, of the term "Islamization," which is commonly utilized to gloss the heightened salience of Islamic symbols, norms, discursive traditions, and attendant practices across one or more domains of lived experience.[1] I suggest that as it is generally used by Western social scientists and other observers since the late 1970s and the 1979 Iranian Revolution in particular, the term obscures an understanding of recent developments bearing on Malaysia's increasingly powerful *sharia* judiciary, especially those implicated in its actual workings and the directions in which it is currently moving. Many of these latter developments involve bureaucratization, rationalization, and corporatization, rather than a "return to tradition," as the term "Islamization" is sometimes taken to imply. And they are heavily informed by common-law norms and sensibilities (associated with the legal traditions inherited from British colonizers); by the rebranding of long-standing Malay practices in specifically Islamic and Arabic terms; and, more recently, by Japanese systems of management and auditing that Malaysian state authorities have embraced. In order to make sense of the vicissitudes of change in the realm of Islamic law and governance, I find it useful to regard Malaysia's *sharia* judiciary as a global assemblage in Ong and Collier's (2005) sense of the term, especially if we keep squarely in mind that it is simultaneously "a project, a terrain and target" (Cohen 1995, 39), and that it is situated in a more encompassing juridical field (Bourdieu 1987) dominated by the civil judiciary, the secular constitution, and the global forces impinging on them.

Brief clarification of the term "assemblage" will be helpful here. The *New Oxford American Dictionary* (Jewell and Abate 2001) explicates the concept with entries such as "a machine or object made of pieces fitted together" and "a work of art made by grouping found or unrelated objects." Rough analogs include a conglomeration and a miscellany. Claude Lévi-Strauss's (1966) notions of *bricolage* and *bricoleur* are both apposite, even though what Lévi-Strauss means by *bricolage* and what Ong, Collier, and the contributors to their edited volume mean by assemblage are very different, as are the contexts in which the terms are invoked and the objectives of their use. *Bricolage* is relevant because of its attention to processes and products of assembling, constructing, or creating "by means of a heterogeneous repertoire," i.e., fiddling, tinkering, and, by extension, creatively utilizing "whatever is at hand," regardless of its provenance or original purpose (Lévi-Strauss 1966, 17); *bricoleur* because it emphasizes that the processes and products are the result of creative human agency involved in doing odd jobs, repairing. Of more immediate relevance is Deleuze and Guattari's (1987) work, which builds on Marx, Kafka, and Foucault, and informs both the Ong and Collier (2005) volume mentioned above and this book. Deleuze and Guattari's concept of assemblage highlights "diversity, differentiation, and mobility" as well as multiplicities, metamorphoses, and anomalies (1987, 503). Unlike Lévi-Strauss's corpus, Deleuze and Guattari's is practice-oriented, drawing attention to assemblages as power-laden and "imbricated heterogenous forms" that "may open onto and . . . [be] carried off by other types of assemblages" (1987, 509, 530–31n39), and that are in any event "contested, temporal, and emergent" (Clifford 1986, 19; Rabinow 1999; Latour 2005, 2010; Marcus and Saka 2006; Sassen 2008; Dovey 2010; Tsing 2015).

To characterize Malaysia's *sharia* judiciary as a global assemblage is to suggest, further, that it is profitably viewed in relation to the global circulation of goods, services, discourses, and structural imperatives and constraints of various kinds, including those associated with neoliberal globalization. From this perspective, Malaysia's *sharia* judiciary is composed of a congeries of contested sites characterized by the interplay of a number of heavily freighted, globally inflected discourses, practices, values, and interests of disparate origins. The content of this assemblage will be empirically unpacked as I proceed. Suffice it to add that its heterogeneities and contingencies, like its mutually contradictory transformations, are the "product of multiple determinations that are not reducible to a single logic" (Collier and Ong 2005, 12). To put some of this differently, the concept of global assemblage is valuable both because the *sharia* judiciary is a good example of a global assemblage, and because the notion of global assemblage helps us comprehend features of the judiciary that have been poorly understood or elided in most accounts of Malaysia's Islamization and modernity.

A few words on the terms "globalization" and "neoliberal globalization" are also in order. Like *sharia,* albeit for other reasons, they are invoked by different scholars in different ways, certain of which involve starkly dissimilar assessments of their putative benefits and effects, some arguably utopian, others decidedly not. By "globalization" I refer to processes commonly held to date from the 1970s that have involved the rapid acceleration and increasingly pronounced (though locally variable) impact of transnational, planet-wide flows of capital, labor, goods, services, information, and discourses of various kinds. These processes entail deregulation—a weakening if not dismantling of the national and other barriers to such flows—as well as what David Harvey (1990) famously glossed as "time-space compression" (see also Comaroff and Comaroff 2000).

I use the term "neoliberal globalization" to designate the variants of these processes that are inflected by doctrines of neoliberalism. These doctrines extol the virtues of a number of analytically distinct, sometimes mutually contradictory, phenomena; we are not dealing with a single, undifferentiated "it entity." These include:

(1) the restructuring and reform of government or the paring back of social-welfare services and state agencies through business models developed in the private/corporate sector, or both;

(2) the privatization, corporatization, and commodification of enterprises, activities, and resources formerly owned or managed by the state;

(3) the shifting of wealth to those at the top of the social-class hierarchy;

(4) market-based technologies of governance coupled with policies geared toward "responsibilizing" citizen-subjects and fostering subjectivities conducive to self-management and self-actualization; and

(5) private enterprise pursued by innovative, risk-taking, flexible, adaptable selves.

It is useful, following James Ferguson (2009), to distinguish between neoliberal doctrines and neoliberal cultures, projects, and techniques. This is partly because elites may profess fealty to neoliberal doctrines but may not necessarily evince a commitment or ability to realize the full range of such doctrines in the projects or techniques of governance they implement. Malaysian political and economic elites, for example, are generally speaking strongly (but at times ambivalently) committed to many doctrines widely associated with neoliberalism, but they do not embrace all of them. One they do not embrace has to do with the notion that state agencies should be trimmed back; another involves the idea that the primary responsibility for redressing poverty (e.g., among Malays) and the redistribution of wealth (e.g., from non-Malays to Malays) lies with "the market," and that the state should play a negligible role in these matters.

The heterogeneity of projects and techniques implemented in ostensible accordance with neoliberal doctrines leads some scholars to speak of neoliberal or global assemblages (Ong and Collier 2005; Ferguson 2009; see also Tsing 2015). I find this approach useful, partly for reasons mentioned earlier. I consider it all the more valuable in light of the fact that the "anthropology of Islam" (Asad 1986; Eickelman and Piscatori 1996; Osella and Soares 2010; Bowen 2012) has only recently begun to seriously engage neoliberalism (notable exemplars of such engagement include Rudnyckyj 2010; Fischer 2016; Hoesterey 2016).[2] Even when doing so, moreover, it has not usually engaged neoliberalism's punitive features, their pastoral counterparts, or the mutually constitutive nature of these phenomena.

Scholars in a number of academic fields have shown that neoliberal globalization is commonly associated with, and perhaps directly entails, a "punitive turn" in both cultural-political and more narrowly legal realms (Garland 2001; Pratt et al 2005; Wacquant 2009; Alexander 2010 [2012]; Lancaster 2011). The surge in punitiveness is by no means uniform across cases or within them, and is variably evident in a number of analytically distinct domains. These include: the expanded scope and force of technologies of surveillance, discipline, and control; the criminalization of activities previously held to be legal; harsher punishments and increased rates of incarceration; the expansion of post-detention regimes of surveillance and shaming; the erosion of presumptions that persons formally charged with or merely suspected of crimes are innocent until proven guilty; and increased fears and anxieties bearing on Others, Otherness, and attendant indices of potentially menacing irregularity (Lianos and Douglas 2000).

The correlation between the onset and entrenchment of neoliberalism and a rising tide of punitiveness is strongly positive but not universal; Canada, Scandinavia, and Italy are among the exceptions that prove the rule (Pratt et al 2005). Might Malaysia be yet another exception that proves the rule? In the 1980s and 1990s, after all, it enjoyed a previously noted reputation for representing the best of Islam and modernity. And what kinds of evidence from Malaysia's *sharia* judiciary might help us answer this important and generative question?

The short answer to the first of these questions is that like many Western nations (the United States, the United Kingdom, France) Malaysia has indeed become more punitive in recent decades. We see abundant evidence of this if we examine continuities and transformations in micro-political processes in the *sharia* courts over the past few decades. It is important to appreciate, however, that a rising tide of punitiveness commonly goes hand-in-hand with developments that Foucault (1979 [2000], 2007) refers to as "pastoral." The latter term designates types of care, leadership, and governance that emphasize beneficence, salvation, and the well-being of both the unique individual and the group as a whole. In his analysis of the workings of the postcolonial state in India, Akhil Gupta (2012) argues that the pastoral face of some government programs in rural areas distracts citizen-subjects' attention from, and in this and other ways helps legitimize, a wide variety of highly unsavory state effects. Some of these entail bureaucratized structural violence on an exceedingly large scale, resulting in more than 250 million and perhaps as many as 427 million persons living below the poverty line and the "excess deaths," due to poverty, malnutrition, and largely preventable diseases, of some two million Indians annually (2012, 1, 5). In her work on Southeast Asia, Aihwa Ong (1999, 2006) takes a different approach, emphasizing "graduated sovereignty" and the kindred notion of "graduated citizenship." Both of these involve the state "making different kinds of biopolitical investments in different subject populations, privileging one gender over the other," for example, and "in certain kinds of human skills, talents, and ethnicities" (1999, 217), some of which are encouraged and rewarded while others are effectively punished. Whether one focuses on state effects and structural violence or on clines of sovereignty and citizenship, the cautionary points are clear: the punitive and the pastoral are different sides of the same coin of governance, and, as such, should not be viewed in zero-sum terms.

The same is true of punitive and rehabilitative (or restorative) justice, though in any given empirical case one may be hegemonic in relation to the other(s). Phrased more generally, because punitiveness and pastoralism, like social justice and pluralism, are invariably graduated, our investigations must be attentive both to the intricacies of context and to their sometimes subtle historical transformations.

The political and religious elites charged with overseeing Malaysia's *sharia* judiciary and charting its (to them, ideally enhanced) future are clearly concerned with the dispensing of justice, both punitive and pastoral, as are judges and other officers of the court. Most of these elites are Malays who hold influential positions in (or have been carefully vetted by) the secular and religious bureaucracies of the state apparatus, although some are prominent in opposition parties, Islamist organizations, think tanks, advisory boards, and consultancies (Liow 2009; tan beng hui 2012; Sloane-White 2017). Operating under the watchful gaze of the Prime Minister's Department, which has direct jurisdiction and control over the *sharia* judiciary, they also tend to share a pronounced concern with augmenting the legitimacy accorded *sharia* courts and *sharia* law generally both by members of the civil judiciary and by society at large, including, not least, the country's non-Muslim citizenry. Non-Muslims, who are mostly Chinese and Indians, comprise nearly 40 percent of the nation's population; in accordance with the Federal Constitution, they are not subject to *sharia*. But a number of controversial cases and high-profile programs introduced in recent decades, such as "The Harmonization of Laws," formerly known, more controversially, as "The Islamization of Laws," have made clear that their immunity from Islamic law and normativity is increasingly contingent, and that they could well come more squarely under the jurisdiction of *sharia* in the years to come. It is partly with an eye toward winning the hearts and minds of non-Muslims that state authorities, whom I sometimes refer to as social engineers, have undertaken a systematic rebranding of the *sharia* judiciary since the early 1990s. Kindred concerns to upgrade its image as a backwater or poor cousin in relation to the more powerful and prestigious civil judiciary are also in play, as is the goal of attracting the foreign capital necessary to secure Malaysia's place at the center of global Islamic banking and finance, whose assets in 2017 were estimated to exceed US$2.1 trillion.[3]

This rebranding is part of a story of cultural production, more specifically of juridical production in Bourdieu's (1987) terms, and is a major concern of this book. So too is the relative efficacy of the rebranding and whether it might involve, as some critics suggest, what the business and advertising literature refers to as "ambush marketing" (Hoek and Gendall 2002). For our purposes, such marketing involves the promotion of a new product by capitalizing on the popularity, prestige, or legitimacy of one or more well-known entities—Nike athletic shoes; the Olympics; iPhones; Malaysia's civil judiciary—in ways that are (contractually) illegal, unethical, or politically suspect.

Courts and more encompassing juridical fields almost everywhere are heavily gendered spaces. The Muslim world is no exception: key laws and norms are skewed in favor of men; most judges are men; most plaintiffs are women; and most defendants are their current or former husbands (Hirsch 1998; Peletz 2002; Tucker 2008; Osanloo 2009; Zainah Anwar 2009; Mir-Hosseini et al 2015; Rosen 2018). Circumstances such as these, along with mass-mediated accounts of "honor killings" and other real or imagined forms of Oriental excess and irrationality, help explain why politicians, journalists, and others in the West often argue that "Muslim women need saving" (Abu-Lughod 2013). One problem with these kinds of arguments is that they gloss over gender biases in Western and other non-Muslim legal arenas that provide the implicit comparative point of reference (see, e.g., Merry 1990, Conley and O'Barr 1998).

Partly so as to avoid the pitfalls of such arguments and the perspectives associated with them, I start with a clean (gendered) slate and pose a series of questions deriving from my ethnographic and historical research since the late 1970s. The most general question is: How are we to understand changes (and continuities) in women's and men's experiences in the courts, along with shifts in the courts' engagements with heteronormativity, since the late 1970s? Subsidiary questions concern whether women are currently getting more (alternatively, less) justice than previously, and how these developments might relate to the rise of an increasingly rigid heteronormativity in *sharia* legal arenas and society at large. The punitive turn taken by the courts in recent decades is relevant here inasmuch as the majority of defendants are men, and since their mistreatment of their wives and children is more heavily penalized than in times past. This is one of the grounds on which to argue that women are getting more justice than in earlier decades (assuming they embrace increasingly salient strictures of "obedience" and heteronormativity), though there are others, including the foregrounding and valorization of women's rights in discourse and practice alike.

Developments such as these merit serious attention both in their own right and in light of their implications for dynamics of kinship, gender, and sexuality. They also provide useful counterbalance to my data and arguments bearing on Malaysia's punitive turn. As such they leaven the "dark anthropology that focuses on the harsh dimensions of social life (power, domination, inequality, and oppression)" (Ortner 2016, 47), which presentation of this material necessarily entails. Put differently, they make hope practical, to paraphrase Raymond Williams (1982) when he argued that scholarly observers of the human condition have a moral obligation not just to document dynamics conducive to social injustice and destruction, but also to draw attention to possibilities that encourage hopefulness. I would not want to overstate the point, however, by claiming that, overall, this book exemplifies an "anthropology of the good" that centers on such themes as how our interlocutors in the field engage "value, morality, well-being, ... empathy, ... [and] care" (Robbins 2013, 448) or freedom, virtue, dignity, and "the good life for humanity" (Lambek 2010, 6).

FIGURE 1. In the field: *Sulh* officer in conversation with the author, his research assistant Najat (to author's immediate right) and others, Rembau, Negeri Sembilan, 2013. Photo by *Sharia* Court Staff.

Readers will encounter material relevant to these important concerns in the pages that follow, but the thrust of the discussion lies elsewhere.

A final introductory comment bears on methodology. I conducted eighteen months of ethnographic fieldwork in Malaysia during 1978–80, by which time I had already attained good working proficiency in Malay (the national language); seven months in 1987–88; and seven months since then, primarily in 2010–13 and 2018. During the first two stretches of fieldwork I engaged in participant observation and carried out (mostly informal) interviews on a daily basis, and also undertook village-wide household surveys and archival research. In the second and third periods of fieldwork I observed and took extensive notes on approximately 185 motions and hearings in the *sharia* courts, chiefly in Rembau and Kuala Lumpur. During this time my research assistants observed another twenty-five *sharia* court hearings, providing me with relatively complete transcripts and other notes. In addition, I interviewed over sixty current and former judges, lawyers, and other officials in the *sharia* judiciary (many of them on multiple occasions), some of whom shared crucial historical perspectives and other longitudinal data discussed below. I also attended more than 120 motions and hearings in the nation's civil courts for comparative purposes.[4]

ORGANIZATION OF THE BOOK

This book is composed of five chapters, in addition to this introduction and a conclusion. Chapter 1 lays out the case for viewing Malaysia's *sharia* judiciary as a global assemblage. It does this by describing and analyzing the empirical complexities and heterogeneity of the *sharia* judiciary and the multiple directions it is moving, especially in terms of its day-to-day operations and the ways that the nation's social engineers and brand stewards are endeavoring to rebrand and otherwise represent it to variously defined publics. Here I begin to illustrate *sharia's* complex entanglements with phenomena of highly variegated provenance that simultaneously highlight its relations of exteriority as distinct from its internal "essences" (DeLanda 2006). These phenomena include: myriad elements of common law, reflecting the legacy of British colonialism and the postcolonial centrality of the common law in the nation's constitution and more encompassing juridical field; e-governance, an emergent feature of governmentality built around densely networked channels of electronic communication and surveillance; and a much celebrated system of Japanese management and auditing that authorities in the *sharia* judiciary and the governmental apparatus as a whole have recently embraced. I also develop the more general argument, subsequently fleshed out in more detail, that analytically distinct processes of bureaucratization, rationalization, corporatization, and neoliberal globalization are at least as relevant, and arguably far more salient, than those commonly subsumed under the gloss of "Islamization," though I also make clear that by various criteria the *sharia* courts are "more Islamic" than they used to be.

Chapter 2, "A Tale of Two Courts," provides ethnographic and historical perspectives drawn from two distinct periods of fieldwork separated by nearly a quarter-century. I begin with background material on the training of Islamic judges and then present an overview of micropolitical practices of conflict management in the *sharia* court of Rembau, a small town located about sixty miles south of Kuala Lumpur (the nation's capital), as I encountered them in my fieldwork in the late 1980s. I proceed with a discussion of changes (and some continuities) in the appearance, discourses, and practices of that court that I observed during subsequent fieldwork conducted during 2011–13. Ensuing sections of the chapter include the transcript of a hearing that took place in 2012, followed by commentary aimed at highlighting its broad relevance. The remainder of the chapter engages the punitive turn that is evident in the latter case and in the transcript from a 2013 hearing involving a man's unauthorized repudiation of his wife. The surge in punitiveness, as we shall see, is also apparent in new forms of criminality and what I refer to as "creeping criminalization."

The comparative-historical approach I adopt in this chapter and subsequently, along with insights generated by usage of a modified version of Bourdieu's (1987) notion of the juridical field, allows us to productively situate some of the oftentimes abstract, hypothetical, and free-floating *sharia*-talk heard in different quarters of Malaysian society and globally. It is beyond the scope of my discussion to consider how and why *sharia*-talk often acquires these (abstract, hypothetical, free-floating) qualities globally, but a few comments will be helpful in providing additional context for this chapter and those that follow. Part of the dynamic has to do with the heterogeneity of symbols, idioms, norms, moral registers, discursive traditions, and related phenomena that are associated with the Quran and *hadith* (see note 1). Additionally, both popular and elite Muslim understandings of what is congruent or compatible with such texts vary considerably through time and space, as do some of the ambiguities, ambivalences, and contradictions linked with them (An-Nai'm 2008, Hallaq 2009, 2013, Ahmed 2016). Many contemporary interpretations of Islam and of *sharia* in particular, moreover, tend to be both "contingent and conjunctural" (Hefner 2016a, 3), embedded as they commonly are in the legal and ethical regimes of modernizing postcolonial states with unique histories (of legal pluralism and much else) and distinctive visions of and for the future. Amplifying these dynamics is the fact that *sharia* and *sharia*-talk (sometimes focusing on the higher principles and aims of *sharia* [*maqasid al-sharia*], other times on legal codes and their details) are increasingly pressed into service by different groups of Muslim political and religious elites (some absolutists, others not) to negotiate juridical fields and competing social imaginaries, and to advance diverse projects keyed to moral renewal, nation-building, and state formation. The twofold bottom line here is that, globally speaking, there is significant variation in the ways Muslims imagine, understand, and talk about *sharia;* and that *sharia*-talk is often rather radically untethered to—and otherwise free floating vis-à-vis—the empirical realities of the state-controlled *sharia* judiciaries that are tasked with managing key features of modern Muslims' lives.

My approach also allows for a clear, explicitly historicized view of how the relevant discourses and social forces play out "on the ground," in relation to an ever more corporate Islamic governmentality and the rise in punitiveness that is evident both in legal domains and in the nation's cultural-political realms generally. My understanding of "relevant" discourses and social forces is quite broad. For as is true in other Muslim-majority nations, many of the crucial streams of thought and congeries of social forces bearing on *sharia* and ethics are of wildly disparate provenance and have less to do with debates over the intricacies of belief, ritual, and sacred text than with expansive questions of governmentality, asking how best to discipline and control the nation's citizenry and help guide them to a more prosperous and secure future.

Chapter 3, "What Are *Sulh* Sessions?," engages the pastoral face of the *sharia* judiciary. It focuses on *sulh* (mediation) sessions, formally introduced in the early years of the new millennium, that are designed to provide litigants, especially women, with a forum to air their grievances in their own voices, in a no-holds-barred sort of way. Social engineers and brand stewards have represented this juridical innovation to the Malay/Muslim public in heavily Islamic and Arabic terms, as a "return to (classical) tradition." This despite its longstanding Malay precedents, formally unacknowledged; its heavy borrowings, also generally unacknowledged, from the alternative dispute resolution (ADR) movement that has its proximate roots in the United States and dates mostly from the mid-1970s (Nader 2002); and the fact, also generally glossed over, that the push for mediation as an alternative to formal adjudication began to feature prominently in Malaysia's civil-court arenas around the same time it began to take shape in their *sharia* counterparts. These latter dynamics are part and parcel of the global dissemination of Euro-American legal models to streamline legal proceedings, unclog the courts, and facilitate the flow of transnational capital (Dezalay and Garth 2002, 2010).

My interests in *sulh* stem in part from these dynamics. They also reflect debates within the scholarly community concerning whether there is a distinctively "Islamic" mode of "doing" law. Many distinguished scholars have argued that a uniquely Islamic legal mode has long existed and was evident in classical *sharia* practice that prominently featured *ijtihad,* a polyvocalic term referring to judicial creativity (Rosen 1989, Hallaq 2009). Other eminent scholars contest this claim (An-Na'im 2008). Still others contend that whichever position may be more meritorious, the empirical operation of *sharia* in the Muslim world is so complex that it is exceedingly reductionist to confine one's ethnographic and historical investigations to matters of "authenticity" (Agrama 2012, 179). I share this latter perspective, but I also think that aspects of the debates outlined here warrant consideration. Partly for these reasons, this chapter presents the transcripts of two *sulh* hearings I attended in 2013, along with commentary on each case as well as a discussion of officials' views concerning both the merits of *sulh* and the ethical dilemmas of formal adjudication, which some regard as an unwelcome feature of the "culture of litigation imposed on Muslim societies during the colonial days" (Syed Khalid Rashid 2008, 10).

Chapter 4, "Discourse, Practice, and Rebranding in Kuala Lumpur's *Sharia* Courthouse," deals with the aesthetics and the legal, socio-spatial, and cultural-political dynamics of the new *sharia* courthouse serving Kuala Lumpur that opened in 2011. These phenomena provide valuable perspectives on nationwide developments both within and far beyond *sharia* arenas that have occurred or are likely to do so in the years ahead. This is largely because Kuala Lumpur, in addition to being the nation's capital and largest metropolis, is the center from which formal enactments and promising juridical experiments "trickle down" to jurisdictions throughout the country. Especially noteworthy are three related sets of dynamics. The first is the ascendancy in Kuala Lumpur's *sharia* courtrooms of lawyers, illustrated by the transcript of a hearing I attended in 2012. The second is lawyers' effective sidelining of litigants and (to some extent) judges in hearings, and the relative outsourcing and privatization of justice involved in these developments. The third is the state's myriad efforts to rebrand the *sharia* assemblage, which are particularly evident in Kuala Lumpur though certainly not limited to the nation's capital.

Building on themes taken up in earlier sections of the book, this chapter elaborates on how the state's sartorial advisors and other social engineers have sought to rebrand *sharia* judges and the courts over which they exercise relative dominion. One way they have done this is by introducing black business suits as judges' new uniform, to replace their more "traditional" Malay attire. This rebranding operates on a number of contrasting though related levels. It involves the sharp demarcation of differences between new and old *sharia* judges and the simultaneous muting of dissimilarities between *sharia* judges and their more prestigious and powerful civil counterparts. It also effaces the distinction between loyalty to a specific ethnic group (Malays) and religion (Islam), and allegiance to a cosmopolitan, global ("trans-eth-nic") community that does not prioritize "primordial" sentiments associated with a particular language, culture, ethnicity/race, or religion. More generally, the rebrand-ing aims to reassure non-Malays, especially the non-Muslims within their ranks, that the *sharia* judiciary embraces increasingly universal standards and normativi-ties bearing on justice and due process, and that they need not be apprehensive about Islamization, *sharia*tization, or the further advance of Malay supremacy. The con-cluding sections of the chapter examine the extent to which the rebranding has been effective and whether it might be said to involve subterfuge or "ambush marketing."

Chapter 5, "Are Women Getting (More) Justice?," addresses themes that emerge in previous chapters, albeit in a more explicitly historicized and otherwise system-atic way. A question here is why family law ostensibly grounded in religion is frequently represented by Western scholars, local activists, the international human-rights community, and others as deeply unfriendly to women, if not back-ward-looking and anachronistic. One goal of the chapter is to complicate this imagery by describing and analyzing a relatively "female-friendly" pattern of his-torical shifts in the domain of Islamic family law since the late 1970s. A second, related goal is suggested by John Borneman's (1992, 75) research on kinship, family law, and belonging in Berlin shortly before the reunification of the city in 1990. To paraphrase, this involves illustrating how states endeavor to define, codify, and normalize particular kinds of relations and particular kinds of selves that political and religious elites see as essential to the constitution of citizens as subjects. In pursuit of this goal, I examine the role played by *sharia* courts, which are integral features of the state apparatus and the components of the state that I foreground in this chapter, in the cultural politics of marriage and gender pluralism as a whole.[5]

The conclusion provides a summary of the book's main arguments, particularly those concerning global assemblages, punitive turns, and rebranding, along with brief comments on some of their comparative and theoretical implications. It also addresses the value of the kind of historical-anthropological perspectives that I have brought to bear on *sharia*, law, and cultural politics, and offers some thoughts on useful directions for future anthropological research relevant to juridical fields, legal liberalism, and "extremism" in the Muslim world and beyond. In closing, it speaks to some of the limitations of the assemblage analogy.

Sharia Judiciary as Global Assemblage

Islamization, Corporatization, and Other Transformations in Context

You begin with assemblages that look vaguely familiar and you end up with completely foreign ones.
—BRUNO LATOUR (2005)

What is often described as 'globalization' involves competition in laws, approaches to law, and approaches to the state and governance.
—YVES DEZALAY AND BRYANT GARTH (2002)

Malaysia has been a model of success in the Muslim world and the Global South generally throughout much of its postcolonial history. There are a number of reasons for this. They include the rapid development since the 1970s of the nation's middle classes; its stunning levels of urbanization and educational attainment; and the enviable rates of industrialization and overall economic growth it has sustained in recent decades, which are probably second to none in the Muslim world.[1] Malaysia also enjoys a reputation as the "crossroads of Asia." This is due partly to its strategic location along the waterways connecting China, India, the Middle East, and points beyond (Map 1). Relevant as well is its rich ethnic and religious diversity that government slogans foreground in marketing the nation to foreign visitors as "Truly Asia—the Essence of Asia." Ethnic Malays, nearly all of whom identify as Sunni Muslims, constitute 50–51 percent of Malaysia's population of approximately 33,000,000 people.[2] According to state-sanctioned discourse, the two other major ethnic designations are the "Chinese," who comprise roughly 23 percent of the nation's citizens and are mostly Buddhist or Confucian/Taoist (though some are Christian); and the "Indians," including Sri Lankans and most others of South Asian ancestry, who make up approximately 7 percent of the citizenry and are predominantly Hindu (others are Sikhs, Muslims, or Christians). "Others," a rubric that encompasses the remaining 12 percent of the nation's

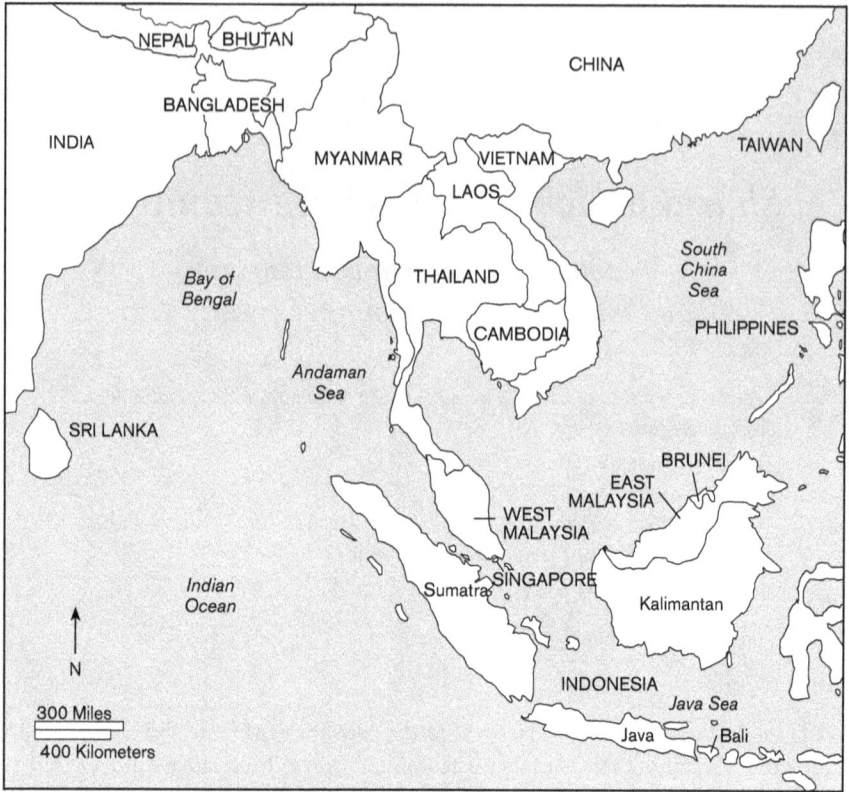

MAP 1. Malaysia and surrounding regions. Produced by Ellen L. Walker.

citizens, includes aboriginal groups, Eurasians, and others, who generally follow animist, Islamic, Christian, or other religious traditions. Non-citizens, who make up roughly 8 percent of the nation's population, are of variable ethnicity and national origin, but hail mostly from Indonesia, Pakistan, Bangladesh, and other Muslim-majority nations, thus bringing the total percentage of Muslims in the country to approximately 60 percent.[3]

Once known for its moderate and relatively progressive Islam, Malaysia is also a place where state-sponsored Islamization and analytically distinct though culturally interlocked processes of bureaucratization, rationalization, and corporatization have proceeded apace. These processes have raised questions in some quarters of the nation, especially but not exclusively among non-Muslims, about the co-imbrication of law, politics, and religion and what the expansion of state power and its sanctification via symbols, idioms, and discourses of Islam means for current and future generations of its citizens. For reasons such as these, and because

Malaysian political, economic, and religious elites have endeavored to position the nation as the global center of Islamic banking and finance, an inquiry into recent developments in Malaysian *sharia* should be of broad interest to scholars and policymakers alike.

I am an anthropologist by trade—more precisely, a historically-oriented anthropologist. My understanding of *sharia* in Malaysia is based on more than three years of ethnographic fieldwork and archival research that I have conducted since 1978. One of the research projects that I undertook in the late 1980s focused on the Islamic court in the small town of Rembau, Negeri Sembilan, one of eleven states in West Malaysia (Map 2). Partly because I was able to return to this same court in 2011, 2013, and 2018, continuities and transformations in its discourses and practices since the 1980s serve as my point of departure for this chapter and subsequent sections of the book. I hasten to add that I am ultimately concerned with national-level trends in Malaysia's *sharia* judiciary and the juridical field as a whole, and with theorizing from them, not simply about them.

This chapter provides an overview of continuities, transformations, and cultural politics in Malaysia's *sharia* judiciary during the past few decades, and in the new millennium in particular, that I flesh out later in the book. Most of the chapter focuses on transformations, but there are important continuities that we need to also bear in mind lest we operate under the erroneous impression that virtually all aspects of the judiciary have changed in recent decades. In the following section I thus outline a range of important continuities. I then proceed to a discussion of Islamization, how the *sharia* judiciary has been transformed, and why it is usefully conceived as a global assemblage.

CONTINUITIES IN GENDER, POWER, PRESTIGE, AND LAWFARE

We might begin with brief consideration of what, by many criteria, is a sacred text for Malaysians of all religious orientations and from all walks of life: the Federal Constitution. The constitution of the Federation of Malaya, drafted by the Reid Commission on the eve of independence from the British in 1957, specifies that Malaya, which became Malaysia in 1963, is a parliamentary democracy with a constitutional monarchy, with both a prime minister and a king (the former by far the more powerful) at its helm. It also stipulates, in Article 3, that "Islam is the religion of the Federation." This provision was apparently intended primarily to ensure that state ceremonies and pageantry, associated with celebrations of the nation's independence and rituals of investiture and inauguration, for example, would be Islamic in character—featuring Islamic prayers (*doa*), (Malay) Muslim dress codes, and *halal* food, for example—in order to respect the nation's Malay/Muslim majority (Fernando 2006, Harding 2012:233–236).

MAP 2. The states of West Malaysia. Produced by Ellen L. Walker.

Importantly, albeit with one critical but partial exception noted below, the constitution does not go on to specify that *sharia* is or should be a basis for the nation's legislation, let alone *the* main (or sole) basis for legislation, and it explicitly guarantees freedom of religion (Articles 3 and 11). Indeed, the constitution and the texts to which it refers make abundantly clear that the extant, British-derived system of secular law, based on the common law, is the law of the land, except within the narrowly delimited jurisdictional domains of the nation's *sharia* courts, which are subject to state rather than federal control (and within "native" or "customary"/*adat* courts, which are not relevant here). According to the constitution, the *sharia* judiciary has no jurisdiction over the affairs of non-Muslims, who currently comprise nearly 40 percent of the nation's citizenry. Its jurisdiction over Muslims, moreover, is confined largely to "family law" and other personal status law: matters of marriage, divorce, custody, child support, spousal maintenance, certain sexual transgressions, as well as consuming alcoholic beverages, observing Ramadan, "respecting Islam," etc. Virtually all other offenses, including traffic violations, theft, assault, murder, treason, drug smuggling, and human trafficking, are dealt with in the nation's far more powerful and prestigious secular courts, generally known as civil courts (*mahkamah sivil*), in accordance with secular/civil law, regardless of the plaintiff's professed religion.[4] These are critically important, and in some instances intensely contested and politicized, features of the national juridical landscape to bear in mind, especially as we proceed to a consideration of gendered themes.

As in times past, the vast majority of plaintiffs in Islamic courts both in Rembau and in Malaysia as a whole are women of modest or meager means, just as most defendants are men, from generally comparable socioeconomic backgrounds, typically plaintiffs' husbands or former husbands (but not men in other kinship or social roles; see Peletz 2002). Noteworthy as well are continuities in the types of cases that women (and to a lesser extent men) bring to the courts, the vast majority of which concern civil rather than criminal matters.[5] As in previous decades, female plaintiffs typically petition the courts to help them resolve problems associated with their husbands' failure to provide spousal or child maintenance (*nafkah*) and/or to clarify the status of their marriages (or to seek either a *taklik* divorce, due to violation of a stipulation in the marriage contract, or a termination of marriage via *fasakh*, variably rendered as "divorce by judicial proceedings," "judicial rescission/voiding of the marriage contract," and "annulment"). The first two sets of issues are often inextricably linked insofar as women who have not received support from husbands who have left home to seek a living do not always know if their husbands have simply been delinquent in providing them with money or news of their whereabouts, or have divorced them via the *talak*/repudiation clause, which need not be recited in their presence or the court's to effect a valid divorce (though failure to do so in the courthouse is illegal). Women seeking *taklik* or *fasakh* divorce are often in the courts for the same general kinds of reasons. Men, in contrast, usually approach the courts to obtain formal approval of their divorces or to seek the court's permission for polygynous unions, but not for clarification of ambiguity or owing to financial hardship. In this too we see considerable continuity with times past as well as important changes that require men to obtain the court's permission to effect a divorce or a polygynous marriage that is legal in the eyes of the state.

Relevant here are quantitative data on court use obtained by anthropologists in the late 1980s and early 1990s, and their congruence with material from the period 2005–10. Data I collected in the course of my study of the *kadi's* (Islamic magistrate's) office in Rembau, Negeri Sembilan during the period 1987–88 indicated that women were plaintiffs in 67 percent (22/33) of the cases (Peletz 2002, 156). Statistics from the District Religious Office in Kempas, Selangor and Kota Jati, Kedah obtained in 1990 and 1991 by Sharifah Zaleha Syed Hassan and Sven Cederroth (1997) indicate broadly comparable patterns; women were the plaintiffs in 79 percent (333/420) and 92 percent (423/459) of the cases, respectively (cited in Peletz 2002, 157–58). There are of course many dynamics that these data do not speak to; for instance, that women were buffeted about by the courts in ways that men were not. But I am primarily concerned with the fact that the vast majority of plaintiffs in all three of these settings (Negeri Sembilan, Selangor, and Kedah) were women.

Aggregate data collected by the Jabatan Kehakiman Syariah Malaysia (JKSM; the Malaysian Department of *Syariah* Judiciary) bearing on the period 2005–10 reveal profound continuities since the late 1980s. In Negeri Sembilan, women were plaintiffs in 73 percent (9,699/13,201) of the cases brought to the courts; the corresponding figures for Selangor and Kedah are 69 percent (35,693/51,566) and 72 percent (4,324/5,975), respectively.[6] These statistics reveal that Malaysia's Islamic courts are still very much "women's courts" in the sense that women constitute the overwhelming majority of those who seek out the court's services to help them resolve domestic (and certain other) problems. One set of reasons for this has to do with gender skewing in Islamic law, coupled with the way Islamic law is codified in Malaysia: women lack the legal prerogatives to resolve marital and related domestic problems without the help of the state-backed courts. Unlike men, in other words, women cannot divorce their spouses unless they have obtained the assistance and cooperation of the courts, hence the state. This is an exceedingly important historical continuity to bear in mind. So too is the fact that women continue to experience discrimination in the workplace and still bear the lion's share of the responsibility for the socialization and care of infants and children. One consequence is that, compared to men, women enter and experience marriage with significantly fewer economic resources to fall back on, and are thus not only much more dependent on their spouses' earnings than vice versa, but also far more likely than men to seek out the court's assistance when their spouse's financial contributions to the household are not forthcoming.

Other gendered continuities include the fact that in various kinds of legal proceedings, women's appearances, bodies, and bodily functions (e.g., when they last menstruated, or whether they are pregnant) are the subject of much greater legal concern than men's. Consider also the gendered composition of court staff, especially judges, and of the judicial hierarchy as a whole. Prior to 2010, all of Malaysia's

Islamic judges were men, a pattern in keeping with many other Muslim-majority nations, where the prevailing sentiment has it that classical Islamic texts prohibit women from serving in this capacity. The hegemonic view on this matter was virtually universal in Malaysia during my early fieldwork, but the years since then have seen a gradual loosening (though not a shattering) of the hegemony. This is due largely to the efforts of Muslim feminist activists such as Sisters in Islam (SIS) as well as female scholars working in prestigious universities such as the University of Malaya and the International Islamic University of Malaysia (IIUM) who do not consider themselves SIS-style feminists but nonetheless share SIS's view that there is ample support for the appointment of women as *sharia* judges in classical Islamic texts such as the Quran and *hadith* (see, e.g., Ramizah Wan Muhammad 2008b).

In July 2010 the government announced amidst much fanfare that two women had been appointed to serve as judges in the Islamic judiciary for the Federal Territories of Kuala Lumpur and Putrajaya. The two women were Suraya Ramli, 31, originally from Sabah, and Rafidah Abdul Razak, 39, who was born in Penang. Suraya had been senior assistant director of the Training Division, JKSM; Rafidah had been assistant director in the same division. Both of them had obtained diplomas from the International Islamic University of Malaysia, a key feeder institution for those seeking appointments in the Islamic judiciary, Suraya having also received a degree at Al-Azhar in Cairo, and Rafidah a degree from the University of Malaya.

In a speech announcing the decision, then-Prime Minister Najib Tun Razak (r. 2009–18) declared that "The appointments were made to enhance justice in cases involving families and women's rights and to meet current needs," and that the decision "was part of the Government's commitment to transform the *Syariah* judiciary." Najib went on to say that "the Government agreed to allocate RM$15 million [around US$5 million] to the Family Support Division to *help those in dire straits due to their husbands' failure to abide by Syariah Court orders*" (emphasis added)—a significant confirmation from the highest office in the land of the view long espoused by Islamic court staff and many others (female and male alike), that (Malay) men in their roles as husbands and fathers are responsible for most of the problems associated with (Malay) marriage and divorce. Najib added that "issues such as the *fight* for custody involving couples from different religions, *battles* over the remains of deceased converts, validation of religious status, [and] *disputes* over property inheritance between Muslims and non-Muslims, . . . and multi-million *ringgit* claims required a high level of expertise and wisdom to resolve" (*Sunday Star* 2010, emphasis added).

Language highlighting the latter kinds of hot-button interfaith cases and the symbolically-laden "fights," "battles," and "disputes" associated with them is in many ways out of keeping with the day-to-day workload and tenor of Islamic courts. Statistically speaking, such cases are so rare that they barely appear in ledgers detailing the relative frequencies of the different kinds of civil and criminal cases that come before the courts, which are oriented toward negotiation, mediation, and compromise in any event, not zero-sum decisions that images of "battles" and such often conjure (Sharifah Zaleha Syed Hassan and Cederroth 1997, Peletz 2002). But they are increasingly central to highly fraught public debates and wars of position bearing on the status and scope of *sharia* in Malaysia. Some of these contests center on whether or not the long-dominant ruling party, the United Malays National Organization (UMNO), committed as it is to a broadly construed "civilizational Islam" (e.g., *Islam Hadhari*) as distinct from the more "*sharia*-minded" approach associated with the Islamist opposition party, the Parti Islam Se-Malaysia (PAS; the Pan-Malaysian Islamic Party), has done enough (or too much) to safeguard the nation's Islamic resources and identity.[7] Perhaps for this reason the article announcing the appointment of the two female judges to the *sharia* bench concludes, in pastoral mode: "The prime minister also said that 76,663 people had converted to Islam between 2000 and 2009" (*Sunday Star* 2010).

Media accounts the next day cited the prime minister's comments that the appointments were "a historic moment" for Malaysia, "show[ing] that women in the country were treated equally as men," and that "Islam does not set limitation[s] for women to advance" (Roslina Mohamad 2010). In the following days, however, the media carried an announcement from *Syariah* Appeals Court Judge Md Yusup Che Teh that "a panel . . . had been set up to discuss the jurisdiction [read: power and prestige] of the two women judges." "Among the concerns were the kinds of cases which . . . [they] could *not* preside over" (emphasis added). "Md Yusup . . . said the demarcation of duties . . . was not gender discrimination, but based on Islamic rulings that could not be disputed." But Md Yusup made no reference to the specific "Islamic rulings" in question: whether they might be found in the Quran or *hadith*, for example; in early, medieval, or subsequent Islamic history; or perhaps in recent Malaysian *fatwa*. Nor did he offer any clarification concerning his statement that the Islamic rulings at issue "could not be disputed" (Ng Cheng Yee 2010).

This bald but exceedingly ambiguous assertion was perhaps intended as a reference to passages and positions in the Quran and *hadith* that might be subsumed under the category of *muhkam*, as distinct from *mutashabih*. *Muhkam* is usually translated as "inherently clear" and intelligible, "beyond doubt, and not susceptible to abrogation," hence "allow[ing] for only one clearly definitive interpretation" and set of juristic opinions, in contrast to *mutashabih*, which pertains to foundational textual phenomena that are "equivocal, ambiguous, susceptible to different interpretations" and a range of different juristic positions (Abou El Fadl 2001, 304–5). At the same time, Md Yusup's assertion might have been intended (and widely interpreted) as a warning that the government would brook no debate on any of these matters, and that anyone seeking to contest the government's position on such issues or any others bearing on interpretations or practices of Islam would be liable for criminal charges under the state's *sharia* enactments or the dreaded Internal

Security Act (ISA), a thoroughly secular provision from the colonial era that allows for indefinite detention without specific charges or the prospects of a trial.

The state's manipulation of these kinds of ambiguities is a key component of strategies of governance involving what John and Jean Comaroff (2006, 30) refer as to "lawfare." Lawfare is typically characterized by a regime's "use of its own rules—of its duly enacted penal codes, its administrative law, its states of emergency, its charters and mandates and warrants, its norms of engagement—to impose a sense of order upon its subordinates [and enemies] by means of violence rendered legible, legal, and legitimate by its own sovereign word." In Malaysia, tactics of lawfare are not confined to those who are part of the state apparatus; they are commonly deployed by conservative Muslim sectors of civil society to silence groups (such as Sisters in Islam) that are perceived as threatening their values and interests, or those of the "race," nation, or global Muslim community (*ummah*). While these strategies build on important historical precedents and thus represent a significant continuity vis-à-vis earlier times, they have become particularly intense in the last decade or so.

The recent appointment of women as Islamic judges is clearly noteworthy and is one of many progressive developments in the *sharia* juridical field that has occurred in recent years. Others include the formal introduction of *sulh*/mediation sessions, the creation of a Family Support Division to help women and children negotiate the trials and tribulations of divorce, and changes in the substance of Islamic family law (discussed in chapters 3 and 5). The fact remains, however, that, at present, women comprise a mere 10.8 percent (17/158) of the nation's Islamic judges, men making up the remaining 89.2 percent (141/158). Corresponding figures for the civil judiciary are far less skewed, and have been estimated at around 40 percent.[8] The more gender-equitable distribution of judgeships that we see in the civil judiciary is likely to contribute indirectly to the increase of female judges in the Islamic judiciary in the years to come (as is the fact that women make up more than half of the "mediation officers" [*pegawai sulh*] in the Islamic courts). This is especially so since the political, religious, and specifically legal elites in charge of modernizing the Islamic judiciary are commonly inspired by civil-court models and the sensibilities and dispositions associated with them. Put differently, and to underscore a point taken up in due course: the gold standard that informs much of the rationalization and reform of Malaysia's Islamic judiciary is the nation's *civil* judiciary—along with innovations in alternative dispute resolution (ADR) processes, family courts, and psychological counseling from the United States, Europe, Australia, and Japan—not *sharia*-based developments in nations such as Saudi Arabia, Sudan, Pakistan, Egypt, Iran, or Indonesia. This even though Islamization—construed as the heightened salience of Islamic symbols, idioms, discursive traditions, and attendant practices in specifically political arenas and in the realms of personal piety—is a goal that Malaysia's political and religious elites, or at least the Muslims among them, share with their counterparts in most other Muslim-majority nations.

These then are some of the continuities in gender, power, prestige, and lawfare that we see in the *sharia* judiciary and the more encompassing juridical field since the 1970s and 1980s. I address others below, though most of the remainder of the chapter focuses on transformations in these arenas.

ISLAMIZATION AND TRANSFORMATION IN THE *SHARIA* JUDICIARY

Islamization/Creeping Desecularization

Malaysia's Islamic resurgence, often referred to as the *dakwah* movement, is a multi-faceted, heterogeneous phenomenon of urban, middle-class origin that dates from the early 1970s, even though it is most appropriately viewed as an outgrowth of earlier developments in Islamic nationalism and reform, such as those associated with the Kaum Muda (Young Group) movement of the 1920s and 1930s (Roff 1967).[9] It has been fueled by state policies in conjunction with religio-political developments elsewhere in the Muslim world, and has involved heightened expressions of piety among Malays (new technologies of the self, new patterns of comportment and consumption, including new styles of dress, new modes of greeting, etc.) in addition to other far-reaching changes. The latter include: the Islamization of Kuala Lumpur's monumental architecture; nation-wide campaigns to build and refurbish prayer houses and mosques; the passage of myriad legislative measures bearing on Islam; the creation of an international Islamic university and a nationwide system of Islamic banking and finance; and the co-optation by the state of charismatic Muslim intellectuals.

In this context it is not surprising that in recent decades Malaysian political, legal, and other institutions have become increasingly inflected by Islamic symbols and idioms and that the scope and jurisdiction of Islamic law have been broadened considerably. More generally, what Clive Kessler (2008, 62) has referred to as "the long march toward desecularization" has proceeded largely unchecked in certain domains. Commonly cited (e.g., by Lee 2010; Liow 2009; Norani Othman et al 2008; Whiting 2008, 2010; Moustafa 2018) as evidence for these trends are the following six sets of mostly legal/political/religious developments, which I mention in rough chronological order.

First, the seemingly straightforward and at first glance relatively innocuous 1988 revision of the Federal Constitution, known as amendment 121(1A). This amendment specified that civil courts have no jurisdiction over matters falling within the purview of Islamic courts. In doing so, it largely eliminated civil-court reviews and repeals of Islamic-court rulings. It also set the stage, as far as many Malaysians and outside observers are concerned, for Islamic sensibilities and dispositions to trump the Constitution.

Second, Prime Minister Mahathir's late September 2001 declaration that Malaysia is an Islamic state. This enigmatic declaration, which was aimed partly at offsetting President Bush's post-9/11 characterizations of Muslim polities as extremist and hostile to the United States, proved to be politically explosive in many (especially non-Muslim) quarters.

Third, Deputy Prime Minister Najib's July 2007 public "confirmation" that Malaysia is indeed an Islamic state, which was followed by warnings from on high that those wishing to avoid detention should avoid public deliberation of whether this is in fact true.

Fourth, the apostasy case of Lina Joy (nee Azlina Jailani), which began when she changed her religion in 1990 and culminated in a 2007 Federal Court ruling that essentially refused to recognize her renunciation of Islam—or her conversion to Christianity—on the grounds that this was a matter to be addressed by Islamic courts. The vast majority of the latter, as it happens, do not countenance apostasy involving the abjuration of Islam (though they do facilitate non-Muslims' conversion to Islam). This decision made clear that the freedom of religion enshrined in the Constitution does not pertain to those, like Joy, born Muslim.

Fifth, a host of incidents since the 1980s that have involved campaigns of Islamically-inflected moral policing, aimed mostly but not exclusively at Muslims, which have reached new heights in recent years. In some instances, these campaigns have been overseen by rapidly growing and extremely well-funded religious bureaucracies like the Jabatan Kemajuan Islam Malaysia (JAKIM; the Malaysian Department of Islamic Development) and the Jabatan Agama Islam Wilayah Persekutuan (JAWI; the Federal Territory Department of Islamic Religion.)[10] In other cases, they have been orchestrated by Islamic NGOs that aim to galvanize Muslim public opinion concerning how and in what specific directions Islamization should proceed.

Sixth, legal strategies on the part of Islamist groups to harass Muslim feminist organizations such as Sisters in Islam and other like-minded reformers by mounting lawsuits against them alleging defamation, blasphemy, apostasy, etc. These strategies have become particularly intense in the past decade or so, and commonly involve lawfare (Harding 1996, 270–74 et passim, 2012, 165–78, 248–51; Whiting 2017).

Several scholars have provided superb documentation of the step-by-step constriction of public and intellectual spaces for discussing issues of public interest that these developments have entailed (Norani Othman at al 2008, Liow 2009, Moustafa 2018). Some have observed that since the early years of the new millennium the key debates among Malay political and religious elites have concerned not whether Malaysia is (or should become) an Islamic state, but what kind of Islamic state it *already* is and what types of additional measures are needed to entrench that status (Farish Noor 2006, Moustafa 2018). These observations point to a rather remarkable shift, which, to oversimplify, occurred mainly after 9/11.

Note, for example, that as recently as 2000, the most eminent scholar of Malaysian Islamic law could write that "officially at least," Malaysia is "a secular state which has not embraced the idea of establishing an Islamic state, nor does it have any agenda of developing a Shari'a-based constitution" (Kamali 2000, 2).

Sharia, *Common Law, and the Islamic Judiciary as Global Assemblage*

It is curious that even when scholars of Malaysian Islam provide magisterial genealogies of these developments, they typically convey little sense of the dynamism of *sharia* or of the hierarchy of religious courts or bureaucratic behemoths, such as the JKSM, established in 1998, charged with managing and auditing their procedures and outcomes. Except when they are addressing matters of *hudud* law, differences between the Shafi'i legal tradition (which predominates in Malaysia) and the other schools of law in Sunni Islam, they often depict *sharia* in rather static, undifferentiated, and monolithic terms, the relevant discussions chiefly confined to the expanded jurisdiction of *sharia* and the border skirmishes with the civil judiciary and defenders of the constitution that such expansions commonly incite. Typically elided in these accounts are discussions of how the *sharia* judiciary is structured and managed; what the routine operations of the *sharia* courts tell us about the local cultural logics of Islamic judicial process; and how on a day-to-day basis the courts deal with male and female litigants, and matters of marriage, divorce, reconciliation, spousal maintenance, conjugal earnings, child support, and custody.

This literature also obscures crucial dynamics that are jarringly dissonant with regard to most scholarly and popular understandings of terms such as "Islamization."[11] Relevant here (and explained in more detail below) is that for many decades now, the political, religious, and specifically legal elites who have been centrally involved in reforming the *sharia* judiciary have consciously endeavored to model it on its far more powerful and eminently more prestigious *secular* counterpart, Malaysia's *civil* judiciary, and the common-law traditions inherited from the British colonial era with which that counterpart is inextricably associated. This is not to imply that elites have abandoned efforts to enhance the operations and legitimacy of the *sharia* judiciary in specifically Islamic terms. Far from it. Nor am I suggesting that all the innovations introduced in recent years, such as the formal mediation processes referred to by the Arabic-origin term *sulh,* which were initiated in 2001, are of non-Islamic origin or design. My point about modeling needs to be understood in relative rather than absolute, mutually exclusive terms. This is especially so since virtually all of the world's major legal systems are deeply hybrid with respect to the historical origins of their characteristic features and the ways these features are currently configured, inflected, legitimized, and contested. Germane here is John Makdisi's (1999) argument that key elements of English common law developed by Henry II in twelfth-century England, including common-law notions of contract, debt, and trial by jury, were adapted from medieval Islamic law of the Maliki tradition practiced in North Africa and Sicily, elements of which were incorporated first into the Norman law of Sicily and subsequently into both the Norman law of England and what came to be known as English common law. Also relevant is George Makdisi's (1985–1986, 15) thesis that classical Islamic schools of learning (*madrasah*) in Palestine, Syria, Egypt, and elsewhere inspired the development and design of the earliest law schools (Inns of Court) in London, which were founded in the twelfth and thirteenth centuries and helped secure London's fame as the "'home of colleges' in the Christian West."

Circumstances of the sort outlined above and in the material presented below help explain why Malaysia's *sharia* judiciary is profitably viewed as a global assemblage. Put differently, the concept of global assemblage is useful both because Malaysia's *sharia* judiciary is a good example of a global assemblage and because the notion of a global assemblage helps us comprehend features of this judiciary that have been poorly understood or glossed over in most accounts of Malaysia's Islamization.

Consider the *sharia* judiciary's modeling on the system of civil law. This modeling is evident in the Islamic court's greatly increased reliance on written evidence (as distinct from oral testimony) and in its heightened concern with written precedent, reflected partly in the rapid growth in the past few decades of Malay- and English-language academic and professional publications that the nation's cadre of Islamic judges and lawyers are expected to read, master, and respect (e.g., *Jurnal Hukum, Shariah Law Reports, Malaysian Journal of Syariah and Law, Jurnal Syariah, IIUM Law Journal*). This modeling is also apparent in the Islamic courts' tendencies toward more adversarial hearings, partly a function of the recent proliferation of lawyers in the courts; and in augmented concerns on the part of court officials and lawyers alike with procedures characteristic of the civil judiciary. These were strikingly obvious in the motions and hearings I observed in the *sharia* courts in Kuala Lumpur, Negeri Sembilan, and Penang in 2010–13 and 2018, in the cases in Kuala Lumpur's civil courts that I sat in on for comparative purposes in 2012–13, and in the various legal documents shared with me during this time. I refer to procedures for lodging complaints; turning problems into cases; maintaining a sense of order and decorum in the courtroom; generating summons, warrants, affidavits, and appeals; discerning what constitutes fact, relevance, burden of proof, hearsay, and legally salient evidence; delivering and recording judgments; and keeping records and managing paperwork and electronic files generally. As one knowledgeable observer who studied court documents put it, the latter procedures "are borrowed wholly from common law, making them almost a carbon copy of laws used in civil (secular) courts" (Maznah Mohamad 2010b, 516).

Recent decades have also seen significant shifts toward common-law sensibilities in the substance of family (and other personal status) law administered by

Islamic courts, even as they witnessed controversial cases involving the imposition (in some instances commuted) of "Islamic punishments" such as whipping or caning for adultery and the consumption of alcohol. Technical examples of this shift in legal sensibilities that occurred in the late 1980s and early 1990s and that could have easily been reversed since that time ("there is always . . . a potential for relations to be otherwise" [Anderson et al 2012, 182]) but have in fact become further entrenched, are delineated elsewhere (Horowitz 1994, Peletz 2002, and chapter 5, below), so I will not dwell on them here. Suffice it to note that several of them bear on the increasingly restricted legality of men's prerogative to enter into polygynous unions and to effect extra-judicial divorce (via the *talak*/repudiation clause); the more liberal division at divorce of conjugal earnings (*harta sepencarian*);[12] and the expanded grounds for certain kinds of divorce initiated by women, such as *fasakh*.[13] Importantly, such shifts have not occurred in a simple unilinear fashion; they have proceeded in fits and starts and have occasionally been temporarily or partially reversed (Kamali 2000, 12–13, 66–68, 306, 317–18; Norani Othman 2008).

Consider too that in contemporary state-sanctioned parlance, Malaysia's Islamic judges are most commonly designated by the generic (Arabic-origin) term for judge or magistrate, *hakim* (sometimes by the more specific *hakim syarie*), whose primary referent in the Malaysian context has long been civil-court judges. The flip side is that the more conventional (Arabic-origin) term for Islamic judge, *kadi* (sometimes rendered *qadi*, *qadzi*, etc.), which was prevalent in Malaysia through the early 1990s and long before, is, for the most part, no longer in official use.

This socio-linguistic engineering constitutes a striking break from Islam's classical juridical past, which is inextricably linked with the term *kadi,* and from the terminologies and symbolics of Islamic judiciaries in most of the contemporary Muslim world. It reflects official strategies to upgrade the status and prestige of Islamic judges *in relation to civil-law judges* in the eyes of the legal-judicial profession and the populace as a whole. Ahmad Hidayat Buang's (2007, 322) observation that Malaysia's "Shariah Court . . . [is] seen by many as a second class, incompetent court" is clearly intended as a relative point: that the *sharia* court is regarded as second-class and incompetent *in relation to the civil court,* which in many respects constitutes the gold standard. So too is Kamali's (2000, 312) convergent, widely shared view that "The Syariah Courts and their judges and personnel . . . exist on the fringes of the system and tend to see themselves as being marginalized."

Official thinking has it that such upgrades necessitate "rebranding," the term half-jokingly used by a high-ranking member of the *sharia* judiciary with whom I discussed these matters in 2011. A key feature of this rebranding involves capitalizing on the legitimacy of the civil-court system by incorporating various features of that system into the *sharia* judiciary, and divesting Islamic judges of the negative connotations of the term *kadi*—rural, backward, capricious, and irrational—some of which were foregrounded in Max Weber's Orientalist caricatures of "*kadi*-

justice" ([1925] 1968). In 2010, when I resumed conducting research on the Islamic courts after many years of being engaged in other projects, I was warned by a Malay scholar and activist conversant with these matters that Islamic judges would be deeply insulted if I referred to them as *kadi* in my conversations with them. I remember being somewhat dumbfounded by the warning, since it signaled such a sharp contrast to the situation that prevailed during my fieldwork in the Islamic courts in the late 1980s, when *kadi* was clearly the most appropriate term of reference and address.

Another noteworthy instance of rebranding involves the promotion of mediation sessions subsumed under the rubric of *sulh,* an Arabic-origin term denoting the end of quarreling with the intention of compromise, that build on centuries-old but largely unacknowledged Malay precedents. The *sulh* process was formally introduced in Kuala Lumpur as a pilot project in 2001 (though it was practiced informally there beginning in 1976), and spread to various states in the following years, as discussed in chapter 3. The formal appointment of *sulh* officers (*pegawai sulh*) followed experiments in courts, schools, and workplaces that were variously informed by U.S.-style psychological and social-work counseling and the alternative dispute resolution (ADR) movement that gained traction in North America and beyond beginning in the mid-1970s (Nader 2002). The immediate goal of these experiments was to reduce the backlog of suits that have long plagued the nation's Islamic courts and to help resolve disputes amicably. It is no coincidence that broadly analogous developments in Malaysia's civil courts date from the same general period, and, more specifically, that the civil courts are the proximate source of the relevant *sharia* initiatives. All such developments reflect the global circulation of legal discourses, emanating mostly from the West, that aim to streamline and otherwise rationalize legal systems worldwide and thus render them more friendly to flows of transnational capital (Dezalay and Garth 2002, 2010; Ruskola 2013).

In light of the variegated legal, administrative, management, and attendant discourses and practices that authorities have drawn upon in rationalizing the Islamic judiciary, it should come as no surprise to find that officials have invested much energy in attempting to legitimize the *sulh* process in cyberspace and through other advertising campaigns that underscore its Arabic and Islamic origins. This is part of a larger process involving efforts to stabilize the (Islamic) identity of the *sharia* judiciary as it is increasingly characterized by its relations of exteriority distinct from its real or imagined "essences," a challenge facing many types of assemblages, or at least the social engineers and brand managers involved in fashioning and marketing them (DeLanda 2006). That said, brochures available from the Islamic courts and on official websites of the *sharia* judiciary commonly refer to *sulh* processes as "mediation," using the English term in the relevant Malay-language texts, partly because many urban Malays are familiar with its general meanings as well as its specific uses in civil-court arenas, but are altogether unfamiliar with the

Arabic-origin term *sulh,* which authorities are endeavoring to popularize, largely against the grain.

In Malaysia, the general processes involved in *sulh,* along with the valorization—both in the courts and other contexts—of mutual accommodation, compromise, and mediation, are in fact of great antiquity. There is nonetheless much that is new here: (1) the formalization and bureaucratization of these processes in the Islamic courts, including policies rendering them more or less mandatory for those who seek to have certain aspects of marriage/divorce cases heard by an Islamic judge; (2) their rebranding in specifically Arabic and Islamic terms, even as *sulh* officers are encouraged to obtain training and certification from Australian mediation consultancy firms and to qualify for membership in the United Kingdom Chartered Institute of Arbitrators; and (3) efforts on the part of the *sharia* judiciary to signal that in addition to being grounded in the Quran and *hadith,* they are compatible with the common-law practices of civil courts. Conspicuously absent from these discourses are references to the traditional Malay precedents for *sulh.* This absence is in keeping with the current thrust of the hyper-rationalist social engineering central to Malaysia's modernity projects, which are more concerned to create modern Muslims than modern Malays, though the distinction between the two is often elided and the term "Muslim" is often a codeword for "Malay" and vice versa, as is also true for the terms "religion" and "race."

Of broader concern in light of the central arguments of this chapter is that the heightened prevalence of *sulh,* which has deep roots in classical Islamic jurisprudence, is an entailment of bureaucratic rationalization and attendant features of Malaysian modernity—rather than a return to tradition—in a Muslim-majority nation in which elites and ordinary folks alike commonly invoke symbols and idioms of Islam to legitimize and/or come to terms with many different kinds of change.

Corporatization and E-Governance

Thoroughly resonant with the foregoing (and with my argument that changes in the Islamic judiciary have little to do with a "return to tradition") are the sartorial styles and professional activities and organizations of Islamic judges and *sharia* lawyers alike. *Sharia* lawyers (generally known as *peguam syarie*) are increasingly involved in hearings in Islamic courts, as might be expected in light of the rapid growth of the Malay middle class, the greater financial stakes in cases focusing on divorce, spousal maintenance, child support, and conjugal earnings (which, taken together, dominate the docket), and the pressures toward bureaucratic specialization, rationalization, and reform spawned partly by these and attendant developments. Not coincidentally, both *sharia* lawyers and Islamic judges organize their professional practices and formal associations on civil-law models, such as those of the Malaysian Bar Council and Lincoln's Inn. Even in small towns far from the capital, moreover, their professional attire is nowadays exceedingly "corporate" in the smartly-tailored, Western black-business-suit sense of the term. Indeed, it is much like (but even more corporate than) the professional apparel worn by their colleagues in the civil judiciary, some of whom donned the long white wigs of their English counterparts and former colonizers through the early 1990s. Here too we see clear evidence of rebranding that capitalizes on the legitimacy of the civil judiciary.

Terms such as "Islamization," like the kindred "*shariatization*" and "desecularization," obfuscate these kinds of dynamics. They sometimes suggest, or are interpreted to mean, certain kinds of homogeneous, homogenizing, or otherwise "fatefully necessary" processes (Cannell 2010, 90) that we think we understand, perhaps because of familiarity with broadly analogous processes in other parts of the Muslim world such as Iran, Pakistan, Afghanistan, or Sudan. The problem here is that if we consider the full range of developments—many of which are mutually contradictory—that have occurred in the Islamic judiciaries and national legal systems of these latter nations in recent years (Otto 2010; Hefner 2011b, 2016b; Massoud 2013), it is not clear whether terms such as "Islamization" or "desecularization" are particularly meaningful glosses. In any case, these terms reveal very little about either the actual workings of Malaysia's Islamic judiciary, or, expanded jurisdictions aside—admittedly no small matter—the directions in which it is moving.

In Malaysia, the relevant dynamics have less to do with one or another variant of Islamization than with contextually variable processes of bureaucratization, rationalization, corporatization, and neoliberal globalization entailing (among other things) the privatization of enterprises, activities, and resources formerly owned or managed by the state, related to healthcare, education, transportation, water supply, etc. (Jomo K. S. 1995, Tan 2007). In light of the scope, force, and overall salience of corporatizing developments in recent decades, I should make clear that my usage of the term "corporatization" takes as its point of departure the hierarchically authorized models, practices, sensibilities, and dispositions, along with the pecuniary and other values and interests animating and sustaining them, that prevail in upper-level management circles in corporate/capitalist business sectors of Malaysia and beyond. Especially relevant is Taylorization involving highly rationalized "assembly-line processes strictly regulated for maximum time-efficiency" and seamless mass production (Newfield 2007, 68). More generally, I am interested in the relative permeation throughout Malaysian society of certain kinds of economistic and attendant administrative/managerial principles and ideals, once associated largely with the upper echelons of rational (industrial) capitalism, that have become increasingly hegemonic and "commonsensical," though variably so, across a wide variety of social, cultural-political, and other domains. Indices of these trends that will be discussed shortly include Japanese management and auditing regimes, ISO protocols, and the fetishization of KPIs in the civil judiciary, universities, and elsewhere, and the spectacular growth of industries centered around *halal* food and body-care products, Islamic management, banking, and finance, and *sharia-*

compliance in the workplace (Fischer 2008, 2016; Sloane-White 2017; Dolan 2019). Worthy of mention as well is the popularity of Indonesian-origin organizations such as ESQ (Emotional and Spiritual Quotient), which meld together Islamic doctrine and spirituality, Western management sciences, and pop-psychology discourses of self-development (Rudnyckyj 2010; see also Hoesterey 2016). Founded by Dr. Ary Ginanjar Agustian, ESQ regularly hosts lavishly choreographed, multimedia-enhanced training sessions at upscale hotels in Kuala Lumpur and beyond, selectively targeting upper-level management personnel, parents, teens, and others; the organization boasts nearly 80,000 members ("alumni") in Malaysia and over a million worldwide.

In these latter initiatives we see a clear commodification and rebranding of Islam—as pro-corporate/capitalist development, friendly to common-law sensibilities, and otherwise modern, progressive, and this-worldly. No "clash of civilizations" here! This rebranding is strikingly evident in the Islamic judiciary, which authorities are marketing by means of (inter alia) densely networked sites in cyberspace; DVDs, books, journals, and other media products; and gifts to conference attendees, visiting dignitaries, curious anthropologists, and others that include handsomely produced brochures, notepads, ballpoint pens, travelling coffee mugs, bath towels, and tote bags variably embellished with the Islamic judiciary's corporate logos and trademarks. As Malaysia further cements its ties to the "power/ knowledge networks of global capitalism" (Zuern 2010, 201), it increasingly resembles a gigantic emporium where everything is being merchandized, albeit not necessarily for enhanced market share in the narrow sense of the term. Contests for legitimacy, which are never fully settled, clearly require strategic marketing as well.

In the past two decades Malaysian authorities, in consultation with international advisors representing a variety of fields in management and information-communication technology and a host of transnational corporations with headquarters in Western or East Asian nations, have embraced globalized forms of e-governance with a vengeance, much as Mazzarella (2006) has documented for India. Before clarifying e-governance, a fascinating example of Islamic modern Malaysian-style, I should mention that these corporations include AT&T, the Bechtel Group, British Telecom, Hewlett Packard, IBM, Intel, Motorola, Nippon Telegraph and Telephone, Peking University, and Sun Microsystems. Conspicuously absent from this list are corporate advisors representing the Muslim world.

The term "e-governance," like the synonym "E-Government," which those who authorize official Malaysian discourse prefer, refers to the use of "high-end, state-of-the-art information and communication technologies to facilitate efficient and effective delivery of government services through . . . [densely networked] electronic delivery channels."[14] Unlike earlier computerization initiatives that were essentially agency-specific, e-governance works across—and systematically integrates—the entire spectrum of state agencies. Ideally it will enable "citizens to access, transact and obtain any government service via a range of multimedia portals over a range of delivery channels such as phone, PC, mobile, kiosk and interactive TV" (Muhammad Rais Abdul Karim and Nazariah Mohd Khalid 2003, 54–55). One rationale for developing e-governance is that in order to remain transnationally competitive—and to keep ahead of the global curve—"the business of government" must be continually reinvented, building on forms of governance that are "at once stable and predictable yet agile and flexible" (2). The move is also squarely embedded in ideologies of "high modernity," which James Scott (1998, 4) characterizes in terms of "a self-confidence about scientific and technical progress, the expansion of production," and "the rational design of social order commensurate with the scientific understanding of natural laws." According to the latter logic, "If the future is viewed as a scientific and technological puzzle, then E-Government will be the integral interlocking piece that completes the picture, at least for now" (Muhammad Rais Abdul Karim and Nazariah Mohd Khalid 2003, 3).

Malaysia's commitment to e-governance is a central entailment of Prime Minister Mahathir's Vision 2020, launched in 1991, which aimed to ensure that Malaysia would join the ranks of fully industrialized nations by the year 2020. As part of this commitment, Mahathir (r. 1981–2003, 2018–present) poured resources into what came to be known as the Multi-Media Super Corridor (MSC). The MSC is a zone of high-tech development fifty kilometers long and twenty kilometers wide, which extends from Kuala Lumpur's City Center in the north to the Kuala Lumpur International Airport in the south; it contains Putrajaya (the government's administrative capital, with offices for over forty-two thousand federal employees) (Muhammad Rais Abdul Karim and Nazariah Mohd Khalid 2003, 85), as well as Cyberjaya (a massive IT-themed town, spread across seven thousand acres, with a science park and university complexes at its core). Sometimes characterized as a mélange of Silicon Valley and Hollywood, the MSC is a key component of the government's strategy to create "a technology-literate thinking workforce that can perform in a global environment and use Information Age tools to support a knowledge-based economy" (32). E-governance, for its part, is promoted in official publications as "the crown jewel of the MSC," though one should add that, according to some scholars (Bunnell 2004), the MSC has fallen far short of government expectations.

E-Syariah *Portal*

In 2002, as part of the e-governance initiative, authorities rolled out an extremely sophisticated, visually stunning, and highly interactive E-*Syariah* Portal. The E-*Syariah* Portal was created with a number of specific goals in mind (in addition to the general objectives of e-governance noted earlier). One goal is to enable Islamic judges, lawyers, state auditors, and others to code, classify, manage, and track cases and their outcomes electronically, thereby reducing the notorious backlog of suits along with widespread criticisms along the lines of "justice delayed is justice denied," which highlight the plight of women, who continue to comprise the vast majority of plaintiffs in the Islamic courts. Another objective of the E-*Syariah* Portal is to facilitate officials' efforts to amass reliable information on the whereabouts and financial resources of litigants and other "persons of interest" to the Islamic judiciary and to the police, the military, and others who help them develop their databases.

The E-*Syariah* Portal is also designed to disseminate legal forms and other relevant information to litigants and others, who are collectively and interchangeably designated in official literature as "users," "customers," "citizen-users," and "change targets." Users can surf the sites accessible through the E-*Syariah* Portal to obtain information both on *sharia* lawyers who are registered with the system, and on any of the 140 or so different types of civil and criminal cases handled by the Islamic judiciary. Users can also access information relevant to the state-specific statutory laws that bear on each type of case. For many of them, moreover, users can activate live links to passages from the Quran and *hadith* that officials have selected to provide authoritative religious rationales for the statutory laws and relevant punishments in question. In addition, the portal prominently displays the exact times at which Muslims are called to prayer each day. The portal's myriad live links also enable users to access the various web-pages created by the Department of Islamic Judiciary, which include (inter alia) an extensive glossary of more than seventy terms relevant to the Islamic courts, many of which are borrowed from the largely English (or English-derived) lexicon of the civil judiciary; e.g., *affidavit, bailiff, injunksi, klient, kontrak, litigan, saman.* One of the reigning ideas is that the portal will serve modern Muslims' needs in much the same way as a "one-stop shopping center."

The E-*Syariah* Portal is thus equipped with critically important pedagogical, legitimating, and regulating tools. These tools are geared, on the one hand, toward encouraging technological and digital literacy, much like the courts encouraged print-based literacy during my fieldwork in the late 1980s; and, on the other, toward enhancing surveillance, discipline, and control. Not surprisingly, the latter goals are omitted from officials pronouncements, which are cast in discourses of reform that "promise and pledge" to "revise and streamline Islamic law" and its administration, to clarify the "visions, missions, and (quality) objectives" of the courts, and to "manage complaints and advice within 14 days of their receipt." According to spokesmen in the Prime Minister's Department, the more encompassing E-*Syariah* Project aims to "introduc[e] administrative reforms to upgrade the quality of services of the *Syariah* Courts by enhancing the effectiveness of the Islamic Justice Department ... in coordinating and monitoring its respective agencies and to improve the productivity and efficiency of the *Syariah* Courts management nationwide" (Muhammad Rais Abdul Karim and Nazariah Mohd

Khalid, 2003, 78–79). Rather hard to miss is the global management-speak suffusing these kinds of official overviews; the point that one objective of such initiatives is to "upgrade and enhance the efficiency and *effectiveness* of the government's administrative machinery" *as a whole* (Tan Sri Samsudin Osman cited in Muhammad Rais Abdul Karim and Nazariah Mohd Khalid 2003, front matter; emphasis added); and the fact, quite familiar to most readers in these neoliberal times, that, in World Bank parlance, "Good governance is . . . [made] synonymous with sound development management" (cited in Rittich 2000–2001, 932; cf. Mazzarella 2006).[15]

Japanese Management and Auditing

More recently, we see evidence of an extension or revival of Mahathir's Look East policy of the early 1980s, which included government and corporate efforts to utilize Japanese management techniques in local industrial production in order to encourage continued Japanese investment and inculcate Malay employees with a version of the Japanese work ethic. I refer to the fact that the *sharia* judiciary and indeed the governmental apparatus in its entirety have adopted Japanese systems of corporate management and financial auditing. This has involved launching widely advertised campaigns that emphasize the 5Ses—in Japanese: *Seiri, Seiton, Seiso, Seiketsu,* and *Shitsuke;* in Malay: *Sisih, Susun, Sapu, Seragam,* and *Sentiasa Amal;* in English: *Sort, Set in Order, Shine, Standardize,* and *Sustain.* These euphemistic glosses do not do justice to the goals or demands of the campaign. Suffice it to say that such campaigns aim to encourage new modalities of self-management, ethical engagement, and "social awareness" (of one's self, one's work habits, one's coworkers, one's workplace) so as to better discipline, motivate, and govern Muslim and other Malaysian citizen-subjects; enhance their efficiency, productivity, personal accountability, and global competitiveness; and help guide them—and the nation—to a more prosperous and secure future (cf. Rudnyckyj 2010).

When I visited the Islamic court in Kuala Lumpur in the (northern) summers of 2010 and 2011, the campaign was in full swing. The walls of the registrar's office, for example, were not only adorned with the usual photographs of the Prime Minister, the King, and the Queen, plaques bearing beautiful calligraphic renderings of the words "Allah" and "Muhammad," and flow charts depicting the organization of the court hierarchy and the stages involved in processing cases. They also featured prominent wall hangings celebrating and explicating the new, Japanese-origin system of management and auditing, some of which enumerated the 5Ses in both Japanese (a language that is unintelligible to virtually all Malays and other Malaysians) and Malay. In their backstage offices, moreover, various members of the judiciary were wearing jackets emblazoned with the 5S logo. Others thumbed through, carried around, or had within easy reach official guidebooks for implementing the 5Ses, such as *Panduan Amalan 5S Sektor Awam (5S Practice*

Guide[book] for the Civil Service); these include glossy color photographs illustrating the proper way to maintain one's bulletin boards, filing cabinets, surge protectors, and toilets.

The more expansive goal is to ascertain how best to manage and audit the workflow, overall operations, and "outcomes" of the *sharia* judiciary and otherwise provide the public with the quality and type of service demanded by total quality management (TQM) protocols and the International Organization for Standardization (ISO). The ISO is, for a great many Malaysian policy-makers, *the* ultimate arbiter with regard to an ever-proliferating range of standards and more, encompassing normativities for business, government, society, and culture alike. This is readily apparent to anyone who has recently spent time in Malaysian universities, government offices, bookstores, or other venues associated with the production or dissemination of official or public culture, including, not least, the museum in Kuala Lumpur's new *sharia* courthouse, which opened for business in October 2011 (see chapter 4).

This last, Japanese-inflected corporatizing development dates from 2010. Systematic assessment of its full impact might thus be premature. It is quite likely, however, that it will affect employee productivity and morale, courtroom procedures, and dealings with the public in some of the same general ways as the studies collected in Marilyn Strathern's edited book *Audit Cultures* (2000) describe for broadly analogous dynamics in the United Kingdom, Greece, New Zealand, and elsewhere. One set of common themes underlying the differences in these cases is that they typically involve "coercive accountability" on the part of those subject to rapidly proliferating audit regimes. Limited resources (time, money, intellectual capital) associated with the provisioning of vital services are subject to compulsory reallocation so as to meet one-size-fits-all assessment protocols based on top-down corporate business models that are patently ill-suited to many of the extra-business contexts in which they are unilaterally imposed. Another common theme is the diffuse, enduring alienation experienced by employees who feel their relative autonomy and authority to make informed judgments about the workplace and the services they provide has been seriously compromised by bottom-line corporate considerations masked in discourses focusing on efficient time-space management or lofty ethical imperatives.

This is precisely what we see in Malaysia's civil courts: the fetishization of key performance indicators (KPIs) has become something of a tyranny for judges and lawyers alike, litigants (especially plaintiffs) being the most disadvantaged (Whiting 2011, 28–30). Should we see similar developments on the Islamic side (some *sharia* judges and lawyers told me quite emphatically that they are already evident in the *sharia* lower courts) the major losers could well be women, who, unlike men, are heavily dependent on the courts (hence the state) to negotiate their relationships with their spouses. On the other hand, the setting of timetables and other goals for the resolution of disputes is a clear plus for women, who in previous years have faced lengthy delays and other obstacles in their efforts to obtain justice.

Authenticity and Identity

Even if systematic assessments of the effects of runaway audit culture in the *sharia* judiciary may be premature, the other dynamics alluded to here have been evident for decades now and merit serious consideration. Some of them raise intriguing, politically sensitive questions about the ontological status of present-day Malaysian *sharia*. One question has to do with the bureaucratized, corporatized, positivized *sharia* that is practiced and experienced in contemporary Malaysia. Does this form of *sharia* have any organic or other connection with the pre- and early modern variants of *sharia* that, in addition to being community-based, were thoroughly grounded in local cultural conventions and certain kinds of "*ijtihad*ic hermeneutics," as scholars like Wael Hallaq (2009), addressing the Muslim world as a whole, have discussed with such insight and clarity? The question is an exceedingly important one in Malaysia and elsewhere in light of heavily freighted debates and wars of position bearing on what is authentically (or quintessentially) "Islamic," what roles one or another conceptualization of *sharia* should play in the nation at present and in the years to come, and who is qualified to engage these debates (Zainah Anwar 2001; Peletz 2005, 2013). Before clarifying the issue of hermeneutics, I might add that as far as the vast majority of ordinary Malays are concerned, "Each of the laws and procedures applied in the [nation's] shariah courts is clearly stated in the Qur'an," and that this kind of popular legal consciousness seriously thwarts efforts by feminists and other non-state actors to critically engage the ways the state has configured the *sharia* juridical field and the legally codified norms of the *sharia* courts in particular (Moustafa 2018, 128–29).

The *ijtihad*ic hermeneutics Hallaq has written about were predicated partly on a set of assumptions running throughout Islamic jurisprudence, to wit, that "each individual and circumstance was deemed unique, requiring *ijtihad* [independent reasoning; innovative legal interpretation of (or on the basis of) sacred texts; judicial creativity] that was context-specific" (2009, 546), and that this reasoning should therefore typically take into consideration (among other things) a relatively expansive range of disputants' actions, intentions, character traits, and biographical data. These assumptions diverge rather sharply from those informing common-law reasoning and the notion of binding precedent in particular—e.g., that individuals are, put somewhat facetiously, "indistinguishable members of a generic species, standing in perfect parity before a blind lady of justice" (546), such that a decision rendered in one instance might be more or less automatically invoked, and potentially binding, in any "like case." Hallaq contends that legal hermeneutics based on *ijtihad* constitute one of the defining features of classical variants of *sharia* as well as the feature of *sharia* that was most adversely affected by its encounter with the political, legal, and epistemological regimes of colonialism, postcolonial states, and modern states generally. The latter assertion is most relevant here, and receives a good deal of support from developments in Malaysia (which Hallaq cites frequently) and most other Muslim-majority nations. For reasons such as these Hallaq speaks of the "epistemic breakdown" and "desiccation and final dismantling" of *sharia* in the modern Muslim world; alternatively, of its "structural death" (15, 535, 547).

These views are well substantiated by contemporary scholarly research, but they are deeply controversial as far as many members of Malaysia's *sharia* establishment—and many ordinary Muslims—are concerned. For some, they are quite offensive inasmuch as they deny the legitimacy of what they take to be a defining feature if not *the* key symbol of both the *sharia* judiciary and a distinctly "Islamic" mode of "doing" law (see chapter 3). Some current and former judges I discussed these issues with in recent years were quick to point out that they do indeed exercise *ijtihad*. But since almost all of the evidence they adduced to support this claim had to do with a single issue—whether a man's repudiation of his wife via a "triple *talak*" should be counted as three distinct *talak* (which is irrevocable) or a single *talak* (which is revocable)—it seems safe to conclude that the exercise of *ijtihad* is not a common feature of contemporary judicial practice in today's *sharia* courts. This would seem to be one of the reasons that political and religious elites seek to bolster the specifically Islamic legitimacy of the *sharia* courts in other ways, by playing up the Arabic-origin notion of *sulh* and its deep roots in Arabic and Islamic history, for example.

The larger issue, alluded to earlier, is that the nation's social engineers and brand stewards have sought to rebrand and reconfigure the *sharia* judiciary by highlighting one of its key features as an assemblage, albeit without explicitly invoking the notion of assemblage or other social scientific terminology or academic jargon. They have done this by emphasizing, partly through processes of rebranding, the ways they have refashioned the *sharia* judiciary by incorporating into its discourses and practices features linked to it through its relations of exteriority (to the common law; the civil judiciary; the corporate world; Japanese management and auditing; ISO protocols and other international standards of management and accountability) as distinct from a reworking of its real or imagined internal "essences" (*ijtihad*, for example). In doing so they have destabilized its identity and risked its authenticity, as least or especially as far as Salafists and other "purists" are concerned, some of whom fear that the *sharia* assemblage with which they are imaginatively familiar has been contaminated and may end up becoming completely foreign, to paraphrase the passage from Bruno Latour (2005, 77) that serves as one of the epigraphs to this chapter.

The latter concerns were made clear to me in the Q & A period following a talk I gave on some of the historical themes outlined in this chapter in October 2013 at the International Institute of Advanced Islamic Studies (IIAIS/IIAS) in Kuala Lumpur. The first set of comments came from Kamal, a middle-aged Muslim man, apparently born and raised in Central or Eastern Europe but now residing in Malaysia with his Malay wife and their children, who identified himself as a former student of political theory currently involved in research on Islamic finance. Kamal's chief concern was whether the adoption by the *sharia* courts of various procedures and other features characteristic of the civil judiciary might have "fundamentally altered the identity of the *sharia* courts," resulting in their "conventionalization," as he felt had regrettably already happened with Islamic finance, "which has moved so closely to the conventional system [of finance] that it has become hardly distinguishable from" it. More specifically, Kamal was worried that the dynamics in question might have already "compromised, jeopardized the essential identity of the *sharia* courts because the *sharia* is based on divine revelation" whereas the common law is "not based on revealed knowledge or divine revelation." He reiterated his disquiet in the form of a question as to whether "there is a risk that the *sharia* courts might *lose their essential identity* if they try to become more and more like civil courts and move closer to common law" (emphasis added), concluding with the remark that it is "very important for a Muslim to maintain his identity."

Later, in the lobby outside the auditorium where I spoke and then over lunch at a nearby restaurant with my hosts, as we continued our conversation, Kamal expounded on some of his Salafi-inflected views by explaining that centuries of "man-made" accretions had diluted and otherwise transformed divine revelation in ways he found altogether unacceptable. He also shared his starkly Manichean perspectives on the differences between the Muslim world and West, which he took to be hedonistic, vice-ridden, and terminally decadent. The latter views derived in part from his experiences teaching in a Western (perhaps Canadian) high school or university (our conversation was a bit disjointed and some of the details of his remarks were lost in the fray, amidst the sharing of food and multiple other interactions I was engaged in at the same time). These experiences were largely unhappy ones, apparently, partly because, as Kamal explained it, his students were inclined to smoke marijuana on their lunch break and returned to class in the afternoon stoned and thus unteachable, all of which he found extremely disrespectful and otherwise beyond the pale.

These are by no means the only conversations I could cite to bolster the point that some Muslims find recent transformations in the *sharia* judiciary unsettling if not altogether unacceptable. (Others are addressed in chapters 3 and 4.) Nor are they the only ones that help illustrate the disjunctions that obtain between assemblage theorists and other scholars who are wary of unitary essences on the one hand, and our interlocutors in the field, on the other, many of whom put great stock in such essences and the identities and ethics bound up with them.

CONCLUSION

My main goals in this chapter have been threefold: to delineate some of the empirical complexities of Malaysia's *sharia* judiciary and the mutually contradictory directions in which it is moving; to problematize the trope of Islamization as a gloss for these phenomena; and to illustrate that this judiciary is profitably viewed as a global assemblage. In these concluding remarks, which focus largely on Islamization, I draw attention to broader issues.

There are important comparative and theoretical implications of my argument that the term "Islamization" is a woefully incomplete and otherwise misleading gloss—partly because it is so reductionist—for the changes that have occurred in recent decades in regard to Malaysia's *sharia* judiciary. Processes of Islamization and *sharia*tization, like those involved in desecularization, and of course secularization, are not monolithic, seamless, or all-encompassing, like a steadily advancing prairie fire or some giant avalanche or tsunami. Their directions, dynamics (in terms of force, intensity, degree of institutionalization, etc.), and overall vicissitudes vary tremendously across the terrain of any particular case and from one case to the next (Starrett 2010; Agrama 2012). Their temporally specific, always emergent, and invariably contested "products," moreover, commonly involve a "reorganization of functions and a regrouping of forces" (Deleuze and Guattari 1987, 320). They are thus usefully viewed as global assemblages insofar as they are forged in relationship with a multiplicity of global discourses, practices, incentives, and constraints, widely disparate in origin, often keyed to analytically distinct processes of bureaucratization, rationalization, and corporatization.

Our descriptions and analyses need to make provision for the variegated nature and provenance of these discourses and practices, their ever-shifting articulations in rapidly changing fields of forces, and the different ways in which legal, religious, and other "orders [take shape and] endure across differences and amid transformations" as well as "how orders change and are reworked" (Anderson et al 2012, 173). If they do so, they can help clarify a number of empirical and conceptual issues, including why, across time and space, the operations and directionalities of global assemblages are "heterogeneous, contingent, unstable, partial, and situated" (Collier and Ong 2005, 12), though variably so. They can also clarify why such assemblages cannot be reduced to a single cultural-political or other logic of the sort often foregrounded or assumed by terms such as "Islamization," "*sharia*tization," and "desecularization."

Development of perspectives along the lines suggested here also helps us understand why terms of the latter variety have often been invoked to explain changes in Malaysia's *sharia* judiciary even as arguments of a rather different if not contradictory sort have simultaneously been advanced to sum up transformations in the same assemblage. The latter arguments include claims that recent years have seen "the [common-law] legalization of Islam" rather than "the Islamization of [common] law" (Horowitz 1994, 257),[16] the development of Malaysian "Anglo-Syariah" law (Hooker 1999, 75), and the "secularization of [Malaysian] sharia" (Maznah Mohamad 2010b). To put some of this more broadly: legal (and other) assemblages have their own unique logics and enjoy a (variable) measure of autonomy or "semi-autonomy" in Sally Falk Moore's (1978) terminology (see also Latour 2010), even when they operate in states characterized by exceedingly top-heavy executive branches that resort to lawfare to manage and control their agendas, personnel, and other resources. This is true whether or not the assemblages are implicated, as they are in Malaysia, in the diminishing space between sharia and civil-law arenas and in related processes that have seen countless features of the civil judiciary incorporated into the realm of sharia, resulting in an increasing fusion of the two domains favoring the enhanced prominence of organized Islam in the public sphere. Expressed as a negative proposition, changes in legal assemblages, including those that are heavily inflected by politics and religion, are not appropriately construed as epiphenomena of dynamics in political domains, where, in Malaysia and most other Muslim-majority nations, processes of Islamization are deeply entrenched. Nor are they usefully viewed as inevitable outgrowths of heightened piety or religiosity in private or public realms, another hallmark of Islamization in much of the Muslim world.

This is not the place to provide genealogies of the term "Islamization," a floating, open-ended signifier with "meanings fluid, variant, and elusive," as Gregory Starrett (2010, 628) has remarked of its presumed antithesis, "secularization." Some clarification will be useful, however, since there are at least two analytically distinct genealogies that warrant attention. Consider first that the term has long been deployed by prominent Muslim intellectuals—Fazlur Rahman, Sayyed Hossein Nasr, Syed Muhammad Naquib Al-Attas, Sayyid Abul-A'la Mawdudi, Sayyid Qutb, Ismail al-Faruqi, to mention a few—to conceptualize various processes in early and subsequent Islamic history (Al-Attas 1969; Ali 2010). Inspired according to some accounts by the pioneering work of Abu Hamid Al-Ghazali (1058–1111 C.E.), these intellectuals have frequently used the term when discussing (1) the deleterious effects on Muslims of Western/secular education, the "root cause of crisis, chaos, corruption, and violence in modern societies" (Ali 2010, 8), and (2) the resultant need to develop an "Islamization of knowledge" that purges education of "foreign elements and errors" so "that what is left [may] be remoulded in accordance with Islam" (15). The larger goal is to assist the "community's striving towards realization of the moral and ethical quality of social perfection achieved during the age of the Holy Prophet" (Al-Attas, cited in Ali 2010, 14). For Al-Attas, a major figure in the intellectual history at issue (about whom more below), Islamization involves "liberation of man first from magical, mythological, animistic, national-cultural tradition, and then from secular control over his reason and his language," hence processes of purging, purification, rationalization, and enlightenment (116). AbdulHamid Ahmad AbuSulayman, like many others, hopes "that Islamization in general and the Islamization of Knowledge in particular become the most important issues on the *ummah*'s agenda in the coming decades," though the more encompassing goal for him and others, as suggested above, is "the Islamization of society" (Ali 2010, 131).

To help convey a sense of the dissemination and circulation of some of these ideas beyond intellectual circles, we might briefly consider the work of Syed Muhammad Naquib Al-Attas, who was born in Java in 1931 to parents of Hadhrami Arab, Sundanese, and other ancestry and later moved to Malaysia (then Malaya). Al-Attas is one of the leading intellectuals in Malaysia and Southeast Asia generally, as well as one of the world's most accomplished and respected scholars specializing in Islamic philosophy, metaphysics, and education, and what has come to be known as the Islamization of knowledge. In 1969 he published a programmatic booklet entitled *Preliminary Statement on a General Theory of the Islamization of the Malay-Indonesian Archipelago*, which bore the imprimatur of the Malaysian government's Dewan Bahasa dan Pustaka (Institute of Language and Literature), hence state recognition if not endorsement of Al-Attas's notion of Islamization. This essay lays out some of the broad contours of the transformations entailed in the spread of Islam throughout insular Southeast Asia beginning around the thirteenth century, and helped establish the author's reputation as an erudite scholar with wide-ranging interests in the fields of history, literature, philosophy, metaphysics, education, and Islamic sciences and theology. His widely acclaimed *Islam and Secularism* (1978) is one of many subsequent writings (he has published more than twenty books and dozens of articles, many translated into Arabic, Persian, Turkish, Urdu, French, German, Russian, etc.) that address the importance of knowledge and education for Muslims' advancement. *Islam and Secularism* includes a discussion of the concept of the Islamization of knowledge and is central to his claims (and those of his followers) that he more or less single-handedly developed the concept,[17] which calls for a reformulation of modern thinking in line with Islamic ethics—and conversely, a purging of Western, especially secular, elements from modern scholarly disciplines.

Scholarly achievements such as these helped Al-Attas attain a number of prominent posts in Malayan (subsequently Malaysian) universities. They also help explain how he came to be the founder and director of the Kuala Lumpur-based International Institute of Islamic Thought and Civilisation (ISTAC). ISTAC is a highly influential and architecturally stunning tertiary institution whose daily classes, weekly seminars, and other activities are devoted to "analysing, clarifying, [and] elaborating . . . the key terms [including Islamization] 'relevant to the cultural, educational, scientific, and epistemological problems encountered by Muslims in the present age'" (Wan Mohd. Nor Wan Daud 1998, 99).

No small matter is that Al-Attas has also been the main spiritual and intellectual inspiration for the Angkatan Belia Islam Malaysia (ABIM; the Malaysian Islamic Youth Movement), which has been one of the most powerful and high-profile of the organizations promoting Islamic resurgence in Malaysia since its founding in the early 1970s. ABIM provided the institutional context in which a steady stream of charismatic Muslim intellectuals who went on to make their mark in national political arenas honed their organizational and other skills and otherwise cut their teeth. Such intellectuals include Anwar Ibrahim, who was head of ABIM before Mahathir recruited him to UMNO and rewarded him with a succession of prestigious political posts; Fadzil Mohamed Noor, the longtime leader of PAS and the head of the opposition alliance in its entirety at the time of his death in June 2002; Haji Abdul Hadi Awang, the Chief Minister of Terengganu, who assumed the mantle of PAS leadership on the death of Fadzil Mohamed Noor; and scores of other nationally prominent Muslim intellectuals who command important positions both within and outside state-run (or state-friendly) Islamic institutions.

In sum, Al-Attas's ideas and sensibilities have played a dominant role in shaping the intellectual and political contours of contemporary Islam both in Malaysia and far beyond. It is thus not surprising that terms such as "Islamization" (*Islam-isasi* in Malay) have gained wide currency among ordinary Muslims, particularly in Malaysia. They have also become part of the everyday language of non-Muslims, including, in particular, those who feel threatened by the developments that such terms signify.[18] To put some of this differently, terms like "Islamization" are widely utilized by our interlocutors in the field, however fluid, variant, and elusive their meanings might be. We are thus well advised to engage them in our accounts, regardless of the fact that, or, rather, precisely because, their myriad usages involve floating, open-ended signifiers.

My interest in the concept of Islamization focuses less on the genealogy sketched out in the preceding pages than on the invocation of the term (and of related notions such as "Islamism" and "political Islam") since the 1970s by Western social scientists and other observers concerned with the late twentieth-century resurgence or revitalization of Islam and the mainstreaming or co-opting of *dak-wah*/piety movements by state forces and agents of governmentality.[19] This is an analytically distinct genealogy, though the two are intertwined and mutually constituting, both undergirded by essentialized notions of purging, purification, and social and cultural transformation (Cornell 2014). I argue that during this time Islamization has become a "gate-keeping" concept in Arjun Appadurai's (1986) sense. Such concepts (e.g., Islamic fundamentalism, political Islam, Islamism) "define the quintessential and dominant questions of interest in the region" (357). In doing so, however, they sometimes "limit anthropological [and other] theorizing about the place in question" (357)—in this instance, the Muslim world in its entirety. Similar gate-keeping has occurred with many valuable anthropological studies focusing on topic-locale icons such as "lineage in Africa, exchange in Melanesia, caste in India, . . . and Aboriginal [Australian] marriage systems" (Fardon 1990, 26). Like these and other concepts used with reference to societies broadly distributed across space and time (totemism and kinship are classic exemplars), the term "Islamization" often discourages recognition of the complexity of the phenomena to which it is purportedly relevant: social, cultural, and political change among contemporary Muslims.

A partial explanation for scholars' continued usage of the term "Islamization" has to do with the fact that it is a simple, easy, and convenient one-word gloss for sociohistorical and cultural-political processes that are at once complex, wide-ranging, and increasingly prevalent in today's world. I refer, as mentioned earlier, to processes entailing the heightened salience of Islamic symbols, idioms, and more encompassing discourses and normativities across one or more domains of lived experience that sometimes include variously defined political arenas (in which case observers commonly invoke rubrics such as Islamism, political Islam, or both). "Islamization" is a term that links and condenses a number of distinct but ostensibly related phenomena, and is thus a key symbol in Sherry Ortner's (1973) sense of the term; more precisely, it is what Ortner refers to as a summarizing symbol, as distinct from an elaborating symbol. These kinds of symbols summarize, combine, or condense a variable number of disparate phenomena by means of a single expression or other signifier. The American flag is a classic if well-worn example in some of the literature in that it symbolizes a number of disparate (analytically distinct) phenomena, even from the perspective of a single social actor. For many U.S. citizens, the American flag signifies not only democracy but also "free enterprise," "the land of the free, the home of the brave," the separation of religion and state, and perhaps baseball or football, motherhood, and apple pie. To many of America's critics, domestic and foreign alike, the same flag may symbolize rampant individualism, unbridled sexuality, and unregulated capitalist intrusiveness, if not neo-imperialist policies geared toward suppression of the Global South in general and Muslims in particular. The main issue here is not that the American flag—or Islamization—signifies different things to different people, though that is clear. Rather, the twofold point is that even from the perspective of a single social actor, the flag, like Islamization, signifies many different things simultaneously, and that it does so *metonymically* in the sense that one part stands for the whole (as when, in media accounts, the Kremlin stands for the Russian government in its entirety). It is thus endowed with the capacity to influence social actors in important ways, by canalizing their cognitive and affective orientations and otherwise mobilizing their thoughts and sentiments.

As a quick shorthand, the concept of Islamization has few rivals and will most likely enjoy a longer shelf life than previously used cognates such as Muslimization and Arabization. The latter terms were used in the English-speaking world prior to

World War II to cover semantic domains that were in many ways comparable to that of Islamization insofar as they referred to the spread or diffusion of Islam across space and time—alternatively, to what Geertz (1964 [1973]) famously referred to (in the Hindu Balinese context) as "internal conversion," involving variants of "folk Islam" becoming less "traditional" and more "rationalized" in a Weberian sense. Many, perhaps most, Muslims find the last of these terms (Arabization) deeply offensive, if only because the vast majority of Muslims are not Arabs—and conversely, not all Arabs are Muslim. It is less pejorative, though, than the more archaic Muhammadization, which postulates a cultural-historical process analogous to Christianization, erroneously assuming along the way that the fully-human though divinely-inspired Prophet Muhammad can be likened to Jesus Christ, God the Son incarnated. In sum, because the notion of Islamization currently has few if any rivals, and because, as noted earlier, it is also widely used by contemporary Muslim intellectuals and unlettered Muslims alike to refer to cultural-political and other processes in Muslim-majority settings (and among Muslim minorities), many of us who write about the Muslim world find qualified usages of it convenient in some contexts, and, in any case, exceedingly difficult to avoid.

Some eminent Western scholars of Islam have proposed alternative terminologies in an effort to disaggregate phenomena that, while related, are analytically distinct. Perhaps best known is Marshall Hodgson's introduction of the term "Islamicate," in his magisterial three-volume *The Venture of Islam* (1974–1977), to designate developments which occurred in areas of the world where Muslims were culturally dominant, but which were not, strictly speaking, religious or in accord with *sharia* (at least in Hodgson's understanding of the domains of religion and *sharia*; see Ahmed 2016, 157–75 and passim). One of Hodgson's examples is the development among Persian Muslims living in medieval times of genres of poetry that extolled the virtues of wine. Since the Quran expressly prohibits the consumption of intoxicating beverages, Hodgson viewed it as inappropriate to classify such poetry as Islamic. He nonetheless felt it important to acknowledge these and similar literary, artistic, and related developments pioneered in regions of the world where Muslims were culturally ascendant. Hence his coining of the term "Islamicate," which is analogous to the descriptor "Italianate" in the designation "Italianate architecture." Such architecture maintains a real or imagined connection with things or people Italian, inspired as it was by sixteenth-century Italian Renaissance architecture, even though it developed mainly outside of Italy (e.g., in Northern Europe, parts of the British Empire, and the United States) in the nineteenth and early twentieth centuries. For the most part, terms such as "Islamicate" never took hold (but see Afsaruddin 1999 and Babayan and Najmabadi 2008; see also Ahmed 2016, 157–75). And I am disinclined to deploy them or their derivatives here—"Islamicatization" strikes me as quite awkward—or to introduce yet another set of descriptors that may quickly be relegated to the dustbin of history.

Many transformations presently taking place in the Muslim world have little if anything to do with Islam per se, though some clearly do. The fact that social, political, and other changes involve Muslims does not automatically render them good candidates for inclusion under the rubric of Islamization, unless we are ready to make the problematic twofold claim that Muslims are necessarily "more religious" than Christians, Jews, Hindus, Buddhists, and others, and that virtually everything they do, say, think, or feel is ultimately motivated by or otherwise keyed to a feature of Islam. Such claims commonly involve what Frederic Volpi (2010, 29) characterized as "the overflow of orientalist thinking into political theorizing," leading to what Maxime Rodinson (1988, 102) referred to as "'theologocentrism,' namely the assumption that [in Muslim-majority contexts] 'almost all observable phenomena can be explained by reference to Islam'" (cited in Volpi 2010, 29). In the absence of hard data supporting these kinds of claims, we are best advised to proceed empirically, on a case-by-case basis, with the aim of generating fine-tuned ethnography and the kinds of richly comparative sociohistorical and analytic insights for which Weber, despite his problematic depictions of "*kadi*-justice" and other "essences" of Islam, was justly famous.

In their 2009 review of anthropological studies of Islam and politics, Soares and Osella caution against "automatically privileging religion as the principal—or perhaps unique—foundation for Muslim identity and political practice" (2; see also Schielke 2015). They encourage a focus on *islam mondain,* "which could be translated as 'Islam in the present world'" (Soares and Osella 2009, 11) and the development of a more nuanced, ethnographically grounded appreciation of the many different ways of being Muslim. "*Islam mondain,*" they write, "does not privilege Islam over anything else, emphasizing instead the actual worlds in which Muslims find themselves. This allows us to avoid, on the one hand, narrowly instrumentalist analyses of the relation between Islam and politics, and, on the other, analyses that reduce the politics of Muslims to an epiphenomenon of Islam or the micropolitics of ethical self-fashioning" (12).

Broadly similar approaches, according priority to the everyday lives and quotidian religious and other practices of "ordinary Muslims," have gained currency in recent years, as have related, practice-oriented perspectives on Islamic law in highly centralized judiciaries (Messick 1992; Peletz 1997, 2002; Bowen 2003; Ahmad and Reifeld 2004; Marsden 2005; Agrama 2012; Schielke 2015; Kloos 2018). I find the concept of "ordinary Muslims" (developed in Peletz 1997, 2002) more useful than *islam mondain* or "ordinary (or everyday) Islam." This is partly because, by definition, it takes as its point of departure the practices and lifeworlds of ordinary folks who self-identify as Muslims but are neither political or religious elites nor in the forefront of political or religious movements. This strikes me as more appropriate than starting with a focus on and thus effectively privileging Islam per se, as is the case with emphases on "ordinary (or everyday) Islam" and *islam mondain,* despite the disclaimers of some of their advocates.

Sociologist Baudouin Dupret's (2007) study of Islamic law in Egypt is relevant here, especially because his observations are germane to Malaysia, neighboring Indonesia (the world's most populous Muslim-majority nation), and many other Muslim contexts. Dupret observes that when Egyptian judges deal with cases involving Islamic law, "Explicitly 'Islamic' considerations are few" (97), despite the Islamization of many features of Egyptian politics and everyday life. Arguing that scholars of Islamic law need to focus "much more on living phenomena and actual practices," Dupret underscores "the overwhelmingly routine character . . . of professional practices which are oriented to nothing but the accomplishment of the law" (83, 85). His other points are worth quoting at length.

> At the very place where it is supposed to be massive and overwhelming, that is, in personal status law, references to Islamic law are conspicuous for their paucity. This suggests that the issue of Islamic law in contemporary Egyptian law does not proceed from what the scholarly tradition generally claims. Reference to Islam is occasional; moreover, it is always mediated through the use of Egyptian law's primary sources, that is, legislation and case-law . . . . [T]his reference takes place in the banality and the routine of a judge's activity, which consists mainly in legally characterizing the facts submitted to him . . . . [T]he judge is . . . more interested in manifesting his ability to judge correctly—according to the standards of his profession, the formal constraints that apply to its exercise, the legal sources on which he relies and the norms of the interpretive work his activity supposes—than he is to reiterate the Islamic primacy of the law he implements. There is no doubt that, if asked, the same judge would underscore the conformity of his activity and the law he applies with Islamic law. However, such an attitude would only be retrospective, a posteriori and justificatory. In the course of his work, the judge does not orient himself to the necessity to assess the Islamic dimension of any object, even in this domain of law where the Islamic genealogy of rules seems most evident . . . . [L]aw is a practical accomplishment, rather than an archaeological search for the Islamic pedigree of the norm (97–98).

Approaches like these reveal that in dealing with Islamic law, the everyday discourses and operations of courts in Egypt are not too dissimilar from their Malaysian and Indonesian counterparts, and that, certain obvious differences aside, all such courts have a good deal in common with lower courts in the United States as described by Sally Engle Merry (1990). These kinds of approaches thus go a long way toward de-exoticizing *sharia* and the varied assemblages in which it operates.

2
—————

A Tale of Two Courts

Judicial Transformation, Corporate Islamic
Governmentality, and the New Punitiveness

People do the history of law, and the history of the economy, but the history
of the judicial system, of judicial practices, . . . this is rarely discussed.
—MICHEL FOUCAULT (1980)

Big histories are always best told through insistent, if humble, details.
—ANNA LOWENHAUPT TSING (2015)

Change need not be headline-grabbing to be radical. In parts of the Muslim world,
radical change is taking a less abrupt course than it has in Egypt and other nations
involved in the "Arab Spring." One place where this is happening is Malaysia,
which as we have seen is probably the most successful Muslim-majority country in
the world in terms of its burgeoning middle classes and the stunning rates of
urbanization, economic growth, and educational attainment it has sustained over
the past few decades. In the mid-to-late 1980s and early 1990s, however, Malaysia
was arguably best known among anthropologists not for these developments but
as a *locus classicus* of ethnographic studies of resistance. This was due largely to the
celebrated work of James Scott (1985) on everyday forms of peasant resistance to
the Green Revolution and of Aihwa Ong (1987) on women's involvement in spirit
possession and other forms of opposition to capitalist industrialization and male
control of the workplace. These studies made hope practical even as they documented circumstances giving rise to despair, to paraphrase a point made by Raymond Williams (1982, 85) in another context.

At present, though, owing largely to trends in neoliberal govermentality and
state-sponsored Islamization (documented by Farish Noor 2005; Ong 2006; Willford 2006; Baxstrom 2008; Norani Othman at al 2008; Liow 2009; Peletz 2009; tan
beng hui 2012; Sloane-White 2017; Whiting 2017, and others), Malaysia is better
known among anthropologists and scholars in related fields as a site of constricted

pluralism—with respect to ethnicity, "race," religion, gender, and sexuality, for example—and moral policing. In the circumstances described in these latter accounts, hope seems less practical, though this is a relative point, especially since some studies document robust civil-society activism that manages to ameliorate, subvert, or elude the dominant trends. This change in the focus and tenor of scholarship indexes far more than a shift in the vagaries of academic discourse and its fluid styles, fashions, and zones of prestige, though some of this is involved. It mostly reflects the ways in which the Malaysian state has become more corporate, intrusive, and punitive as it has embraced neoliberal globalization and the forms and norms of Islam and Islamization held to be most compatible with it.

The chapter has two, related goals. The first is to describe and analyze continuities, transformations, and cultural politics in Malaysia's *sharia* judiciary during the past few decades and the new millennium in particular. This goal is facilitated by viewing the *sharia* judiciary as a component or sector of a more encompassing "juridical field" in Pierre Bourdieu's (1987) terminology, a field that is informed by (inter alia) the civil/secular law (British common law) prevalent in most legal arenas in Malaysia, a legacy of British colonialism. Bourdieu's notion of a juridical field is incisively outlined by Richard Terdiman (1987), who translated and provided a forward to Bourdieu's main (1987) text on the subject and offers a summary definition that is at once more clear and more succinct than anything Bourdieu provides in a single passage (see also Bourdieu 2014; Bourdieu and Wacquant 1992, 94–115; Dezalay and Madsen 2012). For Bourdieu, a juridical field is "an area of structured, socially patterned activity or 'practice,' in this case disciplinarily and professionally defined, . . . organized around a body of internal protocols and assumptions, characteristic behaviors and self-sustaining values—what we might informally term a 'legal culture,'" which "exerts a [magnet-like] force upon all those who come within its range." Such fields have fluid, historically contingent boundaries, are "not simple 'reflections' of relations in . . . [political or economic] realms," have their "own complex, specific, and oftentimes antagonistic relation to . . . [state] power," and are also heavily informed by the "internal politics of the profession," a politics given shape and meaning by competitions and conflicts within larger arenas of power (Terdiman 1987, 805–08). This is partly to say that some juridical fields are internally riven, and that their key features or components may be linked through relations of complementary and/or hostile opposition. Bourdieu develops the concept of a juridical field chiefly in relation to Western European, especially French, data from the nineteenth and twentieth centuries, but the geographic and historical referents for his formulations are oftentimes unspecified or unclear. In these situations, I treat the formulations of his that I cite below as pertaining to nineteenth- and twentieth-century France, his primary frame of reference.

The second goal of the chapter, essentially a feature of the first but also analytically distinct, involves focusing on the micropolitics of judicial discourses and the processes associated with them (Messick 1992; Hirsch 1998; Mir-Hosseini 2000; Bowen 2003; Dupret et al 2008; Agrama 2012) so as to elucidate the ways that corporatizing and punitive trends are intertwined with culturally interlocked processes of bureaucratization, rationalization, and Islamization. The logic and genealogy of this intertwining are an important part of a story of cultural production, more precisely, of juridical production in Bourdieu's (1987) terms. Suffice it to add that my approach is more ethnographically grounded and less mechanical, schematic, and abstract than Bourdieu's, and further differs in other ways, especially in its greater concern with governmentality (Foucault 1977, 1991) and religion. More specifically, this chapter offers comparative-historical perspectives afforded by two distinct periods of ethnographic observation, spanning a quarter century, bearing on the same (but ultimately very different) court. The comparative-historical approach I adopt allows me to productively contextualize some of the frequently abstract, hypothetical, and free-floating *sharia*-talk encountered in different quarters of Malaysian society and globally, and, more broadly, is intended to speak to Foucault's (1980, 14) lament, cited as the first epigraph to this chapter, that histories of judicial practices are rarely undertaken. My approach also facilitates a clear view of how the relevant discourses and social forces play out on the ground, in relation to an increasingly corporate Islamic governmentality. Last but not least, it resonates with Anna Tsing's important (2015, 111) contention, bearing on narrative style and method alike, that serves as the second epigraph for this chapter.

In terms of organization, the first section of the chapter presents background material on the training of Islamic judges and the texts cited in courtroom proceedings. The second provides an overview of micropolitical practices of conflict management in a *sharia* court located in a small town about sixty miles south of the nation's capital as I encountered them in my fieldwork in the late 1980s. The third discusses changes (and some continuities) in the appearance, discourses, and practices of that court that I observed during subsequent fieldwork conducted during 2011–13. The fourth presents a detailed transcript of a hearing that took place there in 2012, followed by commentary aimed at highlighting the broad relevance of the case. The fifth and six sections of the chapter engage the new punitiveness that we see both in the latter hearing and in a subsequent (2013) case that I discuss, and in national-level data bearing on new forms of criminality and what I refer to as "creeping criminalization." The conclusion briefly addresses some of the comparative and theoretical implications of my material and Bourdieuian insights on juridical fields and related phenomena.

THE TRAINING OF ISLAMIC JUDGES AND THE TEXTS CITED IN COURTROOM PROCEEDINGS

One of the basic requirements for those seeking appointment to the office of *sharia* judge (*hakim syarie*) in present-day Malaysia is that they earn a four-year degree, such as a Bachelor of Arts (B.A.) in *sharia*, from an accredited tertiary institution, as well as a subsequent Bachelor of Laws (LL.B) degree (or post-graduate diploma) focusing on *sharia*, typically involving two to three semesters of work, also from an accredited tertiary institution. The provenance of such degrees is instructive. Information made available to me by the Department of *Syariah* Judiciary (JKSM) in 2012 indicated that 70 percent (103/148) of the nation's *sharia* judges received their initial training locally, and that the remaining 30 percent (45/148) obtained their first degree outside of Malaysia. Eighty percent (36/45) of those who studied beyond Malaysia's borders did so in Egypt, typically at Al-Azhar University in Cairo; the other judges trained in Jordan (11.1 percent of the overseas total) or elsewhere, such as Iraq or the United Kingdom (8.9 percent of the overseas group).

These figures provide a clear sense of the national contexts in which judges received their initial university-level education, but they are misleading as indicators of current (and presumably future) trends. The vast majority of those who studied overseas are of the older generation (55 years of age and above); virtually all of the younger judges (30–35 years of age and below) received their initial (and subsequent) education in Malaysia. Trends such as these, which can be viewed either in terms of the repatriation of *sharia* judges' formal instruction or as the phasing out of foreign-trained *sharia* judges, are viewed in positive term in many different quarters both in the *sharia* judiciary and beyond. This is because it is widely assumed that domestic training means standardization of education, quality control, and, no small matter, commitment to modern, state-friendly interpretations of Islamic law and normativity.

All but one of the 103 judges who received their initial academic training in Malaysia graduated from one or another of three different institutions. Forty-six percent of them (47/102) received their degree from the Universiti Kebangsaan Malaysia (UKM; the National University of Malaysia;) roughly 34 percent (35/102) hailed from the University of Malaya (UM); and nearly 20 percent (20/102) obtained their degree from the International Islamic University of Malaysia (IIUM/UIA). The remaining judge graduated from the recently established Islamic Science University of Malaysia (USIM).

Having focused thus far on the initial (four-year) training of Islamic judges, I need to reiterate that an additional two- to three-semester period of education and certification is also necessary if one seeks a position on the *sharia* bench. I do not have precise figures for the distribution of students across different institutions, but I was told that most Islamic judges received their second period of instruction either from UKM or the IIUM. The latter two institutions, plus the University of Malaya, where, as we have seen, around 34 percent of locally trained judges receive their initial education, thus constitute the main feeder institutions for those who work as judges in the Islamic judiciary.

What of the curriculum that judges engage in the course of their formal studies? The curriculum for the four-year degree consists of courses in both *sharia* and civil law, so that students learn from, and develop a comparative sense of, both systems of jurisprudence. There is some variation from one institution to the next in terms of course requirements, course contents, and language(s) of instruction—typically Malay, as well as Arabic and/or English—but both the Malaysian Qualification Agency, which oversees academic programs in all of the nation's public and private institutions, and the Department of *Syariah* Judiciary monitor and otherwise regulate the curriculum to ensure consistency and quality. As might be expected, the second period of training is more specialized.

Let us consider course requirements for the Diploma in Law and Administration of Islamic Judiciary (DAIJ) offered by the IIUM, which is geared toward those who have already earned a B.A. or LL.B in *sharia* and seek to join the civil service as *Sharia* Court Officials, a designation that includes *sharia* judges, *sharia* prosecutors, and *sulh* officers. Obtaining this diploma involves two semesters of full-time study. Courses taken in the first semester, all of which are taught in Malay, unless otherwise noted, include Islamic Legal Texts (taught in Arabic); [Islamic] Family Law; Managing Muslim Estates; The Islamic Legal System; The Malaysian Legal System; and Principles and Rules in the Study of Islamic Law. The second semester includes courses on Islamic Legal Texts (taught in Arabic); Criminal Matters in *Sharia* Courts; Laws of Evidence; *Fiqh* Principals and Rules; Civil Matters in the *Sharia* Courts; and finally, a Term Paper Project.[1]

Those seeking additional training, as roughly 12 percent (18/148) of the nation's *sharia* judges have done, might pursue a Master's Degree in the Administration of Islamic Law at the IIUM or elsewhere. Obtaining this degree at the IIUM involves coursework on Islamic Legal Maxims; International Law and Its Impact on the Administration of Islamic Law; Alternative Dispute Resolution; Techniques of Legal Writing; Conflicts Between *Sharia* and Civil Law; and related topics.

One cannot necessarily infer the intellectual content of course offerings from the titles of these courses, but it is clear from interviews I conducted with faculty at IIUM and from university brochures and published accounts (e.g., Najibah M. Zin 2012) that students enrolled in programs such as the above engage a wide range of literature relevant to Islamic law and its administration in contemporary Malaysia. The classical texts of Islamic jurisprudence most widely utilized in Malaysian universities involved in the training of *sharia* judges include the weighty set of tomes (running to roughly 3,500 pages in some versions) focusing on the Shafi'i school of Islamic law that were compiled by the sixteenth-century Egyptian religious scholar al-Imam Shams al-Din Muhammad ibn Ahmad al-Khatib al-Shirbini (al-Shirbini for short); these are titled *Mughni Al-Muhtaj ila Ma'rifat Ma'ani alfaz Al-Minhaj* (*The Enrichment of the One in Need of Knowledge of the Meanings of the Words of the Minhaj*), commonly known as *Mughni al-Muhtaj*

(The Necessary Enrichment) (al-Shirbini n.d. [2014]). Contemporary materials on Islamic jurisprudence include, most notably, the eight-volume *al-Fiqh al Islami wa Adillataha [Islamic Jurisprudence and Its Proofs]* written by Syria's Wahba Mustafa al-Zuhayli (1932–2015), who until his recent death was one of the world's leading scholars of Islamic law (al-Zuhayli 1997). They also include a Malay translation of al-Zuhayli's text prepared by Syed Ahmad Syed Hussein et al, bearing the title *Fiqh dan Perundangan Islam [Islamic Jurisprudence and Law]* (1994).

These and related texts provide the philosophical, theological, and conceptual mooring for a good deal of future judges' coursework. But they comprise but one portion of the material in the curriculum that judges-to-be must master. Put differently, those who aspire to positions on the *sharia* bench must develop competence with respect to at least two other bodies of literature, each of which is arguably of far greater significance than the texts noted above for the fulfillment of day-to-day judicial responsibilities and the execution of attendant professional duties.

The first body of literature consists of the summaries of *sharia* court cases and the decisions relevant to them that appear in locally published *sharia*-oriented legal journals such as *Jurnal Hukum, Malayan Law Journal, Shariah Law Reports, Malaysian Journal of Syariah and Law, Jurnal Syariah,* and the *IIUM Law Journal.* (Students are also expected to read selected cases drawn from relevant journals published overseas, such as the *Pakistan Legal Digest* and the *All Indian Report,* but these are ultimately less important.) Recent decades have seen a proliferation of such journals in Malaysia, as elsewhere in the Muslim world, raising questions about the precise role that the published decisions of *sharia* judges play in the disposition of subsequent cases. Such issues are of interest in light of the fact that one of the much-cited differences between the common law and *sharia* is the presence of a notion of binding precedent in the former, its absence in the latter. Suffice it to say here that *sharia* judges are expected, as one highly ranked member of the JKSM told me, to "read, master, and respect" the decisions contained in these journals, a point to which I return in due course.

The second body of literature is arguably of greatest importance for a judge to master; it consists of formally gazetted laws bearing on the *sharia* courts and their administration that are published locally by the International Law Book Services. These laws vary from one jurisdiction to the next, and are compiled in inexpensive, widely available booklets with glossy covers, each of which focuses on a specific state (or the Federal Territory) and on a subset of the laws that obtain in a particular jurisdiction. The booklets are sold in university bookstores, in bookshops specializing in religious texts and books for high-school students, in the upscale bookstores (such as Kinokunia) that are located in Kuala Lumpur's glitziest malls (like Suria KLCC), and in other venues; they are also available online where they can be freely viewed and downloaded, via the E-*Syariah* Portal, for example. They commonly contain both Malay and English versions of the text, though one can also purchase booklets solely in Malay or English. The booklets that are most relevant to the Federal Territory of Kuala Lumpur, to take one jurisdiction as an example, include:

1. *Administration of Islamic Law (Federal Territories) Act 1993 (Act 505) and Rules,*
2. *Islamic Family Law (Federal Territories) Act 1984 (Act 303),*
3. *Syariah Criminal Offenses (Federal Territories) Act 1997 [Act 559],*
4. *Syariah Criminal Procedure (Federal Territories) Act 1997 [Act 560],*
5. *Syariah Court Evidence (Federal Territories) Act 1997 [Act 561],* and
6. *Syariah Court Civil Procedure (Federal Territories) Act 1998 (Act 585) and Rules.*

At present, these are the kinds of texts that are most in evidence in Malaysia's Islamic courts. Their glossy, colorful covers, standardized graphic design, and uniform dimensions make them easy to spot amidst the bundles of papers and other printed material that *sharia* lawyers clutch to their chests or strain to carry under their arms as they hurry from one courtroom to another. And they are easily recognizable amidst the documents that lawyers unpack from their bulky briefcases (many of which, equipped with wheels and long handles, resemble the carry-on bags that airline passengers struggle to fit into overhead compartments) and spread out on the table in front of them as they prepare to represent a client, prosecute a criminal case, or otherwise formally engage a judge in conversation.

More to the point is that these are the written texts that lawyers, judges, and prosecutors most commonly cite in the course of their formal deliberations. Put differently, it is relatively rare for a *sharia* lawyer to make reference to the Quran, *hadith,* or other specifically religious texts, though it is more common now than in times past. This is not because texts such as the Quran are altogether irrelevant. It is, rather, that their importance is greatly superseded by the formally gazetted laws bearing on the *sharia* courts that are compiled in the booklets under discussion. The latter booklets include state simplifications of Quranic provisions, bearing on *nusyuz* (spousal recalcitrance), reconciliation, and divorce, for example, which is to say that the specifically religious doctrines that are most important in the *sharia* courts are those that have been greatly simplified by the state. State authorization of religious practice, is, in any event, crucial, even when the practice is legitimized by the Quran, as in the case of divorcing one's wife via the *talak*/repudiation clause outside of the courtroom, which is a violation of state law in present-day Malaysia even though it does not invalidate the divorce.

Like the lawyers who increasingly appear before them, Islamic magistrates are also more inclined to make explicit reference to formally gazetted enactments than to specifically religious texts such as the Quran or *hadith.* Some of the reasons for this have been noted above, though additional issues are also involved. Due partly to the increased presence in the courtroom of lawyers, who are professionally committed to furthering the rights and interests of their clients, judges must be closely attuned to procedural correctness and related considerations. They do not want their courtroom conduct questioned by lawyers or those they represent, and they certainly do not want their decisions appealed by disgruntled litigants and those whom they hire (or who have been appointed) to represent them. Especially in densely urban areas such as Kuala Lumpur, moreover, judges tend to have heavy caseloads that conduce toward rather formal, business-like hearings and motions that are often of short duration. Procedural appropriateness is one of the top priorities here, though basic fairness is also of great concern. Hence it is not uncommon to see judges making explicit reference to—even reading from, holding up, or waving around—one or another of the published booklets of gazetted laws. Specific provisions from these booklets, moreover, are sometimes cited by judges when they render a decision in a hearing, just as *sharia* prosecutors typically cite one or another of these provisions (bearing on gambling, drinking alcohol, or failing to fast during the month of Ramadan, for instance) when they charge a defendant in a criminal case, as in the hearing involving a man accused of gambling discussed below. Put simply, lawyers and judges alike appear to feel that, in most of the cases in which they are involved, there simply isn't sufficient time to cite specifically religious texts or to make overt reference to explicitly Islamic concerns; alternatively, they feel that there is no need or rationale to do so. In this regard Malaysia's Islamic judges have much in common with Egyptian magistrates adjudicating matters that fall within the ambit of Islamic law in Egypt, as described by Dupret (2007).

I should point out that disinclination or failure to make overt reference to an explicitly Islamic concern or concept does not mean that such a concern or concept has no bearing on a judge's practice or disposition of a case. It is nonetheless curious that the written summaries of *sharia* court cases and the decisions relevant to them that appear in journals such as *Jurnal Hukum*, the official organ of the JKSM, give a very different impression of courtroom proceedings and the discourses that prevail in them. This is because the summaries and decisions presented in such journals are heavily laced with quotes from the Quran, *hadith*, and other specifically religious sources, thus giving the impression that legal maxims and other relevant passages from these kinds of sources are frequently invoked in hearings.

The striking disjunction raises important methodological issues, one of which is that we cannot rely on law-journal summaries of court cases or decisions relevant to them to arrive at a sense of the atmosphere of the court or the types of discourses that commonly prevail within them. If we do, we are likely to end up with a very distorted view of how the courts operate and what kinds of discourses and considerations predominate in their proceedings. Conversely, if we rely primarily on observations of courtroom proceedings in our efforts to develop a sense of how and when Islamic laws and more encompassing normativities may be relevant to *sharia* court proceedings and the decisions rendered in them, we may also fall short in our efforts to understand the relevance of Islam in *sharia* court contexts. I say "may" twice here because it is not entirely clear to me if the Islamic laws and normativities cited in law-journal articles are relevant to the *sharia* judges' comportment, including the specific decisions they render in particular cases, or whether they are included primarily for heuristic or other purposes, such as to increase the likelihood that future generations of *sharia* judges and lawyers will keep *sharia* considerations in mind as they go about their daily professional tasks.

Students studying to become *sharia* judges and lawyers are among the primary readers of *sharia* law journals, a fact that is of course widely known to the judges and other *sharia* professionals who write and edit articles for these journals. The editorial boards of journals such as *Jurnal Hukum,* which, as already noted, is the official *sharia*-law journal of the JKSM, include current and former *sharia* judges as well as members of the IIUM and other Islamic institutions of higher learning that serve as feeder institutions for the Islamic judiciary. I would suggest that one of the most important jobs of such journals is to foreground the relevance of Islam in the law articles and other scholarly publications and online material devoted to the *sharia* courts and their operations, and that this particular set of tasks is all the more crucial in light of the ever increasing tendencies of the *sharia* courts to rely on British-derived, common-law procedural guidelines, Japanese systems of management and auditing (the 5Ses), and other obviously non-Islamic sources, such as KPIs, TQM rubrics and protocols, and ISO recommendations. Debates about Islamic authenticity are both of great import and heavily freighted in the Malaysian context, as Horowitz (1994), among others, has emphasized. This is especially true when they bear on whether or not—and if so, the degree to which—the practices and orientations of the nation's Islamic courts are informed by Quranic or other classical Islamic considerations as distinct from non-Islamic sources that Salafists and other "purists," including many in the Islamist opposition party, PAS, view as harmful, polluting accretions that should be purged.

This brief overview of the formal training of *sharia* judges and the texts cited in courtroom proceedings provides useful context for considering dynamics of judicial transformation during the period 1987–2013, which I explore in the remainder of this chapter. The ethnographic material that I engage below bears most directly on changes that have occurred in the Islamic court located in the small town of Rembau, Negeri Sembilan. The formal training of the two judges that I discuss— one of whom (b. 1942) presided over cases I observed from 1987 to 1988, the other of whom (b. 1980) heard cases during my return visit to that same court during 2011–13—was broadly analogous, although many rough contemporaries of the first judge had far less formal training, a controversial and otherwise problematic situation that began to be rectified in the mid-1980s (Horowitz 1994). Both had obtained four-year university degrees focusing on *sharia* (the first from Al-Azhar in Egypt, the second from a local Malaysian university) and both had apparently received additional training from accredited institutions (at least one of which resulted in an LL.B degree). But the ways they engaged litigants and ran proceedings was strikingly dissimilar, as was the overall professional atmosphere they endeavored to maintain. Islamic judges, after all, "are not a homogenous class," as Morgan Clarke (2012, 107) observed for Lebanon. Some of these differences may be due to contrasting details and emphases of their formal training. Others are keyed to analytically distinct but culturally interlocked processes of Islamization, bureaucratization, rationalization, and corporatization that have occurred since the late 1980s. Still others illustrate related, more or less contemporaneous processes of neoliberal globalization, including the surge in punitiveness that commonly goes hand in hand with them, a subject I discuss in the penultimate section of the chapter.

REMBAU'S *SHARIA* COURT IN THE LATE 1980s

My aim in this section is to provide a sketch of the micropolitical practices of dispute management in the *sharia* court I studied in the small town of Rembau, Negeri Sembilan, in the late 1980s, starting with the atmosphere of the courthouse.[2] (Readers interested in seeing how these dynamics played out in specific hearings may want to refer to some of the thirty-six cases presented in Peletz 2002; see also Sharifah Zaleha Syed Hassan and Cederroth 1997.) For the most part, I do not use the term "courtroom" here because in my experience, involving dozens of visits to the courthouse during the period 1987–88, the Islamic judge, known then and for centuries prior to that as a *kadi* (an Arabic-origin term variably rendered *kadzi*, *qadi*, etc.) preferred that disputes be aired in the less formal and less intimidating atmosphere of his private chambers, rather than in the courtroom itself.

There were two clusters of furniture in the judge's chambers: a low wooden table adorned with plastic flowers and surrounded by four pastel chairs and a matching couch; and the *kadi*'s large wooden desk and black chair, along with three or four other chairs that were usually arranged so that they faced the *kadi*'s desk and were only a foot or two away. Litigants sat in these chairs (as did the anthropologist), hence within a few feet of the *kadi*, and necessarily sat quite close to one another as well. The same goes for witnesses and others involved in hearings. These spatial arrangements contributed to the informality of the proceedings. So too did a half dozen other factors that I outline here, commenting on other important issues along the way.

First, the *kadi* dressed in "everyday (Malay male) attire." He never wore a sports jacket, necktie, or the heavy judicial robes that hung from a coatrack behind him.

Instead, he preferred a more commonplace but respectable outfit, typically consisting of loose-fitting trousers, sandals, baggy shirt, and a white skullcap that signified his having made the pilgrimage to Mecca.

Second, the *kadi*'s three- or four-year-old son frequently played in his chambers (as on a few occasions did his five- or six-year-old daughter), even when disputes were being aired, commonly banging on the *kadi*'s desk, slamming doors, and otherwise creating a good deal of noise and distraction. This gave the impression that the *kadi* was a "family man," that he understood the challenges of balancing the entailments of family and work, a matter of no small significance insofar as the court dealt primarily with matters of Islamic family law and disputes between husbands and wives, and did so at a time when kinship and other social roles were very much in flux due to processes of urbanization, industrialization, and the like.

Third, congruent with the above, and as was customary in rural contexts and many urban settings at that time, the *kadi* and his staff used classificatory kinship terms (*makcik* ["auntie"], *pakcik* ["uncle"], *kakak* ["elder sister"], *abang* ["elder brother"], etc.) when addressing and referring to persons involved in a case. This was in lieu of more formal alternatives such as generic second-person pronouns (*kamu, awak*), terms such as "Mr." or "Mrs." (*Encik, Puan*), or the more technical "petitioner"/"plaintiff" (*sipeminta/plaintif*) or "respondent"/"defendant" (*sipenjawab/defendan*), which were nonetheless commonly utilized in written documents. It should be noted that these usages were not embedded in simple or straightforward discourses that might be glossed "pro-family" (or "pro-kinship"). The courts were key players in the revalorization and narrowing of kinship, deemphasizing the relevance of extended kinship relations as well as those filial ties and sibling bonds that sometimes posed problems for wives and their husbands (as when a mother or sister[s] encountered difficulties with a woman's husband or vice versa).

Fourth, neither the *kadi* nor his superiors felt it necessary to post lists of guidelines or regulations (bearing on styles of dress and comportment, for example) at the entrance to the courthouse, or to instruct those with business there how to address the *kadi* and what kinship terms to use when referring to themselves in the *kadi*'s presence. The partial exception to these generalizations was a small sign posted at the entrance to the courthouse that advised women to cover their heads appropriately before entering the building. This is an Islamic injunction involving covering the *aurat* (parts of the body that should not be exposed or revealed in public), but was not explicitly designated as such.

More broadly, there was not much that materially marked the courthouse as a specifically Islamic space, aside from the name on the front of the building designating it as a *sharia* courthouse and the small framed calligraphic renderings of the words "Allah" and "Muhammad" that hung on the wall in the main room of the building, just below the much larger block-letter sign "*Kepimpinan Melalui Teladan*" ("Leadership Through Example"). The latter slogan appeared throughout government offices in the late 1980s, marking them as spaces of a state that was generally held to be secular (though the latter term was not widely used at the time). The civil-service nametags commonly worn by about half of the staff (but not the *kadi*) further underscored that the premises and all that went on there were under the direct jurisdiction of the state.

Similarly, specific references to classical texts of Islamic jurisprudence or to features of *sharia* other than those formally gazetted in secular/common law and directly relevant to the case at hand were exceedingly rare, as to a large degree were explicit references to more encompassing Islamic codes of normativity enshrined in or otherwise directly associated with the Quran or *hadith*. This does not mean that the latter codes were irrelevant, or that there was little invocation of the semantically expansive concepts of sin (*dosa*) and wrong (*salah/kesalahan*), both of which refer to transgressions defined by Islam as well as other religious traditions and ethical systems (i.e., they are not "Islam-specific.") My point is that even passing reference to the Quran, *hadith,* and classical works in Islamic jurisprudence was highly unusual, and that in judicial discourses in particular there was little mention of Islam and even less of *sharia* (unless formally gazetted and immediately relevant). Put differently, these quintessentially Islamic phenomena were not discursively marked, explicit, or elaborated. On the other hand, the *kadi's* assistant (*penolong kadi*), who counseled and otherwise aided the mostly female plaintiffs (and other women who came to the courthouse), saw as one of her main tasks the dispensing of *nasihat* (morally corrective advice), a central concept in Islamic theology and jurisprudence, as Talal Asad (1993, 214) has noted.

Fifth, there were no lawyers involved in hearings, hence litigants spoke directly to the *kadi* (and his staff) and vice versa. Put differently, even though court clerks (most of whom were male) provided plaintiffs with important advice on how to convert a domestic or other problem into a legally salient case (so that it could proceed through proper channels), litigants' narratives were not packaged or managed by third parties (like lawyers) who relied on specialized, technical language to earn their keep or achieve their professional objectives.

The discourses of the *kadi,* moreover, were oriented directly toward the litigants before him and were heavily pragmatic, fashioned "in response to the requirements and *urgency* of practice," as Bourdieu (1987, 824; emphasis in original) has said of some judicial narratives in nineteenth- and twentieth-century France. They were also commonly couched in terms of Malay "family values" that included the valorization of mutual respect, familial obligation, negotiation/mediation, and mutual accommodation.

Sixth, the *kadi* and his staff permitted and sometimes encouraged relatively wide-ranging, "no-holds-barred" airing of grievances, providing female plaintiffs in particular with opportunities for cathartic and otherwise therapeutic venting toward (or about) their husbands or former husbands, typically the most important authority figures in their lives. These kinds of opportunities were largely unavailable elsewhere at the time and entailed little if any risk of reprisal.

We should not romanticize these and other features (e.g., the relative informality) of the hearings. They sometimes disadvantaged those who depended on the court's services to help them resolve potentially intractable problems in their lives. The cultural logic of judicial process that emphasized negotiation, compromise, and mutual accommodation clearly worked against women seeking to divorce their husbands on the grounds that they did not support them or their children, because women were typically encouraged to work out their differences and to give their husbands more time to "see the light." The relative informality of hearings and record-keeping, moreover, sometimes involved what from a common-law or bureaucratic point of view might be termed "procedural laxity." This could cause problems for litigants. So too could both the *kadi*'s proclivity to refrain from imposing all of the sanctions at his disposal on those guilty of breaches of *sharia*, and the weak follow-up and implementation of court orders that was a widespread problem throughout the country at the time (and previously), and that is still a cause for concern, though less so than in times past.

This brief overview of the handling of disputes in Rembau's *sharia* court in the late 1980s could of course be extended. It should be sufficient for present purposes, however, so long as we bear in mind one additional set of issues that is not explicit in this thumbnail sketch. In the 1980s, as before, *sharia* courts in Malaysia (including Rembau's) were plainly engaged in disciplining and controlling litigants and, albeit to a lesser extent, other members of the Muslim community, although due partly to the limitations of available technology they did not carry out much surveillance. They also helped further what national-level political and religious elites touted as projects of development and modernity (*perkembangan, kemodenan*), notwithstanding the fact that they did not typically see themselves as agents of social change. Under the New Economic Policy (NEP; 1971–90) and subsequently these projects occasioned a greatly expanded role for the state, ostensibly in order both to eradicate poverty, which disproportionately plagued the predominantly rural Malays, and to transform the latter community into an urban middle class that could compete successfully with Chinese and other Malaysians as well as capitalists worldwide. Such projects involved policies of affirmative action, privatization, etc., aiming to insure that Malays would eventually control at least 30 percent of the nation's corporate equity (a goal that is still unrealized, despite the revamped and heavily contested policies aimed at its attainment). The specific ways in which the Islamic courts helped further these projects included their relative devaluation of extended kinship (as noted earlier), long seen in official circles as a drag on economic effort; their related emphasis on the individual, individualism, and agentive notions of personhood and subjectivity; their encouragement of literacy and their stigmatization of both non-literacy and lack of fluency in the national language; and the ways their (usually implicit) definitions of work and livelihood valorized wage labor and salaried employment in urban settings over agricultural work (e.g., rubber tapping, fishing, and related activities). I have discussed these matters elsewhere (Peletz 2002).[3] The key point here is that the striking changes in the court's orientations and activities that I observed in the new millennium, especially its involvement in state projects of rationalization, discipline, surveillance, and control, build on these earlier structural precedents and thus involve continuity as well as transformation. Put differently, they are by no means a complete rupture from the earlier period I have described.

RETURN TO REMBAU, 2011–2013

In 2011 I returned to the same Islamic court. The changes in its appearance, discourses, and practices in the intervening twenty-three years were quite striking, as were certain continuities; the same is true of the town of Rembau, which boasts a population of some 29,000 people (according to the 2010 census), more than a ten-fold increase since the late 1980s. For starters, the courthouse was altogether new, down the road from the now abandoned shell of its former self, much better appointed, and more spacious. In many ways, moreover, it was exceedingly high-tech: the noisy old typewriters, for instance, had been replaced by a bevy of top-notch Dell PCs. These large, imposing machines provide staff with instantaneous access to nationwide (electronic) databases maintained by the *sharia* courts, the police, and other state agencies. More generally, they allow immediate access to the E-*Syariah* Portal—part of the e-governance initiative described earlier—which showcases the services of the courts on lavish websites 24/7.

The *kadi* I came to know in the late 1980s, who was born in Johol, Negeri Sembilan (around 1942) and was thus a relative insider, had retired, as had many members of his staff. His replacement was born in the state of Terengganu (in 1980), and was thus an outsider by local criteria. He was far more business-like in his appearance and approach to the law. In sharp contrast to his predecessor, for instance, he did not wear "traditional" Malay attire. Rather, like all of his contemporaries and successors, he donned the corporate garb worn by white-collar employees in the Malaysian civil service and by corporate executives worldwide, a smartly tailored black business suit, white button-down shirt, fashionable (but conservative) necktie, etc. Completing his outfit was a civil-service nametag (see figure 2 and figure 3).

The figure he cut, his "aura," was decidedly different than that of his predecessor and arguably unrecognizable if viewed through an optic focusing on *sharia* judges in the highlands of Yemen in the mid-1970s as described in Brinkley Messick's influential (1992) account. So too were the sentiments and dispositions, the *habitus,* informing his practice, which struck me as remarkably similar to—albeit even more formal than—that of *sharia* and civil-court judges in the nation's capital.

FIGURE 2. Mohd Abu Hassan Bin Abdullah, judge of *Syariah* Lower Court, District of Rembau, Negeri Sembilan (2010–2015), 2013. Photo by author.

FIGURE 3. Wan Mohamad Helmi Bin Masran, judge of *Syariah* Lower Court, District of Rembau, Negeri Sembilan (2015–present), 2018. Photo by Hariz Shah.

In contrast to the late 1980s, all hearings are nowadays held in the large impersonal courtroom rather than in the judge's private chambers. And the designation *kadi* has been officially retired in favor of the generic (Arabic-origin term) *hakim,* whose primary referent in Malaysia has long been civil-court judge(s), a clear instance of "rebranding"—the latter being the term half-jokingly used by a high-ranking member of the *sharia* judiciary when he explained the terminological shift to me, as mentioned earlier. The walls of the courthouse are decorated with beautiful calligraphic renderings of the words "Allah" and "Muhammad," as was also true in the late 1980s, along with a Quranic verse commanding judgments based on justice (from Surah An-Nisa [4:58]), which is a relatively recent addition. But these Islamic adornments now compete for the viewer's attention with plaques outlining the Vision, Mission, and Objective (*Visi, Misi, Objektif*) of the courts; a Client's Charter (*Piagam Pelanggan*) promising "friendly, fair, timely, and satis-factory service"; and banners celebrating the commitment of the court to proto-cols of the ISO, which many Malaysian businessmen and policymakers alike regard as *the* ultimate arbiter with regard to an ever-proliferating range of stand-ards and more encompassing normativities for business, government, society, and culture alike. Banners and commitments of the latter sort are among the many indices (others of which are discussed below) of the greater interest we see in the court with the models, practices, and sensibilities that prevail in upper-level man-agement circles in corporate/capitalist business sectors in Malaysia and beyond. More generally, they point to the relative permeation throughout Malaysian soci-ety of economistic and attendant administrative/managerial values and interests, once associated largely with the upper echelons of rational (industrial) capitalism, that have become increasingly hegemonic, though variably so, across a wide vari-ety of social, cultural-political, and other domains.

Embellishments such as these convey both secular and specifically Islamic mes-sages that are seamlessly interwoven: the plaque outlining the court's vision, mis-sion, and objective asserts that the *sharia* court is "an excellent agency in imple-menting justice based on Syarak law for Muslim communities in Negeri Sembilan," doing so "in accordance with the Enactment of Islamic Religious Administration (Negeri Sembilan) 2003"; and that it aims to "implement justice based on the boundaries of power vested by the Law and Constitution in line with the require-ments and principles of Islam as contained in the Al-Quran, As-Sunnah, Ijmak, and Qias." Broadly analogous interweaving is evident in commemorative volumes highlighting the welcoming nature of the *sharia* courts (see figure 4).

The signboard at the entrance to the courthouse contains a list of twelve rules pertaining to the proper comportment of those visiting the courts, a significant departure from the single admonition posted there during the late 1980s. The new, greatly expanded list includes rules enjoining visitors to respect the judge and the court, to bow their heads when entering and exiting the courtroom during pro-ceedings, to sit courteously, to refrain from protesting the court's decisions, and, last but not least, to "always control your emotions."

This greatly expanded list of do's and don'ts is emblematic of the more regulated relationship to authority and to the enhanced management of the self (increased self-governance) that political and religious elites have sought to normalize in the

FIGURE 4. "Welcome to the *Sharia* Court." From *Jabatan Kehakiman Syariah Negeri Sembilan: 5 Dekad Merentasi Zaman, 1960–2014* (*Negeri Sembilan Department of Syariah Judiciary: Five Decades Through Time, 1960–2014*) (Seremban, Negeri Sembilan: Jabatan Kehakiman Syariah, Negeri Sembilan, 2014), iv.

years since my earlier fieldwork, part of their aggressive commitment to neoliberal globalization and the creation of a class of entrepreneurially oriented "new Malays" (*Melayu baru*) who can successfully compete in both national and global economic arenas (Ong 2006; see also Rudnyckyj 2010). Another sign of the times was the gifts the judge kindly instructed his staff to provide me as I was leaving: glossy brochures highlighting the work of the courts, along with a notepad, a ballpoint pen, a travelling coffee mug, and a colorful, sturdy tote bag—many of them emblazoned with the corporate logos, slogans, and trademarks of the Islamic judiciary.

Readily apparent from the design of these gifts is the corporate rebranding of the *sharia* judiciary and its highly sophisticated marketing in print media, cyberspace, and elsewhere. This rebranding, which is strikingly evident in the E-*Syariah* Portal (discussed in chapter 1), complements, and, indeed, is of a piece with, then-current government campaigns to promote "1Malaysia." This slogan was meant to suggest a single, unified Malaysia that is home to a single, unified Malaysian "race" (*bangsa*), as distinct from three separate "races" (Malays, Chinese, and Indians), increasing numbers of whom have deserted the long-dominant ruling coalition and its mainstay UMNO party in favor of the opposition. This trend has been particularly evident in the general elections of 2008, 2013, and 2018, the last of which saw the ruling coalition's first defeat since independence in 1957. Perhaps more to the point, "1Malaysia" involved the promotion of a single, monolithic, top-down, and increasingly constricted interpretation of Islam, dubbed "1Islam" by some critics (tan beng hui 2012), a (neo)classic example of what James Scott (1998) refers to as "state simplification."

The *sharia* judiciary, which is under the direct control of the prime minister's department, is a key player in all such campaigns. So too is the more encompassing and far more powerful and prestigious civil judiciary that, while formally independent, is also highly susceptible to political meddling and attendant pressure from the prime minister's department. In recent years the latter judiciary, aided by constitutional amendments such as Article 121(1A) (1988)[4] and the ascendance of Islamist groups, including associations of *sharia* lawyers and other Muslim professionals advocating greater Islamic supremacy, has ceded jurisdiction and control to its *sharia* counterpart in highly controversial, landmark decisions (bearing on apostasy involving the renunciation of Islam; custody disputes over children born to non-Muslim couples that are complicated by one parent's embrace of Islam around the time of marital dissolution; and the proper burial of those who have allegedly undergone late-life conversion to Islam). Such concessions have met with strong opposition from the Malaysian Bar Council, Muslim feminists (e.g., the members of Sisters in Islam), and a multitude of activist human rights groups and other NGOs (many with strong ties to the West) that seek to defend religious freedoms and the rights of non-Muslims. These and other organizations have actively protested the redrawing of boundaries between the two judiciaries and the oftentimes implicit blurring of lines between law, politics, and religion (and the secular and the sacred) thus entailed. As Hussein Agrama (2012) has shown for Egypt, such redrawing and blurring is central to the ways the state endeavors to enact its authority, legitimacy, and sovereignty in the name of public order, morality, and national security.

More broadly, the negotiation and competition between these two judiciaries (and their allies) "for control of access to [and interpretation of] the legal resources inherited from the past," in this instance primarily the Federal Constitution, is at once complementary and hostile, to paraphrase Bourdieu's (1987, 817, 821) observations concerning contestations within juridical fields in France during the nineteenth and twentieth centuries. In Malaysia, competition within the juridical field has "foster[ed] a continual process of rationalization" (817)—as occurred in France—at least or especially within the *sharia* judiciary. The fact that many of these same basic dynamics were evident in the juridical fields of "strongly secular" France, at a time when headscarf controversies and other fraught matters involving Muslims were not yet of national political concern, is revealing. It indicates, on the one hand, that such developments are by no means unique to Muslim-majority settings such as Malaysia or Egypt (Agrama 2012; Mahmood 2012), and, on the other, that the invocation of religious/secular binaries does not necessarily help us understand the dynamics at issue and may obscure more than it illuminates.

I turn now to a criminal incident that came before Rembau's *sharia* judge in 2012. By way of brief background, Malaysia's *sharia* courts have dealt with certain offenses currently classified as criminal or *jenayah* (e.g., *zina* [fornication/adultery]) since their inception in precolonial times. But even through my earlier fieldwork in the 1980s, such matters comprised a negligible percentage of the cases on the docket. They were, in any event, typically viewed by court staff as best handled through negotiation, compromise, and mediation, much like the far more numerous civil disputes (*kes mal;* usually involving Islamic family law on divorce, reconciliation, failure to provide spousal maintenance, child support, etc.) that they endeavored to resolve. Nowadays, however, especially in Rembau's *sharia* court, criminal cases are quite common, partly because of the state's increasingly expansive definition of what constitutes *sharia* criminality. Indeed, criminal matters sometimes dominate the docket in Rembau, though aggregate data (bearing on the period 2005–10) suggest that, at least until recently, they might not have exceeded 20 percent of *sharia* cases nationwide. I hasten to add that we should not exaggerate the importance of this civil/criminal distinction, particularly since the structure, discursive practices, and overall tenor of both types of hearings are more or less the same and since men comprise the majority of the defendants in civil and criminal hearings alike (as discussed in more detail in chapter 5). More generally, the micropolitics involved in the handling of the following case typify many (but not all) of the changes discussed in the proceeding pages, especially those having to do with the ways that the state, through the discourses and practices of *sharia* courts, is currently interpellating Malays and other Muslims and otherwise endeavoring to reconfigure kinship, personhood, and subjectivity. It is, in short, widely generalizable in a theme and variation sense.

CASE 1

The Pensioner with a Penchant for Gambling

This case, heard in the month of Ramadan, 2012, involved a sixty-year-old male defendant, who was among seven or eight Malay men caught in a 2011 raid on a locally well-known "gambling spot" (*premis perjudian*) by enforcement officers from the state's Islamic Religious Affairs Department. The defendant was subsequently charged with the criminal offense of gambling (*berjudi*), under Section 79A(1) of the Negeri Sembilan Syariah Criminal Enactment, which carries a maximum penalty of a RM$3,000 fine (about US$950) and two years in prison. Present at the hearing, in addition to the defendant and the judge, were the registrar, the prosecutor, two police officers serving as bailiffs, five or six members of the public, and my research assistant (Ikmal Adian Mohd Adil), a gifted university student born and raised in Negeri Sembilan who accompanied me to (and worked with me in transcribing) dozens of hearings in 2012 but attended this one on his own since I had to return to the United States a few weeks earlier.[5]

There seems to have been a prior hearing in this case, which may explain the seventeen-month time lag between the raid on the gambling premises and this session. It merits note in any event that this hearing had to be postponed by a few hours because the defendant was not present at the time it was scheduled to begin. When he did appear, he was clad in jeans and a t-shirt and had somewhat disheveled hair.

The proceedings began with the registrar reading the case number and the defendant's name, and informing the judge that the accused was (now) present. The remainder of the hearing proceeded as follows.

Judge (hereafter J): Why [are you] late?

Defendant (hereafter D): I could not find the letter [requiring me to be present].

J: Are you [*kamu*] ready for the proceedings?

D: Yes.

Prosecutor (hereafter P): I request that the charges be read.

Registrar (hereafter R) [addressing the defendant]: With the permission of Your Honor, on the 30th of March 2011 around 4 P.M., you [cites the defendant's name and identity-card (IC) number], were found in a gambling establishment [a storefront that sells lottery tickets], and are accused of committing a crime under Section 79A (1) Negeri Sembilan *Syariah* Criminal Enactment 1992, 2004 amendment. You can be fined up to RM$3,000 or sentenced to up to two years in jail, or both. Do you understand the charges against you?

D: Yes.

J: [Do you] understand? [Is it] clear?

D: Yes.

J: Do you plead guilty or not guilty?

D: I plead guilty.

J: Are you confessing willingly?

D: Yes, no one forced me to confess.

J: Do you know the punishment?

D: Yes.

J: Explain.

D [the defendant stutters and then says]: RM$3,000 fine or two years [in jail], or both.

J: *Encik* [Sir], are you ready with the punishments?

D: Yes.

P: On [March 29, 2011], at about 9:30 P.M., an official of the Islamic Religious Affairs Department of Rembau received a *laporan* [report or tip; apparently from a member of the public] [relevant to the *sharia* enactment bearing on gambling noted above]. A group of officers from the Islamic Religious Affairs Department . . . went to the scene the next day; [they encountered] a lot of people on the premises. . . . As the officers entered the building they identified themselves and formed a barrier to block people from exiting. Some of the men ignored the orders and tried to knock down the barrier, but they were caught. Among them was the defendant, who was wearing a t-shirt and trousers. The defendant was brought to the District Police Headquarters and a police report was lodged. [She continues speaking of the relevant gazetted law and the punishment for breaking it.]

J [to the defendant]: Do you understand everything?

D: Yes.

J: Do you agree?

D: Yes.

J: Time, date, etc? Do you agree with all of it?

D: Yes.

J: Do you still want to plead guilty?

D: Yes.

The judge then instructed one of the bailiffs to "escort" the defendant into the dock (*kandang pesalah*), where he is normally expected to stand while the judge passes sentence.

J: The court is satisfied with the charges read against you, and declares that you have committed a crime under . . . [Section 79A(1) of the Negeri Sembilan *Syariah* Criminal Enactment 1992, 2004 Amendment]. Before the punishment is read out, do you want to appeal?

D: I accept any punishment that will be given.

J: Please continue, prosecutor.

P: I request a strict punishment because the defendant has previously committed this same crime. [She continues by reading parts of the Negeri Sembilan *Syariah* Criminal Enactment 1992, 2004 Amendment, as before.] As a Muslim, being in a gambling premise is wrong. At the entrance to the premises, there is also a notice prohibiting Muslims from entering.

She proceeded to paraphrase a passage from the Quran, emphasizing that intoxicants and gambling are an abomination, of Satan's handiwork, to be eschewed (Surah Al-Maidah [5:90]).

P: This issue cannot be taken lightly. [Even intending to gamble] indicates that the defendant does not practice Islam properly. The accused is an old man; . . . he should know better. I request a punishment that impresses itself upon him so that he won't do it again.

J: Mr. B., the crime [of gambling] in front of me today . . . [he cites portions of the Negeri Sembilan *Syariah* Criminal Enactment 1992, 2004 Amendment]. I refer to the charges mentioned earlier; during the raid, the officers created a barricade . . . and you were . . . arrested. Your presence on the premises indicates your intention to gamble. Even being there is an offense, and will be punished. Okay?

I often pass by the establishment, and it is always full [of people], but the mosque is never full. I see that the majority of the people [in those establishments] are Malays, meaning Muslims. I see young ones, old ones, and really old ones. This should not happen. We should evince good attitudes as Muslims. For me, there is a need for a punishment intended as a lesson for the offender . . . . I will deliver a reasonable punishment. You have pleaded guilty. The consequences are very significant. That is the essence of the *ikrar* [oath]. [There is] a *hadith* by the Prophet, *sallallahu alaihi wasallam* ['peace be upon him'], involving Ma'iz [bin Malik al-Aslami] that concerns adultery and repentence. [He provides a brief overview of the story of Ma'iz.] When you plead guilty, there are a lot of implications. In this court, first time offenders don't usually receive a jail sentence. But if or when a fine is issued as punishment, and the defendant is unable to pay, he/she must go to jail. Then you may not be able to celebrate Eid [the end of Ramadan, which was fast approaching].

It is very easy to put your name in the records. If you access E-*Syariah* after this, your name and IC number will be in the records. Do not come before me again. If you do, I will send you straight to jail. Gambling is *haram* . . ., one of the big sins. If you have done something wrong, repent (*bertaubat*). Allah expects repentance.

Are you ready for me to deliver the punishment? Do you want to sit down? [The judge instructs the main bailiff to give the defendant a chair.] I see that you are already an old man. Repent for what you have done in the past. Do not go anymore to . . . [gambling establishments]. You are fined RM$2,000 and if you fail to . . . [pay the fine], you will be jailed for three months.

At this point, which was around an hour and a half or so into the morning's proceedings, the judge used his gavel for the first time that day.

Commentary

I confine my remarks here to six sets of issues, bearing chiefly on the ways this session and other *sharia* civil and criminal cases I observed in Rembau and elsewhere in Malaysia in 2010–13 and 2018 differ from those I attended during my research in this same court in the late 1980s. I list most of them in the rough order in which they emerge in the transcript, commenting very briefly on the first few issues, which I take up in more detail when addressing subsequent themes.

There is an explicit, highly elaborated commitment to formal procedure and transparency, based on protocols drawn from the civil judiciary, the ISO, etc. This is exemplified (inter alia) in the court's concerns to specify which portion of the Negeri Sembilan *Syariah* Criminal Enactment the defendant had violated (evident in its repeated references to the particulars and number of the enactment in question) and to ensure that all went according to formal code with respect to a host of related issues: that the defendant understood the charges against him; that his plea of guilt was clear and entered voluntarily; and that he understood the punishments the court could impose on him.

All such procedure is drawn directly and proudly, and certainly not defensively or apologetically, from the civil courts, as, more generally, are formal protocols for turning a problem into a case, maintaining order and decorum in the courtroom, generating arrest warrants and summonses, maintaining paperwork and electronic files, etc. (Horowitz 1994; Maznah Mohammad 2010b). This situation is not unique to *sharia* courts in Malaysia and is indeed old news to scholars who have studied legal practices in the Islamic heartlands of the Middle East and North Africa (Brown 1997; Hallaq 2009). It is nonetheless important to note here, partly because it has resulted in women (female plaintiffs) experiencing fewer (and shorter) delays and other obstacles in their efforts to manage their disputes and obtain justice from the courts.

Officers of the court make frequent reference to their power, authority, and legitimacy (e.g., with respect to meting out punishment). These references began with the registrar's opening remarks and included not only the judge's subsequent elicitation from the defendant of the punishment the court is entitled to impose, but also the prosecutor's request for harsh penalties and the judge's ensuing (relatively lengthy) remarks leading up to the sentencing. A key dynamic here is that the judge and the prosecutor underscored their power and authority to punish transgressions of the law with heavy sanctions. More on this below.

The judge and the prosecutor ground their power, authority, and legitimacy both in gazetted statutes that are part of civil/secular law and in specifically Islamic sources. This double grounding, in gazetted positive-law enactments (specifying that gambling is an offense under Negeri Sembilan's *sharia* laws) and in the Quran, *hadith,* and other specifically Islamic sources and codes of normativity, was quite seamless; there are no firewalls between the secular and the religious here, to paraphrase a point made by Saba Mahmood (2012, 59) with reference to family courts and religious law in Egypt. This double grounding culminated, at the conclusion of the hearing, in the judge's use of a gavel, a heavily freighted symbol in both the *sharia* and the civil judiciary.

The court is actively involved in the reconfiguration of kinship, personhood, and subjectivity.   The judge (and others) addressed the defendant with formal terms such as *Encik* (Sir; Mr.) or *kamu* (you), rather than classificatory kin terms like *abang* (elder brother) or *pakcik* (uncle). Classificatory kinship terms were typically utilized by the *kadi* and his staff during hearings and other contexts in the late 1980s, as mentioned earlier. Because the defendant in this case was late to his hearing, he was not present at the orientation the registrar provided to litigants and visitors who had arrived at the courthouse prior to the beginning of the day's business. This orientation included instructions to address the judge as *Tuan Hakim* (Lord Judge; Your Honor) and to refer to oneself with the generic first-person pronoun *saya*, in addition to information on regulations concerning when to sit and stand, etc. Although the registrar did not add that the use of classificatory kinship terms was discouraged or forbidden, his instructions concerning how to address the judge and oneself made the court's stance clear.

The court's current position concerning the use of classificatory kinship terms is an extension or elaboration of its earlier devaluation of extended kinship and certain aspects of filial ties and siblingship, insofar as the emphasis then was on individuation, which is even more evident now. This despite the fact that the court deals mostly with Islamic family law (and increasingly with transgressions of Islamic family law that are classified as criminal as distinct from civil offenses) and is in principle strongly committed to "the family."

A more general theme is that the modalities of interaction within the courtroom are regulated by behavioral codes and more encompassing normativities that are quite different from those obtaining in social fields outside of it, a marked contrast with the situation in the late 1980s. This point is driven home by the exceedingly formal, corporate attire of court staff and the fact that orientation sessions such as those outlined here are seen by staff as necessary to maintain a sense of order and decorum in the courtroom. As previously discussed, in the late 1980s the attire of court staff was not much different than that of the (Malay) public; there were no orientation sessions; and there was but a single rule posted near the entrance to the courthouse, rather than the dozen that existed at the time of this trial.

A related issue is that neither the judge nor the prosecutor raised any questions concerning the defendant's place of birth or family background, where he was currently living, whether he was married and had children, and what kind of work he did prior to retiring. The answers to queries along these lines would have given the judge and the prosecutor a sense of the defendant's *asal* (*usul*), which is commonly rendered into English as "origins" (or "social origins") but has a much wider semantic range, embracing many features of an individual's biography, character, and disposition—in short, what kind of person he or she is.

In the late 1980s, Rembau's *kadi* was very much concerned with litigants' *asal*. This is partly because the *kadi*, like judges everywhere, sought certitude but could not necessarily determine with any degree of confidence "what really happened" in a particular case—who did what to "whom, when, where, and how" (Geertz 1983, 220). Far more certain was what kind of person(s) the *kadi* was dealing with and "what might have happened" in the case at hand (Just 2001; Dupret et al 2008). Information bearing on the first issue helped resolve questions related to the second, which is why information pertinent to *asal* was commonly accorded legal salience in the late 1980s. More broadly, just as for some eminent scholars *asal* has long been a key component of judicial inquiries in Islamic courts and is in some ways, like *ijtihad*, an important symbol if not a defining feature of the Islamic juris- prudential tradition (see, e.g., Rosen 1989; Hallaq 2009), so too does it index a cluster of notions bearing on personhood and subjectivity that are increasingly irrelevant in late modern Malaysia.

The absence in this hearing of any concern on the part of the court with the defendant's place of birth, family background, marital and work history, etc., was not a reflection of the defendant's guilty plea, which eliminated uncertainty regarding the nature of the offense. Nor was it a function of the fact he had previ- ously been charged with and apparently convicted of gambling, and was thus a repeat offender who "does not practice Islam properly," as the prosecutor phrased it. Concerns with *asal* did not emerge in any of the dozens of civil or criminal cases that I (or my research assistants) sat in on during 2011–13 or 2018. This shift, toward the view that *sharia* judges should (or need) not take issues of *asal* into consideration when they gather information and render decisions in proceedings, has myriad causes and consequences. Many of them are keyed to the increased hegemony of positive-law models bearing on (ever more narrowly defined) legally salient evidence, coupled with the further erosion or decline of "*ijtihad*ic hermeneutics" (Hallaq 2009, 381). As scholars like Rosen (1989), Kamali (1991), Bowen (2003), and Hallaq (2009) have explained with reference to founda- tional texts and diverse regions of the Muslim world, these hermeneutics are oriented toward grasping the particularities of litigants' lives so as to better under- stand how best to utilize the resources of *sharia* to help them creatively manage their disputes and ideally get them back on course to renegotiate their relation- ships with one another (in the instance of an estranged husband and wife, for example) and/or to conduct their lives in greater accordance with Islamic ethics and normativity (in a case of gambling, for instance). These issues need not detain us. Most relevant is that in Malaysia's *sharia* judiciary, longstanding concerns with *asal* have been relegated to the dustbins of history, much like the term *kadi* and the attire long associated with it.

To the degree that concerns with *asal* used to distinguish the practices of Malaysia's *sharia* judges from those of their civil-law brethren, we see greater congruence in *sharia* and civil-court hearings at present than at any juncture in times past. A related point is that, as legal subjects, defendants and other litigants who appear in *sharia* courts are being interpellated in vastly different ways than their predecessors—and very much like those who find themselves in today's civil courts. The more general theme is that the *sharia* courts are centrally involved in state-sponsored projects of corporate Islamic governmentality that presuppose (among other things) the reconfiguration of kinship, personhood, and subjectivity. There is much evidence for these contentions above and beyond non-considerations of *asal* and the fact that plaintiffs and defendants alike have seen their direct, verbal interactions with judges significantly curtailed, their wide-ranging and potentially cathartic narratives commonly reduced to passive verbal acknowledgments of the veracity of court officers' renditions of issues relevant to their hearings. (The latter dynamic is partly a function of the heightened presence in the court of *sharia* prosecutors and lawyers, absent in this hearing, but involved in 15 to 20 percent of all cases in Rembau's *sharia* court and more than half of all hearings in its Kuala Lumpur counterpart. Along with judges, they increasingly dominate hearings by dictating whose turn it is to speak, how long one is allowed to speak, and the appropriateness of the tone and content of that speech [Conley and O'Barr 1998]; see chapter 4.) Suffice it to recall the more formal terms of reference and address utilized in the courtroom (in lieu of classificatory kinship terms) and the devaluation of kinship thus entailed; the lengthy list of regulations concerning courtroom etiquette and protocol posted at the entrance to the courthouse; the presence in the courtroom of police officers; the densely networked channels of e-governance that include the E-*Syariah* Portal, coupled with the greatly increased severity of the sanctions at the disposal of *sharia* judges; and the heightened salience of Islam (discussed below).

Overall, the discourses of the court are far more explicitly Islamic in terms of the symbols, idioms, and metaphors embedded within them, in addition to being more congruent with the discourses of the civil judiciary, where Islamic symbols, idioms, etc. are largely absent. The more explicitly Islamic dimension of the court's discourse was evident throughout the hearing: e.g., in the prosecutor's specific, unambiguous reference to gambling being a sin in Islam; in her paraphrasing of a passage from the Quran linking gambling, the consumption of alcohol, and Satan; in the judge's warning that the defendant would not be able to celebrate *Eid* if he was jailed for being unable to pay his fine; and in his invocation of a *hadith* underscoring the virtue of repentance.

There is another context in which this pattern is strikingly apparent and worthy of brief mention, even though or especially because it is not evident in the hearing concerned with gambling, which, as noted earlier, illustrates many but not all of the continuities and transformations we see in the courts since the late 1980s. I refer to the mediation sessions subsumed under the rubric of *sulh* that were formally introduced in the nation's *sharia* courts beginning in 2001. As discussed in chapter 3, these sessions normally begin with prayer and are more or less mandatory for couples experiencing certain types of problems in their efforts to settle property and other issues attendant upon divorce. More generally, *sulh* is an Arabic-origin term, denoting compromise and the settling of disputes, that officials have endeavored to popularize, largely against the grain. Glossy brochures and entries on websites prepared by authorities tout its specifically Arabic and Islamic origins, its grounding in the words and spirit of Quranic passages and *hadith,* and its likeness to civil-court mediation; ironically, there are no references to the fact that *sulh* sessions build on centuries-old Malay precedents valorizing negotiation, compromise, and mutual accommodation.

We might summarize the most general, twofold point as follows: compared to their predecessors in the late 1980s, the discourses and practices of the *sharia* court are far more overtly Islamic and, simultaneously, far more consistently and explicitly informed by procedures and other phenomena drawn directly from the secular, common-law judiciary. This paradoxical trend, the *sharia* courts evincing both "more Islamic law" and "more common law," was incisively delineated by Donald Horowitz (1994) based on his research in the early 1990s. Horowitz's observations have no necessary bearing on the twenty or so year period since he completed his investigations, but they are highly relevant to developments during this time.

The court—and the state—have greatly expanded toolkits and realms of jurisdiction.   Toward the end of the hearing, the judge told the defendant that he could review the particulars of his case via the E-*Syariah* Portal, and that he would see his name and IC number there. But it is unlikely that the defendant would have any specific reason or general inclination to access the E-*Syariah* Portal, which seems geared toward the younger generation(s), much like the IT Center and Internet Café strategically situated on the grounds of Rembau's mosque and prominently advertised to all passersby. Far more relevant is the implicit warning to the defendant that this information is now widely available to powerful authorities associated with the *sharia* judiciary, other religious bureaucracies as well as the police, the military, and officials who administer retirement funds, including, presumably, the defendant's. This warning was coupled with a threat from the judge that if the defendant ever came before him again, he would send him straight to jail. Tellingly, I have witnessed similar warnings and threats during hearings focusing on *sharia* family law, including some that were convened because a husband repudiated his wife (by means of the standardized divorce formula) without the court's permission; such actions are currently defined as *sharia* criminal offenses but they were legally acceptable in the late 1980s and before (see case 2, below).

Such warning and threats, coupled with the realities to which they refer, index a major transformation both in the *sharia* judiciary's involvement in surveillance, discipline, and control, and its—and the state's—greatly augmented capacities and initiatives in these realms of governmentality (though there are 1980s-era structural precedents for these changes, as we have seen). Among the chief selling points and achievements of e-governance, including the E-*Syariah* Portal, is that it makes possible instantaneous data retrieval and electronic communication *across*, and not simply *within*, disparate state agencies, thus providing Muslims and other Malaysians with a one-stop shopping center for information concerning Islam and facilitating more efficient governmental machinery as a whole. E-governance initiatives resonate with the much celebrated Japanese-origin management and auditing regime (the 5Ses), to which court staff and all other civil servants are expected to adhere for purposes of maintaining their files, workspaces, surge protectors, and toilets (as discussed in chapter 1). The 5Ses campaign aims to inculcate new subjectivities encompassing self-management, ethical engagement, and heightened awareness of one's self and one's coworkers alike in order to more effectively discipline and govern Muslim and other Malaysian citizen-subjects, enhance their productivity, accountability, and global competitiveness, and thus help ensure that the nation enjoys a more prosperous and secure future.

The 5Ses are appropriately regarded as an extension or revival of Prime Minister Mahathir's "Look East" policy, introduced in 1981. This policy drew inspiration from "Japanese and South Korean success in . . . economic development such as state intervention to develop heavy industries, . . . state encouragement of Japanese-style *sogoshosha* trading agencies, efforts to get the government bureaucracy to better serve private sector interests ('Malaysia Incorporated'), and . . . [the] 'privatization' . . . of potentially profitable economic activities previously undertaken by government," even though "the more immediate inspiration for 'privatization' in Malaysia was the dismantling of the public sector in the West identified with 'Thatcherism'" (Jomo Kwame Sundaram and Wee Chong Hui 2014, 22, 24). We should also consider the 5Ses in relation to the Clients' Charter promising "friendly, fair, timely, and satisfactory service" posted on the walls of Rembau's courthouse. Each in its own way reflects the *sharia* judiciary's efforts to rebrand itself as a service organization prominently grounded in the "ethos of 'customer relations' that is so pervasive in the commercial sector, and so central to business management," as David Garland (2001, 117) has observed for broadly analogous corporatizing trends in the penal-welfare complexes of the United States and the United Kingdom.

As an additional step toward enhancing surveillance, discipline, and control, and engaging the public in self-governance, thereby further blurring the historically contingent lines obtaining in Malaysia between state and society, public and private, authorities have increasingly encouraged their famously well-wired citizenry[6] to embrace state initiatives aimed at crime prevention and moral policing.

These include public campaigns urging citizens to report vehicular and other crimes they see by texting pertinent information on their cell phones to police hotlines. Others involve the dissemination, through print and electronic media, of guidelines to help the public identify persons allegedly inclined toward same-sex relations, even in the absence of specific criminal actions on their part. Buff male youth wearing v-necked sweaters have been singled out for pastoral concern, discipline, and diffuse surveillance, as have women with "tomboyish" appearance and comportment. These initiatives are intertwined with government efforts to greatly expand auxiliary police forces known as RELA (discussed below). They also resonate deeply with (Malay) political and religious elites' efforts to impress upon all Muslims that proper observance of their religion requires them to take (more) seriously the foundational Quranic injunction to enjoin good and forbid wrong (*amar ma'ruf, nahi mungkar*).

Interpretations of this injunction in the late 1970s (when it first gained prominence in national religious discourse), the 1980s, and the early 1990s focused on the enjoining good (*amar ma'ruf*) part of the equation. So too did government policy measures aimed at building and refurbishing mosques and prayer houses, and developing the infrastructure of explicitly Islamic institutions of education, banking, and finance. This was largely because during this time the government sought both to counter and coopt the proselytizing activities of Islamist groups such as ABIM and other piety/*dakwah* organizations it perceived as a threat to its hold on power, and to undercut the appeal of the Islamist opposition party PAS, which has long depicted UMNO as having dubious religious credentials and being ethically bankrupt.

For a variety of reasons, the past two and a half decades have seen a significant change in the ways that the Quranic injunction in question has been interpreted and realized in practice. The reasons have to do with the government's commitment to the deregulation and privatization of enterprises, activities, and resources (related to healthcare, education, transportation, water supply, etc.) formerly owned or managed by state agencies; the attendant shifting of the responsibilities and burdens of economic and overall social welfare onto individuals and their households; rising rates of crime, violence, and economic and psychological insecurity; the state's inability to stem the tide, especially with regard to epidemics of purse snatching, "baby dumping," child abuse, sexual offenses like rape and sodomy, and moral turpitude; and widely ramifying societal frustration with these and related dynamics, some expressed as moral panic and authoritarian populism (cf. Lancaster 2011; see also Pratt et al 2005; Wacquant 2009). The emphasis is now on the forbidding of wrong (*nahi mungkar*), harsh sanctions geared toward deterrence, and the escalating costs incurred by those who misbehave, rather than the enjoining of good. One consequence (and also a cause) of this turn is that ordinary (and other) Malays are not only increasingly on the lookout for behavior falling outside the range of state-defined normativity, but are also more likely than in times past to bring real or imagined ethical and other transgressions to the attention of mosque officials, the police, or authorities in the employ of massively expanded religious bureaucracies. Recall that the defendant's arrest was triggered when enforcement officers from one such bureaucracy received a tip, apparently from a member of the public.

The heavy sanctions the *sharia* judge imposed on the defendant is by some criteria unremarkable. Fines of RM$2,000 are not currently considered out of the ordinary. The magnitude of the punishment reflects the judge and prosecutor's three-fold concerns that the defendant was a repeat offender; that it was necessary to send a clear message to him and other Malays who might be inclined to gamble; and that in the future there would ideally be fewer Malays in gaming establishments, maintained for the nation's non-Muslim population and the revenue they generate for the state, and more of them attending mosque services, thus ameliorating the current ethical imbalance and damaged social fabric the judge deplored.

The weighty sanctions at the disposal of present-day *sharia* judges are usefully viewed alongside their greatly augmented jurisdiction compared to the 1980s, a trend that was evident in the hearing at issue insofar as gambling, though proscribed in the Quran, was not formally designated by authorities as a *sharia* offense until the late 1990s, following the privatization and flourishing of lottery enterprises (Jones and Fadil Azim Abbas 1994). Recent decades have seen the passage of a multitude of enactments bearing on Muslims' behavior that authorities in everexpanding federal- and state-level agencies have come to construe as *sharia* criminality. These enactments, which promise harsh punishment as distinct from rehabilitation, encompass nearly everything under the sun that might possibly bear on the religious or moral comportment of Muslims. To be clear, though, this is part of a more expansive dynamic involving the proliferation of government bureaucracies (to promote and monitor citizen-subjects' health; to protect children, consumers, the disabled, and the environment; to combat drug use, human trafficking, threats to communal harmony and national security, etc.) and the legal, administrative, and specifically regulatory machinery associated with them. They are symptomatic, more broadly, of a fetishization of the jural and the bureaucratically construed normative (Comaroff 2009). It may be a cliché to say that bureaucracies take on lives of their own, but this has certainly occurred (with a vengeance) in late-modern Malaysia: the number of government bureaucrats rose "from 800,000 in 2003 to 1.2 million by 2011," an astonishing increase of 44 percent in a mere eight years, both reflecting and furthering a "government-is-best approach" and "making for a very top-heavy style of governance" (Welsh 2013, 334).

This situation constitutes a dramatic change since my previous fieldwork and helps explain the important shift in the focus and tenor of the scholarship of anthropologists and others working in Malaysia over the last few decades that I outlined in the introduction to this chapter: from celebrated treatises on resistance that made hope practical (even as they documented states of affairs occasioning despair), to studies highlighting the constriction of pluralistic sensibilities and dispositions (with respect to ethnicity, "race," religion, gender, and sexuality) and the attendant rise of moral policing that render hope arguably less practical. As noted earlier, this change in the thrust and tone of scholarship on Malaysia is only partly attributable to shifts in the vagaries of academic discourse and its fluid styles and zones of prestige. It mostly bespeaks the ways in which the Malaysian state has become more corporate, intrusive, and punitive as it has embraced neoliberal globalization and the forms and norms of Islam (including *sharia*) and Islamization held to be most congruent with it.

For additional perspectives on the punitive turn that is evident both in the nation's *sharia* courts and in various realms of culture and politics, we might consider the following hearing, which occurred in the same courthouse as the gambling case that I have just described, albeit about a year and a half later.

CASE 2

*The Man Who Is Handcuffed and Taken into Custody for Divorcing
His Wife without the Court's Permission on Two Separate Occasions*

This case, prosecuted in December 2013, was the third of the morning, the first two of which were basically no-shows on the part of male defendants. It concerned a formerly married man, perhaps in his forties, who pleaded guilty to two separate criminal offenses having to do with the way(s) and location(s) in which he divorced his wife. The former wife was not present at the hearing, which involved, in addition to the defendant (D), the judge (J), the registrar (R), the *sharia* prosecutor (SP), and two bailiffs who struggled awkwardly to handcuff the defendant at the end of the hearing so as to take him into police custody. I was also present, as was my female research assistant (Najat) and a few others, who were probably waiting for their cases to be called or were family members of litigants scheduled to appear that morning. The Registrar spoke first, as is typically the case.

> R: *Bismillah al-rahman al-rahim* [In the Name of Allah, the Most Gracious and Most Compassionate]. With your permission, *Tuan Hakim* [Lord Judge], the court continues with case number . . . . The accused is Mohd Rosila.
>
> J: You may proceed.
>
> SP: The accused is present. This case is mentioned under Section 125 [of the Islamic Family Law (State of Negeri Sembilan) Enactment 2003, which carries a penalty of up to RM$1,000, imprisonment up to six months, or both]; that is, divorce outside of the court [and without the court's permission]. There are two [sets of] charges for the same case; I request that they be heard simultaneously.
>
> J [to D]: Enter the dock.

The defendant then approached the dock and stood behind it, but did not enter it until later in the hearing, just before sentencing.

R: With the permission of Your Honor (*Yang Arif*). (1) You, Rosila, at 4 A.M. on December 9 [the year in question was not clear to me] divorced your wife via SMS [text messaging] outside of court and without [the court's] permission. This offense falls under Section 125 [of the previously noted Islamic Family Law Enactment]. If convicted, you will be punished under the same section. (2) With permission, at 12 noon on October 17 [the year was not clear to me], you divorced your wife [on the telephone] with the words *Abang ceraikan emak dengan talak tiga* [I/husband divorce you/mother [of our children] with three *talak*] while travelling from Tampin to Seremban.

J: Mohd Rosila? [Is this true?]

D: Yes.

J: How many offenses [were there]?

D: Two.

J: What were the offenses?

D: Divorce outside of court [and without the court's permission].

J: With respect to these offenses, do you plead guilty?

D: Yes, I plead guilty.

J: Were you forced by anyone [to do so]?

D: No.

J: Do you know the punishment?

D: Yes, I do.

J: Are you ready?

D: Yes, I am. [Around this time the defendant entered the dock.]

SP: With the permission of the Lord Judge, on December 9 [?] the head of our investigation unit received a report regarding a divorce outside of court [and without the court's permission] that occurred on the road from Tampin to Seremban; i.e., that the accused had divorced his wife [on the telephone]. The accused can be convicted under the offenses of: Utterance of divorce; utterance of divorce outside of court [and without the court's permission]; and [violating] a court order.

J: Do you understand the first charge?

D: Yes.

J: How many *talak* were there?

D: One.

J: You agree to this fact and the date?

D: Yes, I agree, but I do not remember the date; it was a long time ago.

J: Alright, continue.

SP: On October 17, [2010?], the accused divorced his wife outside of court [and without the court's permission] . . . .; [the offence consists of] utterance of divorce, utterance of divorce outside of court [and without the court's permission] . . . [via a] telephone call, and [violating?] a court order.

J: Alright, do you understand the second [set of] charge[s]?

D: Yes.

J: How many *talak* were there?

D: Three.

J: Do you agree [with everything that's been said]?

D: Yes.

J: Do you plead guilty?

SP: With your permission, Lord Judge, we request giving the accused a heavy punishment because he has committed two [sets of] offenses.

J: *Bismillah al-rahman al-rahim.* The court is satisfied. Mohd Rosila. The court advises you that you have committed two sets of offenses. Two different sets of circumstances will bring about two different punishments. Do you want to lodge any appeals [mention any mitigating factors]?

D: I request that the Lord Judge consider reducing the sentence, since four of my children are in school and I [only] brought RM$300 with me today.

J [to SP]: You may proceed.

SP: With your permission, Lord Judge, . . . every resident of the state must adhere to the [appropriate laws and] procedures. If we look at the chronology of the case, the divorce occurred through telephone and SMS, which is not considered appropriate (*beradab* [an Arabic-origin term referring to what is proper]). The prosecution requests a heavy punishment that will serve as a lesson.

J: *Encik* (Sir), you have committed two offenses with regards to divorce. Alright, regarding divorce through SMS: according to a 2005 national *fatwa*, divorce via SMS is a criminal offense (*jenayah*). It is regarded as *talak bilkitabah,* which is [a form of] divorce by means of writing. But [most importantly] the *fatwa* council decided that such divorce is inappropriate.

The first offense will be penalized with an appropriate fine; the second one will be punished accordingly. It will be a lesson to [others who might be involved in] cases of divorce outside the court [and without the court's permission]. If [the defendant] fails to pay the fines, he will go to jail. Alright, the verdict. For the first offense: a fine of RM$300; if [the defendant] fails [to pay it], fifteen days in jail. For the second offense: a fine of RM$1,000; if [the defendant] fails [to pay it], thirty days in jail.

At this point, the bailiffs become embroiled in the unfolding drama. The older of the two, a man in his late fifties or early sixties, who had been standing near the defendant throughout the hearing, moved closer to him, removed his handcuffs from his belt, and tried to fasten them around the defendant's wrists. In a clear gesture of submission, the increasingly forlorn-looking defendant offered his raised wrists to the bailiff so that he could cuff them. He did not resist the bailiff's efforts to take him into custody, but the bailiff struggled awkwardly to secure the handcuffs, perhaps because they were not in good working order; alternatively, because the bailiff was not in the habit of using the cuffs and was not adept at quickly locking them. The other bailiff, a highly decorated police officer in her forties or early fifties, who usually sits at a desk at the other entrance to the courtroom, came to her colleague's aid with the handcuffs she carried. Together they managed to handcuff the defendant, as those of us who were present continued to watch the drama unfold in awkward—and for me, stunned—silence. The defendant was then directed out of the courtroom by the elder male bailiff. Shortly thereafter he paid the fine in full (thus giving the lie to his earlier contention that he only had RM$300 with him), and was uncuffed and released from custody.

Commentary

Most striking about this case is the use of handcuffs at the end of the hearing for the purposes of restraining the defendant and taking him into custody until such time as he paid the fines that the judge imposed on him, or, in the event that he could not afford to pay, until he was processed for his incarceration. Prior to this case, I never saw handcuffs deployed in a *sharia* courtroom.

A more general and arguably far more telling point is that the actions for which the defendant stood trial in this case—divorcing his wife outside the courthouse and without the court's permission—*were not classified as crimes* in the state of Negeri Sembilan during my fieldwork in the late 1980s, and were, in fact, very common and altogether legitimate occurrences then and previously. Partly because of pressure from women's rights groups like Sisters in Islam, such actions were nonetheless subject to increased state scrutiny during the late 1970s and 1980s. This is because they were widely seen as unfair to women (as wives and mothers). They came to be criminalized in Negeri Sembilan in 1988 with the (delayed) implementation of the Islamic Family Law Enactment of 1983, which took effect in every state in the nation during 1983–91. This despite the fact that according to classical Islamic jurisprudence and the relevant *fiqh* literature, a husband is entitled to divorce his wife simply by uttering the *talak,* and need not do so in the presence of court officials (or his wife) or with the court's permission. Suffice it to reiterate here that while the defendant's actions were deemed criminal in terms of state law, they did not invalidate the divorce. This is because of their validity from the point of view of *fiqh,* which is accepted by the court as a source of action that is legitimate in the eyes of God.

The fact that the defendant in this case was issued a summons to appear in court, formally charged, tried, convicted, slapped with a heavy sentence, handcuffed, and taken into police custody for behavior that was not even criminalized in Negeri

Sembilan during my earlier fieldwork is one indication of the increasingly punitive turn that the *sharia* courts have taken since the late 1980s. Before elaborating on the larger cultural-political dynamics animating and sustaining this turn, and the ways it is manifest in the secular judiciary, the realm of policing, and elsewhere, I should clarify that the defendant was apparently guilty of additional offenses that were not charged. One such offense, mentioned in passing in a conversation over tea and cakes I had with the judge and another court official right after this hearing, involved failing to reconcile (*rujuk*) with his wife after the first *talak*, or at least neglecting to formally register the *rujuk* with the court, both of which are required by current law. (The first but not the second is also an offense according to the *fiqh* literature.) If the defendant failed to *rujuk* with his wife before they resumed cohabitation and sexual relations in particular (assuming they did so), both parties would be guilty of sexual offenses such as *zina* (coupling outside of marriage).

The other transgression, though not technically a criminal offense, involved simultaneous or back-to-back recitation of three *talak*, or saying something like "I divorce you with three *talak*." The court and the state strongly discourage this kind of behavior, partly because it is often assumed that it occurs in a fit of (male) anger, that it therefore might not be fully intended, and because it has potentially dire consequences (a man may fly into a rage and "go crazy" when he realizes that he cannot undo these actions [Peletz 2002, 96]). It can also create additional work for judges, who are already overextended and pressed for time, and are not always clear whether they should treat it as a single *talak*, which is revocable by means of *rujuk*, or a triple *talak*, which is irrevocable. (In the case of a triple *talak*, whether uttered simultaneously or on three different occasions separated by months, even years, the former husband and wife cannot remarry unless and until the wife has been married to someone else, has consummated that union, and then has that union formally dissolved.) Although factors such as these were not mentioned in the hearing, they might help explain (1) why the prosecutor sought a heavy sentence that would serve as a warning to others who might engage in the kind of behavior for which the defendant was on trial; and (2) why the judge heeded the prosecutor's advice and likewise mentioned that he wanted the sentence imposed in this case to serve as a lesson for others who might be inclined to divorce outside of court, and thus disregard the relevant laws bearing on the state's prerogatives with respect to the dissolution of marriage.

The theme of sanctions geared toward deterrence rather than rehabilitation looms large in the cultural logic of prosecution and sentencing both in this hearing and that of the previous case involving the retiree with a penchant for gambling. In many, perhaps most, contexts, proponents of deterrence support harsh punishment on the grounds that punishments that are not severe will not deter those who might be inclined to break the law. More broadly, in this and many other present-day cases, harsh punishment geared toward deterrence is part and parcel of neo-

liberal state policies aimed at making individuals and communities more responsible for regulating and governing their own conduct, so that (ideally) the state and
other agents and institutions of governmentality need not do so. Harsh punishments aimed at deterrence are thus key components of strategies that, to borrow a
phrase from Foucault (2003, 265), seek to "responsibilize" individuals and communities.[7] Hence the "Three Strikes and You're Out" mandatory sentencing guidelines that took root in the United States beginning in the late twentieth century;
the exceedingly heavy sentences meted out for drug offenses, curfew violations,
loitering, and the like that contributed to the explosion of the prison population in
the United States from 1970 to 2010; and the related, twofold fact that the United
States has both the world's largest prison population and the world's highest rates
of incarceration per capita (Wacquant 2009; Alexander 2010 [2012]).

    In Malaysia, the emphasis on deterrence, and the punitive turn more generally,
has not resulted in rates of incarceration of a scale similar to what one sees in
countries like the United States, though, not coincidentally, there is a strong racial,
class, and gender skewing of the prison population in both instances. It has, however, seen a restructuring of "liberal ideas about burden of proof" that is in some
ways similar to what Roger Lancaster (2011, 147) has documented for the United
States. In both cases there has been significant erosion of the idea, enshrined in the
Constitutions and other foundational documents in both nations, that one is innocent until proven guilty. The latter theme is not evident in the hearing at issue here
(recall that the defendant pled guilty as charged). But it is strikingly obvious in
other realms of Malaysian political culture, many of which share deep resonance
with recent trends in *sharia* courts and may well influence them in years to come.

    As one example, on October 5, 2013, the nation's top law-enforcement official
(Home Minister Datuk Seri Dr. Ahmad Zahid Hamidi) proclaimed that the police
should shoot suspected gang members first and ask questions later.[8] Gang members are disproportionately of Tamil-speaking Hindu/Indian background and
poor. For these and other reasons, they are viewed in exceedingly negative terms
by middle-class Malay Muslims who tend to see the Indian community as embod-
ying many things from which they seek to distance themselves, including in particular their pre-Islamic Hindu-Buddhist/animist, overly-ritualistic and otherwise
"superstitious" and rural past (Willford 2006). Less controversial though equally
disturbing to many was the December 2013 contention by one government minister that it was up to PAS leaders charged with "Shia deviationism," which carries
very heavy penalties in present-day Malaysia and can result in indefinite detention
without trial, to prove that they were innocent, in lieu of the government having to
demonstrate in court that they were guilty as charged, a task it sought to facilitate
by media blitzes trying them in the court of public opinion. Around the time I was
leaving the field in mid-December 2013, the mainstream media carried a number
of stories indicating that a stepped-up crackdown on "Shia deviationists" was

underway, and that a number of cases would soon be heard in the nation's *sharia* courts (*Sunday Star* 2013b; see also Mohd Faizal Musa and tan beng hui 2017).

Three other sets of issues warrant brief remark. The first has to do with *fatwa;* the second bears on the symbolics of handcuffs and gavels; the third concerns gender and notions of masculinity in particular.

Toward the end of the hearing, right before the judge announced the sentence, he made brief reference to a national (i.e., pan-Malaysian) *fatwa* issued in 2005. The *fatwa* decreed that divorce via SMS constitutes a form of marriage termination involving writing (as distinct from a verbal utterance) that is both inappropriate (*tak beradab*) and a criminal offense (*jenayah*). Some clarification is in order here since, technically speaking, in Islamic jurisprudence a *fatwa* is a legal opinion issued by a *sharia* legal expert such as a *mufti* that believers are enjoined to respect, but it is not binding. In Malaysia, however, things are not that clear cut or "flexible." For while some *fatwa* conform to the classical definition, being merely expert "opinions," others enjoy the formal status of binding state law. The difference is that *fatwa* of the former type, even if issued by state-certified *mufti* and publicized in official venues in print or online (e.g., on the E-*Fatwa* website), have not (yet) been formally accorded the status of law by government officials at the state or federal level. (Recall that most religious affairs in Malaysia fall under the jurisdiction of state rather than federal authorities, an enduring legacy of the colonial era.) That is, they have not (yet) been "gazetted," to use the colonial-origin terminology that is deeply relevant in Malaysia, even though, to further confuse the issue, the general meaning of the latter term in Britain is "the official pub-lication of a government organization or institution, listing appointments and other public notices," which would mean that they are in fact legally binding. There are, moreover, state-level *fatwa* and national-level *fatwa;* the former are only relevant in the state in which they were issued while the latter are applicable throughout Malaysia.

I do not know if the defendant in this case was aware of the national-level *fatwa* in question, or, if so, whether he understood it to be legally binding as distinct from merely advisory. If he was aware of it, chances are he would have assumed it to be legally binding, because for many Malays and other Muslims in Malaysia, anything a *mufti* says has the formal status of law, regardless of whether it is pub-lished in one or another official venue or simply pronounced in passing in a village mosque or at a marriage feast.

A more general point is that in this hearing, as in the gambling case considered previously, *sharia* court officials grounded their narratives both in formally gazet-ted positive law (Section 125 of the Islamic Family Law Enactment of Negeri Sem-bilan) and in quintessentially Islamic sources (e.g., a *mufti's fatwa*). This double grounding bolsters the legitimacy of the *sharia* courts, as did the conspicuous and dramatic deployment of the gavel at the conclusion of the former hearing and the use of handcuffs in the latter case. Both are key material symbols not only of the civil judiciary that the *sharia* court hierarchy endeavors to emulate, but also of

FIGURE 5. Malaysian Department of *Syariah* Judiciary (JKSM) poster depicting gavel and handcuffs and "*Syariah* Is the Basis of Justice," 2013. Photo by author.

the state apparatus that the two separate but conjoined assemblages seek to inflect, define, and otherwise position in complementary yet increasingly opposed and politically divisive ways. It should come as no surprise to find that one of the more conspicuous visual (self-)images that brand managers of the *sharia* judiciary have sought to promote in recent years takes the form of a large rendering of a gavel and handcuffs above the words *Syariah Asas Keadilan* ("*Syariah* Is the Basis of Justice") (figure 5; see also chapter 4).

As for issues of gender and notions of masculinity in particular, one of the more striking features of the two cases examined in this chapter, especially considered alongside one another, is that, as litigants, men do not appear in a very good light in the *sharia* courts. Part of the reason for this is that most male litigants appear in the court as defendants (not plaintiffs), having been charged by *sharia* prosecutors or their current or former wives with one or another criminal or civil offense. And we have seen, at least in the two cases considered here, that men commonly plead guilty to the charges of criminal wrongdoing that result in their court appearances. The gender skewing of criminal charges is also instructive. In the case of gambling, over 99 percent of those charged are men.[9] This is not to suggest that most men gamble—or drink alcohol, another criminal offense that is overwhelmingly male—but it is to say that virtually all cases of gambling and drinking involve charges against men, and, conversely, that women are rarely involved (in the sense of being participants or charged) in these criminalized activities. Divorcing outside the court and without the court's permission is another offense that involves men but not women as defendants, as in most cases is taking a second spouse without the permission of the court. Partly because wives are far more dependent on their husbands' contributions to the household coffers than vice versa, women are also far more likely to take men to court for failing to contribute to household maintenance than the other way around. The bottom line, deeply ironic in light of the fact that the upper levels of the *sharia* court hierarchy are overwhelmingly male and that the courts are generally seen as a bastion of male privilege, is that they are key sites in the production of views of masculinity that are highly unflattering to men.

More to the point is that *sharia* courts are deeply implicated in the production of counterhegemonic views of masculinity that subvert the official, Islamically inflected view that men have more reason (*akal*) and less passion (*nafsu*) than women. In the late 1980s, when I looked into these matters in some detail, a number of villagers, men and women alike, rejected part or all of the official line, doing so with arguments to the effect that if men really had less passion than women, they wouldn't gamble, drink alcohol, squander household resources at coffee shops, take second wives, or misrepresent their actions in informal settings or formal venues (Peletz 1996, 2002). As my adoptive aunt put it in one of her classic comments (in a January 1988 conversation), "Men, they all lie; . . . that's what you see all the time at the *kadi*'s office." After I chided her for what I took to be a rash generalization, pertaining to *all* men, she thought for a moment and then proceeded to qualify her pronouncement by saying, "Okay, well, nine out of ten of them."

CRIMINALITY AND CREEPING CRIMINALIZATION

I have noted that the past few decades have seen successful efforts by Malay political and religious elites to augment the criminal jurisdiction and penal power of the

Islamic judiciary to encompass nearly everything under the sun that might be construed as involving the religious or moral comportment of Muslims. I have also emphasized that this is one dimension of the new punitiveness illustrated by (among other things) transformations in courtroom operations such as those that have occurred in Rembau. A critical caveat bearing on the first of these generalizations (concerning the recent augmentation of the criminal jurisdiction and penal power of the Islamic judiciary) is that, for the most part, this has had no direct bearing on the myriad offenses that fall exclusively within the jurisdiction of the civil courts, such as theft, murder, stock-market fraud, drug trafficking, illegal assembly, etc. These offenses are already heavily criminalized, and, not coincidentally, are far more severely punishable than in times past.

This turn resonates with the popular normative and ethical trend, well documented for urban Malays, whereby concerns with the binaries of *halal* and *haram* (that which Allah permits and forbids, respectively) have increasingly filtered into all areas of public and private life, such that "more and more is taken in, valorised, and then subjected to a normative *halal/haram* judgment" (Fischer 2008, 30). This is not to suggest, however, that most urban (or rural) Malays necessarily lend their unequivocal support to all state strategies involving criminalization in the name of Islam. The sentiments, dispositions, and ethical orientations of ordinary Malays (as distinct from political and religious elites and those at the forefront of social movements) have long been more pluralistic than those associated with advocates of Islamization, state-sponsored or otherwise (Peletz 1997, 2002). That said, the robust (but graduated) pluralism associated with "traditional" Malay culture has become increasingly constricted, as evidenced partly by the heightened cultural centrality of *halal/haram* binaries. In short, state strategies of the sort outlined here have clearly impacted the ethical imaginaries of ordinary Malays and other Muslims (even as they have built upon long-standing cultural precedents), just as they have contributed to ethnic and religious polarization throughout the nation (Norani Othman et al 2008; Liow 2009; Peletz 2009; Lee 2010).

Before delving into matters of criminality, it is essential to distinguish between the kinds of criminal cases (*kes jenayah*) that the *sharia* judiciary is currently empowered to deal with but does not engage on a regular basis, on the one hand, and those that it commonly adjudicates, on the other. Both sets of cases are important, but they should not be confused. One reason for this is that the greatly expanded scope of religious, moral, and other offenses subject to the jurisdiction of the Islamic courts has not had an appreciable impact on the everyday practices, caseload, litigant base, or overall tenor of the courts, which are among my main concerns in this book. The enhanced purview is nonetheless significant in terms of the cultural-political atmosphere, including relations between Muslims and non-Muslims, and the directions that assemblages of religion, law, and governance are moving. Let us first consider the kinds of criminal cases the Islamic courts typically deal with.

TABLE 1 Major Types and Number of Criminal Offenses
Handled by Malaysia's *Sharia* Courts, 2011–2012

	Offense	Number	% of Total
1	"Illicit Proximity" (*khalwat*)	12,740	36.9
2	Marriage offense with respect to part II of the Islamic family law [enactment] (*berkahwin bersalahan dengan bahagian dua undang-undang keluarga Islam*)	6,520	18.9
3	Divorce without the permission of the court (*perceraian tanpa kebenaran mahkamah*)	3,207	9.3
4	Polygamy [polygyny] without the permission of the court (*poligami tanpa kebenaran mahkamah*)	2,282	6.6
5	Activities that are inappropriate in public places (*perbuatan tidak sopan di tempat awam*)	2,181	6.3
6	Collusion, being an accomplice/collaborator (*subahat*)	1,911	5.5
7	Fornication/adultery (*bersetubuh luar nikah*; literally, "coupling/coitus/copulation outside of marriage")	1,369	4.0
8	Gambling (*berjudi*)	1,067	3.1
9	Not appearing before the NCR Registrar [Registrar of Marriage, Divorce, Reconciliation] (*tidak hadir di hadapan pendaftar NCR*)	1,061	3.1
10	Out of wedlock pregnancy (*hamil luar nikah*)	1,058	3.1
11	Not respecting Ramadan (*tidak menghormati Ramadan*)	382	1.1
12	[Drinking] intoxicating beverages (*minuman yang memabukkan*)	325	0.9
13	Failing to file a report regarding the Islamic family law [enactment] (*tidak membuat laporan berkaitan undang-undang keluarga Islam*)	153	0.4
14	Teaching [religion] without certification (*mengajar tanpa tauliah*)	152	0.4
15	A male posing or behaving as a female (*lelaki berlagak perempuan*)	121	0.4

SOURCE: Malaysian Department of *Syariah* Judiciary

* N = 34,529

According to the JKSM, the vast majority (over 98 percent) of the criminal cases that came before the nation's Islamic courts during 2011–12 fell into one or another of fifteen official categories. Table 1 presents the relevant categories followed by the number of cases and the percentage for each category in relation to the total number of these cases, listed in descending order of frequency.

"Illicit proximity" (*khalwat*), involving a man and a woman who are not married to one another and who are not *muhrim* (barred from intermarriage by genealogical considerations) being alone in a secluded or confined locale, is by far the most common criminal offense handled by the *sharia* judiciary. This is evidenced by the fact that there were nearly 13,000 new charges of *khalwat* lodged during

2011–12, nearly twice the number of the second most common type of criminality to come before the Islamic courts, "marriage offenses with respect to part II of the Islamic family law [enactment]." The latter tend to involve marriages that were "non-registerable" either because they were not solemnized properly or because they violated the minimum age for Muslim marriage (eighteen for men, sixteen for women) or consent requirements for one or both parties. Consider also that cases of *khalwat* are more than nine times as frequent as those involving charges of fornication/adultery, formerly referred to as *zina*. This is partly because *khalwat* is much easier to prove and is in some ways more obvious than fornication/adultery, requiring only one or or more credible witnesses to the couple being alone in a secluded or confined locale (or other relevant evidence), as opposed to either a witness who actually observed sexual relations of the illicit sort at issue here or evidence of other varieties, such as an out-of-wedlock pregnancy.

I was curious why the Malay expression *bersetubuh luar nikah* (coupling/copulation outside of marriage) has increasingly replaced the more conventional Arabic-origin *zina* in official discourse bearing on fornication/adultery. According to a high-ranking member of the JKSM with whom I discussed these matters in 2010, the main reason is that "We don't have *hudud* laws here." This is a short-hand reference to a complicated religious/legal/political nexus: (1) *zina* is an offense falling under the Quranic rubric of *hudud* law (along with theft, highway robbery, intoxication, apostasy, and false accusations concerning *zina*); (2) *hudud* laws have never been implemented in Malaysia, despite efforts by political and religious elites in Kelantan, Terengganu, and elsewhere to have them introduced; and (3) if they had been implemented in accordance with widespread interpretations of Quranic jurisprudence, their infraction could result in one hundred lashes for fornication that does not involve adultery, and death by stoning for adultery. Because these particular sanctions (one hundred lashes, death by stoning) do not exist in Malaysia, the *sharia* judiciary has good reasons to formally avoid using the term *zina*, even though it was the designation of choice for the offenses in question until quite recently and is still found in some official publications. Significantly, while this instance of sociolinguistic engineering is motivated partly by concerns to ensure that the Islamic judiciary avoids inconsistencies with classical *sharia*, it nonetheless involves jettisoning a terminological cornerstone of the classical jurisprudential tradition. We have seen that a similar scrapping has occurred with the recent rebranding of Islamic judges as *hakim*, for this has entailed relegating the term *kadi*, a key symbol in and of Islamic jurisprudence since the time of the Prophet, to the ash heap of Malaysian history.

Both types of offense (*khalwat, bersetubuh luar nikah*) involve heterosexual couples, as do "activities that are inappropriate in public places" (holding hands, hugging, kissing), the fifth-most common type of offense. Same-sex couples believed to have engaged in sexual transgression are not charged with any of these offenses and do not typically come before the Islamic courts in any event. Rather, if charged with a crime, they are hauled before the *civil* courts, in some instances under Section 377 of the National Penal Code, which provides for imprisonment up to twenty years and whipping for any acts, whether or not consensual, of "carnal intercourse against the order of nature."[10] This is despite the fact that the Islamic courts are authorized to deal with cases of *liwat* (sodomy).

More generally, the three types of *sharia* criminality that I mention at the outset of the previous paragraph represented 47.2 percent of the criminal cases heard by the Islamic courts during 2011–12. Taken collectively, cases involving marriage offenses with respect to Part II of the Islamic Family Law Enactment, divorce without the court's permission, polygamy without the court's permission, collusion, and gambling comprise another 43.4 percent of the court's workload during that period. This is to say that over 90 percent of the court's criminal caseload centered on these eight categories of offense.

Two of the six infractions (illicit proximity, fornication/adultery) have long been designated as *sharia* crimes. Items on the top-eight list that have come to be defined as criminal behaviors since the early 1980s include activities that are inappropriate in public places, collusion (e.g., in facilitating an illegal marriage or another type of criminality), divorce or polygamy without the court's permission, and gambling, the first two of which are exceedingly vague and for this reason alone of great concern to women's groups, human rights organizations, and others wary of moral policing by the state and/or conservative sectors of Muslim society. Items on the more expansive list of fifteen criminal offenses that are new include "a male behaving or posing as a female," which is also quite vague and problematic.

Charges against males posing or behaving as females are in fact rarely brought before the *sharia* judiciary; there were only 121 newly registered lawsuits involving accusations of this sort during 2011–12, compared to over 25,000 suits involving alleged infractions of heterosexual (including marriage/divorce) codes, over 1,000 instances of reported gambling, and nearly 200,000 civil suits in the *sharia* courts during the same period. Such charges pertain to transgressions of gender codes (dressing as a female, for example), not those bearing on sexual activity per se, though some *mak nyah* (the general term for male-bodied individuals who consider themselves to be "females born/trapped in male bodies" and who typically dress in women's attire) sometimes engage in prostitution with normatively gendered males to support themselves and are thus involved in homosexual relations. Men who dress or behave as women are also liable to be charged in the civil judiciary (e.g., for creating a public nuisance or "outraging decency"). More generally, they are more likely to encounter difficulties with the police than with authorities directly associated with the *sharia* judiciary, though it is also true that investigators associated with other state religious bureaucracies—e.g., JAWI or the Jabatan Agama Islam Negeri Selangor (JAIS; the Selangor Department of Islamic

Religion)—appear to initiate many of the cases against *mak nyah* through raids on the venues they frequent, following which they turn their investigations over to the police or to officials in the *sharia* judicial establishment for processing. Police, I might add, usually deal with them "extra-judicially," i.e., by harassing, arresting, detaining, humiliating, and sometimes assaulting them, and then letting them go without formal charges.

Alternately, at least if they are of middle-school age, feminized males may be shipped off to "reeducation centers" to be toughened up and otherwise resocialized in accordance with increasingly narrow and martial notions of Malay masculinity. Official concerns with the prevalence in high schools and college settings of "soft males" (*lelaki lembut*) are so pronounced that in the early years of the new millennium the International Islamic University of Malaysia sponsored an elaborate research project to investigate this highly visible phenomenon on its own campus, to target those who "deliberately become effeminates" (as distinct from "genetically effeminate males," about whom much less can be done), so as to "eliminate their sexual identity confusion" and "protect society" (Noraini Mohd Noor et al 2005). As discussed elswhere (Peletz 1996, 2009), ordinary Malays have long been far more generous in their dealings with male-bodied gender transgression than these initiatives suggest. One of the larger issues is that ordinary Malays have long practiced and espoused a relatively inclusive and progressive Islam; another is that when it comes to gender and many other areas, there is a good deal of tension between ordinary ethical sensibilities and dispositions on the one hand, and authorized or authorizing legal and ethical discourses on the other.

JKSM officials I interviewed in July 2018 indicated that in most states there are no laws on the books stipulating that a female behaving or posing as a male constitutes a *sharia* offense (see also tan beng hui 2012, 63). But this may not be true for long given the current cultural-political climate and the telling fact that 2008 saw the Majlis Fatwa Kebangsaan (National *Fatwa* Council), made up of *mufti* and *ulama* representing the entire Federation, issue a condemnation of *pengkids* ("tomboys," or females dressing or behaving like males). "Sexual relations between female persons" (*musahaqah*) is already listed as a *sharia* crime, having been designated as such since the moral panics of the mid-to-late 1990s. Like *liwat,* it is currently punishable in the *sharia* courts of some states by a fine of up to RM$5,000, imprisonment up to three years, or whipping with up to six strokes of a rattan cane. According to my sources in the JKSM, as of late July 2018 no women had ever been charged under these provisions in Malaysia's Islamic courts, though early September of that year saw two women sentenced for such an offense. Women believed guilty of infractions of the sort at issue here are sometimes dealt with in other venues (e.g., the civil courts) and, far more commonly, by other, usually less formal means—teasing, gossip, ostracism, police harassment, etc.—as is also true of males held to be involved in gender-transgression and/or same-sex relations.

As we are now addressing *sharia* crimes that are rarely if ever adjudicated by the Islamic judiciary but are nonetheless of great symbolic and political import, it bears repeating that we need to dinstinguish between the types of infractions that commonly come before the courts on the one hand, and those the courts are empowered to deal with but do not usually address on the other. An additional (twofold) point to reiterate is that the past few decades have seen vastly expanded definitions of what kinds of behavior constitute *sharia* criminality, and that this bodes ill for Malaysians (Muslims and non-Muslims alike) insofar as the nation's exceedingly top-heavy executive branch increasingly utilizes whatever resources it has available to stifle dissent and otherwise neutralize its real and imagined adversaries and critics.

The greatly augmented jurisdictions and penal powers of the Islamic courts now cover more than eighty different types of criminal offenses. This number is sure to grow in the years ahead. The sanctions the courts are empowered to impose for such crimes will in all likelihood be increased in severity as well, as has been the trend in recent decades. Some of these crimes are relatively unambiguous and are not new, such as failure to perform Friday prayers and disrespecting Ramadan. Others, many of which are of recent provenance, are highly ambiguous (or at least potentially so), given the government's insistence on monopolistic definitions and state simplifications, which are not usually explicit and do in fact change over time but are not necessarily clearly broadcast in advance or even after the fact, of what constitutes acceptable Islamic doctrine and ritual practice. That said, Shia, especially Iranian Shia, teachings and practices are definitely out, at least for Malays (but not necessarily for Muslims of presumed Shia/Pakistani background) (Mohd Faisal Musa and tan beng hui 2017); and groups such as Darul Arqam and Ayah Pin's Sky Kingdom are banned as "deviationist," as are various Sufi orders (*tarekat*), despite the absence in the Quran of any clear basis for deviationism (An-Na'im 1999).

The current list of *sharia* criminal offenses includes wrongful worship; teaching false doctrine; the propagation of religious doctrines other than Islam among Muslims; making false religious claims; insulting or bringing into contempt the religion of Islam; deriding Quran verses or *hadith;* printing, publishing, producing, or disseminating material contrary to Islamic law; instigating neglect of religious duty; teaching or professing religion without a *tauliah* (formal authorization); expressing contempt or defiance of religious authorities; defying a *sharia* court order; expressing an opinion contrary to *fatwa;* instigating a husband or wife to neglect spousal duties or to divorce; indecent acts in a public place; gender-transgressive behavior on the part of males; same-sex relations involving either males or females; and collusion, as we have seen. This list is far from exhaustive, but it should suffice to convey a sense of how political and religious elites have endeavored to position the Islamic judiciary to better discipline and control Muslims and others in Malaysia and ostensibly help guide them to a more secure and prosperous future.

There are important ironies here worthy of brief consideration. Ever since independence in 1957, national-level political and religious elites associated with the party (UMNO) that dominated Malaysian politics through 2018 have promoted what Robert Hefner (2011a) refers to as a broadly "ethicalized" Islam and have been at pains to distinguish this orientation from the more legalistic, *sharia*-minded policies championed by the Islamist opposition party, PAS. The UMNO approach has typically been keyed to expansively-cast moral principles: "Faith and piety in Allah; [a] just and trustworthy government; [a] free and independent people; . . . balanced and comprehensive economic development" (Abdullah Ahmad Badawi 2006, 4). In theory, UMNO's approach contrasts sharply with that of PAS, which has tended to focus on the virtues and necessity of implementing narrowly defined legal codes (e.g., *hudud* laws), and on other legalistic fixes such as revamping the Federal Constitution so that the Quran and the *Sunnah* comprise its core. One irony is that UMNO's twin commitment to the instantiation of broadly construed ethical values and to being both different from and better than PAS also entails a strong commitment to *sharia*tization (in the form of creeping criminalization as well as landmark concessions to the *sharia* courts regarding their jurisdiction in hot-button cases involving the abjuration of Islam, interfaith couples, and the proper burial of those whose late-life conversion to Islam is in dispute),[11] albeit of a contrasting—"kinder, gentler," and more gradual—sort than that proposed by its nemesis. A second, related irony is that as different groups (particularly UMNO, PAS, and their respective supporters) spar over the pros, cons, and interpretations of various legal initiatives and symbolics bearing on *sharia,* the underlying ethical considerations and attendant political implications, including not least for the nation's non-Muslims, are sometimes eclipsed or altogether ignored, much like the situation in Pakistan described by Muhammad Qasim Zaman (2016). As one Chinese Malaysian lawyer commented, "PAS has put the frog into the pot of hot boiling water. UMNO put the frog in the pot and then boiled the water. Either way we're going to get burned" (cited in Lee 2010, 89).

CONCLUSION

This chapter has addressed the co-imbrication of law, politics, and religion, illustrating (among other things) how neoliberalism and the punitive turn that commonly goes hand-in-hand with it have been instantiated and experienced in various realms of Malaysian society since the 1970s and 1980s. Neoliberalism, as noted earlier, has many diverse, potentially contradictory, entailments; this is one reason it is often conceptualized as an assemblage. A surge in punitiveness, such as I have documented here, is but one of them. And of course in some cases, a rise in punitiveness may long predate, or otherwise have nothing to do with, neoliberalism. In this chapter, I have explored certain kinds of elective affinities between the two phenomena.

Four features of Malaysia's new punitiveness merit brief note in these concluding remarks. First, recent decades have witnessed stepped-up efforts on the part of
Malay political and religious elites to delegitimize and stigmatize many variants of
Otherness, some of which have been unambiguously criminalized. This is readily
apparent in laws, policies, sanctions, and (Malay) attitudes bearing on Chinese,
Indians, and other non-Muslims, though it is also evident in legal and cultural-
political developments bearing on Shia Muslims as well as gays, lesbians, and others (regardless of ethnic and religious background) who transgress heteronormative expectations and ideals. Second, ordinary Malays are increasingly on the
lookout for behavior falling outside the ever more narrow range of state-defined
normativity. Third, they are much more likely than in times past to bring real or
imagined ethical and other transgressions to the attention of religious officials and
the police.

A fourth feature of the surge in punitiveness, which I discuss in more detail, has
to do with the deputization of large numbers of the public so that they can provide
ancillary services to the police and others involved in community watches and
crime control. Most relevant in this context is the organization Ikatan Relawan
Rakyat Malaysia (the Malaysian People's Volunteer League), known as the RELA
Corps (*rela* means "willing," "ready," and is sometimes used as shorthand for
sukarela ["voluntary," "voluntarily," "willingly"]). The RELA Corps traces its origins to the Home Guard that operated as "the eyes and ears of the government"
(*mata dan telingga kerajaan*) during the period of the Emergency (the communist
insurgency of 1948–60) and the ensuing Confrontation (*Konfrontasi*) with Indonesia (1963–66), though it was not formally inaugurated under its current moniker
until 1972. Its easily recognizable uniformed members, typically clad in green
army fatigues and yellow berets, enjoy a broad mandate. This includes formal
authority and responsibility to carry out raids at factories, restaurants, hotels,
etc.;[12] to conduct interrogations; to detain people without passports, proper work
permits, and other required documents; and to otherwise aid the police in fighting
crime, managing vehicular traffic, and providing community service. High-
ranking members of RELA, including the thousand or so officers who occupy the
most powerful and prestigious positions in the organization and hail primarily
from military backgrounds, have at times been authorized to carry firearms, like
conventional police. But their authority in this regard has been widely contested
due to the organization's reputation for heavy-handedness, which has on occasion
resulted in charges of armed robbery and culpable homicide against overzealous
volunteers (Goh 2013).

Interestingly, the two high-ranking RELA officials I interviewed at their headquarters in Putrajaya in July 2018 were adamant, in responding to my questions on
the subject, that RELA is *not* an auxiliary police force, let alone a para-military
organization. Indeed, they bristled at this suggestion, giving me the distinct

impression that I had committed a major faux pas in raising the issue. This despite the organization's mandate (as outlined above) and the fact that RELA is run by former military men, has both a formal structure (with variably-starred generals, platoon leaders, sergeants, etc.) and sartorial codes that replicate those of the military, and was characterized by the officials I interviewed (and in their 43-frame Powerpoint presentation) as "the eyes and ears of the government." My interlocutors and their staff preferred to conceptualize RELA as a community service organization, sometimes referring to RELA members as "first responders," as when they assist communities beset by floods, and alternatively, as the "second line of defense," as when backing up police and military forces dispatched to secure international borders.

According to figures provided by RELA's Deputy Director General, there were 3,078,631 RELA members as of July 17, 2018, men comprising 59.2 percent of the total, women making up the other 40.8 percent. More than 68.4 percent of RELA members are Malay (the remainder are mostly Chinese, Indian, Iban, and others from the states of Sarawak and Sabah in East Malaysia). Roughly one million members of RELA are "active" members; the others, presumably including the RELA-affiliated taxi drivers encouraged as a matter of civic duty to eavesdrop on their passengers and report suspicious conversations, are classified as "dormant" or "inactive." Since Malaysia's population in 2018 was roughly 31 million, this means that nearly 10 percent of the country's population are members of RELA. If we confine ourselves to the demographically and politically dominant Malay population, which provides most of the recruits, the percentage of RELA members is around 14 percent, roughly one in seven of all Malays. And if we focus on Malays over the age of eighteen (the minimum age for joining RELA), the latter percentage increases to nearly 23 percent, almost one out of every four adult Malays. These are striking figures, especially since RELA is but one of many organizations involved in community watches and crime control. Others include *Rakan Cop* ("Friends of Cops"), an organization of motorcyclists formed in 2005 that works closely with the police ("as their eyes and ears") and was said to have around 535,000 members nationwide in 2013 (*Sunday Star* 2013a).

Not surprisingly, these dynamics and the attendant proliferation of private security firms hired to patrol and safeguard shopping malls, apartment complexes, gated communities, upscale homes, and the like have coincided with a boom in incarceration. The number of people imprisoned in Malaysia doubled in size between 2000 and 2016 (from 27,358 to 55,490), and increased more than twenty-fold in the forty-four years from 1972 to 2016.[13] As percentages, these increases are much larger than their counterparts in the notoriously punitive United States during the same general intervals (see, for example, Wacquant 2009, 114–15), even though Malaysia incarcerates a much smaller proportion of its overall population than does the United States (177 per 100,000 vs. 655 per 100,000, respectively).[14] More broadly, the Malaysian state's treatment of its mostly Tamil-speaking Indian minority, which is disproportionately represented in the nation's prisons and squatter settlements, is clearly punitive, bordering on ethnic cleansing (Willford 2006, 2014; Baxstrom 2008). And there is clearly much greater involvement on the part of the public in the penal framework, which is currently equipped with greatly enhanced technology and pervasiveness, to paraphrase a point made by John Pratt et al (2005, xxv) in another context.

Important to mention, too, is that these broad trends have occurred alongside counter-currents and orthogonal developments, including relatively female-friendly reforms in the Islamic judiciary that make it easier for Malay and other Muslim women to get justice in the cases they bring against their husbands or former husbands for failing to support them and their children (chapter 5). The larger issue here is that both cross-culturally and historically, a rising tide of punitiveness commonly coincides with developments that Foucault (1979 [2000], 2007) refers to as "pastoral." The latter term designates certain modalities of ethical care, guidance, and governance oriented toward the protection and welfare of both the singular individual and the larger community. The punitive and the pastoral, in other words, should not be viewed in zero-sum terms, as discussed in more detail in subsequent chapters (Gupta 2012). Nor should punitive and rehabilitative or restorative justice, though in any given empirical case one may be hegemonic in relation to the other(s).

Here it is useful to briefly consider comparative material bearing on the rising tide of punitiveness in the Indonesian province of Aceh, in northern Sumatra, just across the Straits of Melaka from the Malay Peninsula. Before addressing specifics, I should mention that Indonesian initiatives involving the embrace of neoliberal doctrines and the implementation of projects associated with them are broadly comparable to those that have occurred in Malaysia. So, too, are some of their unintended consequences (Li 2007; Long 2013).

The Acehnese are well known in the literature for their Islamic piety, and because they waged a protracted struggle against central authorities in postcolonial Indonesia to achieve a measure of regional autonomy. They also suffered horrendous losses of life and property as a consequence of the 2004 Indian Ocean tsunami that is estimated to have killed at least 160,000–170,000 people in their province alone. Recent studies bearing on Aceh's implementation of Islamic by-laws beginning around the turn of the new millennium are of interest here (Feener 2013; Kloos 2018). These studies indicate that, as in Malaysia, there has been a recalibration of the Quranic injunction to enjoin good and forbid wrong, such that the "forbidding wrong" part of the equation has come to be accorded more salience both in relative and absolute terms. This is especially obvious from the activities of the Wilayatul Hisbah, or "*Sharia* Police Force," created in 2002. This organization is charged with a number of related tasks. They include enforcing compliance with newly introduced *sharia* provisions bearing on illicit sexual relations, female dress codes, gambling, and alcohol; providing morally corrective advice; and, when necessary, administering physical punishment such as flogging with a thick rattan cane.

The *Sharia* Police created significant local controversy and garnered much bad press, both nationally and internationally, as a result of some of the more dramatic public floggings they oversaw or were seen as having encouraged during the early years of the new millennium. Michael Feener's careful (2013) analysis indicates, tellingly, that the impetus to impose harsh punishments was greatly amplified by the tsunami. This is because the tsunami was seen by many Acehnese as divine retribution for their widespread errancy and sinfulness. Feener (2013) and Kloos (2018) also make the crucial point that public punishments administered by the *Sharia* Police need to be distinguished from acts of vigilantism undertaken by village youth. Some of the latter clearly violated *Sharia* Police guidelines bearing on discipline and punishment, inasmuch as they occasionally beat heterosexual couples believed to be guilty of *khalwat* ("illicit proximity") with wooden clubs and flogged them with as many as one hundred strokes of a rattan cane.

At the risk of oversimplification, what we see here is a florescence of sentiments and dispositions conducing toward fearful vigilance and a punitive turn in both narrowly legal and more expansive cultural-political terms. These developments might be expected for a variety of reasons. Foremost among them is that Acehnese are painfully aware of their vulnerabilities, their victimization by political, economic, and natural forces beyond their control, and the precarities of their individual and collective lives. Such painful awareness would likely incline them to perceive their social and natural environments to be full of danger, as Michalis Lianos and Mary Douglas (2000, 110) explain in another context. It would also likely incline them to apprehend and analyze the world through categories of menace. The latter categories, to paraphrase, encourage not only continuously detecting threats and assessing potentially adverse circumstances, but also continuously scanning the environment for indices of potentially threatening irregularity (118). We see much the same thing in Malaysia, albeit on a reduced scale compared to Aceh.

Issues of menacing irregularity and punitiveness aside, this chapter has also brought Foucauldian and other concerns to bear on Bourdieu's work on juridical fields to chart the rise of an increasingly corporate Islamic governmentality as it is revealed through a consideration of continuities and transformations in the micropolitical practices and attendant reorientation of Malaysia's *sharia* judiciary during the past few decades and the new millennium in particular. Bourdieu's scholarship encourages close attention to the heterogenous components of discourses in juridical fields, their unstable and contested configurations, and their historically contingent genealogies and realignments in the fields of state power (but see Dezalay and Madsen 2012, 438). Hence I want to draw attention to some of the complications that would arise if we followed the many protagonists and observers of current struggles over law, politics, and religion in Malaysia and elsewhere who seek to delimit clear, sharp, or enduring divisions between things "secular" and "religious." Bourdieu's main text on juridical fields does not explicitly engage such matters, partly because it dates from the 1980s, when it was not yet clear that assertive public religions and the political and policy challenges they pose to secularity—and vice versa—might be here to stay, though the larger issue is Bourdieu's relative neglect of most things religious, even or especially in his early scholarship on Algeria, which largely ignores the influence of Islam (Goodman and Silverstein 2009). The complications are patently obvious when we focus, as I have here, on transformations in the discourses, practices, and micropolitics of late-modern *sharia* courts. In Malaysia and many other parts of the Muslim world, the discourses and practices of these courts evince a seamless interweaving of elements of Islam (drawn from or otherwise associated with the Quran, *hadith,* and, in some instances, newly invented traditions of *sulh*) and features derived from civil law and other, ostensibly secular sources—sources that, in the Malaysian context, include corporate business templates, Japanese and other systems of audit and normativity, and e-*sharia* governance.

Circumstances such as these point to the difficulties of the signifiers "Islamic" and "Islamization." Compared to the late 1980s, for example, are Malaysia's present-day *sharia* courts ultimately more, or less, Islamic? By what—or whose—criteria? The questions make considerable sense in the ethnographic/historical context and will undoubtedly be debated for years to come. But, analytically, they have no simple or correct answers. Just as, for Agrama (2012), secularism presupposes an always ongoing exercise in the (re)drawing and blurring of lines, so too, arguably, do processes of Islamization.

The interweaving at issue here does in any event have a distinct genealogy. A key feature of the genealogy is that *sharia* courts often derive their charters from independence-era constitutions, largely intact or substantively revised, that were originally crafted by representatives of colonial regimes. These officials typically acted in accordance with secular-liberal imperatives that in many settings effectively quarantined *sharia* to (Islamic) family law and other personal status law, even as they made formal provision for Islam in the realm of state ceremony but not elsewhere in the corridors of power. Postcolonial concerns to rectify the marginalization of *sharia,* its courts, and the norms and ethics of Islam have taken many forms. But they are commonly interwoven with expansive yet context-specific and otherwise highly variable processes of state-sponsored Islamization, which are largely inseparable from processes of state formation, and which have their own unique genealogies and mandates concerning *sharia* and much else. My description and interpretation of transformations in the cultural logic of judicial process in Rembau's *sharia* court between 1987 and 2013, and my fine-grained commentary on two hearings in 2012–13 in particular, provide a sense of the historical vicissitudes of these dynamics and how one such mandate is currently realized in practice. This account is thus offered partly as a contribution to the historical anthropological literature on law, politics, and religion. More generally, it is intended as an illustration of the potential value of long-term fieldwork grounded in the methodologies of deep hanging out that are conducive to "experience-near" understandings (Geertz 1983, 57) and the kind of comparative-historical perspectives for which Weber (1925 [1968]), despite his problematic views on "*kadi* justice" and Islam, was deservedly famous.

One of Bourdieu's more interesting observations concerning juridical fields in nineteenth and twentieth century France is that they were internally riven, their key components oftentimes linked to one another through complementary and/or hostile competition, and that they were also heavily informed by the internal politics of the profession, a politics that was inseparable from the profession's positioning in the fields of state power and in relation to the global dynamics inflecting them. This observation has wide-ranging comparative and theoretical implications (Dezalay and Garth 2002). And it certainly rings true in Malaysia, where *sharia*-court judges have long been accorded less prestige and power (in terms of sanctions and jurisdictions) than their civil-law brethren, and have long been relegated to lower standing in civil-service hierarchies and the schemes of remuneration associated with them. Efforts to rectify the situation have involved an array of strategies to make the *sharia* judiciary more like its (idealized) civil-law counterpart— more "civil-ized." Some have focused on professional ethics, formal procedure, Japanese and other audit protocols, accountability, and transparency, including, as we have seen, judicial attire and nomenclature. Others have sought better pay, weightier sanctions, and expanded jurisdictions. More broadly, the main reason why the civil judiciary (minus its corruption and other shortcomings) and many of its laws (bearing, e.g., on procedure) and symbolics constitute the gold standard for the system of *sharia* courts—but not vice versa—is that, in accordance with the Federal Constitution, the civil judiciary, sometimes in response to or in conjunction with legislative initiatives, defines and occasionally expands (or otherwise revises) the constitutional charter of the *sharia* courts, and is thus, in a very concrete sense, their political patron. It is, at the same time, their main competitor and adversary, as well as the primary source of models in comparison with which they are often held to be lacking by members of the judicial profession (broadly defined) and those outside it.

In an important sense, then, there is only one serious game in town, and that game defines not only the field of play and its rules, but also the most cherished prize: control over the valorization of legal texts and their interpretation and implementation, or alternatively, over society's nervous system, as Durkheim

(1893[1964], 128) famously viewed law. To secure the prize, one must engage the other team on its field of play, in accordance with its rules, and beat it at its own game. For the *sharia* judiciary, this means developing a potentially winning "feel for the game" that includes both the anticipation and the crafting of amended codes that may define its shifting, ideally expanded boundaries and possible futures, hence comprehensive processes of rationalization involving bureaucratization and corporatization that are inflected by the common law and are exceedingly friendly to capitalism and neoliberal governance alike.

Finally, we might consider a broadly cast contention, inspired in part by Bourdieu (1987, 830–31), that many of the decisions, self-representations, and symbolics evident in juridical fields are usefully viewed in terms of struggles, negotiations, and compromises, simultaneously political and pragmatic, involving potentially irreconcilable social forces (and the imperatives and constraints associated with them), interest groups (large and small), and the disparate ethics, social imaginaries, and demands they have helped fashion. Formulations such as these serve as useful correctives to Foucault's sweeping generalizations, elisions, and silences concerning both the specific driving forces behind particular instantiations of governmentality and their actual social-engineering "achievements." Conversely, Bourdieu's work on juridical fields has more analytic purchase if it is informed, on the one hand, by explicitly historicized Foucauldian concerns with governmentality, and, on the other, by meaningful consideration of the scope, force, and content of religious sensibilities and commitments, which both theorists tend to ignore when engaging law and related phenomena. The value of these formulations will be increasingly evident in the following chapters.

3

What Are *Suhl* Sessions?

After Ijtihad, *Islamic ADR, and Pastoral Power*

If a wife fears cruelty or desertion on her husband's part, there is no blame on them if they arrange an amicable settlement between themselves; and such settlement is best.

—QURAN, SURAH AN-NISA (4:128)

The culture of litigation imposed on Muslim societies during the colonial days must be replaced by the Islamic ways of amicable settlement.

—SYED KHALID RASHID (2008)

Western-style lawyering runs counter to the Islamic notion of ADR.

—WALID IQBAL (2001)

We have seen that Malaysia's *sharia* judiciary has undergone a number of significant transformations in recent decades, especially in the new millennium. Perhaps most evident, it has become more globalized, rationalized, and corporate as well as more intrusive and punitive. It has simultaneously become more pastoral, inasmuch as it provides compassionate care, supervision, and governance concerned with the salvation and overall welfare of both the unique individual and the group as a whole (Foucault 1979 [2000], 2007). This is particularly apparent in the formal introduction of *sulh* (mediation) sessions. These sessions tend to be run by female officers of the court and are more or less mandatory for couples experiencing certain kinds of problems in maintaining, or, alternatively, dissolving, their marriages, unless they have already participated in counseling or mediation sessions sponsored by the Jabatan Agama Islam (Department of Islamic Religion).

My interest in ethnographic descriptions and analyses of *sulh* sessions derives partly from their pastoral dimensions and partly from debates within the scholarly community as to whether or not there is a uniquely "Islamic" mode of "doing" law, and, if there is, what its constituent features might be. Many eminent scholars have suggested that a distinctively Islamic modality of law has long been evident and was clearly discernable in classical variants of *sharia* practice. Other reputable scholars dispute this claim. Still others argue that regardless of which position may have more merit, the practice of law in the Muslim world is exceedingly complex and that it is thus quite reductionist to limit one's ethnographic and historical inquiries to issues of "authenticity." I am of the latter view, but I also find some of the previously noted debates worthy of contemplation.

In support of the first set of arguments, that a uniquely Islamic legal mode has deep temporal roots and was apparent in classical variants of *sharia* practice, some scholars cite *ijtihad,* which as we have seen refers to innovative legal interpretation of (or on the basis of) sacred texts in order to deal with unprecedented cases, hence independent reasoning/judgment and/or judicial creativity (see, e.g., Kamali 1991; Hallaq 2009; see also Rosen 1989; Bowen 2003). Some of them also cite judges' pronounced concerns with, including the juridical weight they accord, litigants' *asal* (*usul*). The latter term is commonly rendered into English as "origins" or "social origins." But it has a much wider semantic range insofar as it embraces many features of an individual's social relations, biography, character, and disposition; in short, what kind of person he or she is or might be (Rosen 1989). For these scholars, *asal* has long been a key component of Islamic judicial inquiries and decisions, and simultaneously distinguishes them from many of their non-Islamic, especially common-law, counterparts. More broadly, a number of scholars have argued that *asal* is a key symbol if not a defining feature of the Islamic jurisprudential tradition, much like *ijtihad.*

In his magisterial volume entitled *Shari'a: Theory, Practice, Transformations* (2009), for example, Wael Hallaq argues that legal hermeneutics grounded in *ijtihad* comprised one of the defining attributes of classical modalities of *sharia.* Hallaq also maintains that *ijtihad* was the feature of *sharia* that was most negatively affected by its engagement with the political, legal, and epistemological regimes of colonialism and modern states generally. The latter contention is most germane here, resonating as it does with data from many Muslim-majority nations, including Malaysia, which Hallaq discusses at various points in his text. More broadly, in his 2009 work and subsequently, Hallaq has highlighted the "epistemic breakdown" and "desiccation and final dismantling" of *sharia* in the modern Muslim world; alternatively, its "decimation" and "structural death" (2009,15, 535, 547; 2013, 167).

These bold assertions are "good to think," to borrow a phrase from Levi-Strauss (1962, 89), though I have suggested that they may need qualification. In an essay published in 2013, I offered a friendly amendment to Hallaq's thesis based on my long-term ethnographic and archival research. My position was twofold. I argued, on the one hand, that Hallaq's thesis seems valid in light of data on judicial processes involving Islamic judges (*kadi, hakim*) in Muslim-majority settings. I also argued, on the other hand, that his thesis *might* merit qualification if we shift our focus to the mediation sessions orchestrated by those referred to in Malaysia as *sulh* officers (*pegawai sulh*). I knew from the secondary literature and from court documents that, compared to formal proceedings run by *sharia* judges, almost all of whom are men, *sulh* (mediation) sessions, which tend to be overseen by women, are highly informal. I also knew that they are much less constrained by the florescence of bureaucratic regulations and positive-law models that the *sharia* judiciary has embraced in recent decades to enhance its legitimacy and efficiency. Partly for that reason, but also because I sat in on many counseling sessions in a *sharia* courthouse in the late 1980s that were the forerunners of modern-day *sulh* hearings, I assumed that *ijtihad* might be alive and well in these latter settings.

These arguments were not central to my 2013 essay, which focused on the *sharia* judiciary as a global assemblage (and provided part of the framework for early versions of chapter 1 of this book). Moreover, I was careful to emphasize that data from *sulh* sessions, which were formally introduced in the early years of the new millennium, *might* lead us to qualify Hallaq's arguments, not that they *necessarily* did so. The reason I phrased things this way is that, unlike regular hearings in Islamic courts, which are open to the public, *sulh* sessions are designed and guaranteed to be highly confidential. They typically involve only a *sulh* officer and the two litigants, who are invariably husband and wife. As such, they are largely inaccessible to local and foreign researchers who might want to observe them firsthand; Malaysian scholars who have written entire doctoral dissertations on *sulh*, for instance, have been barred from attending them (see, for example, Sa'odah binti Ahmad 2010, 15). To mix metaphors, at the time I wrote the essay in question, the jury on the matter of *ijtihad* and *sulh* sessions was still out.

A few months after the 2013 essay was published, I returned to Malaysia for an additional six to seven weeks of fieldwork. I had many different goals for that period of research, but I was hoping that my contacts in the Islamic judiciary would facilitate my access to *sulh* sessions, so that I might be able to see if my arguments about *ijtihad* were valid. Thanks to them and to the cooperation of *sulh* officers and the litigants involved, I was allowed to sit in on five *sulh* sessions in the fall of 2013. My observations of those sessions and my interviews with *sulh* officers and other officials led me to the realization that I was probably wrong in assuming that one might find evidence of *ijtihad* there, though much depends on how one defines *ijtihad*. This is despite the fact that *sulh* officers do deploy a variety of psychologically creative and emotionally compelling discursive strategies to help them realize their goal of guiding couples to a mediated compromise, rather than a settlement that, in the absence of successful mediation, requires potentially costly and time-consuming adjudication by a judge and involves lawyers and other court staff (registrars, court recorders, bailiffs, etc.).

If we take *ijtihad* to refer to judicial creativity in a very broad and non-technical sense—as resourcefulness, originality, initiative, artistry, individuality, and imagination on the part of those in charge of *sharia* proceedings—then one can perhaps reasonably contend that *sulh* officers exercise *ijtihad* (see cases 3 and 4, below). One problem here, however, is that a broadly construed creativity of this sort is by no means unique to practitioners of Islamic law as distinct from, say, common law. Arguably more important is that in my conversations with them, *sulh* officers categorically denied that they exercise *ijtihad,* a view shared by judges and most others I spoke with. This position is typically based on the twofold argument that *sulh* officers lack authorization to formally adjudicate disputes, and that the agreements they coax, prod, and cajole litigants to reach must be formally approved by a judge in order to be legally binding. Technically speaking, in other words, *sulh* officers cannot render binding decisions, and this capacity is a prerequisite for the exercise of *ijtihad.* In this view, only duly appointed *sharia* judges and *mufti* (who issue *fatwa*) are capable of exercising *ijtihad.* Since nearly 90 percent of Malaysia's *sharia* judges are men, and since all the nation's *mufti*s are men, this means that *ijtihad* is, in effect, an exclusively male prerogative.[1]

More generally, in this view, both the prerogative and the actual practice of *ijtihad* is confined to a very small group of (overwhelmingly male) elites in the employ of the state. Conversely, those outside the ranks of this tiny group of state-approved specialists have no right to engage in innovative legal interpretation of— or on the basis of—sacred texts or any other form of independent reasoning and/ or intellectual creativity with respect to *sharia.* Needless to say, these views pose considerable obstacles to reform-oriented activists, including Muslim feminists such as Sisters in Islam. They are also consistent with the fact that "Malaysia has one of the most tightly regulated religious spheres in the world" (Moustafa 2018, 4; see also Osman Bakar 2008, 82; Pew Research Center 2018).

Looking at *sulh* sessions for evidence of *ijtihad* may be misguided. So too may be the idea that there is—or ever has been—a distinctively Islamic mode of doing law, though for many Muslims there is no question that a distinctively Islamic mode of doing law has existed since the time of the Prophet. Hussein Agrama's (2012) scholarship on Egyptian *fatwa*s is relevant to the first set of issues insofar as he reminds us that "*fatwa*s [like *sulh* sessions] are heterogeneous things; given their highly plebeian character, it would certainly be a mistake to reduce them to a single thing, whether this be a form of *ijtihad* or a form of pedagogy" (179). I concur on this point and will argue in the pages that follow that the heterogeneity of *sulh* sessions and the timing of their formal implementation in Malaysia encourages us to range far beyond issues of *ijtihad, asal,* and related matters. Concerning the second set of issues, we might briefly consider the position of Abdullahi An-Na'im, who is among the most distinguished and vocal critics of the idea that there is a uniquely Islamic mode of doing law (see, e.g., An-Na'im 2008 and much of the rest of the scholarship he has produced over the last decade or so). As he recently put it to me,

I am against the notion that there is a distinctively 'Islamic' mode of 'doing' law, simply because there is no way of defining it authoritatively and conclusively. What is this alleged Islamic mode of doing law, and what makes it Islamic to the exclusion of all other modes of doing law? There is too much diversity and complexity in every sense (theological, philosophical, ideological, political, cultural, etc.) among the Muslims of the world for anything so-called 'Islamic' to be distinctively identified. If I may suggest, please ask any one of those who claim that there is a 'distinctively Islamic mode of doing law,' to define or even describe what that mode is and [to clarify] where . . . we find its difference from other modes clearly illustrated.[2]

Whatever one's position on the existence of a uniquely Islamic mode of doing law—and on how much if any of our analytic attention ought to be devoted to such things—*sulh* sessions merit serious consideration in their own right. This is partly because they are heralded as an ethically appropriate alternative to Western-style litigation and a return to "Islamic ADR," and partly because they provide important perspectives on morally corrective advice (*nasihat*) and pastoral governmentality in late-modern Malaysia. I thus proceed with a brief overview of some of the characteristic features of *sulh* sessions and then consider transcripts from two *sulh* hearings that I attended, one from Rembau (overseen by a female *sulh* officer) and one from Kuala Lumpur (overseen by a male *sulh* officer). The penultimate section of the chapter focuses on my follow-up interview with the *sulh* officer who presided over the latter case, raising issues bearing on intentional deception in the course of one's profession as an officer of the court and other ethical conundrums, as well as KPIs and Islamic ADR. The conclusion returns to some of the themes broached at the outset of the chapter and also provides brief comments on the importance of expanding one's purview beyond the realm of "leading actors" to encompass those Bourdieu (1977, 35) refers to as "utility men," many of whom are women. The larger issue has to do with the gendering of religious authority in the new millennium.

SULH SESSIONS: AN OVERVIEW

Sulh services and "products," as they are sometimes referred to in government circles and official publications, are strategically advertised and branded to the public in a variety of ways: through glossy brochures and other informational handouts available in *sharia* courthouses; via information posted on official government websites; by means of Islamically-themed radio and television broadcasts and DVDs directed at married or formerly married couples and the *ummah* more generally; and through articles that appear in mainstream print media, much of which is government-controlled (if not government-owned). Registrars and clerks at *sharia* courthouses and local Departments of Islamic Religion also provide information to potential litigants about *sulh* insofar as they are tasked with clarifying the kinds of claims that, according to official policy, *must* be referred to the *sulh* division for processing at the time they are formally registered with court staff. According to a national directive that was issued by the head of the JKSM in 2010 to *sharia*-court staff throughout the county, there are eighteen types of claims that must be assigned to authorities in the *sulh* division for possible resolution in lieu of—or prior to—a formal court hearing, unless the couple has already undergone counseling or mediation sessions sponsored by the Department of Islamic Religion. These include claims for: (1) a wife's maintenance (either in general [*nafkah isteri*] or for the three-month *edah* period following divorce [*nafkah edah*]); (2) maintenance for children (*nafkah anak*); (3) the obligatory consolatory gift due a wife who is divorced without fault (*mutaʾah*); (4) conjugal property (*harta sepencarian);* (5) guardianship of children (*jagaan anak*); and (6) custody of children (*hadanah*), which frequently includes claims bearing on visitation.

Much of the advertising and branding of *sulh* services is oriented toward legitimizing *sulh* hearings and explaining the basic meanings of the Arabic-origin notion of *sulh,* which authorities are endeavoring to popularize, largely against the grain. The term is not widely known to Malays and apparently never has been. Indeed, I never encountered the word during my village-based fieldwork in Malaysia during the late 1970s, and never came across it during my ethnographic and archival research in the *sharia* courts in the late 1980s. Moreover, none of the half-dozen or so Malay-language dictionaries I have collected since the late 1970s, some of which are of relatively recent provenance (dating from 2010, for example), include entries for the term. They do, however, include Malay-language entries for related phenomena such as mutual understanding, negotiation, compromise, reconciliation (*berunding, muafakat, persetujuan*) as would be expected in light of the fact that forms of mediation have long been valorized in Malay communities.

The most widely available brochure on *sulh* that is distributed by the *sharia* judiciary illustrates the diverse kinds of legitimacy work authorities are undertaking to smooth the implementation of the *sulh* process and establish its authenticity to a number of different (mostly Muslim) constituencies. The initial section of the brochure, under the heading of "understanding *sulh*" (*pengertian sulh*), grounds the practice in moral and specifically Islamic language. It does this by clarifying, in the very first sentence of the text, that *Al-Sulh* is an Arabic term denoting the end of quarrelling/disputing (*putus pertengkaran*) with the intention of compromise, adding that it involves an agreement among Muslim parties to end conflict. The brochure goes on to note that in civil law *sulh* is known as "mediation," using the English gloss in this context. This implicitly legitimizes the practice in common-law discourse as well, simultaneously effecting the kind of double legitimization that one sees in many domains of the *sharia* judiciary. That the overall thrust of this legitimization is in Islamic idioms is evident from the relatively lengthy sec-

tion that follows, titled "*Al-Sulh* from the perspective of Islamic law," which clari-
fies *sulh* from the vantage point of the Quran and *hadith*. This section includes a
passage from Surah An-Nisa (4:128) of the Quran, emphasizing that "If a wife fears
cruelty or desertion [*nusyuz*] on her husband's part, there is no blame on them if
they arrange an amicable settlement between themselves; and such settlement is
best." Next is a reference indicating the necessity for Muslims to seek peace or
compromise, followed by a *hadith*, also exhorting peaceful resolution of differences, especially between husbands and wives.

Brochures such as the one described briefly here, like the manuals distributed
to *sulh* officers (*Manual Kerja Sulh*) and the large informational boards displayed
in the public areas of *sharia* courthouses, often contain flowcharts depicting the
various steps in the process from initial registration of a complaint or problem to
its outcome, as either "successful" or a "failure." Such binaries are strongly favored
by those who manage and audit the *sharia* judiciary and many other domains of
law, politics, and culture in present-day Malaysia.

To the best of my knowledge, there is no additional information given to couples experiencing marital problems who come to the court to file a claim or otherwise obtain assistance. But "(pre)marriage courses" have been mandatory since
the early years of the new millennium and do, I am told, provide some information
bearing on the legal remedies available to those whose marriages have become
problematic.

As for the hearings themselves, one of the characteristic features of *sulh* sessions, as noted earlier, is that they are highly informal. (This is of course a relative
point, the frame of reference here being formal *sharia*-court hearings.) They occur
behind closed doors in *bilik sulh*, or "*sulh* chambers," which are basically small,
generic, sparsely appointed offices (see figure 6). And unlike formal *sharia*-court
sessions, which take place in large, highly impersonal, and intimidating courtrooms (modeled on the courtrooms of the civil judiciary), they do not involve
judges, lawyers, bailiffs, registrars, witnesses (or members of the public), or oath-
taking of any sort, though they invariably begin with recitation of the first chapter
of the Quran (Al-Fatihah, "The Opening"). Equally important, *sulh* officers provide a forum for the articulation of issues bearing on *asal*, which judges in formal
hearings no longer deem relevant or appropriate to engage. And they both allow
and encourage wide-ranging airing of differences on the part of plaintiff and
defendant alike. This is true even when the airing of such differences has little
direct bearing on the legally salient issues that brought the litigants to court—and
even when it involves, as it frequently does, litigants trading very rude and
demeaning insults and accusations.

This too is a sharp contrast to how things work in hearings overseen by *sharia*
judges. The kinds of narratives enunciated by litigants in the latter contexts are
thoroughly controlled by officers of the court, especially judges and lawyers. These

FIGURE 6. *Sulh* session in progress, depicting a *sulh* officer and her clients. From *Jabatan Kehakiman Syariah Negeri Sembilan: 5 Dekad Merentasi Zaman, 1960–2014* (*Negeri Sembilan Department of Syariah Judiciary: Five Decades Through Time, 1960–2014*) (Seremban, Negeri Sembilan: Jabatan Kehakiman Syariah, Negeri Sembilan, 2014), 59.

officials not only dictate whose turn it is to speak and what questions and topics litigants are to address; they also control the length, tone, tenor, and appropriateness of their responses (Conley and O'Barr 1998). Indeed, nowadays lawyers in particular so dominate *sharia*-court hearings that litigants often have little if any opportunity to speak, other than to monosyllabically confirm or deny lawyers' (or judges') versions of what did or did not transpire between them (see chapter 4).

The plaintiffs both in *sulh* sessions and in more formal hearings in the *sharia* courts are overwhelmingly married (or formerly married) women bringing charges against their husbands (or former husbands) for reasons of the sort noted earlier: e.g., because their husbands have abandoned them and/or failed to provide them and/or their children with the material or other sustenance required by Islamic law enactments, though other issues, bearing on custody/visitation, for example, are sometimes raised as well. Some women turn to the *sharia* judiciary to get justice, others to get even. Regardless of which of these (or other) objectives may be primary, many of them want their "day in court." What I mean here is that they seek a forum in which they can articulate their grievances, ideally in their own voices, to ostensibly neutral parties in the employ of the court (hence the state) who can help them renegotiate the terms of their relationships with their husbands (or former husbands), who in many instances are or were the most important authority figures in their lives. This kind of direct articulation of one's grievances in one's own voice is, for the most part, no longer possible in formal *sharia*-court hearings, monopolized as they are by lawyers and judges. It is possible, indeed more or less expected, in *sulh* sessions, however. This is one of the reasons these sessions appeal to female litigants. Since most *sharia* judges are men and most *sulh* officers are women, it is tempting to think of formal adjudication as a masculinized phenomenon and mediation as feminized. Different modes of conflict management in the *sharia* judiciary are indeed gendered in this fashion, but there are limits to these gendered associations, as I will discuss in a moment.

Consider, first, that the jurisdiction of the *sharia* judiciary and the sanctions at its disposal have been greatly expanded in recent decades. Like the more encompassing state apparatus of which it is a part, the *sharia* judiciary has become more extensively involved in surveillance, discipline, and control, just as it has become more corporate, intrusive, and punitive. *Sulh* sessions, on the other hand, have a more pastoral character, though they too are heavily bureaucratic, routinized, and rationalized, and are very much part of governmentality in present-day Malaysia. In characterizing *sulh* sessions as "pastoral" (or as having a more pastoral character than formal *sharia*-court hearings), I am again drawing on Foucault's work, especially his 1977–78 lectures at the College de France that were published in English in 2007 under the title *Security, Territory, Population* (see also Foucault 1979 [2000]). Foucault uses the term "pastoral" to designate modalities of ethical care, management, and governance foregrounding beneficence, salvation, and the flourishing of both the community and the unique individual. He underscores both the distinctiveness and the intertwining of pastoral and (more formal) political power in the history of Christianity, his major frame of reference (albeit in relation to Greco-Roman antiquity as well as ancient Hebraic and other eastern Mediterranean traditions), sometimes speaking of the pastorate as a "prelude to governmentality," alternatively as the "inner depth and background of the governmentality that begins to develop in the sixteenth century" (2007, 184, 215). A key question for Foucault is "how the crisis of the pastorate opened up and how the pastorate ... broke up, and assumed the dimension of governmentality, or how the problem of government, of governmentality, was able to arise on the basis of the pastorate" (193). My historical concern, which I address later in this chapter, is somewhat the opposite: what kinds of dynamics in Malaysian governmentality or beyond led to the formal implementation of pastorally-oriented institutions such as *sulh* at the turn of the new millennium?

One should not assume from the ethnographic facts outlined here that female *sulh* officers and other women in the employ of the *sharia* judiciary invariably seek mediation, compromise, and the avoidance of punitive sanctions, whereas their male counterparts are oriented toward formal adjudication and zero-sum decisions that carry the possibility of harsh punishment. The two prosecutors I observed in the *sharia* court of Rembau in 2013, for example, were both young women (probably in their twenties); indeed, one was so young that she still had braces on her teeth! In the half dozen or so cases where I and my research assistants observed them in action, they consistently implored the (male) judge to impose the heaviest penalties that the law allowed. One of these hearings involved the man who on two separate occasions had repudiated his wife outside the court and without the court's permission. At the end of the hearing, recall, he was taken away in handcuffs, though he was subsequently released upon paying his fine. Interestingly, the elderly male bailiff who was instructed to take the defendant into custody was unable to properly secure the handcuffs, even though the defendant offered no resistance. The other bailiff, a middle-aged woman, came to his aid, enabling him to achieve his goal. The male bailiff who led the errant husband away in handcuffs was clearly the leading actor in this (very) awkward part of the courtroom drama. But without the assistance of the female bailiff, it is not at all clear that he would have been able to perform the role given to him.

This summary sketch of *sulh* sessions could of course be amplified. More useful for present purposes is to turn to the transcript of a *sulh* hearing I attended in the fall of 2013.

CASE 3

*A Sulh Session Initiated by a Woman Seeking More Security
in Her Marriage and Better Treatment from Her Husband*

This hearing occurred in the small, bustling town of Rembau, Negeri Sembilan in September 2013. It involved a decorously dressed married woman (wearing a mini-*telekung* [prayer cloak], tunic, and long skirt) who appeared to be in her late thirties or early forties; her husband of sixteen years, who was around the same age but less appropriately attired (in cargo pants and a collared t-shirt); and the *sulh* officer (SO), Puan Khadijah, a woman in her thirties who wore a long black sport coat with civil-service nametag over her stylish ankle-length outfit. I was also present at the hearing, as was my female research assistant (Najat) who, like me, took extensive handwritten notes that we later typed up and discussed. The session began at 9:10 A.M., after the SO obtained the couple's consent for my research assistant and me to observe the proceedings ("for the study they are doing"), and took place in the SO's modestly-sized office, which was cluttered with files but otherwise fairly nondescript and unadorned (without the flags and calligraphic renderings of the words "Allah" and "Muhammad" that typically grace *sharia* courtrooms, for example), with the door closed. The husband, wife, and SO sat around the small round table in the office that is the usual venue for *sulh* sessions; my research assistant and I arranged our chairs behind them, so that our presence would be somewhat less intrusive.

The husband and wife interrupted one another constantly, trading insults and accusations that in the Malay context are quite serious, occasionally beyond the pale, and often spoke at the same time, though this is not evident from the transcript of the hearing since the interruptions were so frequent that we could not keep track of how often and exactly when they occurred. The wife, who had initiated the hearing, was crying audibly throughout much of the session, and was obviously distressed about her marriage, her husband's behavior, and the circumstances of her life generally. The husband was also visibly distraught and seemed to resent being present at the hearing, though he had agreed to attend the session and had, moreover, consented to participate in at least one counseling session prior to this hearing. As with a great many men who appear in *sharia* courts as defendants, he was somewhat surly and seemed more angry—the term "pissed off" is perhaps most accurate here—than hurt.

Following the session, which lasted around forty-five minutes, the SO typed up the agreement they reached, so that the couple could have it formally approved and certified by the judge. About ninety minutes later, the couple appeared before the judge, who duly certified the terms of their agreement. The *sulh* hearing proceeded as follows.

> *SO: Assalamualaikum,* we open our *majlis* (session, ceremony) with Surah Al-Fatihah [the first chapter of the Quran, generally referred to as "The Opening" or "The Exordium," which consists of seven *ayat* or verses praising Allah and asking for His guidance along the straight path].

The SO then led the couple in silent recitation of the prayer, which tends to be more "low key" when done by female officers of the court, partly because women leading men in prayer is a contentious issue in Islam (Mahmood 2005, 86–91).

> *SO:* I would like to introduce Professor Michael Peletz from the U.S., and Ms. Najat Nabihah from the University of Malaya. Are you comfortable [with them being here]?
>
> *Defendant (the husband; hereafter D):* No problem, since I do not know them.
>
> *SO:* Madam (*Puan*) and Sir (*Encik*) have you gone through *sulh* before?
>
> *Plaintiff (the wife; hereafter P)* and D: Yes, once in the Office of Religion.

SO: *Sulh* is a peaceful resolution [of disagreement, conflict]. In this session, Madam [the plaintiff] will go first; then Sir [the defendant]. Each of you must be respectful [to each other] and discuss [things] appropriately. If an agreement [is reached], there is no need for a [formal court] hearing later. The *sulh* process involves up to three sessions. If the first session is insufficient, you can go to the second . . . . I cannot be a witness in any event between the two of you [should the case go to court] . . . . Okay, Madam R., what do you feel (*apa yang Puan R. rasa*)?

P: I am petitioning for money, because I don't have any security (*tak terjamin*).

SO: Money for what?

P: For expenses, for the children's expenses, for studying and school.

SO: How much?

P: It depends on my husband. Throughout [our marriage], I have never felt that my life is secure.

SO: In other words, you're petitioning for *nafkah* [maintenance]? How much do you usually receive?

P: It depends, because as long as there is enough for food and drinks [milk, tea, etc.], it's alright.

SO: Mr. H., how much can you give?

D: Read the order [an apparent, arguably rudely put, reference to a written document]; RM$1,000 [per month; 200 each for the wife and four children].

SO: Did you mention this?

P: No.

SO: So how much?

D: I will give RM$1,000, but with the condition that you do not disturb me while I am working. I return home exhausted, and she *membebel* (chatters or yaks incessantly). If I don't pick up the telephone [when she calls], she calls me a pig (*babi*). I can give RM$1,000. But I want tranquility, to calm down (*bertenang*). We each need to calm down; if we feel calm, we can live together again. Don't bring up stories from the past.

SO: In the sixteen years of marriage, how much did you provide?

D: I give as much as I get [from working]. But when she acts that way, I can't even meet my friend(s). When I'm slow to answer the phone, she calls me a *babi* (pig) and a *sial* (loser, jerk, dumbass). What is that? If [there is something] you don't like, calm down first. When ready [when the time is right], we'll [?] return to ourselves.

SO: You are living together now?

P: Yes. I do not want a divorce.

D: Then why do you behave (like) that? You humiliate me, impugn my dignity/ honor/self-respect [*malukan maruah den*]. You do not cook, or feed the children; but all the blame is heaped on me. You do not see your own wrongdoings.

Around this point in the hearing, the defendant's cell phone rang; it was supposed to have been turned off before he entered the building, as is made clear by the list of rules and regulations posted at the entrance to the courthouse. He answered it, speaking briefly, thus compounding his flaunting of courthouse etiquette. Later in the hearing, his phone rang again. After he answered it, the SO gently requested that he turn it off.

P: How many years did you lie to me? Just this past two months ... [you've been better (?)]. I have been mistreated like this for a long time. I do not feel secure. I haven't been able to save any money; I use it for the children. It is just recently that he's provided some money.

D: I regret [that]; I have regrets.

P: Every night you go out. I am the one who takes care of the children; other women have their husbands [by their side].

SO: So, you, Madam, want *nafkah*, right? And you, Sir, want tranquility, [things] to calm down?

D: Yes, tranquility. We [can?] separate for a while, repent, and ponder our mistakes.

P: I do not want to separate, I am patient. I want a resolution. I do not want to separate.

SO: Have you discussed [things] properly at home?

P: No. Because it has been three weeks like this. I do not want to separate. I have been patient for sixteen years; of course I can be patient.

D: You humiliate me.

P: I do not; even my siblings do not know [about any of this].

SO: I only listen, I only write down what's important. This is a place to discuss things.

P: I want to discuss things; I don't mind. But you spend tens of thousands [of *ringgit*] on that other woman. And I do not ask for anything. Please pay attention to me and the children. [Regardless of] what he did to me, I do not want to divorce. I love the children. My mother passed away; I do not have a mother. I am under a lot of pressure. I don't get mad if you're out looking for money [working].

SO: So, Sir?

P: I didn't cook [on some occasions] when there was nothing to cook with [because the husband didn't provide any money for cooking supplies, groceries].

SO: So [Sir]?

D: I will give RM$1,000; but don't interfere with my life and work (*jangan ganggu hidup dan kerja saya*).

P: I don't interfere.

D: I cannot stand it; because I always need to find another person to prove [to her] where I've been.

P: How can I trust you? You've been lying to me for years.

D: I feel degraded. There's a lot of income (sustenance) now. She's quiet when there's a lot of income. When I come home, you should greet me with a smile, not with a sour expression on your face. Alright, I will deposit RM$1,000 every month; the account book can be kept here for easy proof. I will even take her on the *umrah* [the minor, non-compulsory pilgrimage to Mecca that, unlike the *haj,* may be performed at any point during the year].

P: Madam, I have been depressed for a long time; I do not want to talk about it.

D: In 2007, there was a lot of income, every weekend I found work.

P: Since the fasting month [which had ended about five weeks earlier], I have asked Allah [for His assistance].

D: You have sought help from Allah, but when Allah gives you guidance, why don't you want to follow it?

P: Madam, I have not disturbed him; really.

SO: How many times have you gone for counseling, Madam?

P: Once . . . . He cheated on me for years.

SO: I ask you, Madam, when he gives you money, what do you feel (*rasa apa*)?

P: There must be a reason [he has ulterior motives].

SO: You still haven't discussed it at home [?].

D: I have changed, but my wife keeps pestering me. I want to change; what else does she want?

P: He challenges (*cabar*) me.

D: I am stressed/depressed by her (*tertekan*). As bad as I have been, I [always] remember my children and wife.

P: In 2008, he married a second wife; they divorced after a month. Then in 2010, he married another one. My life is stressful. When we got married, we worked together to find money. But when he gets rich, he marries other women.

SO: Umm, I feel it's like this. Madam, you don't want a specific amount of money, but just want to express to your husband what you feel (*apa yang dirasakan*) . . . . I am just helping; I will not make the judgment.

D: I work for myself, cutting wood, arranging things with machines and whatnot. When I come home, she *membebel* (yaks and yaks; chatters/gossips/babbles).

P: I do not yak and yak. [*Mana ada membebel?*]

D: During the fasting month, she babbled until I couldn't take it anymore. I have changed. Just pray for me (make *doa* for me), cook, and [make sure] the house is not messy, that there is food [on the table], that the children are healthy. If you want more income (sustenance) for us, do not interfere with my work.

SO: Alright, the amount that is needed?

D: I will bank in [deposit] RM$1,000 on the 17th of every month. I want to pay now.

At this point the husband produced a wad of bills that he attempted to put on the table or hand to his wife.

SO: You cannot do that, Sir; you have to make payments in front of the judge. I will prepare a draft [of your agreement] first. Sir and Madam, please wait outside. Thank you.

With these latter remarks, the SO ended the session and the husband and wife left the *sulh* chamber. After an hour and a half or so, as mentioned earlier, they appeared in the courtroom, where the judge formally certified the agreement that the *sulh* officer had coaxed them to reach.

Commentary

The aim of the hearing, as the *sulh* officer made clear to these litigants at the outset, is to arrive at an agreement that is acceptable to both parties, so that the case need not be formally adjudicated by a judge (thus adding to the judge's and the court's workload and wasting the couple's time and money). It is not intended to be adversarial, though clearly there is much contestation and trading of accusations between the litigants, whose relationship seems anything but amicable.

Partly for these reasons, the *sulh* officer evinces no interest in ascertaining the veracity of the charges traded back and forth between husband and wife. Some of these charges are quite serious: most notably, the husband taking a second and then a third wife, without the first wife's—or presumably the court's—prior permission, which are heavily sanctioned criminal offenses; the husband's failure to provide his wife and children with adequate maintenance for extended periods of time, another serious violation of the law; and, on the wife's part, her failure to properly perform her duties as wife and mother by not maintaining the house properly, not providing appropriate meals, and so forth, which are also legally salient and could, if true, render her guilty of *nusyuz* (wifely or spousal recalcitrance) and therefore make her ineligible for support.

The *sulh* officer's lack of concern with "the truth," with "what really happened" between husband and wife, is emblematic of *sulh* hearings. Of comparative-historical significance is that such disinterest also typified the attitude and orientation of the *kadi* in Rembau who I observed in action on many occasions in the late 1980s. He too was less concerned with what really happened than with working out a compromise between husband and wife so that they would remain married, unless it was patently obvious from their narratives and interactions that the marriage could not be salvaged. The *kadi*'s present-day counterpart, now referred to as *hakim*, does not share this orientation; rather, much like judges in civil-court hearings, he is more oriented toward adjudication than mediation, though he too seeks to maintain marriages whenever possible.

The SO used her "soft skills" (Ramizah Wan Muhammad 2008a) both to encourage a broad airing of differences on the part of husband and wife alike, and to guide them along a path that might lead to resolution of their differences. She was clearly concerned with their feelings, especially the wife's. This is evident in her initial question, "Okay, Madam R., what do you do feel?"; in her later query, asking the wife how she feels when her husband gives her money, which may have been aimed at eliciting a comment from the wife that she still cared for her husband; and in her comment toward the very end of the hearing that summed up her view of what the wife really wanted, perhaps as much as (or even more than) the *nafkah*: "Um, I feel its like this. Madam, you don't want a specific amount of money, but just want to express to your husband what you feel."

Readers unfamiliar with Malay culture may not appreciate that the SO's frequent exhortations to the litigants that they focus on articulating their feelings is exceedingly un-Malay, and that Malays typically evince a strong preference for keeping their feelings and inner thoughts to themselves. The alternative, giving voice to those feelings and thoughts, risks both causing hurt or offense to others and incurring their wrath or retaliation (possibly through potentially deadly mystical/occult means). A good deal of everyday Malay speech, both within the household and beyond, is oriented toward ensuring smooth interpersonal relations and is otherwise "pressed into service to affirm the social order," as Mary Douglas (1970, 22) once phrased it in another context. That said, the kind of training and certification that *sulh* officers undergo, which increasingly includes social-work-oriented mini-courses, modules, and exercises developed in Australia, the United Kingdom, and the United States, tends to valorize the untrammeled "sharing of feelings," just as it emphasizes that successful *sulh* officers are those who use their soft skills to elicit their clients' emotions.

The use of such soft skills by the SO may be seen as resourceful, creative, and imaginative, and thus partaking of a kind of judicial creativity, albeit a judicial creativity which does not necessarily qualify as *ijtihad* in a narrow, technical sense. It is, moreover, so generic as to be more or less indistinguishable from its analogues in non-Islamic (e.g., common-law) venues and therefore of questionable analytic value for our purposes. In this connection we might also note that the issues that motivated the wife to bring the case to court—to obtain more security in her marriage and better treatment from her husband, both of which were arguably condensed or symbolized in the request for *nafkah,* and to articulate her grievances in an ostensibly neutral, family-friendly forum—are by no means unusual, let alone unprecedented. More generally, the kinds of issues aired in *sulh* sessions tend to be quite routine and rather pedestrian from the point of view of court officials, though of course anything but from the perspectives of the litigants. As such, they do not require innovative legal interpretation of—or on the basis of—the Quran or other sacred texts. Indeed, just as there was no mention of specifically Islamic texts in the *sulh* session at issue here, other than the brief Quranic prayer (Surah Al-Fatihah) that was recited by the SO and the litigants at the outset of the session, there is no reason to believe that the SO's goals involved any other objectives than the purely pragmatic one of helping the couple reach an agreement that she could type up for the judge's formal approval. One is reminded here of Baudouin Dupret's (2007, 85) remarks concerning how Egyptian judges typically deal with cases involving Islamic law; specifically, that we need to better appreciate "the overwhelmingly routine character . . . of professional practices which are oriented to nothing but the accomplishment of the law."

As for issues of *asal*, the SO did not ask either husband or wife to discuss what kind of person they were (or were married to), the fields of social relations in which they were enmeshed, or the broader social or moral context(s) of their concerns. But by repeatedly encouraging them to focus on their feelings, she effectively elicited information on these matters and thus helped ensure that they would comprise a central part of the *sulh* discourse and experience. From the wife's perspective, the relevant dynamics included her mother's death; her feelings of being alone (despite having a husband, four children, and at least two siblings); her longstanding depression; her husband having secretly wed two other women in the course of his marriage to her; that he cannot be trusted to provide for her or their four children in the months or years ahead; and her overall lack of life options. From the husband's point of view, the relevant dynamics seem less expansive. They focused more on the physically demanding nature of his work; that at the end of the day he cannot bear his wife's chattering; that she is so mistrustful of him that he cannot spend uninterrupted "quality" time with his friends; that she seriously insults and maligns him; and that she does not properly perform her duties as mother and wife.

There was, I might add, very little if any morally corrective advice (*nasihat*) proffered by the SO in this session. One might counter, however, that her repeated insistence that the husband and wife focus on articulating their feelings was intended as a meta-message to them: that, among other things, they need to take one another's feelings more seriously, and that a meaningful (companionate) marriage involves discussing things properly at home. Many of these issues emerge in a "theme and variation" sense in case 4, to which I now turn.

CASE 4

A Sulh *Session Initiated by a Woman Aiming to Clarify Her Marital Status Vis-à-Vis Her Estranged Husband and Secure Custody over Their Young Daughter*

This hearing unfolded in October 2013 on the third floor of Kuala Lumpur's new *sharia* courthouse, an architecturally stunning complex that opened for business in 2011. It took place in an area of the building designated for *sulh* sessions and the offices and adjoining chambers of those in charge of them. My female research assistant (Najat) and I arrived in the chambers of the SO (Encik Ahmad) who oversaw this case around 10:30 A.M., a minute or two after the hearing had begun. (We had been attending another *sulh* session across the hall and were thus late to this one). By this time, the heavy-set, avuncular forty-something SO, who had worked as a *sharia* lawyer before becoming a *sulh* officer and was dressed in a black business suit—but no necktie, *songkok*, or shoes—had already obtained the couple's permission for us to sit in. Also by this time he had presumably recited the Surah Al-Fatihah and provided the couple with a brief overview of the *sulh* process, as is both customary and required at the very beginning of *sulh* sessions and clearly specified in *sulh* manuals.

Najat and I were invited to sit in the SO's office, rather than in the adjoining room formally designated as the *sulh* chamber; hence we observed and listened to the proceedings from that vantage point, through the open door and window. This arrangement gave the couple a bit more privacy and was more than adequate for our purposes, but it prevented me from being able to observe facial expressions and body language.

The hearing involved a thirty-five-year old woman (as plaintiff), who was born in Indonesia but had lived in Malaysia for some time and had obtained Malaysian citizenship, and her well-to-do British husband (as defendant). The husband was in his fifties and had converted to Islam to marry the plaintiff, albeit as his second wife; his first wife, to whom he was still married, lived in the United Kingdom. According to my conversation with the SO after the hearing, one aspect of the case involved clarification of the wife's marital status; she wanted to know whether the *talak* that the husband pronounced in the midst of an argument or quarrel (outside of court and without the court's permission) was valid or not. A second aspect of the case concerned custody of their young daughter, Kelly, who, according to the *sulh* officer, might have been conceived prior to the couple's marriage. None of the issues relating to the status of the *talak* were discussed while we were present at the hearing, probably because a SO does not have authority to certify the status of a *talak* and thus dispensed with this issue at the outset of the session, before we arrived. The primary concern throughout the bulk of the hearing was, ostensibly, custody of the daughter and what kinds of visitation rights were going to be granted to the husband/father (visitation tends to be subsumed under custody). But as we shall see, a number of other issues were aired, bearing on the character of the husband and wife and whether or not they lived as Muslims; these were mainly in the form of serious insults and accusations, many of which had little if anything to do with custody or visitation. Most of the hearing was conducted in English, though both the SO and the wife sometimes spoke in Malay. The husband spoke entirely in English and gave no indication that he was able to speak or understand Malay.

I turn momentarily to the transcript of the hearing, but first want to reiterate that my research assistant and I arrived a minute or two after the session had begun and thus did not hear the SO's introductory remarks. The latter comments

probably resembled those that his fellow *sulh* officer (and boss) down the hall provided when she explained the *sulh* process to first-timers in a session I observed
about ten days earlier, since the relevant guidelines are explicitly formulated in
widely disseminated *sulh* manuals that all SOs are expected to follow. Hence they
would have gone something like this:

> SO: *Assalamualaikum.* Is this your first time? I will explain [how things work]. In some
> cases, when a plaintiff requests a divorce, *sulh* is required. The advantages [compared
> to a formal court hearing]: you save time, it save cases [from having to go to court],
> and you save money. You just need to take care of the court fees and pay for the court
> order. There is no need to attend a prolonged hearing [in court]. If you come to an
> agreement today, I will . . . [prepare a draft of your agreement], and will be present in
> court for the [perfunctory] hearing [in which the judge formally certifies the
> agreement].
>
> First, the plaintiff, the one who initiated the case, begins; you have seven
> minutes [to state your case]. When the plaintiff speaks, the defendant cannot
> interrupt. Do not cut in on each other, . . . allow a duration to calm down [for
> both of you]. You need to keep quiet, and [deal with] one issue at a time. Both
> sides are prohibited from condemning each other and [should come?] in a
> composed manner. Okay Madam, you may proceed.

These are the kinds of introductory remarks that SOs typically provide before signaling to the plaintiff and the defendant that it is time to state their case. What follows is the transcript of the remainder of the hearing that Encik Ahmad oversaw.

> SO: . . . . Concerning custody (*hadanah*): normally, if the child is less than seven
> years old it goes to the mother, especially for girls. At age nine, she will be able to
> choose [which parent] gets custody.
> *Plaintiff (the wife; hereafter P):* He can only see Kelly once [in a while].
> SO: Okay, for the time being, that's okay. But it will be different in another five years
> [when the child is seven years old].
> P: I want to make a condition if he's [going to get] to see Kelly. He must live in an
> Islamic way, as a Muslim. He must practice Islam in his life.
> *Defendant (the husband; hereafter D):* You too [have to practice Islam properly].
> SO [*to P*]: Is it true [that you don't practice Islam properly]?
> P: No, its not [true]. He's the one who doesn't follow the Muslim way.
> SO: How long have you been married?
> D & P: [Almost] three years.
> P: I don't eat pork or drink alcohol.
> D: No [that's not true]. She does eat pork and drink alcohol.
> P: No I don't. Well, yes, [once?] I drank alcohol because people pushed me to do so.
> But after that, I never did. And I swear I never eat pork. But he always eats pork
> in front of me.

SO: Where?

P: In restaurants, not in the house.

SO: Wait; okay, when there's a divorce [and children], custody normally goes to the mother, unless she's remarried or crazy, deemed unfit, or involved in prostitution, in which case she will lose custody. But if the mother is okay and good, she's entitled to custody. But please don't deny the father his rights, even though he's not originally a Muslim. In Islam we cannot deny the rights of the father.

P: I know; that's why I filed for custody, because he doesn't live in the Muslim way, and he has his first wife in the UK, who is non-Muslim. He wants my child; his wife there can't have children. That's my concern; I'm afraid that he will take the child with him because he has money [the means to do so].

SO [to D]: When was the last time you saw your child?

D: Three months ago.

SO: So, you will go and see the child?

D: Yes.

SO [to D]: Is it okay if you just leave the child to the mother, because she's still only five months old? [The SO sometimes referred to Kelly's age as five months; other times as around two years old.]

D: No.

SO: So?

A brief discussion followed, concerning where the husband might be allowed to visit Kelly other than where the wife is currently staying.

SO: Is there another place [that would work for you]?

P: My mother's house. I never rent, because I can't afford it.

SO: Your siblings' or friend's house?

D: I was attacked by my wife's sister; they tried to put something [poison] in my drink.

P: No, he has attacked me [there]; I don't feel comfortable.

SO: Your sister's house?

D: She wants to control everything; I hate it.

P: I have a friend . . . .

SO [to D]: Okay, how often do you want to see your child?

D: Every time I come back to Malaysia [from business trips to China and other foreign travel].

SO: Once a month?

D: No, every two weeks.

P: I'm not sure [about that], because the atmosphere, with his family and friends, is not good.

D: How do you know?

P: It's true; many of his friends are bikers [motorcycle enthusiasts].

SO: Now, even if the parents divorce, the child needs to see both of you. The money is not the real issue. Why not forget about going to court, because it wastes money. Let's settle outside the court. The court suggests that Kelly stay with her mother, and every time the father comes back to Malaysia he can see Kelly at the place [not yet specified] until she is twelve years old. After that, she can choose whom she is comfortable to live with.

P: But after what he's done. After Kelly was born, I gave him access to visit, until he asked me to enroll [in courses] at the University. I was so relieved; I had a lot of time to spend with Kelly. But then I found out that he brought a prostitute to our house; I sent copies [of incriminating SMSs] to his friends. He said the woman was married. But in Islam if a married man is with a married women [who is not his wife], it's heavier, right? So at that point, okay, I took Kelly . . . . I never slept with other guys.

D: She lied to me when I asked her how she knew about it.

P: Of course; I'm not going to tell you that.

D: She said she found out from the guard; but no, some gossipy neighbor[s] told her.

SO: [Does this] involve Kelly?

P: Yes; it involves Kelly. I'm only concerned about my child. Once he takes her, I don't have money to get her back.

D: The child has been registered [as a British subject/citizen], but I have no intention to take her [away].

P: Yet . . . . [?]

D: I do not [have any intention of taking her away]. [Though shortly after this he said he has elderly parents in the United Kingdom, that they're too old to travel to Malaysia, and that he wants to take Kelly to see them.]

P: You want to take care of me? No. You want to give Kelly money for her expenses? No. He just says he does.

D: She cannot trust me. I will ask my lawyer to do more.

P: He never pays me; I've only got [RM$]50,000 to support myself. His money is just for the apartment, a five-star apartment; can you imagine the *cukai pintu* [condo fees]? You can ask me to . . . [provide additional documentation], but the fee and everything else was all paid for with my money. When I got pregnant, all of the expenses associated with the pregnancy came from me. He just gave me RM$1,000.

D: No, I gave RM$5,100.

P: Yes, he gave me the money; but I had only asked for expenses [associated with pregnancy and giving birth]. But what about me? Don't I need to eat and drink?

D: I pay for everything, but it's not enough. What else does she want?

P: Your Honor, it is true. There's a condominium and a new BMW. But if I do anything wrong, for example, like scratch the car, he gets mad; and in our apartment I cannot even take out our wedding picture or anything. I just feel like none of it belongs to me.

SO: That's common, Madam. For a man, his car is his first wife, and the real wife is a second wife.

D: What does she expect?

SO: You guys are talking about cars, houses, and not living in a Muslim way. Right now, nothing you are saying involves custody. Madam, why not have Kelly stay with you and just give access to the father? I will write [up an agreement indicating that] no one can have access [visit her] without permission. And he can't ask others to take Kelly on his behalf.

P: Who will take action if he takes my daughter to Britain?

SO: That cannot happen.

P: I'm just asking: Who will take action if he takes Kelly from me?

SO [to D]: For the time being, you can't take Kelly traveling. She's still small; it's not suitable to take her [out, like] to the market.

The conversation then turned to issues of citizenship and passports.

P [in response to a question from the SO about her background]: I was born in Indonesia. [After moving to Malaysia] I had to choose the country [of citizenship].

SO: No need for Kelly . . . . [?]

P: . . . The officer asked me to choose my citizenship.

SO: Where was that?

P: At the JPN [National Registration Department], in Putrajaya. Of course I wanted to choose Malaysian [citizenship].

D: No. But she [Kelly] is a British [subject/citizen].

P: Look, he wants to take Kelly.

SO: No, no, this is going too far [getting too far afield]. We're not discussing passports; we're discussing custody. Kelly must stay with her mother until she is 18 years old. In the meantime, the decision should come from both of you . . . . [?] In Islam, custody [of a young child] goes to the mother.

P [to D]: So?

SO: Okay, it's going to be like this. Custody goes to . . . [the wife], until Kelly is old enough to choose. The father will be able to visit her until she is nine years old; you can spend time together outside. But, Kelly is still only five months old, I can state [all of this] in the agreement.

D: I'm not happy [with this arrangement].

P: See!

SO [to D]: So you want to go to the [Sharia] High Court?

D: Yes.

SO [*to D*]: Okay, who is your lawyer? Okay, I just want to reconfirm. It's difficult because of the technical problem(s). A lot of personal matters come out. It's very confidential so you have to go to the High Court. If possible, we'll settle outside the court. If not, I will send it [the case] to the High Court. Madam, do you agree?

[*P doesn't answer.*]

SO: Okay, let's say that after that [going to court] you want to settle here. You can ask the High Court to send you back here. Okay, now you can wait outside and confer with your lawyers, and I will mention you [your case] to my staff. Thank you.

With this the session ended, the couple left the *sulh* chambers, and the SO came into his office to meet with me and Najat to discuss the background of the case and various other matters.

Commentary

This hearing is profitably viewed in relation to the *sulh* session in Rembau that involved the woman who sought more security in her marriage and better treatment from her husband (case 3). In both cases women petitioned the court to help them negotiate dynamics of their relationships with their estranged and far more powerful and resource-rich husbands; and in both cases the issues aired by the women and their husbands were not only wide-ranging, but also, from a narrow legal point of view, somewhat irrelevant to the ostensible focus of the hearings. The accusations and insults that the parties to the hearings heaped upon one another were quite grave, involving charges of serious criminal wrongdoing, especially on the part of husbands: e.g., failing to maintain one's wife and children; taking second and third wives without informing the first wife and concealing the relationships for extended periods of time; engaging in extramarital relationships with other women; consuming pork and alcohol; and so on. Whether these hearings were cathartic or otherwise therapeutic as far as the plaintiffs were concerned, I can't say with certainty, since I did not interview them. But I concur with the SO in the first of the two cases that one of the principal objectives—if not the overriding goal—of the plaintiff in that hearing appears to have been to air her widespread dissatisfaction with her husband and her anxiety and depression concerning the circumstances of her marriage, and to do so in the presence of a potentially empathetic third party (a SO). All of this gets lost in a formal court hearing, especially if lawyers are involved, as they increasingly are. In such cases, as we shall see in the following chapter, women's voices tend to be silenced.

Note in any event that the first of the two hearings was officially classified as "successful" (*berjaya*), because it did not necessitate a formal airing of grievances in front of a judge charged with adjudicating the dispute (as distinct from his simply endorsing a mutually acceptable agreement arrived at voluntarily by both parties, with the help of the SO), regardless of whether or not the terms of the agreement were truly equitable. The second hearing, in contrast, went down in the books a "failure" (*gagal*), since the two parties did not arrive at a mutual satisfactory agreement and ended up taking their grievance to the *Sharia* High Court to be settled by a judge.

The question of "success"—how to gauge it and what the relevant criteria are or should be—is complicated, with most of the available information on the subject limited to what can be gleaned from aggregate, "auditor friendly" (i.e., more or less binary) data presented in tables disseminated within the *sharia* judiciary or made available on official websites. One account, which appeared in the widely-read English-language daily *The Star* on December 28, 2006, under the headline "Mediation Reduces Backlog" and was subsequently published on government websites, reported that 70 percent of cases had been resolved through *sulh* since the beginning of the program in 2001 (Ramizah Wan Muhammad 2008a, 43). Aggregate data shared with me in 2013 by the chief *sulh* officer in Kuala Lumpur's *sharia* court indicate that 2,272 *sulh* cases were completed or finished (*selesai*) there during 2011–12, and that 54.8 percent (1,244/2,272) were classified as successful (*berjaya*), 24.2 percent (549/2,272) as failures (*gagal*), and 21.1 percent (479/2,272) as no-shows (*tidak hadir*). As mentioned earlier, official classifications bearing on whether a *sulh* hearing is successful depend entirely on the binary issue of whether or not the case proceeds to court. If it does, it is regarded as a failure, whatever the outcome of the subsequent court hearing(s). If, on the other hand, the case does not go to court, officials classify the *sulh* session in question as successful. Importantly, this is regardless of whether or not the husband and wife resolved their differences in the *sulh* session or simply dropped the claim. Since the vast majority of plaintiffs in *sulh* sessions (and formal hearings) are women, this means that a case involving a woman who participates in a *sulh* hearing that entails no resolution and who subsequently decides not to take the matter to court would be counted as a success. The logic of the metric makes sense only if one keeps squarely in mind that much of the rationale for the formal introduction of *sulh* was to reduce the backlog of court cases by drastically cutting the number of new cases that land on judges' desks.

Another, potentially more promising source of data bearing on the question of *sulh* "success" derives from research conducted by Sa'odah binti Ahmad for her 2010 doctoral dissertation on the effectiveness of *sulh* in the state of Selangor. Due to previously noted concerns with privacy and confidentiality, Sa'odah was not allowed to sit in on any *sulh* hearings, despite her research being carried out under the auspices of the International Islamic University Malaysia (IIUM); she was thus unable to provide her own firsthand assessment of the efficacy or general success rate of the process (Sa'odah binti Ahmad 2010, 15). Instead, she sent written questionnaires to men and women who had recently participated in *sulh* sessions.

Eighty-seven percent (87/100) of those returning her questionnaires reported a "high degree of satisfaction" with the process, 13 percent (13/100) responding that they were "moderately satisfied" (206, 209).[3] Men, who are usually defendants, as we have seen, tended to be somewhat ("minutely") more satisfied with the process than women, who are typically the plaintiffs (213, 240–41), but the reasons for such differences were not explored and need not detain us here.

These findings are important to take seriously, but we should also bear in mind two caveats. First, there is an extensive body of crosscultural literature on the ways that ostensibly neutral, "family-friendly" mediation commonly disadvantages women who, compared to men, tend to be less aware of their rights and the laws relevant to them, and are also, due to gendered patterns of socialization, more inclined toward compromise, patience, perseverance, and making do, even when it means putting up with poor treatment from spouses and foregoing access to spousal or domestic resources to which they are clearly entitled (Fineman 1991; Grillo 1991). And second, in formal questionnaires, perhaps especially those devised by highly educated strangers associated with elite institutions of higher learning that collaborate with the government, Malay respondents may be even more inclined than interlocutors in other settings to give the answers they think those with social standing and authority might want to hear. The problems are perhaps compounded when one is associated with an elite institution such as the IIUM. The IIUM works very closely with the *sharia* judiciary, particularly in developing new programs, services, and "products"—such as *sulh*—that are the focus of the questionnaires at issue, and that judiciary, recall, is under the direct control of the Prime Minister's Department.

In the "failed" Kuala Lumpur hearing I attended, both husband and wife may have been predisposed to proceed to court to try their luck with formal adjudication, for each of them had secured the services of a lawyer prior to the *sulh* session. (Lawyers, it should be noted, are barred from attending *sulh* sessions.) A good deal was indeed at stake, even though the hearing focused on custody, or rather, the kinds of visitation rights, if any, the husband would enjoy on his return trips to Malaysia from China and the United Kingdom. The stakes included the condo the couple shared, their BMW, child support for Kelly, and property (including stock, money, etc.) acquired by the husband or the couple working together or separately in the course of the marriage, which, on divorce, tends to be split evenly between husband and wife. The heightened stakes involved in the divorces of middle-class urban dwellers, including especially upper-middle-class litigants like those involved in this hearing, are among the main factors driving the demand for *sharia* lawyers. There is also the related fact that judges in Kuala Lumpur, in both civil and *sharia* venues, increasingly advise those who appear before them that because of the technical and otherwise complicated issues involved, they should not proceed with their cases unless they have appropriate counsel.

To put some of this differently, the material life-circumstances of the couples involved in the two *sulh* hearings described here could not be more disparate. The Rembau case turned on the trials and tribulations of a couple whose primary breadwinner ekes out a living by "cutting wood, working with machines, and whatnot"; his long-suffering wife, in turn, sought only 1,000 *ringgit* a month for herself and her four children, a mere 200 *ringgit* (US$60) per person per month. This is in sharp contrast to the Kuala Lumpur session, which was suffused with talk of condos, luxury cars, university education, and international business travel. Despite these sharp social-class contrasts, there is an important commonality running through the two cases and most others I have observed since the late 1980s. This is that due largely to the gendered division of labor, including the allocation of responsibilities for the care of infants and children, women are far more strongly tied to the domestic realm than are their (much more mobile) husbands; are more economically dependent on men than vice versa; and thus, compared to their husbands, are more reliant on the courts to help them resolve problems stemming from their spouses' failure to make financial contributions to the household.

The Kuala Lumpur hearing was also more contentious and anxiety-ridden for reasons unrelated to social class and gendered divisions of labor. For one thing, religious conversion is an exceedingly fraught and heavily politicized phenomenon in Malaysia, especially if it involves either conversion to Islam or abjuration of Islam in favor of another religion such as Christianity or Buddhism. (The issue is much less fraught, or at least far less politicized, if the conversion involves a Buddhist, Hindu, or Sikh converting to Christianity or a Buddhist or other non-Muslim converting to Hinduism, Sikhism, or some other non-Muslim religion.) Cases of conversion that are widely reported in the media, some of which have become hot-button and deeply divisive political issues, tend to be of three varieties:

1. The exceedingly rare instance of a Muslim renouncing (or seeking to renounce) Islam in favor of Christianity, usually in order to marry a Christian. Lina Joy is the most famous exemplar of this category.
2. A non-Muslim headed for or in the throes of divorce who converts to Islam around the time of marital dissolution; these are usually husbands seeking custody arrangements from the *sharia* courts that are more advantageous than they might receive from the civil courts. *Shamala v. Jeyanganesh* is perhaps the best known of these cases.
3. A non-Muslim who may have embraced Islam shortly before his (or her) death, even though close family members claim that he (or she) did not, and is quickly given a proper Muslim burial by authorities. Moorthy Maniam, a member of the first Malaysian team to scale Mount Everest, who subsequently became a national hero, exemplifies this pattern.[4]

What is often lost in the flurry of media reports, political posturing, and saber-rattling—and the genuine fear, anxiety, and hurt associated with such cases—is that while officials in the *sharia* courts and elsewhere, at least if they are Malay/Muslim, are in principle heartened by the conversion of non-Muslims to Islam, they are deeply ambivalent about these conversions if they are motivated primarily by a desire to marry a Muslim, as they commonly are. One reason for this ambivalence is that divorce rates among Malaysia's Malay/Muslim population have long been rather high,[5] and officials thus worry that the spouse who converts to Islam in order to marry a Muslim will renounce his or her faith should the marriage break up. Put simply, one's religious faith and status as a Muslim should not, but in the case of converts to Islam sometimes clearly does, rest on the shaky bed of marriage.

There is another issue, more implicit though no less real. It has to do with the diffuse Malay view that various kinds of identities—keyed to ethnicity, "race," religion, and gender, for example—are "carried in the blood" and otherwise ascribed rather than achieved in the sociological sense and therefore more or less immutable (Peletz 1996, 2002). According to this view, those who convert to Islam cannot possibly be "real Muslims." Hence the awkward, nervous laughter I observed in Rembau's *sharia* courthouse in the late 1980s when a Chinese woman who had embraced Islam (*masuk Melayu*) to marry a local Muslim man mentioned that her surname was Abdullah, a name commonly given to (male) converts. The idea that she was "binti Abdullah," the daughter of a man named Abdullah, was clearly a legal fiction, one that officials were willing, indeed required, to abide. But it did not sit comfortably with their views concerning how one becomes a Muslim, who is an authentic or legitimate Muslim, and who is not (Peletz 2002, 218–19).

More generally, the *sulh* session at hand can be read as a morality tale about the temptations and perils of upward social mobility, particularly upward mobility predicated on marriage to someone who is a Muslim by conversion rather than birth and who is a foreign national and "white person" (*orang putih*) to boot. Relevant here is that the husband did not deny any of the serious charges of Islamic criminality that the wife leveled against him. He had, moreover, behaved, if we accept the wife's accusations at face value, in ways that confirm the worst stereotypes that Malays hold of Westerners: that they have a penchant for alcohol and pork, engage in extramarital relations, and are excessively materialistic and otherwise lacking in virtue. The wife benefitted in a material sense from the relationship, at least temporarily, but ultimately she paid a heavy price—being forced to eat pork, discovering that her husband had brought other women to their home, and facing the very real possibility that he might abscond with their young daughter, and that, as a consequence, she might never see her again.

Morality tales aside, we should also consider Encik Ahmad's discursive strategies, techniques, and procedures, how they compare with those of the SO (Puan

Khadijah) in case 3, and what the contrasts might tentatively suggest about the gendering of religious authority in practice—that is, what is "male" about "male religious authority" and "female" about "female religious authority"? Perhaps most striking is that Encik Ahmad was far more verbally assertive and directive than Puan Khadijah. Additionally, unlike Puan Khadijah, he responded to some of the litigants' charges and accusations by seeking to elicit more information (e.g., "*Where* does your husband eat pork?"), in some instances to confirm whether the accusations were based on fact, as when he asked the wife, "Is it true [that you do not practice Islam properly]?." More generally, Encik Ahmad was involved in a greater degree of "toing and froing" than Puan Khadijah, and also provided more information about Islamic laws and normativity than Puan Khadijah (concerning custody and visitation, for example).

Unlike Puan Khadijah, moreover, Encik Ahmad sometimes referred to his views by characterizing them as the views of "the court," which is something judges, but not *sulh* officers, regularly do. Similarly, he did not correct the wife when she referred to him as "Your Honor," a form of address that is generally reserved for judges and never in my experience extended to *sulh* officers, except in this instance. In these ways Encik Ahmad traded on the respect and fear that members of the *sharia* judiciary expect litigants and other members of the public to feel toward *sharia* judges and the juridical apparatus they oversee. Encik Ahmad's black business suit looms large here as well. For as he told me in our interview following this hearing, the black business suit symbolizes both the professionalism of the *sharia* judiciary and the fact that, due to its enhanced standing vis-à-vis its (still far more powerful and prestigious) civil counterpart, those called to appear in the *sharia* courts face charges of contempt if they fail to show up and are thus nowadays afraid to disregard summonses and other *sharia*-court orders. The threat of punitive adjudication is clearly in evidence here.

Encik Ahmad's concern that litigants fear him stems not from his interest in—or any satisfaction he might derive from—punishing their errant behavior. Instead, it reflects his desire to steer them to a successful mediation of their problems so that they need not experience the trials and tribulations of formal adjudication at the hands of judges and lawyers. Such adjudication, in his view, is ethically problematic.

Compared to Puan Khadijah, Encik Ahmad also admonished the litigants more directly to stick to the central issues: "You guys are talking about cars, houses, and not living in a Muslim way. Right now, nothing you are saying involves custody" (or visitation, the key issues in the hearing); and "No, no, this is going too far [getting too far afield]. We're not discussing passports, we're [supposed to be] discussing custody." And he provided more reassurance than did Puan Khadijah, as when he (dubiously) reassured the wife that her husband cannot possibly take Kelly to Britain without her (the wife's) consent. He also endeavored to alleviate her misgivings about her husband's materialism, asserting that it is "common for a man," nothing to be overly concerned with, explaining further that "a man's car is his first wife, and the real wife is the second wife."

In addition, in contrast to Puan Khadijah, Encik Ahmad proposed solutions to the dilemmas before him: "Madam, why not have Kelly stay with you and just give access to the father? I will write up [an agreement indicating that] no one can access [visit her] without permission. And he [your husband] can't ask others to take Kelly on his behalf. . . . Kelly must stay with her mother until she is 18 years old." Then, finally, "Okay, it's going to be like this. Custody goes to . . . [the wife] until Kelly is old enough to choose. The father will be able to visit her."

In these latter respects, Encik Ahmad behaved more like a judge than a mediator, albeit with the goal of enhancing the likelihood that the couple would not elect to take their problems to a judge (and lawyers) for formal adjudication. Some of this orientation derives from his experience as a lawyer, as discussed below. A more general point, raised by sociolinguistic studies of mediation in Malaysia's civil courts, is that when active or retired judges are appointed to serve as mediators, they sometimes (unwittingly or otherwise) impose their adversarial and adjudicatory orientations on both the participants and the overall process, thus partially or totally subverting the logic and goals of mediation (Powell and Azirah Hashim 2011). A similar dynamic is at play here. This is partly to say, more abstractly, that the "judicial model," which Foucault frequently defines in opposition to "the pastorate" (even while he acknowledges the generalized intrusion of judicial elements into pastoral practice by, and in some cases long before, the eleventh and twelfth centuries in certain Christian communities (2007, 203–4), is sometimes less antithetical to practices and more encompassing assemblages deemed "pastoral" than ideal-typical characterizations might suggest.

Despite the particularities of this case, the central issue (visitation rights) is a rather common one in *sulh* sessions (and more formal hearings), and according to Encik Ahmad, is unambiguously covered by Islamic law. As such, its resolution does not require any technical form of *ijtihad* on Encik Ahmad's part, though one can arguably make the case for the broadly construed kind of judicial creativity I observed in the session overseen by Puan Khadijah. It is also readily apparent that issues of *asal* were a central feature of the discourse and experience of this hearing, even though Encik Ahmad did not explicitly encourage their articulation and, not being a judge, was not in a position to accord them juridical weight.

More broadly, and in sharp contrast to present-day *sharia* judges, both Encik Ahmad and Puan Khadijah allowed and at times encouraged their clients to express their feelings in their own voices and to delve into highly personal and particularistic matters bearing on character, disposition, and past behavior, both their own and their spouse's. As they undoubtedly knew from previous experience, many of the issues their clients went on to raise would have no necessary or direct bearing on the legally salient issues at hand. In this regard and because the resolutions Encik Ahmad and Puan Khadijah proposed were presented as tailored to their clients' unique experiences, feelings, needs, and desires, the individualized care and governance they sought to provide is appropriately glossed as "pastoral." Such care and governance, after all, was touted as beneficent and was geared towards the wellbeing and salvation of the clients before them, who, like most others, experienced their own unique problems but were generally assumed to be better off if they avoided not only formal adjudication but also, at least in the first case, the formal dissolution of conjugal ties.

ETHICAL CONUNDRUMS, KPIs, AND ISLAMIC ADR: FOLLOW-UP INTERVIEW WITH ENCIK AHMAD

I turn now to some of the issues that emerged in the context of my interview with Encik Ahmad, which, as noted earlier, occurred right after the session's conclusion. One of the issues I raised had to do with the ways that the each of the litigants responded to, in some instances by essentially ignoring, the various accusations made by the other party. I mentioned finding it interesting that the husband had not denied having an affair with a married woman, bringing the woman to the house he shared with his wife, or eating pork or consuming alcohol, all of which are grave offenses in Islam and could easily undercut his assertion of rights to spend time with his young daughter should the case go to court. Encik Ahmad confided that the husband smelled strongly of liquor, adding that he could smell it on his breath (recall that during the hearing Encik Ahmad and the litigants were sitting around a small round table, separated from one another by a few feet at most), and that he had apparently been drinking before the hearing. Encik Ahmad also remarked, in response to a question of mine about whether, in his opinion, false allegations were more likely to come from female or male litigants, that in this case, the wife seemed to be more truthful than the husband, but that, overall, women are more inclined than men to make false statements in hearings because they are so "influenced by their emotions" (*terpengaruh dengan emosi*). (He quickly apologized to my research assistant, Najat, for possibly offending her with this statement.) His view, which I might simplify as "women lie more than men," is out of keeping with my findings in the late 1980s. Most of the court officials and villagers I spoke with then felt quite strongly that men were much more likely to lie than women, and, more generally, that most of the problems in marriage and its dissolution via divorce stem from the inappropriate behavior of men in their roles as husbands and fathers. Overall, I think these views still prevail, but I shall not pursue the point here.

The issue of overt, intentional deception (lying) is one that all court officials and people in nearly every walk of life have to come to terms with one way or the other. Indeed, officers of the court and litigants alike must not only contend with overt deception on the part of their adversaries, but must also weigh just how far they are willing to go, in terms of "stretching the truth," to win the cases in which they are involved. Encik Ahmad was formally trained and practiced for a while as a *sharia* lawyer, as noted earlier. When I asked him whether he enjoyed his work as a SO more than lawyering (or vice versa), he broached the subject of lying head on, focusing on intentional deception in the course of one's profession (rather than lying on the part of litigants), raising broader ethical concerns that encouraged him to abandon the practice of *sharia* law in favor of his current occupation as a *sulh* officer. His remarks also point to deep ambivalence about hearings overseen by *sharia* judges, especially if they involve lawyers, as they increasingly do, and whether the *sharia* judiciary has gone too far in its emulation of practices in the civil courts, which clearly comprise the gold standard.

> Both [kinds of work] are enjoyable, but I am more comfortable being a *sulh* officer because it is not as stressful as being a lawyer. When you become a lawyer, if you take a case, you need to win it. Sometimes, people fabricate facts to win. If a lawyer says that he or she never lies in a case, that [in itself] is a lie . . . . So, [as a lawyer,] whether you want to or not, you have to lie at least once [in a while]. I wanted to find a *halal* way of making a living for my wife and children, and I got the chance to work here, *Alhamdulillah*.

Encik Ahmad did not state explicitly that working as a *sharia* lawyer invariably involves behavior, such as lying, that is expressly forbidden in Islam; that is, he did not put the matter as simply or directly as I have here. But that is precisely the point he was making when he explained that he opted out of the practice of *sharia* law (as a lawyer) in order to find work, like being a *sulh* officer, that was *halal*.

It remains to add that especially in present-day Malaysia, many things that are not formally certified as *halal* are, by definition, forbidden and anathema to Muslims; and that there is increasingly little if any middle ground (Fischer 2008). This is despite the fact that foundational Islamic texts bearing on these matters are much more nuanced, distinguishing among phenomena that are mandatory (*wajib*), encouraged (*mustahak*), permissible (*halal*), discouraged (*makruh*), and forbidden (*haram*). Settling disputes "in a good way" (*secara baik*), moreover, means settling them by means of mediation, not by going to court, which is stressful for everyone concerned and is expensive (wastes both time and money), as *sulh* officers frequently point out in their opening remarks to their clients.

I encountered various iterations of Encik Ahmad's critical views when I spoke with other *sharia* lawyers, some of whom also hold prestigious academic positions in the nation's major universities. Among the most common charges is that the sensibilities, dispositions, and practices of *sharia* lawyers are overly informed by a "time is money" ethos. A related critique is that they overcharge clients, partly by insisting on excessive retainers. They are also allegedly inclined to "open separate files," as one of my interlocutors put it, for each dimension of a case (such as clarifying one's marital status and dealing with issues of custody/visitation, which may be entailments of a single nexus of problems from a litigant's point of view, but are formally classified by the courts in accordance with separate codes and classifications) and charging accordingly. Sometimes, moreover, they fail to honor the contracts they've worked out with their clients and don't even show up in court when their cases are scheduled to be heard. These "internal" critiques clearly complicate *sharia* lawyers' collective image of themselves as doing God's work, toiling for justice on behalf of their Muslim brethren, and contributing to the advancement of Islamic law and normativity in the nation-state and the *ummah*.

Encik Ahmad's deeply felt concern to reconcile his obligations as a Muslim (to engage only in conduct that is *halal*) with the practical requirements of successfully representing clients in a court of law not only forced him to abandon the practice of (*sharia*) law. It sometimes leads him to ignore the expectations and demands imposed on him by supervisors and auditors concerned with KPIs, which are heavily fetishized in the *sharia* judiciary, throughout the civil service, and in many other venues in present-day Malaysia (cf. Clarke 2012).

Generally speaking, he feels that having KPIs in the sense of performance targets is positive, "good for management (*pengurusan*)," as he tellingly phrased it. But they have a downside because they can entail more or less arbitrary, "one-size-fits-all" deadlines and other stipulations that, if not met, can condemn married couples to the trials and tribulations of formal court hearings.

> They [KPIs] require us to be organized in handling cases. So every time a new case [is registered], we know that there has to be a meeting/session [resolution of the case] within three months. If not, our record will be tarnished. But there are cases that I intentionally prolong for up to four months, because I see that they have the potential to be resolved in *sulh* sessions [as distinct from formal court hearings]. As long as many of our cases can be solved within three months, our record will [still] be good [even if we allow or effectively encourage some cases to drag on longer than that].

The formally codified requirement that all *sulh* cases be resolved within three months thus sometimes flies in the face of the ethical imperatives underlying Encik Ahmad's commitment to the idea that couples should resolve their marital differences "in a good way" (*secara baik*), rather than through one or more formal court sessions, which, according to this perspective, are "other than good" or "less than good," though not necessarily or explicitly *haram* per se. In this view, practices of negotiated settlement arrived at by the litigants themselves, albeit with the assistance of a mediator, resonate with Islamic ethical sensibilities, whereas those associated with adversarially oriented hearings entailing formal adjudication do not. More generally, like a good shepherd, Encik Ahmad "sacrifices himself" or at least risks tarnishing his record "not only for the flock in general, but also for each sheep in particular" (Foucault 2007, 152).

Encik Ahmad's disdainful view of formal court hearings is a key feature of a relatively elaborated critique of prevailing hegemonies, a critique that may well be gaining traction in Malaysia and other Muslim-majority nations even while it flies in the face of entrenched hierarchies of power and prestige, both national and transnational. The main thrust of the critique, as noted in two of the epigraphs to this chapter, is that "Western-style lawyering runs counter to the Islamic notion of ADR" (Iqbal 2001, 1045), and that "the culture of litigation imposed on Muslim societies during the colonial days must be replaced by the Islamic ways of amicable settlement" (Syed Khalid Rashid 2008, 10). Proponents of these views typically combine scriptural exegesis with textbook-like discussions bearing on the do's, don'ts, and idealized virtues of ADR to make the important point that while "It is popular belief that ADR has emerged and originated in the West during the last few decades, . . . ADR processes like Negotiation, Mediation, [and] Arbitration, . . . are as old as Islamic law itself, that is, 1400 years old" (Syed Khalid Rashid 2008, 1). But they don't usually address issues of timing bearing on the recent "(re)emergence of Islamic ADR," the relevant economic and cultural-political dynamics that help explain the timing, or the fact that the most immediate/proximate models for *sulh*-style mediation came directly from the civil judiciary and from Singapore, the United States, the United Kingdom, Australia, and Japan, rather than one or another Muslim setting. More specifically, local advocates of Islamic ADR do not usually explain why the formal introduction of *sulh* occurred in Malaysia around the turn of the new millennium, following experiments with the practice of *sulh* beginning around 1976. Nor do they usually consider why the final quarter of the twentieth century and the early years of the new millennium also saw widespread experimentation with and implementation of mediation in the *civil* judiciary, where it has been promoted not in Islamic terms but in accordance with celebratory discourses associated with the ADR movement that was formally launched at the now-famous Pound Conference held in St. Paul, Minnesota, in April 1976. As Laura Nader (2002, 49) has discussed, this conference occurred at a time when social activists were increasingly utilizing courts in the United States and elsewhere to press claims that threatened the status quo; ADR initiatives were thus designed in part to keep such claims out of the courts and to pacify plaintiffs with therapeutic treatment rather than formal legal remedy (see also Merry 1990). More generally, the conference set the stage for the global marketing of ADR by emphasizing that "adversarial modes of conflict resolution were tearing the society apart," and that "alternative forums were *more civilized* than the courts" (Nader 2002, 52; emphasis added).

My primary aim in raising these points is not to substitute sociohistorical explanations bearing on the rise of Islamic ADR (including *sulh*) for those cast in more Islamic terms. It is, rather, to provide partial context for the emergence of the latter sorts of discourses, which emphasize the virtue and necessity of adopting alternatives to formal court hearings that are "more civilized," which, in this case, clearly means "more Islamic."

For additional context and an explanation for the emergence of formal *sulh* sessions that is at once more expansive and more focused than the bourgeoning literature on the rise of *sulh* and Islamic ADR generally, we might turn to P. G. Lim (1915–2013), one of Malaysia's first female lawyers and the longtime director of the Kuala Lumpur Regional Centre for Arbitration, founded in 1978 (and formally rebranded in 2018 as the Asian International Arbitration Centre). As Lim (2008) notes, "The growth and use of mediation is being promoted in Asia, which has been caught up in the rising swell of Western-style mediation in its more structured form" (106). "All over Asia," she continues, "workshops are being conducted by mediation experts and practitioners . . . to show how mediation works according to the Western mould," adding that "the tidal wave of legal reform . . . [involves] a complete and unreserved accommodation by Asians of Western concepts in the interests of expanding trade and investment with Western partners" (106–07). Lim goes on to remark that "emerging markets in the Asia Pacific region . . . have seen the need to open up their markets and liberalize trade," that "Expanding trade gives rise to trade disputes which have to be resolved," and that "It was also in the national interest to provide a favourable venue and an internationally accepted framework for dispute resolution within the countries themselves" (108).

Lim's remarks help clarify some of the motivation for the introduction and expansion in Malaysia of mediation and of ADR generally, just as they encourage us to appreciate that the groundswell of interest in ADR coincided with the massively expanded opportunities for trade and investment that were a direct entailment of Malaysia's late twentieth-century embrace of neoliberalism (Dezalay and Garth 2002, 2010; Nader 2002). According to this view, the pressure on litigants in the *sharia* courts to resolve their disputes by means of *sulh* will both reduce the politically sensitive backlog of cases and free up the courts to deal with "more important" matters related to trade. Crucial to bear in mind here are efforts by proponents of Islamic law to expand the jurisdiction of the *sharia* courts to cover matters of Islamic finance. These are currently handled by the civil courts since the latter courts have jurisdiction over virtually all types of contracts—including those made by Islamic banks and related institutions—other than those entailed in Muslim marriage (Ahmad Hidayat Buang 2007).

These, in any event, are among the key dynamics that have fueled the development of pastorally-oriented institutions such as *sulh*. So too, more generally, are state policies that have encouraged large-scale urbanization and the rapid development of a middle class, especially a Malay/Muslim middle class. These policies greatly increased the financial stakes and complexities involved in marriage and divorce. The states' failure to make the necessary resources available to manage these and other matters of Islamic family law in a timely manner through formal court hearings, coupled with its efforts to clothe as many state initiatives as practicable in Islamic terms, paved the way for the introduction and subsequent spread of mediation sessions in the form of *sulh* and their promotion in explicitly Islamic idioms.

Much more could be said about the latter issues, but I want to return to Encik Ahmad's comments, particularly his altogether unambiguous and unapologetic admission that he intentionally prolongs some *sulh* cases beyond the three months that are available to him for their resolution. There are two ironies here. First, by intentionally prolonging *sulh* cases beyond the three-month limit so as to save couples from having to undergo formal trial, Encik Ahmad violates protocol and engages in a kind of bureaucratic deception, one that introduces ambiguities into and otherwise muddies the waters of formal ledgers maintained for auditors, annual reports, and public-relations purposes, including the increasingly ubiquitous clients' charters posted in *sharia* courthouses throughout the nation. This presumably requires a cooking of the books broadly analogous to what I observed in Rembau in the late 1980s. At that time, court clerks frequently "forgot" to record certain kinds of marriage payments if the sums involved were so small as to be embarrassing to one or both parties to the union, even though the formal recording of all such payments was required by state law. In addition, they commonly listed husbands as plaintiffs in the documentation of cases in which they were clearly defendants, so that they would have to bear the burden of court fees. This was done on the widespread assumption that husbands cause the majority of problems in marriage and are at fault in most cases of divorce, even though some staff also recognized that "among the [Malay] poor, poverty itself appears to dissolve marriages," as the anthropologist David Banks (1983, 100) once observed. This kind of deception might be said to involve "whites lies," "benign untruths" in J. A. Barnes's (1994) terminology, since they cause no direct harm to anyone, serve the public good, or both. Intentional fabrications on the part of *sharia* lawyers, in contrast, cannot be so characterized. This is partly to say that Encik Ahmad's previously noted stance regarding overt, intentional deception is more nuanced than his explicitly phrased comments about lying suggest.

The second irony has to do with some of the changes in the *sharia* judiciary that Encik Ahmad criticizes, such as the increased reliance on lawyers and formal adjudication as well as the adoption from the civil courts of terminology like "plaintiff" and "defendant." Such changes are precisely what lends today's *sharia* courts a measure of enhanced respectability—both within and beyond the juridical field—vis-à-vis their counterparts of times past. This, in turn, is crucial to the expanded role—in relation to the civil courts—that he hopes and expects them to play in the future.

The *sharia* courts [today] are a lot different than before. There have been lots of improvements. In the past, when one mentioned the *sharia* court, people thought of it as a second-class court; there was no fear. When a summons was issued requiring someone to appear in court, the person was not afraid and [might not appear if he] did not feel like showing up. But now it's different, the court is coming into its own. When called, the respondents will come; if they don't, it will be considered demeaning to the court, and they could be charged [with a criminal offense] .... [These days] the *sharia* courts collaborate with the National Registration Department, the Royal Malaysian Police Force, the Immigration Department, and probably the Employees' Provident Fund, to identify [i.e., locate, track down] particular individuals .... We have seen a lot of improvements. But more time is needed to render the *sharia* courts equal to the civil courts.

These comments suggest (among other things) that the *sharia* courts are—and are seen, especially from "the inside"—as a "work in progress." One of the other interesting features of these remarks is that they were offered partly in response to my question to Encik Ahmad about the attire of *sharia* judges—why they wear black business suits, like the one he was sporting—which he opined was "maybe to make the judges and the *sharia* department look professional." Although he did not elaborate on these points, the wearing of black business suits is, in this view, part of the professionalization of the *sharia* judiciary that has helped overcome some of the stigma associated with it being a second-class system of courts that no one fears or respects.

To a significant degree it is the civil judiciary—more precisely, the Federal Constitution—that is most directly responsible for the stigma borne by the *sharia* judiciary, for as Encik Ahmad put it, "the *sharia* courts can only hear cases when the civil courts *allow them to*" (emphasis added). This shorthand reference to the fact that the civil rather than the *sharia* courts enjoy the mandate enshrined in the Federal Constitution to interpret the constitutional provisions bearing on the jurisdictions of the two judiciaries and their boundaries and sanctions indexes a deeply contentious issue in present-day Malaysia. Suffice it to add that like most Malays, Encik Ahmad was no doubt heartened to hear what he referred to in passing as "rumors that cases on Islamic finance will be placed under the jurisdiction of the *sharia* courts" (they are currently handled by civil authorities, as noted earlier, much to the dismay of a good number of Muslims). Judging from the overall thrust of his comments, however, he probably has deep misgivings that the decision in question and many features of its implementation would ultimately come from highly placed officials in the civil judiciary, many of whom are non-Muslims.

CONCLUSION

In these final remarks I want to return briefly to the issues of *ijtihad* and *asal* that I mentioned at the outset of this chapter. Based on my fieldwork in the fall of 2013, I am less confident that Hallaq's thesis concerning the demise of *ijtihad* in modern Muslim societies might merit qualification if we switch our focus from formal adjudication in *sharia* courts to the informal *sulh* sessions that complement them. Much depends on how one defines *ijtihad*, as we have seen. *Sulh* sessions do provide a forum for the articulation of issues bearing on *asal,* however. As such, they evince an important, albeit qualified, convergence (perhaps even a continuity) with classical variants of *sharia* practice. They also allow much greater scope and latitude for the agency of women as litigants than do regular *sharia* hearings. For these reasons, and because *sulh* sessions valorize the mediation, compromise, and negotiation that has long been a hallmark of Islamic jurisprudence and politics alike, they merit more serious consideration on the part of scholars and others concerned with the entanglements of law, politics, and religion in the Muslim world and beyond. The fact that *sulh* sessions tend to be overseen by women is another reason to accord them more significance. This is especially so since research on female religious authority in the Muslim world is still in its infancy, and very much in need of more robust scholarship addressing women's discourses and practices in contexts other than mosques, Sufi orders, and activist organizations like Sisters in Islam.

Two related, but more general points: First, it behooves us to focus less attention on those Bourdieu refers to as "leading actors," and to accord greater descriptive and analytic priority to those he characterizes as "utility men" (1977, 35). Despite Bourdieu's androcentric terminology, these are often women, toiling behind the scenes, or at least in less glamorous or prestigious contexts, to make possible the social and other achievements credited to men in their roles as leading actors. In Malaysia's *sharia* judiciary, these "utility men" include women employed as bailiffs, *sulh* officers, and in myriad other capacities, some of whom are tasked with the research and writing of articles published in prestigious *sharia* law journals under the names of male judges.

Second, and finally, there is an important comparative-historical point to be made about the gendering of religious authority and of the *sharia* juridical field in late-modern Malaysia. Recall that in 2010 officials announced the appointment of two women to the *sharia* bench, thus ending men's long-standing monopoly of *sharia* judgeships. This was a momentous though contested development, to be sure. But in suggesting enhanced pluralism it also deflects attention from the fact that in recent decades Islamic religious authority and the more encompassing juridical field have become unforgivingly heteronormative.

In emphasizing the latter point I am not referring to the protracted Anwar Ibrahim affair (1998–2015), which saw the former Deputy Prime Minister (and longtime head of the opposition movement) thrown out of office, charged with multiple counts of sodomy, and imprisoned on numerous occasions, though it is certainly relevant to my argument.[6] I am thinking instead, at least in part, of the proliferation of *sharia* enactments in the past few decades that have criminalized same-sex relations and various kinds of gender non-conformity (see chapter 2). I am also thinking of an intriguing case from the northern state of Kedah that occurred in the early 1980s, which is largely unthinkable in the present cultural-political climate.[7] The case involved a locally well-known transvestite seamstress and dancer by the name of Ismail who, after a series of visions and trance episodes, gave up his transgender practices and took on the role of *alim* (Islamic religious scholar, man of learning; pl. *ulama*), despite having no religious education. Ismail drew such a large following as an *alim* that authorities feared he would soon be accorded the status of a prophet. The Kedah State *Fatwa* Committee that was convened to look into the matter recommended that the state's Religious Council prohibit Ismail from expounding his religious views in public. In some ways most intriguing is that Ismail went on to assume "a new and more prestigious role . . . as a healer" (Sharifah Zaleha Syed Hassan 1989, 63).

There is no way of determining how Ismail's well-known history of engaging in transgender practices may have figured into the legitimacy accorded him in either his new role or his previous role as *alim*. But it seems evident that his transgender past was not an obstacle to his assumption of either role. On the basis of my field research in Malaysia since the late 1970s, I would contend that it probably enhanced his legitimacy in both roles, at least as far as the lay public—the community of ordinary Muslims—was concerned. This case does in any event have deeply allegorical features. It highlights not only the relative permeability and interchangeability of different kinds of religious authority, but also their variable gendering, at least through the 1980s. The historic differentiation and segregation of such roles that has occurred since the 1980s is also striking. So too is the fact that the gender nonconformity on the part of a religious authority that featured in this case is largely unthinkable at present. This is true even though the nation's *sharia* judiciary, warts and all, is arguably more responsive and friendly to (heteronormative) women than at any point in times past, as discussed in chapter 5.

Discourse, Practice, and Rebranding in Kuala Lumpur's *Sharia* Courthouse

In order to understand symbolic systems, you have to understand the systems of agents struggling over these symbolic systems.
—PIERRE BOURDIEU (2014)

Dynamics in Kuala Lumpur's *sharia* courthouse—such as the ascendancy of law-yers, their effective sidelining of litigants and (to some extent) judges, and the state's myriad efforts to rebrand the *sharia* assemblage—provide valuable lenses on nationwide developments in and beyond *sharia* arenas that have taken place or are likely to occur in the years to come. This is partly because of Kuala Lumpur's status as the nation's capital, its largest metropolis (with a population of nearly 1.8 million residents),[1] and the context from which gazetted enactments and successful jurid-ical experiments that are relevant exclusively or primarily to Kuala Lumpur are developed for jurisdictions throughout the country.

The architecturally stunning *sharia* courthouse that is the focus of this chapter opened for business in 2011, more than three decades after I began my research in Malaysia; this is one reason I sometimes refer to it as Kuala Lumpur's "new *sharia* courthouse." The eclectic but unmistakably Islamic design of the building's exterior is complemented by a large sign posted at its entrance that advertises the complex as a zone where women's private parts are to be covered (*Zon Menutup Aurat*) in accordance with sacred texts in the form of a *hadith* about the Prophet Muhammad. The symbolics of the exterior of the building might be said to contrast rather sharply with the messages conveyed by the building's interior, which emphasizes the *sharia* judiciary's extensive borrowings from and overall compatibility with its main patron and competitor—the civil judiciary—and their mutual embrace of international standards of management, accounting, and audit. Rather than seeing the two sets of symbolic statements (one keyed to the building's exterior, the other to its interior) as mutually contradictory, I argue that they are more appropriately viewed as variably inflected features of a single statement to the effect that the *sharia* judiciary is a thor-oughly cosmopolitan, global assemblage, albeit still very much a work in progress.

Whichever of these (or other) positions one adopts, there is no question that the state's sartorial advisors and other social engineers have sought to rebrand *sharia* judges and the courts over which they exercise relative dominion. This rebranding, which operates on a number of different though related levels, includes the marking of contrasts between new and old *sharia* judges and the suppression of differences between *sharia* judges and their civil counterparts. It also involves an erasure of the distinction between membership in and allegiances to a particular, regionally defined ethnic group (Malays) and religious community (the *ummah*), and a prioritized sense of belonging to a professionally oriented, cosmopolitan, global "trans-ethnic" community that does not privilege any particularistic "primordial" sentiments associated with language, culture, ethnicity/race, or religion. The rebranding aims partly to convey to Malays and other Muslims that Malayness and Islam can be thoroughly middle-class, modern, global, and cosmopolitan. It also seeks to signal to non-Malays, especially the non-Muslims among them, that *sharia* judges subscribe to more or less universal standards and normativities bearing on justice, equality, and due process, and that, as such, non-Malays have nothing to fear from creeping Islamization, *sharia*tization, or the further entrenchment of Malay supremacy. In this we see a universalizing move, of a piece with the adoption of the gavel and the handcuffs as key symbols of the *sharia* judiciary, that is also directed at current and future foreign investors, whose capital and diplomatic and infrastructural support is crucial to elites' efforts to position Malaysia at the center of global Islamic banking and finance.

The first section of the chapter following these introductory remarks addresses the architecture and exterior of the courthouse. The second considers some features of the interior of the building, including the lobby and museum. The third and fourth sections engage themes bearing on the spatiality, composition, and ambience of courtrooms and the attire of judges and other officers of the court ("black-business-suit fever"). The fifth focuses on judicial process, repudiations, and the increasingly dominant role that lawyers play in *sharia* hearings, as illustrated in the transcript of a case involving a woman who may have been formally repudiated by her husband. The concluding section examines the extent to which the rebranding discussed in this and previous chapters has been effective and whether it might be said to involve, as some critics suggest, subterfuge, or what is referred to in the literature on advertising and rebranding as "ambush marketing."

OF ARCHITECTURE AND *AURAT*

The architecture of Kuala Lumpur's new *sharia* courthouse is profitably viewed in relation to recent trends in the design of public buildings and more encompassing spaces and cityscapes in Malaysia, especially those that have occurred since the early 1990s. A number of architects, geographers, and city planners have discussed these trends (e.g., Yeang 1992; Mohamad Tajuddin Mohamad Rasdi 2005, 2010; King 2008). I will thus be brief here and will focus for a moment on the administrative capital of Putrajaya, which I mentioned earlier in connection with the Multi-Media Super Corridor and e-governance initiatives such as the E-*Syariah* Portal (chapter 1). Putrajaya is renowned for its grand boulevards and imposing architecture. Some features of its design are reminiscent of French Beaux-Arts grandeur, others of the Art Deco movement in corporate American architecture of the 1930s–50s, and still others of classical Middle Eastern mosques and mid-twentieth-century socialist schlock. Perhaps more than any of the other influences, "Putrajaya's Middle East referencing is explicit and intentional. Masjid Putra [the Putra Mosque], certainly the most finely elaborated building in the city, variously claims a source in Uzbekistan [and] attributes its Persian-Islamic architecture to the Safavid period and its minarets to the model of the Sheikh Omar Mosque in Baghdad" (King 2008, 164). Significantly, Putrajaya makes no use of indigenous Malay residential, commercial, or spatial patterns of any sort; as Ross King puts it, "There is nothing identifiably Malay in the styling of Putrajaya" (165).

Many of these same generalizations are relevant to the design of the ("new") mosque in Kuala Lumpur, Masjid Wilayah Persekutuan, which opened in 2000, can accommodate up to seventeen thousand worshippers at any given time, and was inspired in part by the Blue Mosque of Istanbul and by "Indo-Saracenic, Middle Eastern and Art Deco" architecture (King 2008, 189). Many of them also pertain to the architecturally eclectic complex that houses Kuala Lumpur's civil courts, the Kompleks Mahkamah Kuala Lumpur. This massive six-story structure, which opened in 2007, contains more than seventy separate courtrooms that deal more or less exclusively with civil-law matters, along with dozens of offices, meeting rooms, a cafeteria, and a good deal else. It boasts a monumental architectural style known as Late Modern Indo-Saracenic Revival.[2] This is despite its explicit and more or less exclusive civil-law orientation and the fact that—outside the limited purview of the *sharia* courts, which have no jurisdiction over the country's non-Muslims—civil law is the law of the land in this multi-ethnic and multi-religious nation.

Kuala Lumpur's new *sharia* courthouse, for its part, is located on a four-hectare piece of property atop a hill in the upscale Taman Sri Hartamas neighborhood of Kuala Lumpur (a few miles north of the city center), more or less adjacent to the Immigration Department and just down the road from the commanding new palace (the Istana Negara) built for the Yang diPertuan Agong, the King. It is in close proximity to the recently established Government Office Complex off Jalan Duta and is in the same general vicinity as—and readily visible from—a number of the other recently constructed monuments mentioned a moment ago, including both the mosque and the civil-court complex, that have helped establish Kuala Lumpur's reputation as perhaps the most architecturally fascinating city in all of Southeast Asia (King 2008).

The architecturally dazzling six-story building that is home to Kuala Lumpur's *sharia* courts was built at a cost of 96 million *ringgit* (around US$30 million) and opened for business on October 24, 2011 (*Utusan [Malaysia] Online* 2011). It thus brought to a close the twenty-one-year period that saw the courts housed in the colonial-era Art Deco Sulaiman Building (Bangunan Sulaiman), named after Sultan Alauddin Sulaiman Shah, then-ruler of Selangor, which was built by the British in the 1930s and once served as the nerve center of the National Registration Department. In architectural and art-history terminology, the Islamic-themed architecture of the new complex, which is mostly two-tone beige with white trim, would be glossed "Late (or Post-) Modern Indo-Saracenic Revival," but the flat surfaces and framing lines of the stucco edifice are "pure Baghdad," according to one expert who has written extensively about contemporary architectural trends in Kuala Lumpur, Putrajaya, and beyond.³ The massive, fortress-like walls, monumental arched gateways adorned with geometric tiles, and large gold onion domes crowning the building are also reminiscent of iconic Islamic architectural design in Uzbekistan, Egypt, and Iran (figure 7). In this they complement the aesthetic of the Putra Mosque in Putrajaya and further illustrate the ways Malaysian authorities have encouraged architectural firms to incorporate Islamic motifs from both Sunni and Shia traditions into their designs for the monumental architecture of the new millennium. In some cases this is less encouragement than insistence, since it is part of a series of official moves to position Malaysia both as the center of global Islamic finance and of "a pan-Islamic world bloc to stand against others that have long denigrated the Islamic world" (King 2008, 167).

Built around a large open square showcasing a series of fountains and pools meant to suggest the original purpose of Islamic courtyards, as places for ablutions and gardens, the new courthouse is a world unto itself. It contains eighteen separate courtrooms—eleven for lower-court hearings, six for high-court hearings, and one for appellate-court hearings—as well as work space and meeting rooms for more than 130 officers of the court, including prosecutors, lawyers, and *sulh* officers. This is in addition to chambers for producing sworn affidavits; seminar rooms, a library, and an information-technology (training) center; a police station with around three dozen holding cells; a prayer house, a nursery, a grocery store, and a cafeteria that can accommodate up to two hundred patrons; plus a museum, massive parking lots (some of them underground), and much else.

Posted just outside and to the left of the main entrance to the building is a large signboard featuring a cartoon-like drawing of a girl or (very) young woman of indeterminate age with a prominent "smiley face" and Disney-esque doe-eyes, who is attired from head to toe in a bright canary-yellow *jubbah* (kaftan) and *tudung* (headscarf) (figure 8). The eye-catching signage and imagery designate the the building and adjacent grounds as a *Zon Menutup Aurat,* that is, a zone or area where the *aurat,* the "private parts" of a person, especially a female, that must be

FIGURE 7. Federal Territory *Syariah* Courthouse (Kuala Lumpur's *Sharia* Courthouse), 2013. Photo by author.

covered in public according to Islam, are appropriately concealed. In the case of the young female cartoon character in question, this clearly means everything but the front portion of her face and her hands. Telegraphically brief clarification of this injunction appears beneath the words *Zon Menutup Aurat* in the form of a *hadith* about the Prophet Muhammad, narrated by Bazzar and Al Termizi, which explains, with the relevant term rendered in capital letters: "Indeed, women are "PRIVATE PARTS"; every time they go out, Satan will observe/take notice."[4] An identical sign appears on the side of the road even before one turns into the parking lot for the building. The message that one is entering Islamic space, and that that space has clear, gender-variable entailments, is hard to miss.

According to Islam, men too have *aurat*—roughly the part of the body between the navel and the knees—but virtually all *sharia*-court (and other public) references to *aurat* focus on women. Conversely, *sharia*-court references to women commonly focus on women's dress, appearance, and bodily functions (whether or not they are menstruating, hence impure or not, or pregnant; how many times they have gotten their periods since their husband pronounced one or more *talak*, etc.), thus either directly or indirectly alluding to their *aurat*.

FIGURE 8. Sign at entrance to Kuala Lumpur's *Sharia* Courthouse admonishing women to keep *aurat* covered, 2013. Photo by author.

A noteworthy exception to my generalization concerning the more or less exclusive link in public discourse between *aurat* and femininity appeared in a directive issued by the state government of Kelantan in September 2013 (Syed Azhar and Qishin Tariq 2013). The directive proclaimed that, effective immediately, the injunction pertaining to covering or protecting one's *aurat* would also be applicable to male employees of the state secretariat complex in Kota Baru, the capital of Kelantan, even when they were not at work. This was apparently because some of them occasionally donned inappropriate "sports attire" (running shorts, etc.) when coming to or leaving their offices. Consider in this connection the large signboard posted outside the Chief Minister's Office in Kota Baru, advertising that it is a *Zon Menjaga Aurat* and that *Menjaga* ["guarding"/"protecting"] *Aurat* is a command of Allah (*Menjaga Aurat Adalah Perintah Allah SWT*). This signboard shows, as an example of appropriate attire, a (Malay) woman clad in a fashionable black *baju kurung* with red highlights complemented by a full red *tudung,* an outfit which reveals only the front of her face and her hands. To her left is a distinguished looking middle-aged man (also Malay) clad in a black business suit and civil service nametag (figure 9.)

The idea that covering a man's *aurat* is best done with a black business suit was subsequently caricatured in cartoons that appeared in local media, such as one from *Sunday Star,* October 6, 2013 (figure 10). The first frame shows a happy,

'Keep aurat covered' zone

Male civil servants at Kelantan govt complex now included in circular

By SYED AZHAR and QISHIN TARIQ
newsdesk@thestar.com.my

KOTA BARU:The state secretariat complex at Kota Darul Naim here has been designated as a *Zon Menjaga Aurat* which is enforced on both male and female civil servants.

State Women Development, Family and Welfare committee chairman Mumtaz Md Nawi, who launched the campaign, said the state government circular previously applied to female civil servants but it will now be enforced on male employees too.

The circular, issued in 1993 by the state secretary, is now enforced on both genders since Sunday as the *Al-Quran* states that males must also cover certain parts, she said.

She told *Harakahdaily*, the official PAS organ, that although male civil servants were dressed according to Islamic principles while at work, they failed to do so particularly when donning sports attire.

Aurat are parts of the human body which must, according to Islam, be covered from the sight of others with clothing.

Women need to be fully covered

Fully covered: Nur Adleen Mohd Suhaimi, 20, looking at the 'Keep Aurat Covered' poster at the Kelantan Mentri Besar's office in Kota Bharu.

except for the hands and face while the men must cover themselves from navel to the knees.

Mumtaz also said the government had the responsibility to safeguard the dignity of those under its administration, similar to that of a father

overseeing his family in the Islamic context.

When contacted, Mumtaz advised all visitors to the government complex to be decently dressed.

She said no action would be taken against those who failed to adhere to

the dress code for Muslims.

"We are not interested in taking action or penalising anyone. It is only an advisory guideline to educate people.

"It's just like guidelines on dress code in Parliament or the circular to wear batik on Thursdays and so on," she said.

Meanwhile, state MCA secretary Tan Ken Ten said the Muslim dress code propagated by the Kelantan government should be respected as long as it did not involve non-Muslims.

"What we do not want is non-Muslims turned away from government departments because they are ignorant of a Muslim dress code," he said.

Persatuan Ulama Malaysia secretary-general Dr Mohd Roslan Nor said covering one's *aurat* was not a matter of personal choice, but a part of the religion that should be followed by Muslims.

"We agree with the stand to encourage people to keep their *aurat* covered. However, we would like to see the state government encourage it through education, not punishment," he said.

FIGURE 9. Sign designating chief minister's office in Kota Baru, Kelantan as a "'Keep *Aurat* Covered' Zone." From *The Star*, October 3, 2013.

FIGURE 10. Cartoon satirizing new government dress policy for men, by Reggie Lee. From *Sunday Star*, October 6, 2013.

buck-toothed Malay man whistling a tune, clad in a striped sarong and ill-fitting sleeveless undershirt that is rolled up, thus exposing a good portion of his bare belly, who is about to walk past a large, imposing *Zon Menutup Aurat* sign that looks something like a stop sign. The second depicts the same man, clearly alarmed and making a hasty retreat after seeing the large sign. The third frame portrays him smiling, but no longer whistling, now outfitted in a dark, somber business suit, white shirt, and necktie, happily resuming his journey. One of the clear messages conveyed by this cartoon, by others like it, and by the new directives on male attire is that earlier ("traditional") Malay male dress entails a kind of "nakedness . . . [that is] an outward manifestation of inner backwardness"—as Henk Schulte Nordholt (1997, 11) put it for the analogous Indonesian case.

SOME FEATURES OF THE INTERIOR OF THE BUILDING

I proceed to a consideration of some features of the interior of the building, partly as a prelude to my discussion of discourses and practices in the courtrooms. Before delving into specifics I want to emphasize a general point to which I return in due course: the cultural elaboration of formative influences on the courthouse—and by extension, of the work carried out within it—that is suggested by its exterior architecture, which most Malaysians and other observers would instantly recognize as "Islamic-themed," is at sharp variance with the legal and cultural-political work one encounters inside the building. The unmistakable themes emphasized within the building are that the activities and overall orientations of the *sharia* courts share deep resonance with civil-law traditions inherited from British colonizers and otherwise conform to the Japanese-origin 5Ses and the various audit protocols and international standards of operation that have been embraced by state agencies and corporate entities alike. This is readily apparent from the huge flat-screen TV that hangs from the ceiling on the left wall of the lobby and displays information on the classification and venue of hearings and the key players involved in them; from the museum situated off the other side of the lobby that provides visitors with official representations of Islamic law and the *sharia* courts; and from the hearings themselves. The arguably discrepant messages conveyed by the building's exterior and interior reflect efforts to appeal to different constituencies, as I discuss later on.

The Lobby and Flat-Screen Monitor/Directory

Most any ethnographer observing the comings and goings in the main lobby of the courthouse would quickly note that those entering that space fall into two separate, non-overlapping categories: those who know where they are going and those who do not. The former are mostly lawyers (judges have separate entrances so that they need not use the same entranceway as those whose cases they are adjudicating), along with litigants and other members of the public who have visited the courtroom in the past and thus have some sense of the layout of the building; they tend to move quickly through the lobby to their intended destination(s), though they may consult the large flat-screen television monitor hanging on the wall for updated information about the timing or venue of their hearings. Those in the latter category are more inclined to head for the information desk staffed by uniformed police, who are sometimes tending to male prisoners in handcuffs ordered to appear in court. Once there they are either directed to the flat-screen TV for further information or provided with directions on how to get to their desired destinations.

Among the first things one is likely to notice from the rolling images displayed on the TV monitor is that each of the courtrooms in the complex is designated either for lower-court cases (*Mahkamah Rendah Syariah*), high-court cases (*Mahkamah Tinggi Syariah*), or appellate-court cases (*Mahkamah Rayuan Syariah*); and that in any given venue the disputes aired are categorized either as civil cases (*kes mal*) or criminal cases (*kes jenayah*). All such classifications derive directly from the civil courts—and are altogether foreign to classical Islamic jurisprudence—as does the current plan to introduce two new levels of courts into the *sharia* juridical hierarchy so that it will mirror the five-level civil-court hierarchy. This is in keeping with state projects aimed at the "Harmonization of Laws," the latter being a widely heard, seemingly innocuous slogan that replaced the far more controversial "Islamization of Laws."

Further dimensions of the classificatory apparatus that are apparent from the TV monitor include: (1) that each case is classified either as a "mention" (*sebutan*, from the root *sebut*, "to mention"), or as a "hearing" or "discussion" (*perbicaraaan*, from the root *bicara*, "to discuss"); (2) that the principals to the disputes, whose full names are listed on the screen, are either plaintiffs (*plaintif*) or defendants (*defendan*); and (3) that a good many of the litigants are represented by counsel (*peguam*), whose full names are also provided. The monitor also displays information on other broadly relevant matters, such as the precise times that Muslims are called to prayer each day (these vary slightly from one day to the next), so that those with business at the court might more easily plan the timing of their visit(s) to the room in the courthouse that is set aside for prayers (the *surau*).

The Museum

The politics and poetics of the displays within the courthouse museum, formally designated as the *Syariah* Gallery (*Galeri Syariah*), are worthy of a book in themselves, but I confine my remarks to a few salient themes. The first has to do with the depiction of *sharia* as the law of the land in precolonial times. Others concern the ways that the museum represents the present-day operations, orientations, and achievements of the court and the directions in which it is heading.

One of the first exhibits one encounters after entering the enclosed museum space is entitled "*Sejarah Perundangan dan Kehakiman Islam*" ("History of Islamic

Law and Judiciary"). The first two paragraphs of the text may be translated as follows.

> History has proven [*membuktikan*] that Islamic law was the original law in the Malay States. This law was widely adopted as the law for administering various states and it encompassed a broad range of law such as family law, *sharia* criminal offenses, and so on.
>
> The British took over administrative responsibilities in the Malay States from the Malay Rulers in all affairs, except those related to the Islamic religion and Malay customs, through the appointment of British officers as advisors to the Malay Rulers. English law then began to be employed and was later successful in restricting the usage of Islamic law in the Malay States solely to matters related to the Islamic religion. Further, the interpretation of the Islamic religion itself was narrowed by the British power-holders to matters involving only laws relating to the individual, such as marriage, divorce, and so forth.

The display goes on to say that

> English law was brought into the Malay States and replaced Islamic law as the law of the Malay States ... [partly through British "advice" to the Malay Rulers to] devise written laws in accordance with the English law, such as the Penal Code, Evidence Enactment, Contract Enactment, Civil Procedure Code, Criminal Procedure Code, and Land Enactment . . . . In those areas, Islamic law was brushed aside and English law was enforced . . . .
>
> The advent of British law not only restricted the usage of Islamic law in the Malay States, but also influenced the drafting of the Federal Constitution through the Reid Commission, and later affected the development of the administration of Islamic religious affairs in this country through the formation of . . . [constitutional arrangements] that provide complete authority to the states in forming the(ir) Islamic religious administrations. As a result, to this day, most of the provisions regarding the Islamic religion are confined to laws related to the individual.

This representation of the past, which is a cornerstone of the official history conveyed to children in Malaysian schools, is a neo-classical example of what James Scott (1998) refers to as "state simplification" that simultaneously occludes, erases, and obfuscates. It includes some assertions that are largely beyond dispute: that the British colonized the Malay states; that they curtailed the scope and force of extant political and legal arrangements; and that in the process they tended to "substitute" English law for prevailing legal codes, many of which were indeed forcibly "restricted," "narrowed," and "brushed aside." But it also contains other assertions that greatly oversimplify—one might say seriously distort—precolonial realities, such as the opening declaration, presented as something that historians have "proven," as in a court of law, that *sharia* was the original law in the Malay states. This contention elevates Islamic law to a position it did not enjoy prior to the arrival of the British (or at any time since). Precolonial customs and laws pertaining to succession, inheritance, and landownership, like those bearing on determinations of innocence and guilt (judicial ordeals, trials by wager, divinations, and the like) and the punishments to be meted out for criminal offenses, sometimes included features of *sharia,* but in many instances they did not, comprised as they often were primarily if not exclusively of "customary," largely pre-Islamic features of Austronesian and/or Hindu-Buddhist provenance.

It is commonplace in some quarters to point to the *Batu Bersurat (Terengganu),* or "Terengganu Stone" as it is known in English, to support claims that *sharia* was the law of the land in the Malay States for hundreds of years prior to the arrival of the British. The *Batu Bersurat* is a large stone carved with Jawi (Malay-Arabic) script, which dates from around 1303 C.E. and was discovered in the east-coast state of Terengganu in 1899. In addition to specifying harsh Quranic punishments for offenses such as fornication/adultery (*zina*) and sodomy (*liwat*), it proclaims *sharia* as the law of the realm. The Melaka legal codes (*Undang-Undang Melaka*), which are generally believed to have been compiled between 1424 and 1458, are sometimes cited in this connection as well, partly because they contain numerous references to Islamic law. One problem with extrapolating from these texts, however, is that there is no evidence to suggest that they encode models *of*—as distinct from models *for*—reality.[5] A second, related problem is that there is a good deal of evidence suggesting that in a basic sociological sense they are more prescriptive than descriptive (see, for example, Gullick 1958; Yegar 1979; Milner 1983; Peletz 1988, 2002; Reid 1988, 1993; Andaya and Andaya 2001; I. Hussin 2016). One needs to bear in mind that the mere existence of legal codes in written form, fragments and compendia of which were sometimes maintained by Malay rulers as *pesaka*—in this context, "sacred heirlooms"—and sources of spiritual potency, does not necessarily mean they were implemented within the inner realms of Malay polities, or known to exist, let alone widely understood or practiced, beyond them. One needs also to exercise caution in making generalizations based on historical references to the existence of individuals attached to royal palaces who bore honorific titles such as Islamic judge (*kadi*), for it is not at all clear that individuals thus honored actually served in the adjudicatory or other juridical capacity that is nowadays commonly associated with such titles. More generally, the evidence for the existence in precolonial times of formally constituted Islamic courts is inconclusive, some would say largely nonexistent, though much depends on which region(s) of the Malay Peninsula one is talking about (Peletz 2002, 25–38).

The foundational claim that *sharia* was the law of the land in precolonial times is central to variously construed efforts on the part of political and religious elites to expand the scope of *sharia* across the nation, so as to rid it of myriad features from its tainted, colonial-era past—a past that saw Islamic law "restricted," "narrowed," and "brushed aside" by English common law—and otherwise restore *sharia* to its rightful place. It is thus curious that the courthouse museum does not contain any photographs or replicas of the Terengganu Stone (the original is housed in the Terengganu state museum) or of early modern texts such as the Laws of Melaka, especially since we have seen that these are the sources often cited in support of the official line noted above.

Arguably more curious still, the museum does not feature any displays of the Quran or *hadith*, clearly the cornerstones and *ur*-texts of *sharia* by any criteria, or anything at all in the Jawi script, the introduction of which is widely regarded as a defining moment in the early stages of the Malay States' Islamization (Syed Naquib Al-Attas 1969). The only written texts in the form of books or pamphlets that are on display in the museum are bound, gazetted, positive-law enactments bearing on Islamic family law (in English and/or Romanized Malay), and dusty, oversize books maintained by the Registrar, which look like ledgers.

These, in any event, are not the most symbolically significant written texts that are exhibited in the museum. The written texts of greatest import—judging partly from the prominent way they are displayed, including the amount of space devoted to them and their proximity to photographs of Prime Minister Najib (posing with the first two women appointed to the *sharia* bench)—are the numerous certificates and awards testifying to the *sharia* court's implementation and achievement of the standard management and auditing requirements of Quality Environmental Practices, Quality Management Systems, and the ISO. These certificates and awards, some issued by the Malaysian Productivity Corporation, are given pride of place in the museum, as are the adjacent display cases highlighting the objectives and entailments of the Japanese-origin system of management and auditing known as the 5Ses (discussed in chapter 1), and the genealogy, design, and meanings of the 5S logo and the keywords and slogans associated with it. Such are the features of the *sharia* assemblage that the Prime Minister's Department, which directly oversees the *sharia* judiciary, would like visitors to bear most strongly in mind both during their time in the museum and the courthouse more generally, and forever after. Further support for this view derives from the fact that some of these same posters and information boards appear elsewhere in the courthouse, both in places where they are readily visible to the public, clearly one of their intended audiences, and in backstage office areas as well, to help motivate staff and keep them on track. Charts documenting chronologies bearing on the implementation and achievement of audit standards are perhaps the most common, both in public areas and backstage regions.

There is more to the museum than the display of written texts that I have focused on thus far. The exhibition also contains formal photographic portraits of (mostly senior) judges, with brief biographical information below each photo. It also features a heavy wooden desk and chair that was used by the chief judge in Kuala Lumpur's old *sharia* courthouse and black judicial robes of unspecified provenance that, like the desk and chair, look more or less exactly like those used by civil-court judges with the exception, perhaps, of the gold trim on the robes. Noteworthy as well are the numerous photographic depictions of larger-than-life-size, generic gavels, some of which include pictures of larger-than-life-size, generic handcuffs and are the centerpiece of the JKSM posters proclaiming "*Syariah* is the Basis of Justice" (*Syariah Asas Keadilan*).

In sum, if the most culturally and politically salient written texts displayed in the museum are the certificates and awards documenting and congratulating the court on implementing and achieving international standards of and for management and auditing, then the key symbols of both the museum and the *sharia* judiciary as a whole are clearly the gavel and the handcuffs. As with the black business suits worn by *sharia* judges, these are instantly recognizable signifiers in Malaysia and far beyond, much like the terms "*sharia*" and "justice" and the idea that there is or should be a strong positive correlation between all that they signify.

A final ethnographic observation worthy of brief mention is that in the course of my half-dozen or so forays into the museum (in 2012–13 and 2018), I never saw anyone else there, aside from the occasional custodian silently discharging his duties. This situation recalls James Scott's (1990) remarks about the 1985 anniversary celebrations of the Laotian Communist Party, which "virtually no one comes to see . . . save those on the reviewing stand and those marching past" (58–61). Though clearly different in key particulars, both examples point to the importance of processes involving the "self-dramatization of elites" as they endeavor to fine-tune and otherwise craft official narratives of past and present that can be pressed into service to shape both current realities and possible futures.

THE SPATIALITY, COMPOSITION, AND AMBIENCE OF COURTROOMS

The new *sharia* courthouse, like the nearby buildings mentioned earlier in this chapter (the Kuala Lumpur mosque and the Court Complex that houses Kuala Lumpur's civil courts) are both aesthetically stunning and of enormous scale. As with the eighty-eight-story Petronas Towers in the heart of Kuala Lumpur and the overall design of Putrajaya, they are intended to substantiate national political elites' claims that Malaysia has combined the very best of modernity and moderate, progressive Islam, and is thus capable of any technical or other achievement imaginable, a sentiment summed up in the ubiquitous national slogan *Malaysia Boleh!* ("Malaysia Can Do It!"). Those who designed Kuala Lumpur's new *sharia* court complex created monumental structures and spaces that also aim to emphasize the ostensibly unchallengeable nature of the judiciary's power and legitimacy, rather than architectural styles and spatial arrangements of a less imposing and more open sort that might possibly suggest an arm of the state or a type of law, religious or otherwise, that is readily approachable by the public.[6] More generally, the colossal scale of the new complex gives the impression of a monolithic, internally undifferentiated, unchallengeable state that is firmly in control of the nation's Islamic resources and identity and everything else over which it claims dominion. One reason for this may be that the variant of Islam promoted by the Malaysian state *is* widely challenged by the existence of discourses and practices that do not sit comfortably with state-authorized Islam. Some of these discourses and practices are squarely or at least self-consciously Islamic, while others are grounded in the secular frames of the Federal Constitution, as discussed later in this chapter.

From the perspective of my experience in Rembau in the late 1980s, when virtually all hearings were held in the *kadi*'s private chambers, the *dewan* (rooms, halls) designated for hearings in the new building are huge, indeed, cavernous. They are around sixty to eighty feet long and forty feet wide, with thirty-five- to forty-foot ceilings, though this an educated guess, since neither I nor my research assistants were able to measure or photograph them (or to use any video recording or other such equipment). Hearings are typically held in these formal, windowless courtrooms, not in the judge's private chambers or elsewhere. The large space is partitioned in a number of clearly demarcated ways, unlike anything one saw in the spaces commonly used for hearings in Rembau in the late 1980s; the demarcation is also far more formal than, though it bears a family resemblance to, what one sees in present-day Rembau.

Entering the courtroom from the back, as virtually everyone except the judge does, the first thing one is likely to notice is that litigants and other members of the public are expected to arrange themselves in gender-segregated seating areas. On the left is the space reserved for females, marked by a sign that says "*Tempat Duduk Perempuan*" ("Female Seating Area") and, for the benefit of Indian Muslims and others who might not be able to read Malay, an image of the profile of the head of a woman wearing Malay Muslim headgear (the *tudung*), a profile that, interestingly, faces the back of the courtroom. To the right is where men are supposed to sit, appropriately marked both by a sign indicating as much ("*Tempat Duduk Lelaki*," "Male Seating Area") and by an image of the profile of the head of a man wearing the fez-like *songkok*, which, like the *tudung*, is characteristically Malay; this profile faces the front of the court. This public seating area, which includes four long rows of wooden benches on either side of the path one would take to reach the areas designated for officers of the court, can accommodate somewhere between fifty and sixty people, though much depends on how many of them are infants and small children (the majority of whom sit with their mothers). The bailiff, who is typically but not always male and is usually dressed in a police uniform, ordinarily sits in this area of the courtroom as well.

If one seeks to walk past this (back) part of the courtroom toward the judge and the front of the courtroom, one has to pass through a low wooden gate, which separates the public from the areas designated for officers of the court (mainly lawyers, but also court recorders and others) and individuals providing testimony in the case currently being adjudicated (typically one or two litigants and perhaps a witness or someone else providing testimony on behalf of one of the litigants). This is where lawyers tend to congregate while they are waiting for their cases to be called, though this same general area includes the (partially enclosed) dock, where those charged with criminal offenses provide and listen to testimony, and learn of the sentences and other decisions judges read out to them when they have concluded their deliberations. It also includes, off to the right, the Witness Room (*Bilik Saksi*), where key witnesses are on occasion sequestered (each one separately) until they are called to provide testimony.

One of the more noteworthy features of this general (middle) region of the courtroom is that at any given moment, especially early in the morning when the order in which cases will be called is not yet clear, eight to ten or more *sharia* lawyers may be milling about there, talking and joking among themselves, fiddling with their cell phones and other electronic gadgets, rifling through their briefcases and wheeled tote-bags, arranging documents in front of them, and otherwise waiting for the court recorder to call their cases. The lawyers tend to be young, late twenties or thirties, sometimes a bit older, mostly male, and Malay (always Muslim in any event), and invariably attired, at least in the case of the males among them, in black business suits, conservative neckties, black leather shoes, and black *songkok*. In many instances, they wear black robes over their business suits, as *sharia* judges sometimes do (depending on formal rank) as well. Female lawyers in the *sharia* courts dress in similar fashion, insofar as they tend to wear long black sport coats over their conservative long-sleeved blouses and ankle-length skirts; they sometimes opt to wear black robes (that are more or less the same as those worn by their male counterparts) over these outfits, which are completed by appropriate female headgear (the *tudung*).

Some of the lawyers sit in or near the area designated for the plaintiffs' counsel (*Peguam Plaintif*), others toward the other side of the room that is reserved for the defendant's counsel (*Peguam Defendan*). The tables in each of these areas are equipped with top-notch Dell PCs and microphones, as is the table closer to the judge, which, as the sign atop the table makes clear, is reserved for the Court Recorder/Registrar (*Pendaftar*). The responsibilities of the recorder, whose attire typically resembles that of lawyers (except that it includes a civil-service nametag), include maintaining a written record of the deliberations in each case (something the judge may do as well), circulating documents among the lawyers and litigants involved in each case, announcing which case the judge will hear next, and so on. The recorder, who is often but not always a male, usually types his notes directly into the computer in front of him but does not appear to make an audio version of the transcript that might be used subsequently to check the accuracy of his notes.

We come, finally, to the front of the courtroom, which is clearly reserved for the judge and cannot be approached by anyone other than an officer of the court. The judge's huge wooden desk and oversized chair occupy center stage here. So too, to a lesser degree, does the more encompassing symbolic space surrounding the desk, which has been designed so that it is three or four feet higher than the rest of the courtroom. This area is remarkable for its relative austerity. Aside from the computer (or two), the microphone, and the documents the judge may have spread out before him, which commonly include gazetted enactments relevant to the Federal Territory of Kuala Lumpur, the desk is relatively bare. It sometimes includes a nameplate adorned in block letters with the single word *HAKIM* (JUDGE), sometimes the more specific *HAKIM SYARIE* (*SYARIAH* JUDGE), or the judge's full name and title, indicating whether he is a lower-, high-, or appellate-court judge. And it occasionally includes a generic-looking gavel, though this is less common and I never saw one used in Kuala Lumpur, even though, along with the handcuffs, it is the symbol of choice for those seeking immediately recognizable iconography to help rebrand the *sharia* judiciary.

Before turning to the judge's attire, a few comments are in order as to what litigants and others see when they look toward the judge and in the direction of the front of the courtroom generally. What they see is stark simplicity, for the walls of the courtroom are almost entirely bare (though some of the trim includes muted Malay architectural motifs). A key exception is the pair of calligraphic renderings of the words "Allah" and "Muhammad" (in Arabic script), one on the wall behind the judge, just to his right, the other on the same wall, to his left. In addition to these adornments, there are two flags, one of Malaysia, the other of the Federal Territory of Kuala Lumpur (one to the judge's right, the other to his left).

Nothing else hangs on the walls of the courtroom, not even a clock that might orient those present toward the passage of time, and as mentioned earlier, the courtrooms have no windows. More generally, there are no other decorations or distractions—visual or otherwise—that might possibly divert people's attention from the serious business at hand, except of course personal cell phones and other handheld electronic gadgets, which are ubiquitous but are supposed to be turned off before their owners enter the courtroom. Air conditioning units, which throughout much of Malaysia pose problems in large rooms because they generate so much noise that one cannot always make out what is being said (even by someone sitting or standing relatively nearby), are a non-issue in this new building. This is because they are buried deep inside the walls, ceilings, or floors, and create no noise to speak of, though they keep the rooms so cold that many people find it uncomfortable to sit in them for any length of time without a jacket or sweater. The sounds of passing traffic are likewise inconsequential, though they made it exceedingly difficult to follow proceedings in the building that housed Kuala Lumpur's *sharia* court complex from 1990 to 2011. All in all, the sense one gets from these (new) courtrooms is that they are largely cut off from the rest of the (noisy, chaotic) world, rather than being an integral part of it.

THE ATTIRE OF JUDGES AND OTHER OFFICERS OF THE COURT

I have already mentioned that the attire of *sharia* judges is exceedingly corporate, being more or less identical with high-ranking corporate executives in Malaysia and worldwide, with the notable exception of the civil-service nametag that is part of the uniform: sharply tailored black business suits, crisp white button-down shirts, and fashionable but relatively conservative neckties.[7] The black color chosen for these uniforms helps convey "seriousness, steadiness, formality and self-restraint" (Lurie 1981, 192). Put differently, it signals "the gravity of authority, of power in its solemnity," coupled with impersonal expertise and the ascetic "work-ethical values" central to the kind of corporate success Malaysian political and economic elites have foregrounded as necessary for the development and prosperity of the nation in the new millennium (J. Harvey 1995, 55, 248, 252). In this context, "Black is serious and means business, in more senses than one" (63).

A minor caveat I should register here is that judges tend to wear black leather shoes when entering and leaving the courthouse and walking around the grounds of the building, but not necessarily during proceedings. This is because they usually enter their courtrooms from their carpeted chambers and, like everyone else, they typically remove their shoes before entering the latter quarters, just as Malays invariably take off their shoes before entering their own homes or anyone else's. Hence judges preside over cases without their shoes on, usually in black socks, but sometimes barefoot, as is the habit of Rembau's *sharia* judge, though this is not apparent to most members of the public since their vision of the judge's lower half is obstructed by the imposing desk he sits behind. The more relevant point is that judges' disinclination to wear shoes during proceedings is one of the sole concessions to local custom that one sees in their outfits.

During proceedings, some *sharia* judges don the black fez-like caps known as *songkok,* which are part of the formal costume, at least for men (they are also part of the national dress for men, regardless of ethnic group or religious affiliation, though this is a contested and fraught issue), but others do not. The wearing of black judicial robes (*jubbah*) is also somewhat variable, depending mostly on one's formal rank in the *sharia* hierarchy: appellate and high-court judges are supposed to wear them when they preside over hearings, though they do not always do so. In some cases this is because the robes "make them too hot," as one high-court judge told me, even though they are well aware that lawyers—and perhaps other officers of the court—prefer that they do. Lower-court judges are not allowed to wear these accoutrements of power and prestige. Women appointed to the *sharia* bench are similarly attired, though in lieu of black trousers they wear long black skirts, black sport coats over their *baju kurung,* and a *tudung.* This is more or less the same outfit worn by women who work as *sharia* prosecutors, recorders, registrars, and *sulh* officers. Because most cases in Kuala Lumpur and throughout the nation are heard by lower-court judges, and because men make up nearly 90 percent of the nation's *sharia* judges in any event, the attire of *sharia* judges that is most firmly imprinted in people's minds is the black business suit.

The black business suits worn by male judges contrast quite dramatically with the clothing worn by male litigants—most of whom are defendants—and other men who come to the courthouse to provide evidence or support. Male defendants, who often comprise the bulk of the men in the courtroom (or at least its public seating area) at any given time, are commonly clad in blue jeans or cargo pants, t-shirts (mostly with collars, sometimes not), cheap plastic sandals, and the like, or other relatively lowbrow or transgressively casual attire. Their female counterparts are invariably much better dressed. This is partly because there is more public scrutiny of women's appearance and comportment than men's, and partly because, compared to men, women are more reliant on the court to help them negotiate their relations with their spouses and are thus more concerned to remain in the court's good graces.

It is hard not to see in male defendants' attire a conscious gesture of resistance to the authority of courts and to court officials in particular, who typically hear cases that women bring against them (in their roles as husbands, former husbands, and/or fathers of their children). The broader point is that the sharp contrast in male clothing styles indexes the increasingly large social-class gulf that separates highly specialized middle- and upper-middle-class professionals such as *sharia* judges from the working- and lower-middle-class men (and women) whose problems they are charged with resolving. Put differently and more generally, the "magnetic pull" of the encompassing juridical field, a field dominated by the civil judiciary and the foundational texts that accord it supremacy over the *sharia* judiciary, not only leads *sharia* judges to emulate the attire and other trappings of their civil-court counterparts (and businessmen); it also results in an increasingly large chasm separating them from the ranks of the ordinary (in this context, non-elite) Muslims who make up most of the clientele they serve.

The black-business-suit uniform worn by today's *sharia* judges is mandated by the state as part of an effort to rebrand these judges and the courts over which they exercise (relative) dominion, as mentioned earlier. It remains to add that the rebranding operates on at least four different levels, especially since no single item of clothing or outfit, such as "the veil" or that of the "veiled woman," to cite more widely discussed examples (Smith-Hefner 2007; C. Jones 2010), is intended to convey—or is interpreted by others with reference to—a single set of social meanings, let alone one particular meaning. To put some of this differently, "dress is always both over-determined and polysemic" (J. Harvey 1995, 133).

By way of elaboration, the rebranding speaks first, and perhaps most obviously, to a set of contrasts to be overcome within the juridical field and among the fields that impinge on it and give it shape and meaning. On this level, the contrast between the sartorial styles of new and old *sharia* judges encapsulates differences in training, professional competence, *habitus,* ethos, worldview—including commitment to more or less universal values (justice, equality before the law, due process, etc.) as distinct from the more parochial allegiances and commitments thus implied. A related contrast, ostensibly minimized if not altogether visually erased by the *sharia* judges' new uniforms, is that between present-day *sharia* judges on the one hand and both their civil-law brethren and modern-day businessmen on the other, all of whom have been pressed into national service to help facilitate the nation's achievement of full industrialization by the year 2020.

The second set of contrasts involves alignment or identification with the modern, professionally oriented political party, UMNO, that was the mainstay of the then ruling coalition (*Barison Nasional*) and is increasingly dominated by (Malay) businessmen as distinct from (Malay) civil servants and teachers, as was the case in former times. This alignment simultaneously involves dissociation from the more populist and more "traditionally" oriented (Malay) Islamist opposition party, PAS. PAS represents itself and is widely viewed by others as dominated by *ulama* (religious scholars) and other spiritual leaders who are more inclined to dress in "traditional" Malay attire of a kind that is heavily inflected by Islamic, especially Middle Eastern, style: long flowing gowns, *sarong* or billowy pants with *baju Melayu,* turbans or *songkok,* etc. PAS leaders and their supporters are also inclined to sport more facial hair than their UMNO counterparts, in keeping with the widespread belief that Muslim men should emulate the Prophet by growing beards, especially long ones. Many of the latter generalizations about clothing styles and facial hair also pertain to groups that the state has banned as "deviationist sects," for example, Al-Arqam. This is partly to say that, all things being equal, the black business suit worn by Muslims indexes a style or variant of Islam that the state both accepts and encourages, and that some of the more "traditional" and self-consciously "Middle Eastern" styles of Islamic attire are increasingly seen by authorities as deeply suspect.

Of interest in light of these UMNO vs. PAS contrasts are the sartorial symbols invoked in a September 2013 interview posted online in PAS's official English-language newsletter, *Harakahdaily,* concerning who should fill the number-two spot in the party. The then eighty-three-year old Nik Aziz, who was at once the spiritual advisor to PAS, one of the most revered *ulama* in the nation, and the former chief minister of Kelantan, long a PAS stronghold, denied an intra-party wedge that was rumored to exist "between the professionals and the *ulama.*" To drive home the point, he added that "A professional can be an *ulama* and, likewise, an *ulama* can also be a professional. It does not matter whether they wear neckties or *songkok* because as long as they can expound the Al-Quran and the Hadith, they are considered *ulama*" (*The Star* 2013a).

As far as the Malay and overall Malaysian public is concerned, the contrast thus drawn between neckties and *songkok* (or turbans), professionals and *ulama*, is very heavily freighted, keyed as it is to non-Malays' (and some Malays') concerns that the coming years will see an "Islamist capture" of many professions (Welsh 2008). Indeed, it symbolically condenses many aspects of current struggles over interpretations of the place of Islam in the Federal Constitution and what these contests bode for the future. Nik Aziz's (official) view, though, at least as articulated in the brief comments cited here, is that the contrast encodes a false dichotomy.

Leaving nothing to chance interpretation, those in charge of (re)dressing the *sharia* judiciary—the "wardrobe engineers," as Alison Lurie (1981) famously dubs those who dictate sumptuary codes and fashion trends—have gone him one better by insisting that *sharia* judges wear both neckties *and songkok*, along with the iconic black business suit. Based on my observations in courtrooms, however, both the suit and the necktie (like the crisp white shirt) are internalized as mandatory parts of the uniform, whereas some judges feel that the *songkok* is not, often appearing in court without it. Hence *sharia* judges look much more like professionals than *ulama*, though, like *ulama*, they too are in theory trained to "expound the Al-Quaran and the Hadith," and thus, according to Nik Aziz's (in this context, generous) interpretation, "they are [or may be] considered *ulama*." This capacity or inclination of *sharia* judges to inhabit these two distinct subject positions simultaneously heartens Islamists, just as it raises deep concerns among many Malaysians, especially the non-Muslims among them.

The third contrast indexed and ostensibly transcended by the shift in *sharia* judges' uniforms has to do with the distinction between allegiance to a particular ethnic group (Malays) and religion (Islam) on the one hand, and a commitment to a professionally oriented, cosmopolitan, global "trans-ethnic" community that is unfettered by the relatively parochial sentiments associated with a particular language, culture, ethnicity, race, or religion, on the other. This contrast is related to others that I have noted, but it is also analytically distinct. In this context, the style of rebranding aims not only to convey to Malays and other Muslims that Malayness and Islam can be, and in the Malaysian setting are in fact, thoroughly middle-class, modern, and cosmopolitan. It is also intended to reassure non-Malays that the *sharia* judiciary operates on the basis of more or less universal standards and normativities bearing on justice, equality, and due process, and that for these and other reasons they have no reason to be apprehensive about the advance of Islamization, *sharia*tization, or Malay supremacy. In this we see a universalizing strategy, akin to the formal adoption of the gavel and the handcuffs as key symbols of the *sharia* judiciary, that is also directed at current and future foreign investors, especially Japanese, Chinese, Middle Easterners, Americans, and other Westerners, whose capital and diplomatic support is essential to elites' endeavors to secure Malaysia's position as the center of global Islamic banking and finance. Like many of the other messages conveyed by *sharia* judges' new outfits, these latter messages could not be conveyed by the language of the clothes that *sharia* judges used to wear (Lurie 1981, 261).

The fourth and last contrast to which I draw attention, which is also implicated in other distinctions mentioned earlier, is that between "new Malays" (*Melayu baru*) and those from whose ranks they emerged. The latter are variously referred to as "old Malays" (*Melayu lama*) or simply as Malays (*Melayu*), though these latter categories are not usually linguistically marked in a contrastive way vis-à-vis "new Malays." This is essentially a class distinction, as is suggested by the fact that "new Malays" are sometimes referred to as the "new rich people" (*orang kaya baru,* or *OKB* for short). *OKB* is one of the terms commonly used to gloss the large middle-class group that emerged from a less class-differentiated Malay populace as a consequence of the New Economic Policy (1971–90), its successors (such as the National Development Policy [1991–2001]), and related programs. In this context, *sharia* judges' new outfits are sharply distinguished from the Malay male attire long associated with village set- tings and still seen in many rural and urban situations: *sarong, baju Melayu* or t-shirt, and cheap rubber or plastic sandals, with or without a *songkok;* or alternatively, sturdy work clothes, such as one might wear to plant rice, tap rubber, dig graves or trenches, or venture into orchards or the forest in search of fruit or other produce.

The outfits of *sharia* judges are thus the uniforms of men of the new middle class, signaling, among other things, that members of this class are not engaged in agricultural or other manual labor; that they work in air-conditioned offices; that they drive (or are chauffeured to work in) air-conditioned cars; that they live in air-conditioned homes; and that they enjoy the income (along with access to tai- lors, dry cleaners, and the like) that is necessary to maintain the ever-expanding wardrobes required to accommodate the routines of the newly minted "leisure class" to which they belong (Veblen 1899).

We see much the same thing in neighboring Indonesia, where the business suit has become "the male uniform of the new middle class" (Schulte Nordholt 1997, 12), though less to replace other, more conventional attire than to supplement it. There, as in Malaysia, movement up the social-class hierarchy along with mainte- nance of one's position in middle-class strata or above requires a wardrobe that is more extensive than those normally associated with rural folk, one that expands as new occasions and new leisure routines demand. As Henk Schulte Nordholt, writ- ing in the late 1990s, put it:

[T]he wardrobe of male representatives of the emerging [Indonesian] middle class is still expanding: depending on the occasion, one man in a single week may wear a traditional costume at a wedding, a safari suit during an official meeting, a long-sleeved *batik* shirt at a reception, a business suit or long-sleeved shirt with tie during office hours, and a *sarong* when he goes to Friday prayers, not to mention expensive leisure wear on the golf course (25).

The recent history of the black business suit in Indonesia appears to diverge in important ways from what we see in Malaysia, though there has been little research directly on the subject in either setting, especially Malaysia. Indonesian President Sukarno (r. 1946–65) commonly wore black business suits when making speeches and in other public appearances, in keeping with the early revolutionary view that those who wore such garments could demand and might well receive more equitable treatment from the Dutch. Sukarno's successor, military strongman Suharto (r. 1965–98), opted instead for safari suits, batik shirts, and military uniforms as more culturally authentic and politically appropriate garments (Taylor 1997). Suharto's penchant for military outfits led, especially in the 1980s, to what some have referred to as "uniform fever" (Schulte Nordholt 1997, 5; see also Frederick 1997; Sekimoto 1997) and to the relative fall from grace of the black business suit as nationalist symbol. No such fever has ever broken out in Malaysia, due partly, perhaps, to the relative unimportance in governance and public life of the military as compared with Indonesia, coupled with the related fact that Malaysia (then Malaya) attained its independence from the British without the kind of protracted and bloody military struggle that was required for Indonesia to win its independence from the Dutch. The "Sukarno to Suharto" shift in men's sartorial styles, moreover, has no Malaysian counterpart other than a reversal of that pattern, which can be observed when one compares the Mahathir era (1981–2003) to the years since. Mahathir favored batik shirts and safari suits in particular, his successors the black business suit.

"Black-business-suit fever" has reemerged in Indonesia but is nowadays associated with business/corporate culture. And it is clearly endemic in much of East Asia—Japan and its "salarymen" come immediately to mind—just as it is deeply entrenched in Malaysia, both in business/corporate sectors and the civil service (including the *sharia* judiciary), and far beyond. So too is the penchant for golf that is referenced in Schulte Nordholt's previously cited comments about the expanding wardrobe of Indonesia's middle-class men.

In Malaysia (and beyond) the wearing of black business suits at work and the playing of golf in one's leisure time are clearly part of a single "cultural package." This was impressed upon me in September 2013 when, after a year-long absence from Malaysia, I made a hastily arranged and poorly timed visit to Kuala Lumpur's *sharia* courthouse. Despite the information provided on the flat-screen TV monitor in the building's lobby and other signs indicating that a good number of the courtrooms were scheduled for hearings that day, I discovered that this was not the case. The reason: many members of the *sharia* bench assigned to Kuala Lumpur (and other jurisdictions) had been flown by the government to Kuching, Sarawak, to compete in the Malaysian *Syariah* Judiciary [JKSM] Invitational Golf Tournament that was held at Damai Golf and Country Club. According to one press report: "the golfers consist[ed] of senior ranking officers from JKSM and local dignitaries," the tournament being one of "the side activities organized in conjunction with the 15th Malaysian *Syariah* Officers' Conference." Organizing committee chairman Mohammad Mokarat noted that "over 400 delegates from throughout the country . . . [would] be attending the event . . . from Sept 8 to 10, including those invited from neighboring Brunei, Singapore, Indonesia and the Philippines," and that the conference would take place at the Sheraton Four Points Hotel, a luxurious five-star property (*Borneo Post Online* 2013).

On a comparative-historical note, the *kadi* from Rembau I came to know in the late 1980s, who wore relatively plebeian attire, as mentioned earlier, had a penchant for the game of ping-pong that he regularly indulged with male staff during their tea- and lunch-breaks, utilizing the ping-pong table squeezed into one of the staff-only rooms in the courthouse. This relatively lowbrow pastime did not require any special (let alone expansive, luxurious, or ecologically disastrous) facilities, clothes, membership fees, or equipment, other than inexpensive paddles and balls, and the one-time purchase of a cheap ping-pong table that the government may have subsidized. I do not know if the *kadi* also played golf, though I would guess not; and I have no idea if many of today's *sharia* judges play ping-pong in addition to golf. More important is the rise and spread of "a golf-and-country-club" cultural complex in Malaysia and the *sharia* judiciary's close alignment and involvement with it. This is striking evidence of the kinds of social-class transformations that have occurred in recent decades. So too, to summarize, are the black-business-suit uniforms worn by today's *sharia* judges and other officers of the *sharia* court, especially when viewed in relation to the relatively downmarket attire of the majority of male litigants who appear before them.

ON JUDICIAL PROCESS, REPUDIATIONS, AND LAWYERS

Changes in the attire of judges (and other officers of the *sharia* court) discussed in the previous section have coincided with other transformations that have been pursued by political and religious elites seeking to enhance the power and prestige of the *sharia* courts in relation to their main competitor and patron, the civil judiciary. Foremost among the latter changes are those bearing on judicial process. Chapter 2 discussed some of the shifts in judicial process that have occurred in *sharia* courts in small towns such as Rembau—elements of which are readily apparent in large urban areas like Kuala Lumpur as well. In the next section of this chapter I expand the analysis by addressing other dimensions of these changes, particularly those associated with the greatly enhanced role of lawyers in *sharia* hearings in urban settings such as Kuala Lumpur, where they are estimated to be involved in roughly 60 percent of all cases.

I focus on a case involving a female plaintiff seeking clarification of her marital status after her husband may have thrice repudiated her (by pronouncing the *talak*) outside of court and without the court's permission, in a hearing that her lawyer dominated, effectively sidelining both her and the judge. In my commentary on the case, I provide brief remarks on the use of oaths (*ikrar* and *sumpah*) and the *taklik*/conditionality clause that husbands increasingly invoke to threaten, discipline, and control their wives. I then turn to a discussion of the transformative role played by lawyers in *sharia* hearings, elaborating on why some officers of the court (such as Encik Ahmad, profiled in the previous chapter) have grave misgivings about this development.

CASE 5

*A Woman Seeking Clarification of Her Marital Status
in a Hearing Thoroughly Dominated by Her Lawyer*

This hearing, which took place in in July 2012, involved a female plaintiff, probably in her mid-to-late thirties, seeking to clarify her ambiguous marital status some years after her husband, who was around the same age, pronounced three separate *talak* outside of court and without the court's permission. The ambiguity stemmed in part from the conditional nature of two of the three pronouncements, which entailed statements like "I will divorce you if you do that [again]," as distinct from "I [hereby] divorce you." Those present included the (male) judge, the plaintiff, her husband (the defendant), her (male) lawyer, her husband's (male) lawyer, along with the registrar, the bailiff, members of the public (most of whom were awaiting their hearings), perhaps a few other lawyers waiting for their cases to be called, me, and my male research assistant (Ikmal). Neither the husband nor his lawyer spoke during the session, partly because the judge adjourned the hearing immediately after the plaintiff's lawyer finished eliciting her testimony, hence before her husband's lawyer had a chance to cross-examine her or obtain his client's version of what had transpired between the couple and brought them to court.

The hearing began with the registrar reading out the number of the case and the names of the two principals. The plaintiff's lawyer (PL) then rose from his seat and asked the plaintiff (P) to enter the witness box and recite the oath (*ikrar*), the wording of which was indicated on a laminated sheet that the registrar handed to her to read aloud. Throughout the remainder of the hearing, the plaintiff's lawyer initiated all of the dialogue, except for the minimalist but key performative utterance on the part of the judge, at the very end of the session, to the effect that the hearing was adjourned. The plaintiff spoke only when addressed by her lawyer, and confined almost all of her remarks to answering his questions in a narrow, matter-of-fact way. She appeared to have been well coached as to the most efficacious way to convey her message and obtain justice.

P: I . . . [mentions name and IC number] with utmost sincerity and the purity of my heart, acknowledge/pledge/swear that everything I mention in the court shall be the truth, the whole truth, and nothing but the truth.

PL: Answer accordingly. Please [re]state your name and IC number.

P: [Restates this information.]

PL: Can you state your address and occupation?

P: [She provides her address, adding] I work as a freelance trainer.

PL: What is the purpose of your presence in court?

P: I am here to petition for validation of the pronouncement of divorce (*tuntutan pengesahan lafaz cerai*).

PL: Who pronounced it?

P: My husband.

PL: What is the your husband's name?

P: [She provides his name: Ismail bin . . . .]

PL: Is Mr. Ismail present?

P: Yes.

PL: When were you and Mr. Ismail married?

P: On December 28, 2001.

PL: Did you bring the original copy of your marriage certificate as evidence?

P: Yes. [She hands it to her lawyer.]

PL: [He confirms the marriage date but then adds] I request the court's confirmation. It says December 27, 2001. I request an amendment of the marriage date. Is that correct, Ma'am?

P: Just go with [what] the marriage certificate [says].

PL: Are you sure? Your Honor, I retract my earlier request. The date [of the marriage] is December 27, 2001. Do you have any children, Ma'am?

P: Yes, I have three children.

PL: Can I have their names?

P: Yes. [She mentions the names of the children.]

PL: How many *lafaz* are you referring to?

P: Three.

PL: Please explain the first one.

P: In 2004, at 1 o'clock in the afternoon, the defendant said, "If you don't open the door, I divorce you" (*Kalau awak tak buka pintu, saya ceraikan awak*). Concerning the second *lafaz*, he said, "Rusila, I divorce you with one *talak*" (*Rusila, aku ceraikan engkau dengan talak satu*). And the third one, he said, "If you go first, I will divorce you" (*Kalau awak pergi dulu, saya ceraikan awak*).

PL: Where did the first *talak* happen?

P: In a rental house [located at . . .].

PL: Whose house is that?

P: My husband rented the house.

PL: Is it a *rumah kelamin* [conjugal residence]?

P: I do not understand the question.

PL: *Rumah kelamin* is a house where both husband and wife stay together.

P: Yes, then it is.

PL: Where did the *lafaz* happen?

P: Outside the house.

PL: What type of dwelling was it? A terrace house, or a flat in an apartment building?

P: A flat on the ground floor.

PL: What happened before the *lafaz*?

P: We had an argument because my husband was angry and wanted to beat our year-and-a-half-old son with a rattan cane. I brought our son into the first room in the house and locked the door.

PL: Where were you when the *lafaz* was uttered?

P: In the room.

PL: Where was the defendant?

P: He was outside the house. From inside the room, there is a window that looks out of the house. My husband was at the window when he pronounced the *lafaz*.

PL: Were you able to see your husband outside the house?

P: Yes.

PL: How long after you locked the door did you hear your husband utter the *lafaz*?

P: Probably around 15–30 minutes.

PL: Does the house have a living room? What is the distance between the main door of the house and the room you were in?

P: It is very near, as it is only a flat.

PL: When you heard the *lafaz,* was there any possibility that another person uttered it?

P: No. I am sure it was the voice of my husband, who was angry at that time.

PL: When the *lafaz* was uttered, where was your husband?

P: He was going from inside the house to the outside, which is where he uttered the *lafaz*.

PL: After you heard the *lafaz* being uttered, what happened to you, Ma'am?

P: I slumped down on the wall, far from the window, and sat quietly.

PL: After your husband uttered the *lafaz,* did you open the door?

P: No.

PL: How long were you in the room?

P: I cannot remember, but it was a very long time. Probably up to a few hours.

PL: Did you go out at anytime?

P: No I did not, until my husband broke the doorknob from outside.

PL: After he broke the doorknob, did you open the door?

P: No, my husband opened it from the outside.

PL: Did you leave the room?

P: Yes.

PL: After leaving, did you enter the room again at any time?

P: Yes, for daily chores.

PL: After he broke the doorknob, did you ask him the meaning of his *lafaz*?

P: Yes, I did. He said that in order for me to report it to the court, I [would] need to present a witness.

PL: Did you ask your husband if he intended to divorce you by means of the *lafaz*?

P: I said to him, "You just uttered a *taklik* divorce on me." He said I was mistaken.

PL: Did your husband mention that he wanted to reconcile with you (*rujuk*)?

P: Yes.

PL: Were you still with your husband after that?

P: Yes.

PL: Who else was in the house at the time?

P: Only me and our one-year-old child.

PL: Are you sure that was your husband's voice uttering the *talak*?

P: Yes, I am sure.

PL: When your husband was in a state of anger, describe how angry he was.

P: He was definitely very angry, and in his hand he had the long, thin rattan cane that belongs to me as a teacher.

PL: When he entered the room, was he sane (*waras*) or not due to anger?

P: He was sane.

PL: Was he drunk or intoxicated (*mabuk*)?

P: No.

PL: Was there any noise around the time of the *lafaz*? Are there any roads in front of the house?

P: Between the blocks [of apartment buildings] there is a stretch of road. But it was not busy at the time.

PL: Before the *lafaz*, was the television turned on?

P: I am not very sure about that.

PL: Did you tell anyone else about the *lafaz*?

P: No, I did not.

PL: I refer to the defendant's defense statement. Do you agree with it or deny it?

P: No, I do not agree with it. I deny it fully. Only the part where he says I locked myself in the room with our child is true. I do not agree that I'd lost control (*hilang kewalan*) and that he was scared.

PL: For the second *lafaz*, please explain the situation and what was uttered.

P: In 2005, one night [she could not remember date and time] my husband said, "Rusila, I divorce you with one *talak*."

PL: I refer to the defendant's defense statement. Did he reconcile with you (*rujuk*) after that?

P: Yes, in the same year, 2005. It was in Penang; I was assigned to work there for two weeks.

PL: When was it?

P: It was a few weeks after the second *lafaz*.

PL: Do you remember how it happened?

P: My husband came to Penang and said to me, "I *rujuk balik* (reconcile) with you" in the hotel where I was staying.

PL: For the third *lafaz*, please explain the utterance and where it happened.

P: My husband said, "If you leave first, I divorce you" [*Kalau awak pergi dulu, saya ceraikan awak*]. It happened in a house rented by my husband, located at . . . .

PL: What type of dwelling was it?

P: A flat.

PL: When did it happen?

P: In 2008, at 7:30 in the morning.

PL: Did it happen inside the house?

P: Yes.

PL: What happened before that?

P: I was getting ready for work, while also preparing the children for school. I tried waking up my husband before that, but it was only when everyone was ready and the children were in the car that my husband woke up and started preparing for work. He was brushing his teeth in the kitchen sink when I mentioned to him that I wanted to go first with the children. He then asked me to take him to KLCC [Kuala Lumpur City Centre] first. I said that [if I did], I wouldn't make it to work on time, and I immediately went to work. It was before that, when he was still brushing teeth, that he uttered the *lafaz*.

PL: What did you hear when you were about to leave the house?

P: I heard him utter the *lafaz* clearly. He took the toothbrush out from his mouth before uttering it.

PL: How far was it between you and your husband?

P: I was at the door, and he was in the kitchen. It was about 5–6 arms' lengths.

PL: Were you facing . . . your husband?

P: I was facing him because he had called me in.

PL: Was there any noise at that time?

P: The television wasn't on, but the road was quite busy in front of the house.

PL: Is there any possibility that the *lafaz* was unclear to you?

P: No, . . . the *lafaz* was clear.

PL: Was your husband [fully] conscious or not, as he had just woken up?

P: He was brushing his teeth, so I am sure he was wide awake.

PL: Were you talking to your husband when it happened?

P: No, I was busy preparing the children.

PL: After the *lafaz* was uttered, what did you do? . . .

P: [Said something about the third *lafaz* also being a *lafaz taklik*, like the first one.]

PL: After you went to work, did you ask your husband about the *lafaz*?

P: No. Only after coming back from work did I ask him.

PL: What did he say?

P: I asked, 'You uttered a *lafaz taklik*. I want to go to the court to report it. What should we do?' I discussed with my husband our next course of action. He said that there were no witnesses, so it wasn't possible for us to bring it to court. There wasn't anyone at home at the time of the *lafaz*, except for the children who were in the car.

PL: Did you ask anyone about it?

P: I asked [someone] at the religion office (*Pejabat Agama*).

PL: After the *lafaz*, did he reconcile (*rujuk*) with you?

P: No.

PL: Did you continue to have sexual relations (*hubungan kelamin*) with your husband?

P: Yes.

PL: Did you obtain any child through the relations?

P: Yes, one child.

PL: Are there any other *lafaz* you want to add to the existing statement?

P: No.

At this juncture, the judge, who had not uttered a word throughout the entire session, proclaimed that the hearing was adjourned and would resume with the cross-examination of the plaintiff (*soal balas plaintif*, as he phrased it). I did not catch the date chosen for the next hearing in this case; but based on my experience in this courthouse, I would guess that it was scheduled for an early- to mid-morning weekday five to seven weeks down the road.

Commentary

My remarks in this section focus partly on the effects of having lawyers involved in *sharia* hearings and partly on a range of other matters, such as the use of oaths, husbands' use and abuse of *taklik* or "conditional divorce," and the fact that one of the greatest challenges women face in going to court is having to deal with their husbands' manipulations of language and law.

Concerning Oaths.   The *ikrar* enunciated by the plaintiff prior to testifying in this hearing—" . . . with utmost sincerity and the purity of my heart, [I] acknowledge/pledge/swear that everything I mention in the court shall be the truth, the whole truth, and nothing but the truth"—is the more generic and less "weighty" of the two types of oaths administered in *sharia* courts in Kuala Lumpur and elsewhere in the nation. Judges and other officers of the court (such as registrars) must decide whether this oath, the wording of which is drawn directly and proudly from the oaths administered in civil courts, is likely to be sufficient to (help) guarantee truthfulness on the part of those providing testimony, or if a weightier and more specifically Islamic oath may be required in light of the evidence, ambiguities, and gravity of the case. Alternatively, they may decide that no oaths need to be administered. Some of the criminal cases I observed in Rembau in 2013, for example, did not involve any oath-taking. This may have been because the judge knew or assumed that the male defendants in question were going to plead guilty, and was thus not concerned with the possibility of their providing false testimony.

The second of the two oaths mentioned here, which is less commonly administered than the first, involves a declaration known as the *sumpah laknat Allah, sumpah laknat,* or simply *sumpah* (oath or solemn promise involving the possibility of punishment by God in this life and the Hereafter). It tends to be used if concrete, written evidence is lacking, insufficient, or ambiguous, and/or if the case is brought by a female plaintiff seeking *fasakh,* which, in the absence of truly compelling evidence, judges are generally reluctant to effect (though they are increasingly willing to do so; see chapter 5) since it involves undoing a sacred covenant. The most common variant of this oath I encountered is as follows:

> I seek forgiveness from Allah, I seek forgiveness from Allah, I seek forgiveness from Allah. In the name of Allah, the most compassionate, and all merciful. By Allah, by Allah, by Allah, I . . . [name and IC number] swear in the name of Allah [concerning the information] which I have provided . . . regarding . . ., and if I lie, I shall incur the wrath of Allah and His punishment in this world and in the Hereafter.

Another version of this *sumpah* that I encountered in Kuala Lumpur includes all of the above, in addition to the declaration of faith or *syahadah:* "There is no God but Allah, and Muhammad is his Prophet."

For a variety of reasons, female litigants are somewhat more likely than male litigants to be asked to recite the *sumpah,* though in any given hearing judges (or registrars) tend to select a single type of oath for both parties. This gender-skewing is partly a function of the fact that men don't always show up for their hearings, even when they face serious charges that could result in a judge approving their wives' petitions for a *fasakh* divorce, and thus cannot be administered an oath of any sort. Relevant as well is that most plaintiffs are women, and in many instances the charges they bring can result in their husbands or former husbands facing serious criminal charges at a later date (as when a husband has pronounced the *talak* outside of court and without the court's permission, has taken a second wife without the court's permission, and so on). The likelihood of women facing criminal charges in consequence of their husbands' petitions against them is much smaller, indeed, in my experience, largely nonexistent.

The somewhat greater likelihood of female litigants being asked to recite the *sumpah* is not, in other words, attributable to a belief that women are more inclined than men toward overt, intentional deception (such beliefs do exist in some quarters, as we saw in the last chapter, but they pale in comparison to the majority view on this matter), and that, as such, they need to be administered the most weighty of oaths in order to help guarantee their truthfulness. The classical Islamic stipulation that a man's testimony is worth twice the value of a woman's is not germane here either, for this convention has no traction in today's Islamic courts and in my experience since the late 1980s never has. Noteworthy as well is that litigants rarely challenge adversaries they believe to be offering (or likely to provide) false testimony to swear any kind of oath—something that is done on the assumption that a person's failure or reluctance to swear an oath amounts to an admission that his or her testimony violates the canons of truth, as Lawrence Rosen (1989) has reported for Morocco. I saw one such challenge in Rembau in the late 1980s but have never seen once since. This is largely because the prerogatives to initiate and administer oaths lie primarily with the judge and other officers of the court, in other words, the state.

Taklik Divorce. This type of marital dissolution is usually initiated by a woman on the grounds that her husband has violated one (or more) of the conditions specified in writing in the marriage contract (*akad nikah*) prior to the solemnization of marriage and the signing of the relevant paperwork. Conditions commonly stipulated involve matters of considerable consequence, including taking a second wife without the first wife's knowledge or approval; being absent from the conjugal residence for a period exceeding three (sometimes, depending on the state, four or six) months; and failing to provide maintenance or send news of one's whereabouts for a comparable period of time. The idea here is that if conditions enumerated in the marriage contract are violated by the husband, the wife has clear grounds for obtaining a divorce, though she must go to court to prove to the judge's satisfaction that a violation has occurred.

In the hearing at issue, the wife was not seeking a *taklik* divorce, but, rather, the judge's confirmation (or disconfirmation) of the validity of the *talak* pronounced by her husband. But she did recount that two of the three *talak* were conditional (*taklik*) in the sense that the husband reportedly uttered words along the lines of "I will divorce you if you don't open the door," and later, "I will divorce you if you take the kids to school before dropping me off at KLCC"—as distinct from "I [hereby] divorce you." On both occasions she reported responding with words to the effect that "You just pronounced a *taklik* divorce on me," though he denied it in one instance and effectively agreed in another by proceeding to reconcile (*rujuk*) with her, something that is only done in the aftermath of a *talak*.

One of the striking things here is the use and abuse of the *taklik*/conditionality clause by husbands to threaten, discipline, and control their wives in the context of relatively minor domestic disagreements. Another instance of this that I encountered in 2012 in the same (Kuala Lumpur) court had to do with a husband threatening his wife that he would divorce her if she used a cell phone or went to work outside their home. Yet another case, this one from Rembau in 2013, involved a man who had observed his wife sharing an umbrella with another man during a downpour and proceeded to tell her "I will divorce you if I ever see you sharing an umbrella with that guy again." I saw much less of this in Rembau in the late 1980s, and am inclined to interpret what I take to be its increased frequency as evidence of men's heightened sense that they do not enjoy as much control over (or clout with) their wives as they used to—or should have—and that, as a consequence, they need to threaten them with divorce and abandonment in ways that were previously unnecessary.

Note in any event that there is a good deal of linguistic and legal ambiguity created and manipulated by the husband in the case at hand, including his false assertion that his wife could not report his *talak* to authorities because there were no witnesses. Bear in mind too that, as in times past, husbands generally have a better command of language and law than their wives, and are thus far better positioned to exploit such ambiguities and the ambivalences associated with them (Peletz 2002).

On Lawyers and Lawyering.   I mentioned earlier that one of the characteristic features of disputes aired in Kuala Lumpur's *sharia* courthouse is that they tend to involve lawyers, and that the participation of lawyers in *sharia* hearings alters them in significant ways, analogous in some respects to the involvement of *sharia* prosecutors. In this instance, with two important exceptions, the entire hearing was choreographed by the plaintiff's lawyer, albeit in accordance with courtroom protocol as specified in the *Syariah Court Civil Procedure (Federal Territories) Act 1998 (Act 585) and Rules* and other relevant enactments based on the civil-court regimes from which they are consciously and proudly drawn. The two exceptions—the registrar's instructions to the plaintiff to recite the oath and the judge's performative utterance proclaiming the adjournment of the hearing—were more than mere bookends, to be sure, for each in its own way helped define the juridical ritual that was the hearing.

Consider in addition the sharp contrast between the hearing transcribed here and *sulh* sessions, which share deep resonance with court hearings in Rembau and elsewhere in Malaysia during the late 1980s and long before. The wide-ranging narrative of the female plaintiff in the Rembau *sulh* session I discussed (case 3) bears strong resemblance to that of her Indonesia-born counterpart (case 4), as do the relatively far-flung narratives of the husbands in question. In both of those cases, moreover, we saw a good deal of emotion displayed by the litigants (especially the women), frequent interruptions, and a mixed record at best in terms of honoring the *sulh* officers' injunctions that the couples should observe formal turn-taking, should be polite and not insult or interrupt one another, and should remain focused on the central issues in contention. The plaintiff in case 3 in particular seemed primarily concerned to give voice to her feelings of hurt, betrayal, and injustice, and to do so in a relatively public albeit confidential context, as we have seen.

Based on the hearing that is the focus of this discussion and on others that are like it in the sense that they involve lawyers, it would be overly simplistic to claim that the voices of women, especially as plaintiffs, are silenced by present-day dynamics in *sharia* courtrooms. But women's voices are certainly far more regulated, restricted, and otherwise constrained when lawyers are present, even when, as in this instance, the lawyer had been retained by the woman in question. The larger issue is the regulation, restriction, and overall constraint of women's agency, though this is more complicated since one could perhaps just as well argue that women are exercising their agency (and giving voice to their concerns) through or with the help of their lawyers, and that without such ventriloquized assistance their agency is likely to yield little of value. Clearly, much turns on the notion of "value." A narrow materialist rendering of the term would miss the point that what some women seek in going to court is primarily a venue to articulate their objections to the injustices and other mistreatment they have been subjected to at the hands of their husbands, and to do so in their own voices, in terms—figures of speech, intonations, etc.—of their own choosing.

Women's voices and experiences in court are further constrained and transformed in largely negative ways if their husbands have also hired counsel. In aggressively defending their clients, husbands' lawyers, who are typically male, commonly endeavor to discredit (if not belittle and humiliate) the women who have brought charges against them or are otherwise involved as adversaries. (Women's lawyers often subject husbands to the same kind of treatment, as discussed later on, but men seem less rattled by this experience.) This sometimes involves a husband's lawyer cross-examining a wife and proceeding laboriously through a large binder of photocopied receipts submitted to the court as evidence of costs involved in raising children. In such cases, the husband's lawyer demands that the wife verify the date and amount of each specific purchase or expense and confirm that none of the receipts or invoices are duplicates and that each and every one of them was really for (and necessary to) the upkeep and education of the child(ren) rather than for the wife herself. In one case involving child support (*nafkah anak*) that I observed in Kuala Lumpur in 2013, the lawyer for the husband, who was an artist or stage performer and a *haji*, spent an excruciating twenty to twenty-five minutes badgering the estranged wife in this way. He prefaced each query with "And I put it to you that . . . " and concluded each with a very pointed, unnecessarily loud, and belligerently intoned, "Do you agree or not?" ("*Setuju, tak?*"). In another case, in Rembau a few months earlier, the husband's lawyer proceeded in similar fashion, spending a considerable amount of time grilling the wife on the price of milk, diapers, and school expenses.

A quick comparative note is that while in decades past women were sometimes subjected to broadly analogous questioning by *sharia* judges, the judges' goals were generally to keep marriages intact and to find common ground on which an estranged husband and wife might agree and thus be able to reestablish their relationship on an amicable footing. This often meant allowing husbands and especially wives to engage in wide-ranging narratives and accusations, many features of which were not legally salient, as we have seen. A husband's lawyer by contrast does not typically have these ("family friendly") goals in mind. Rather, his aim is to secure the most advantage for his client, by whatever means possible, even if it means fabricating charges of *nusyuz* (spousal, especially wifely, disobedience), and to limit the wife's remarks to short responses to the questions he has strategically chosen to ask. Partly for reasons such as these, it is reasonable to assume that for many women going to court, facing the opposing lawyer is at least as frightening as facing the judge, much as Franz Kafka (1925) famously described for the chief protagonist in *The Trial*.

It is not only the narratives of female plaintiffs, or of litigants generally, that are effectively sidelined by lawyers' increasingly active participation in *sharia* hearings. Judges' involvement is also heavily constrained by the active roles that lawyers assume in questioning litigants and otherwise choreographing what transpires in terms of discourse and practice alike. Relevant here is a hearing in Rembau I attended in 2013 that involved a "conditional *talak*," much like two of the three *talak* at issue in case 5. There were no lawyers involved in the Rembau hearing; hence all of the questions about the exact wording of the *talak* and other matters were framed and articulated by the judge, who spoke directly to the female plaintiff and her husband (the defendant), and vice versa. In that instance, there was more or less complete agreement between the husband and wife as to the wording and conditional nature of what the husband had said some months previously, after he had observed his wife sharing an umbrella with another man during a downpour—which, as noted earlier, was something like, "If I see you with that guy again, I will divorce you." Since the husband made clear to the judge that he did not see his wife with the man again, the judge deemed the couple's marital status to be unchanged by the husband's utterance. In such hearings, it is also the judge, not a lawyer or another third party, who endeavors to ascertain the husband's state of mind at the time he pronounced the *talak,* whether he was angry (and if so, how angry he was), conscious, fully awake, lucid/sane, free of the influence of intoxicants, etc. These two sets of issues—the precise wording of the *talak* and the husband's state of mind when he uttered it—are the most legally salient facts associated with out-of-court *talak* and their validity from the court's point of view.

In the Kuala Lumpur hearing (case 5), in contrast, it was a lawyer, not the judge, who elicited the relevant testimony and established legally salient facts. Does it matter if a lawyer as distinct from a judge assumes center stage here, by eliciting testimony, establishing the facts, and otherwise shaping the narratives of litigants? I would say it matters a great deal, especially in light of some of the negative perceptions of *sharia* lawyers outlined in the previous chapter. The practices and overall comportment of *sharia* judges are generally viewed as informed if not driven by an Islamically-inflected sense of justice and fair play coupled with a commitment to marriage and family, however narrowly, patriarchally, and heteronormatively defined in the view of some critics. *Sharia* lawyers, by contrast, are assumed to be driven by a concern to win the case for their clients—and to keep the meter running so as to rack up large fees. This is despite the fact that they too may be viewed as toiling on behalf of the *ummah* to advance the cause of Islam, partly by mobilizing their professional organizations to lobby the government to expand the scope and force of *sharia.* It is no coincidence that the lawyer in the hearing at issue here spent at least fifteen excruciating minutes eliciting the details of the first *talak,* when two to three minutes surely would have sufficed to convey all of the basics to the judge. Such exceedingly laborious delineation of legally salient facts—along with rigorous, oftentimes highly aggressive, confrontational and dismissive cross-examination of their clients' adversaries or detractors—is by no means uncommon when lawyers are involved in *sharia* hearings.

We have also seen from the *sulh* officer who formerly worked as a *sharia* lawyer but abandoned that trade for a more *halal* way of making a living (chapter 3) that *sharia* lawyers are assumed to lie if necessary on behalf of their clients, so as to win their cases and by extension burnish their reputations and build up their practices and those of the firms that employ them. Indeed, judges and other officers of the court, along with women's rights groups, among others, are well aware that lawyers hired by male defendants in matrimonial cases commonly endeavor to derail or undercut women's petitions for support by charging them with *nusyuz,* even when there is no clear evidence and no belief on their part that *nusyuz* has in fact occurred. My interviews with judges and various members of the *sharia* administrative hierarchy indicate that counter-charges of *nusyuz* are usually unsuccessful. This is because husbands' lawyers typically have no convincing evidence. Moreover, even when *nusyuz* may have occurred, a husband must demonstrate to the judge's satisfaction that he endeavored to educate his wife as to the meanings of *nusyuz* and otherwise bring her back to "the proper path."

Most relevant here is not that the defense tactic of counter-charging a wife with *nusyuz* is generally ineffective from a judge's point of view, or that even threatening to raise the specter of *nusyuz* has a chilling effect on women's commitment to seeking justice (or getting even), although that is beyond dispute. Rather, it is that this tactic feeds into views that lawyers will engage in behavior that is unethical if not overtly dishonest in order to win cases for their clients or at least limit the damages they are likely to incur as a result of being taken to court.

For reasons noted earlier, public perceptions of *sharia* judges are much less likely to entail assumptions that their discourses and practices are tainted by pecuniary and related considerations. The bottom line is that *sharia* judges are mandated to work for the (Muslim) public and the (Muslim) public good; they are, recall, civil servants. *Sharia* lawyers, on the other hand, work for individual litigants, for themselves, and for the increasingly corporate firms that employ them (though some are attached to legal aid bureaus that provide inexpensive or pro bono services). The proliferation of lawyers in *sharia* courtrooms, the effective ceding to them of various features of the judicial process previously controlled by the state—which is analogous to outsourcing—and the relative eclipsing of judges in that process, thus entails an unmistakable process of privatization cum corporatization that dovetails with the massive expansion of RELA forces and other types of community policing discussed in chapter 2. In recent decades we have seen the same general dynamics associated with privatization and corporatization in other domains of Malaysian governance, business, politics, culture, and religion, especially in areas such as health care, water supply, and transportation (Jomo K. S. 1995; Gomez and Jomo K. S. 1997; Tan 2007; King 2008).

Some observers are concerned that with the much greater stakes increasingly involved in the divorces (and inheritance disputes) of wealthy urbanites, celebrities, and politicians, corruption may begin to rear its ugly head on the *sharia* bench, much like what has been widely reported to occur in high-profile civil-court cases involving the awarding of multimillion-dollar contracts to family members and business associates of well-placed (usually UMNO) politicians. Whether or not this proves to be the case, there is no question that the creation of a new Malay middle class and the mindboggling enrichment of Malays situated at the apex of the social-class hierarchy have transformed the stakes and tenor of matrimonial hearings.

An example of the astronomical scope of assets sometimes involved in high-profile divorce cases involving the nation's (Malay) rich and famous was reported in the online version of *The Star* on December 20, 2012, under the headline "Ex-Wife Wants Taib's Son to Pay RM121 mil [around US$40 million] in Maintenance." The article recounted that a few weeks earlier forty-eight-year-old Shahnaz Majid, the sister of nationally famous singer Sheila Majid, had filed a suit in the *Syariah* High Court in Kuala Lumpur against her former husband, Datuk Seri Mahmud Abu Bekir Taib, the son of Sarawak Chief Minister Tan Sri Abdul Taib Mahmud. The couple married in 1992, had a son (Raden Murya) about a year later, and divorced in 2011, by which time their son was enrolled in college in Britain. In a previous hearing, custody of the son was awarded to Shahnaz, but apparently there was no stipulation during that hearing (or any others) concerning his maintenance. Alleging in her 2012 suit that subsequent to their divorce, "her former husband . . . failed to pay any maintenance," Shahnaz petitioned the court for "an education trust fund of RM40 mil and a RM60 mil terrace house in London," in addition to "tuition fees . . . amounting to RM315,000, two Aston Martin cars, air travel for six times a year, RM10,000 for books, RM72,000 for pocket money, RM5mil medical insurance and monthly pocket money for two years totaling RM72,000." The article goes on to note that Shahnaz had earlier filed a claim of "RM300mil in matrimonial property and RM100mil in *mutaah* (gifts) as a divorce settlement," and was also "claiming 50% of all assets owned by Mahmud Abu Bekir." But it never broaches the glaring question: how did the son of Sarawak's Chief Minister get so rich?[8]

Not concidentally, Shahnaz's counsel, Dr. Mohd Rafie bin Mohd Shafie, is one of the most high-profile and successful *sharia* lawyers in the country. The offices of the law firm he runs are located on the seventeenth floor of a prestigious and imposing thirty-nine-story building situated on a prime piece of real estate in the upscale Bangsar neighborhood of Kuala Lumpur. Dr. Rafie's business card and website indicate that he received an LL.B. with Honors in Buckingham, England, and that he obtained certification as a Barrister-at-Law from Lincoln's Inn, London, as well as a Master of Comparative Laws, a PGD in Islamic Banking and Finance, and a Diploma in *Sharia* Law and Practice, all from the IIUM, along with a Ph.D. from Washington International University (USA). I crossed paths and spoke briefly with Dr. Rafie, who appears to be in his sixties and is of South Asian (perhaps Pakistani) ancestry, on a couple of occasions during 2010–12, and also had the opportunity to observe him in action, in a case unrelated to Shahnaz's, during a visit to Kuala Lumpur's *sharia* courthouse in July 2012.

In that case, which involved a divorced couple with two or three children wrangling over property, maintenance, and related matters, Dr. Rafie represented the former wife (the plaintiff) and effectively monopolized the hearing. Virtually all of it was taken up with his highly aggressive interrogation of the former husband (the defendant) about his wages, a subject the latter clearly did not want to broach, judging from his repeated waffling, dissimulation, and evasive answers, though he was forced to acknowledge at one point that they were on the order of RM$8–10,000 per month; his insurance policies (why and when he bought them, who the beneficiaries were); and so on. Dr. Rafie's style of lawyering struck me as more or less identical to that of lawyers in the civil-court hearings I observed. It was in any event exceedingly systematic and rigorous. I should add that in his treatment of the former husband, whose testimony he abrasively interrupted on a number of occasions, Dr. Rafie was highly confrontational, combative, and dismissive—so much so that the opposing counsel, a young lawyer who seemed very much out of his league, strenuously objected to a number of his questions. The judge apparently had no problem with Dr. Rafie's tenor, tone, or overall tactics, inasmuch as he brushed aside the opposing counsel's objections and instructed the former husband to answer all of Dr. Rafie's questions.

One reason for the similarities with civil-court lawyering styles has to do with Dr. Rafie's initial professional training and certification, which was in the common law and at premier English institutions. (Lincoln's Inn, where Dr. Rafie earned his certification as Barrister at Law, is the most prestigious of all law schools in the United Kingdom, and arguably the world, as far as Malaysians and many others are concerned.) Another reason is that he also serves as an advocate and solicitor in civil-court disputes, as do a good many *sharia* lawyers (Whiting 2012),[9] and thus utilizes the same skills and strategies honed in civil-court arenas in the work he does in the *sharia* courts. More broadly, Dr. Rafie's aggressive professional manner (coupled with the erudition and charm he sometimes displays) is a key factor in his success as a *sharia* lawyer, just as it exemplifies the style of lawyering that enjoys the most symbolic capital in the nation's juridical fields. Not surprisingly, it is also broadly congruent with—a model of and for—the modes of lawyering one sees among the younger generation(s) of *sharia* and civil lawyers in Kuala Lumpur and elsewhere in Malaysia.

The larger, threefold issue is as follows: (1) The greater the financial stakes involved in cases bearing on Malay/Muslim divorce (and disputes over inheritance and other matters), the more litigants and judges feel it necessary to share the stage with *sharia* lawyers; (2) The most successful *sharia* lawyers comport themselves much like their civil-court counterparts, swagger, warts, and all; and (3) These are among the primary reasons that *sulh* officers like Encik Ahmad and various well-placed Muslim academics, among others, seek a "return" to what they regard as "more Islamic" styles of managing disputes, via negotiation, mediation, and compromise. This is despite their recognition that the most fractious political issues confronting the courts and the nation as a whole at present and in the future will undoubtedly involve contentious litigation, which many regard as an unwelcome legacy of the colonial era, rather than mediation or arbitration grounded in Islamic ethical values. With regard to pressing political and religious issues such as those involved in the Lina Joy case, I am not sure they would have it any other way, especially since matters having to do with Islam are increasingly seen by most of the nation's Muslims as more or less binary (Fischer 2008, 2016), with little if any room for negotiation or compromise.

My focus in this section of the chapter on the transformative role of lawyers in *sharia* courtrooms and in processes of dispute management generally, especially in Kuala Lumpur, should not lead us to lose sight of discourse and practice in *sulh* sessions, which proceed in Kuala Lumpur and elsewhere without the participation of lawyers, as we saw in chapter 3. We should remember too that while lawyers do not play a direct role in the *sulh* process, they are by no means irrelevant to it. For the success of the process depends partly on *sulh* officers' admonitions to their clients that if *sulh* sessions fail and they continue to press their claims, they will face formal adjudication involving judges, which typically means lawyers as well. Put differently, we need to remember that the *sulh* hearing in which the well-heeled Indonesian woman sought to clarify her marital status (vis-à-vis the wealthy British convert to Islam she married some years earlier) and to secure custody of her young daughter (case 4) took place in Kuala Lumpur, and that the dynamics addressed in my discussion of that case, overseen by a *sharia* lawyer-turned-*sulh* officer, comprise part of the juridical landscape that is the central concern of this chapter. In that hearing, recall, the *sulh* officer was far more formal, directive, and judge-like than his Rembau counterpart, but also explicitly disdainful of *sharia* lawyers (owing to their perceived tendency to be ethically compromised) and of many of the formal, civil-court-origin trappings of the *sharia* assemblage.

It remains to consider the growing importance of *sharia* lawyers as a national cultural-political force. I deal with these dynamics only briefly here, but they merit serious consideration. So, too, more generally, does the rise since the 1980s or so of a Malay/Muslim professional class (Welsh 2008; Whiting 2012). This is part of the emergence of a more encompassing Malay/Muslim middle class, which has gone hand-in-hand with the massive building up of *sharia*-friendly legal capital in the form of Islamic academies, colleges, and universities that train prospective judges, lawyers, *sulh* officers, and others for positions both in the *sharia* juridical field and in institutions of higher learning, the corporate sector, and beyond. Through their professional associations and NGOs—for instance, the Persatuan Peguam Syarie Malaysia (PGSM; the Malaysian *Syarie* Lawyers Association), and Muslim Brothers, an all-male group of *sharia* judges, lawyers, and retirees that was formed to counter the views and influence of Sisters in Islam (Hoffstaedter 2011, 139–45)—*sharia* lawyers and allied experts have brought considerable pressure to bear on politicians and others who make policy and influence public legal sensibilities and dispositions. In this way they have helped transform the workplace of Muslim-run firms so as to make them more "*sharia*-compliant" (Sloane-White 2017). Along with banking and financial institutions in their entirety, they have also been instrumental in molding public opinion (through workshops, books, regular columns in print media and online venues), particularly that of fellow Muslims, and have otherwise been deeply involved in the fields of cultural production.

These developments have not entailed an "Islamist capture" of the Bar Council or the legal profession more generally, let alone the juridical field in its entirety (Welsh 2008; Whiting 2018),[10] as has occurred in Muslim-majority countries such as Iran, Egypt, and Sudan. But they have helped foreground and prioritize Islamic sensibilities and dispositions in national political and legal debates of many varieties. Trends such as these have been welcomed by increasing numbers (though not all) of the nation's Muslims, and simultaneously viewed with growing alarm by the nation's non-Muslims and by Muslim feminists and human rights advocates, many of whom feel ever more marginalized and disenfranchised by them.

Particularly distressing to many Chinese and other non-Muslims are the subtle and not-so-subtle constrictions of pluralistic sensibilities and dispositions that are evident in shifts in majoritarian (Malay/Muslim) subjectivities; these include but are not limited to the increasingly pronounced view that Chinese and other non-Muslims are defiling and polluting and that physical and other contact with them should thus be avoided as a matter of moral and spiritual responsibility and religiously-inflected civic duty. Unlike offenses and injuries of a more strictly legal, political, or economic variety, routine violence involving assaults on the dignity, sovereignty, and cultural priorities of ethnic and religious Others are not readily amenable to judicial remedy, and in many instances are not even actionable, especially when they are encouraged by state directives. In this regard, the law is an exceedingly blunt instrument with respect to its capacity to manage, let alone resolve, a wide variety of social issues (Sullivan 2005). The problem, though, is: what are the other options available to those who seek legitimacy, freedom from discrimination, and justice? "What does anyone persecuted by the law [or ill-treated by law-like norms] want, if not validation by some higher Law [or Norm]? What does the victim of injustice demand, if not justice?" (Lancaster 2011, 136).

This is partly to underscore a methodological point variably addressed in previous sections of this chapter and elsewhere in this book, a highly condensed version of which, provided by Bourdieu (2014, 174), serves as the epigraph to this chapter. The point is that an understanding of the discourses and practices of *sharia* judges and lawyers requires that we range beyond an analysis of what transpires in *sharia* courtrooms, and that we consider these phenomena in relation to their counterparts in civil-secular arenas, legal and otherwise. It is in these latter, especially legal, arenas, after all, that many of the most far-reaching and emotionally and politically fraught battles—over the meaning of constitutional provisions bearing on freedom of religion; the jurisdiction of the *sharia* courts; the ever-expanding reach of the state through the courts (both civil and religious); and checks and balances on the executive branch, for example—are being waged. The concentration of power and prestige in these latter arenas goes a long way toward explaining why the idealized discourses and practices believed to typify them continue to provide the gold standard for their counterparts in the *sharia* judiciary, even when those sitting at the helm or simply in the employ of the latter judiciary consider the civil system of law to be both an unwelcome vestige of the nation's colonial past and morally and ethically bankrupt.

By way of partial summary and elaboration, *sharia* lawyers emerged as key players in the Islamic courts in the 1990s and subsequently, a period that also saw their greater presence both in the fields of cultural production and state power, and in the realms of private and state-controlled enterprise (Dezalay and Garth 2010, 211). As important as this trend is, its recognition should not obscure the fact that in recent decades Malaysia, like many other nations swept up in neoliberal globalization, has seen the relative eclipse within ruling bureaucracies of lawyer-politicians, and the rise to power within the bureaucratic field of economist-technocrats (Dezalay and Garth 2010, 107; Jomo K. S. 1995; Gomez 2009; Sloane-White 2017). Suffice it to recall a few of the contexts discussed in this chapter in which we see clear evidence of the growing influence of such specialists: the courthouse museum, with its prominent displays of awards and certificates attesting to the *sharia* court's adherence to international standards of management, accounting, and audit; the prominence of Japanese-origin 5S logos and information bearing on related management/audit protocols both in the museum and throughout the courthouse; the corporate business attire of judges and other officers of the court ("black-business-suit fever"); and judges' and other officials' embrace of KPIs and various corporate business models to manage both their staff and workload, and the life-problems of those who seek their services or are otherwise required to appear before them.

CONCLUSION: SUCCESSFUL REBRANDING?
AMBUSH MARKETING?

Much of this chapter has engaged the multifaceted rebranding process that (Malay) political and religious elites have undertaken to convey to variously defined publics that the *sharia* judiciary is a thoroughly cosmopolitan, global assemblage, albeit still very much a project under development. A final set of questions has to do with the relative efficacy of the rebranding and whether it might be said to involve camouflage, subterfuge, or what is referred to in the literature on marketing and branding as "ambush marketing" (Hoek and Gendall 2002; Schmitz 2005)—as has been suggested by some detractors of the *sharia* court and some critics of the ways that the entrenchment of Malay supremacy and Islamization have unfolded in Malaysia in recent decades. This trio of concepts (camouflage, subterfuge, ambush marketing) was invoked by a strongly secular British colleague in response to a seminar presentation that I gave (in Bellagio, Italy) on some of the material in this book in the fall of 2012 and the draft of an article (published as Peletz 2013) that I subsequently shared with him. My colleague had a visceral reaction to the Lina Joy case that I had mentioned in the seminar, seeing it as an example of religious and political tyranny via (judicial) bureaucratization. He was alarmed, more generally, by the shrinking space between *sharia* and civil-law arenas, and by the fact that many features of the civil judiciary had been folded into the *sharia* assemblage, such that there was an increasing amalgamation of the two spheres that favored the heightened salience of organized religion (Islam) in public domains.

Especially when taken together and used to gloss some of the dynamics of social engineering aimed at rebranding the *sharia* assemblage, the concepts of camouflage, subterfuge, and ambush marketing have a pejorative ring that I find problematic. Both singularly and collectively they are nonetheless useful insofar as they encourage us to focus on strategies of legitimization and advance, and various other issues bearing on authority, power, and prestige.

To address these issues we might first bear in mind that definitions of the term "rebranding" commonly center on processes that involve transforming the corporate image or identity of a company or organization, or, more specifically, "the creation of a new name, term, symbol, design or a combination of them for an established brand with the intention of developing a differentiated (new) position in the mind of stakeholders and competitors" (Muzellec and Lambkin 2006, 805). This may involve

> radical changes to a brand's logo, name . . ., image, marketing strategy, and advertising themes. Such changes typically aim to reposition the brand/company, occasionally to distance itself from negative connotations of the previous branding, . . . to move the brand upmarket; [and/or to] communicate a new message a new board of directors wishes to communicate . . . . The process can occur intentionally through a deliberate change in strategy . . . or unintentionally from unplanned, emergent situations, such as a "Chapter 11 corporate restructuring," "union busting," or "bankruptcy."[11]

Important to add to this definition, and to make explicit, is that rebranding is ultimately aimed at reconfiguring a relationship with consumers or the public. This is partly because "brands are relationships" (Temporal 2011, 100). The other part of the equation is that their relative success or failure depends on the emotional capital (trust, loyalty, etc.) brand managers endeavor to develop with the public, via strategies that typically involve seductive, noncoercive "soft power," in order to enhance their market share, however broadly or narrowly defined (Temporal 2011, 9; see also Mazzarella 2003; Hoesterey 2016).

"Ambush marketing" (sometimes known as "guerilla marketing" or "parasite marketing"), for its part, refers to certain types of marketing strategies. Such strategies capitalize on the name brand or legitimacy of a high-profile sporting event, such as the Olympics, or on another well-known, popular phenomenon (e.g., an iPhone), to enhance the visibility and market share of a specific product or set of commodities (like particular brands of running shoes or headphones) without paying the contractual fees often required to obtain and publicize such a formal association or endorsement. There are many critics of these marketing strategies, but their advocates, not surprisingly, "see . . . [them] as smart business" (Schmitz 2005, 208). As one American advocate specializing in intellectual property law put it in a discussion of the 2004 Olympics,

> People think ambush marketing hurts the Olympics? Good. Who cares? Are the Olympics going to disappear from the planet? I don't think so. *This isn't religion or virginity here—it's business. Marketing is a form of warfare, and the ambush is a hell of a weapon* (208n40; emphasis added).

The language of this rather remarkable passage would no doubt offend my interlocutors in the *sharia* judiciary (and beyond), both because it glibly mentions religion and virginity in the same breath, presumably on the grounds both comprise "no-go zones" of sorts for critics or at least warrant "delicate treatment," and because it posits an opposition between business and religion. But many of them would agree with the bottom line, that they are engaged in a struggle with wide ramifications, a kind of warfare, for hearts and minds, and that they should make use of all available resources that are both *halal* and legal to prevail in that struggle. The *sharia*-advisors that Sloane-White (2017, 47) has written about clearly feel similarly, though the key resources they draw upon to advance their cause are "business and banks not [laws or] bombs."

Ambush marketing by the *sharia* judiciary would thus involve capitalizing on the legitimacy of the civil judiciary without having received the latter's formal permission to do so. Or, arguably more relevant here, since the specific process involved in the Malaysian case may be viewed as analogous but not equivalent to ambush marketing in the corporate sector, it would involve building on the legitimacy of the civil judiciary without necessarily having any contractual or other commitment to the latter's explicitly codified priorities with respect to justice, due process, and freedom of religion as defined in the Federal Constitution.

Western scholars have occasionally raised these issues with me in the course of presentations I have given in seminar settings and conferences; I mentioned one instance of this earlier. Some of my interlocutors have been vehement in expressing the view that they find the processes I have described in this chapter and previous parts of this book to be "more disturbing" than what they have read or heard about Islamization in other Muslim-majority settings. (Pakistan, Afghanistan, Iran, Saudi Arabia, and perhaps Sudan seem to be the key points of reference here, though they are not necessarily articulated as such). This is because they are camouflaged by micropolitics of power, such as the corporate attire of Malaysia's *sharia* judges and their appropriation of myriad trappings of the civil judiciary. Many of these critics have strongly negative reactions to cases such as that of Lina Joy, and admit to being largely hostile to organized religion, especially when its observance is formally endorsed by the state and prescribed by the Federal Constitution, as is the case with Islam for Malays.

Muslim feminists such as SIS have also voiced some of these concerns, as have some of their allies and other supporters. In language reminiscent of Henry David Thoreau's memorable (1854 [1997], 21) admonition to "beware of all enterprises that require new clothes," some of them warned me not to be taken in by the modern corporate attire of *sharia* judges. This was their way of saying that one needs to maintain a distinction between the brand and the product subject to (re)branding. "Beneath the clothing," as one leader of SIS put it in a conversation in July 2012, they are every bit as conservative and biased against women and, by implication, non-Muslims, as both their predecessors and the conservative *ulama* with whom SIS perennially struggle. In our conversations, some of them added that as part of their public relations campaigns, the nation's *sharia* judges are on their best behavior when they are being interviewed by Western male observers such as myself. One example is their willingness to share archival records and other relevant data with me, something they would not normally do if the requests came from members of Muslim feminist organizations or from non-Muslim Malaysians, a number of whom have in fact been denied access to the *sharia* courts on the grounds that they are not Muslim.

Many of the nation's thirteen million non-Muslims have similar apprehensions and misgivings. This is clear from the available research (e.g., Nonini 1998, 2015; Willford 2006, 2014; Baxstrom 2008), from scores of media accounts, and from the hundreds of interviews and informal conversations I have had, across four decades, with Chinese and Indian lawyers, judges, journalists, academics, activists, actors, artists, taxi drivers, and others. Some of these concerns were shared with me by a group of prominent Chinese lawyers and civil-court judges over a sumptuous lunch in an exclusive Kuala Lumpur venue, The Royal Lake Club, in August 2011. Much of the highly animated luncheon conversation focused on a rapidly unfolding legal case that the firms of some of the lawyers present were involved in. The case centered on a deeply controversial raid and disruption, a week or so earlier, of a dinner function sponsored by a Christian congregation (Damansara United Methodist Church). The raid had been carried out by members of the JAIS on the grounds that a dozen Malays were reported to be among the hundred people present at the event, and were being subject to Christian proselytization, a criminal offense in Malaysia if it is directed at Muslims. At one point one of the lawyers asked about my research in the *sharia* courts and my findings to date. I was eager to hear their reactions as I outlined part of my argument about the "civil-ization" of the *sharia* judiciary and the multiple directions in which it was moving due partly to its increased reliance on common-law procedures and templates coupled with its implementation of Japanese regimes of management and audit. The implicit consensus, polite as it was, was that much of what I outlined was, at best, irrelevant to the bottom line: the *sharia* judiciary's expanded jurisdiction. Indeed, when I mentioned to one member of the group the eminent Tan Sri Datuk Prof. Ahmad M. Ibrahim (1916–99), former Attorney General of Singapore who went on to become a prominent architect of the modernization of Malaysia's Islamic judiciary that rendered it much like the nation's civil courts, he quickly dismissed my remarks as more or less immaterial. In his view Ahmad Ibrahim's most enduring legacy was that he provided much of the rationale and technical expertise for the expansion of the *sharia* system at the expense of the common law and the Federal Constitution. Rather than viewing Ahmad Ibrahim as an important public intellectual and national hero, in other words—bear in mind here that the library of the Law School of the University of Malaya is named in his honor, as is a college within the International Islamic University of Malaysia, which he helped found—my interlocutor regarded him as a traitor to the nation and a chauvinist architect of policies that seriously delegitimized and disenfranchised non-Muslims, albeit in ways that were thoroughly "legal."

I do not recall if issues of camouflage or subterfuge were raised explicitly in these conversations (my notes on the luncheon were not as detailed as I wish they had been), and I am fairly certain that the theme of ambush marketing did not come up. However, these issues and themes were evident in the subtext of many of the remarks made at the luncheon and in previous and subsequent conversations I had with the member of the group I knew best, Robert L., an influential, middle-aged lawyer and one-time academic who had studied briefly in the United States and had become quite active in Kuala Lumpur's Christian evangelical community. In Robert's view, the (Malay) architects of the gradual, piecemeal Islamization process had made sure to devise the blueprints for its entailments and implemenation behind closed doors, without most people's direct knowledge that they were doing so, and to ensure that its realization in practice was sufficiently gradual and ostensibly innocuous that it did not provoke the ire of non-Muslims. On my reading, these remarks point to subterfuge, which, like treason (*derhaka*), is an exceedingly common trope in Malaysian political discourse, especially in narratives about the practices, intentions and desires, particularly if unchecked and allowed to run their course, of ethnic and religious Others.

What disturbs many of the nation's Chinese, Indians, and other non-Muslims is the progressive encroachment on their daily lives and subjectivities of Islamic sensibilities, dispositions, and more encompassing normativities—some of which involve explicit stigmatization of non-Muslims, their religions, and much else that they hold dear—that are increasingly enshrined in formal (*sharia*) law. The expanded jurisdiction and enhanced visibility of the *sharia* assemblage is a key symbol and agent of this encroachment, particularly when it entails the literal destruction of Chinese, Indian, and other non-Muslim community spaces. The anthropologist Donald Nonini (2015) provides one of many examples one might cite (see also Willford 2006, 2015; Baxstrom 2008). That case, from the predominantly Chinese town of Bukit Mertajam in the northern state of Penang, involved the state's appropriation in the mid-1980s of a municipal space long utilized by local vegetable merchants serving the town's mostly working-class residents, to make way for a new *sharia* courthouse. Years of formal protests following the initial announcement of the plan in the late 1970s proved unsuccessful: "The vegetable wholesalers . . . [were] forced to move to the west of the city and abdicate their informal claim over municipal space to the new authority—one they saw as alien, threatening to expand Islamic law to encompass them as non-Muslims" (Nonini 2015, 240).

The concerns at issue here range well beyond non-Muslims' abilities to exercise their "rights to the city" and their desires to be free of "incursions and surveillance on . . . [their] lived spaces" (Nonini 2015, 241). Many of the informal conversations and formal interviews I have had with non-Muslims over the years reveal a widespread and very palpable fear and anxiety that is commonly expressed in idioms of loss and attendant hurt linked to severed ties with children and grandchildren and the threat of failed social reproduction. The specific concern is that a son or daughter will fall in love with and want to marry a Muslim, and will thus convert to Islam prior to his or her wedding in order to effect a union that is legitimate and blessed from the standpoint of Islam and the prospective in-laws. In such a scenario, the parents will forever lose one of their children to Islam—"lose" is the verb of choice in these narratives—since under Malaysian law he or she will be effectively prohibited from subsequently renouncing Islam. And they will also lose all of the offspring from that union because they will be born Muslim, "with no way out," as more than one interlocutor put it.

The following storyline presents broadly analogous threats. A non-Muslim couple experiences serious if not terminal marital difficulties and one of the spouses, typically the husband, converts to Islam either for spiritual or other legitimate reasons, or because he hopes to obtain more favorable treatment from the *sharia* courts than he might receive from their civil counterparts. At present, due to the way constitutional amendment 121(1A) has been interpreted, the husband might succeed in having the *sharia* authorities claim and obtain jurisdiction over the case (though such jurisdiction might well be contested by the civil courts) and would stand a good chance of being awarded custody of the children (if there are any). He could also incur significantly reduced financial obligations to his former wife as compared with those he would face if the divorce were handled by a civil judge. One of the Chinese civil-court magistrates that I had lunch with in August 2011 told me that she had seen cases like this in the family-court arenas in which she operates. She mentioned as an example a hearing she had been involved in where the lawyer for the (non-Muslim) husband argued for greatly reduced spousal maintenance on the grounds that this was in keeping with Islam (the rest of the lawyer's argument was not clear to me—"and that since Islam is the religion of the Federation, Islamic provisions should trump all others"?), despite the fact that neither the husband nor the wife were Muslim.

Thus far, efforts such as these—"a sign of the times" in the view of the Chinese magistrate recounting this story to me—have been largely unsuccessful, even though they are deeply alarming examples of "creeping desecularization" in the form of Islamization in the eyes of the non-Muslim public and experts in the field of civil law, such as my interlocutor. The position that such efforts have been mostly unsuccessful was also conveyed to me by Dato Esah, a Malay judge appointed to the family-court division of the civil judiciary, though she expressed little if any concern about where things might be heading on this front. I interviewed Dato Esah in her chambers in the civil Court Complex (Kompleks Mahkamah) in October 2013 shortly before spending a few hours observing proceedings in her courtroom, which, for reasons explained earlier, are nearly indistinguishable from their *sharia* counterparts, except that they are much more likely to unfold in English or in a mixture of English and Malay, are not adorned with Islamic calligraphy, and do not feature the gender-segregated seating areas one sees in *sharia* courtrooms.

Dato Esah, who is probably in her fifties, is one of the very few Muslim women I have observed in any courtroom or other professional setting who does not wear a headscarf. More directly relevant was her insistence that she would never allow litigants or their lawyers to invoke Islamic legal provisions or related normativities in her courtroom; and that it would be altogether inappropriate and "dangerous" (her term) for anyone to attempt to do so, especially since neither she nor any others officially involved in the hearings over which she presides have any knowledge of *sharia*. I should add that I never observed litigants or lawyers attempt to deploy this strategy in the many hours I spent in her courtroom (or in other civil-court arenas), though there is ample evidence that this has famously occurred—e.g., in the Lina Joy case, and those of Shamala, Moorthy, and others.

Dato Esah's legal education and training had been in London—in the common law, she proudly explained—and apparently involved no coursework on Islamic law, *fiqh,* or related subjects. She regarded jurisdictional disputes of the sort at issue here as having been entirely settled, although the relative finality of her view on the subject may have been an artifact of our brief, informal conversation. She was in a hurry to begin the day's proceedings and was disinclined to grant a formal, lengthier interview without explicit written permission from her superiors (which I sought to obtain with the assistance of my sponsors at the Academy of Islamic Studies at the University of Malaya, but never did receive). The bottom line for her is that jurisdiction in all such cases lies with the court that registered the couple's marriage in the first place. In this view, one spouse's conversion to Islam at a later date has no bearing on the terms of divorce, maintenance, custody, or jurisdictional matters, should one or both parties subsequently seek to terminate the union.

Even if we accept the (dubious) proposition that such matters have been largely settled, it is instructive, I think, that Dato Esah, a Malay/Muslim judge, sees no jurisdictional or attendant problems on the family-law horizon due to this particular feature of Islamization, whereas the Chinese/non-Muslim magistrate I discussed earlier clearly does. Such differences are deeply allegorical, indexing as they do widespread ethno-racial and religious contrasts in attitudes toward Islamization. At the risk of simplification, for most Malays and other Muslims, Islamization is generally a (very) good thing, and obstacles to its further implementation have been or can be rather easily overcome, especially once non-Muslims learn more about the religion and all that it has to offer. For non-Muslims (and some Muslims like Sisters in Islam), Islamization as it has unfolded in Malaysia, though not necessarily Islamization per se, is neither a predominantly good thing nor benign, and is deeply threatening to non-Muslims and to those Muslims who seek a more progressive and inclusive instantiation of their faith.

So, Has the Rebranding Been Effective?

This multifaceted question is rather difficult to answer, despite the impression conveyed in the preceding pages and previous chapters. This is largely because of the relative paucity of relevant longitudinal data that might allow us to compare present-day public perceptions of the *sharia* courts with those that obtained before extensive branding efforts began (in the early 1990s, for example). Suffice it to say that the answer to the question depends on the broadly defined social locations and subject positions of one's interlocutors, and that for some important groups (such as foreign investors, whose capital is clearly targeted by the rebranding) we have no clear evidence.[12] I focus here on those for whom the evidence is fairly unambiguous, though I should first mention one of the major obstacles authorities face across all sectors of Malaysian society: "brand fatigue." In recent decades Malaysian officialdom and their retinues of PR specialists have embarked on so many high-profile, mass-mediated, and seemingly relentless (re)branding campaigns—prominent examples of which include Prime Minister Mahathir's "Vision 2020," his successor Abdullah Badawi's "Islam *Hadhari*" ("Civilizational Islam"), and more recently Najib Razak's "1Malaysia"—that the media-weary, oversaturated public has increasingly tuned out and simply ignored or otherwise failed to take heed of or engage the message(s) (Hoffstaedter 2011, 101–4).

Those in the employ of the *sharia* judiciary, as might be expected, feel strongly that public perceptions of the courts, at least on the part of Malays, are far more congruent with the gold standards to which they aspire than in decades past. Recall

here the *sulh* officer's comment (discussed in chapter 3) that in former times defendants (i.e., Malay males) commonly blew off summonses, "weren't afraid" of and
didn't respect the courts, and that this situation no longer obtains. Recall, more
generally, that I have presented evidence in earlier chapters, including women's generally positive assessments of the *sulh* sessions they have been involved in, that is
broadly congruent with such views. How much of this shift is due to concrete
changes in the actual operation of the courts (e.g., their more timely and substantive engagement with women's claims, or the greater penalties incurred by husbands and fathers who disregard court orders) as distinct from transformations of
their brand image is hard to say. Both sets of dynamics are probably involved.

For reform-oriented Muslim feminists such as SIS, in contrast, the rebranding
is largely a ruse, an unsuccessful and largely transparent and contemptible example of ambush marketing. Other Malay/Muslim women who are active in civil-
society circles, the civil judiciary, or both are sometimes less dismissive of recent
changes in the *sharia* courts and their rebranding efforts but no less pointed in
their criticisms of *sharia* dynamics, thus suggesting that the rebranding has not
been as effective as authorities had hoped.

Relevant here are the views of one of the nation's most esteemed lawyers, a Malay
woman in her seventies who once presided over the Malaysian Bar Council and
continues to be active in the upper levels of Bar Council activities and in a wide
variety of civic affairs. I refer to her as Maryam. Maryam told me in the Bar Council's Kuala Lumpur offices in October 2013 that one difference between the *sharia*
and civil judiciaries is that things are "more stringent in the *sharia* courts," and that
as a woman she feels she would "have to be totally subservient to the *sharia* court"
(e.g., before the judge). She added that she would "feel almost uncomfortable, . . .
might not feel welcome there," presumably because although she is a Muslim, she
does not wear any kind of headscarf. A similar critique was shared with me by a
female High Court (civil) judge, probably in her fifties, who in the course of our
brief encounter at a formal reception (in July 2010) wondered aloud why some
"strongly Islamic" *sharia* judges looked down on her and other Malay/Muslim
women, regarding them as second-class citizens or lower forms of being. Making
matters worse, in Maryam's view, *sharia* lawyers are not subject to disciplinary
review by their peers, in contrast to lawyers working in civil arenas, and they have
no formal or binding code of ethics comparable to that of the Bar Council, which
sanctions and otherwise regulates errant professional behavior on the part of lawyers practicing in civil realms. For reasons such as these, Maryam explained, *sharia*
lawyers sometimes engage in questionable billing practices and other unprofes-
sional conduct with little fear of reprisal, though her larger concern was that *sharia*
lawyers don't evince much interest in Bar Council activities relevant to the legal
profession as a whole and appear more concerned to advance Islamist agendas. She
lamented further that because of political, legal, and religious developments such as

the Lina Joy case, the "Allah controversy"[13] and so on, "lots of people," by which she meant non-Muslim professionals, have already left the country.

Taken as a whole, these comments are quite damning, especially since they come from a Malay woman who moves in the highest circles of the juridical field and is something of a national treasure. It is important to add that she has spent little time in the *sharia* courts, and suggested to me that I probably know more about them than she does, a comment I encountered countless times over the years. That Maryam has rarely had reason to enter *sharia* courtrooms means that her perceptions of these courts are based partly on what friends, relatives, colleagues, and others have told her, perhaps but not necessarily from their first-hand experience; and partly on how the courts are represented in the media—in short, on how they are imagined to exist in the eyes of the public, the very same public the rebranding is targeting.

What about non-Muslims, to whom efforts at rebranding the *sharia* judiciary are importantly directed? The evidence here is altogether unambiguous and overwhelmingly negative. This is suggested both by the remarks of Chinese lawyers and judges outlined earlier and by the perceptions of Chinese, Indians, and others of more modest means than the professionals I have focused on thus far. For these groups, the rebranding is a ruse, a decoy, a subterfuge. It is not necessarily an example of ambush marketing, however, since the civil courts are commonly regarded as deeply complicit with their *sharia* counterparts, sharing many of their orientations and objectives; they are held to be like two sides of the same coin, not a source from which *sharia* officials have illegally or unethically poached. Support for these views derives partly from non-Muslims' assessments of the outcome of cases involving Lina Joy, Moorthy, Shamala, and others mentioned earlier, which commonly involve critiques that the *sharia* courts disrespect all relevant evidence before them, and are yet another vehicle for the advancement of Islamization and Malay supremacy. If the *sharia* judiciary and those in the Prime Minister's Department who are in charge of its rebranding are in the market to enhance the legitimacy that is bestowed on *sharia* courts by the nation's non-Muslims, they have clearly failed.

The Moorthy controversy (2005–06),[14] for example, helped birth the protest movement spearheaded by the Hindu Rights Action Force (HINDRAF), though HINDRAF's emergence was also a response to the displacement in the preceding years of Tamil communities and the destruction of Hindu temples and spiritual landscapes in the course of the creation of Putrajaya, Shah Alam, and various Malay-oriented developments. HINDRAF began as a coalition of some thirty Indian/Hindu NGOs but quickly coalesced into a mass movement aimed at preserving Hindu culture and communities and defending the rights of Indians in a cultural-political and specifically juridical environment increasingly experienced as hostile and discriminatory to Indians in particular and to non-Muslims generally. The fact that this movement arose in direct response to the way the *sharia* court (mis)handled the Moorthy incident—in that case, as one Tamil man put it, "The *shariah* court ignored all of the evidence that was placed before it. We knew we had to do something" (Willford 2014, 240)—speaks volumes about the Hindu community's perceptions of *sharia* courts and their version of justice. The government's harsh treatment of HINDRAF leaders and the mass demonstrations they helped organize did not help.

The Moorthy case is but one of many examples of Islamic religious bureaucracies intruding into the lives of Indian and other minorities in ways that members of these groups find deeply offensive and threatening. Such intrusions are perceived and experienced as part and parcel of more encompassing efforts geared toward cultural if not ethnic cleansing (as discussed below). One Indian observer, S. Nagarajan, merits quoting at length.

> Islamic authorities forcibly separated V. Suresh from his wife, Revathi Masoosai, and their 16-month-old baby. Revathi was born to Muslim convert parents but was brought up as a Hindu by her Hindu grandmother. She was detained at the Muslim rehabilitation centre against her will while her child was handed to Revathi's Muslim mother.
>
> In another case, P. Marimuth's five young Hindu children were taken from their home by Islamic religious officials who said his wife was technically still a Muslim [she was apparently born to Muslim parents but had embraced Hinduism] and therefore their marriage of twenty-one years was invalid . . . . This worrying trend of Muslim officialdom to ignore the religious sentiments and the rights of non-Muslims only served to fuel more fear and unhappiness among non-Muslims. But they had an even more troubling impact on the Indian Malaysian psyche because most of the affected people are from the [Indian Malaysian] community. They not only lost their spouses, but their children were taken away from them and they had no recourse to justice (Nagarajan 2008, 390–91, cited in Willford 2014, 35–36).

In the aftermath of the Moorthy controversy, one of anthropologist Andrew Willford's (2014) Tamil interlocutors claimed that there are "No good Malay lawyers or judges anymore" (184). Another, casting his net much more broadly, asserted categorically that "Malays could not be trusted anymore" (221). This, unfortunately, is a widely held perception on the part of non-Muslims. It poses serious problems both for the prospects of a successful rebranding of the *sharia* courts and of Malaysian Islam generally, and for the iconically bureaucratic view held by *sharia* judges and other proponents of *sharia* that the main impediments to the "Harmonization of Laws" are purely bureaucratic/administrative issues that involve sorting out technical, jurisdictional matters, as distinct from symbolically freighted challenges that are fundamentally political. Brands, recall, are relationships, the relative success or failure of which depends in no small measure on the emotional capital—trust, loyalty, etc.—that brand managers develop with their target audience(s).

The term "anymore" that contextualizes both comments is instructive, pointing as it does to times past that by all accounts, including those not tinged with nostalgia, were more conducive to positive interactions between Malays and non-Muslims. Thus Willford (2014) recounts elderly Tamils' recollections that in the decades before Prime Minister Mahathir (r. 1981–2013), village Malays "participated in Hindu festivals and invited [Tamil] plantation workers to their own festivals and weddings in the *kampungs* [villages]" (106). He adds that

> these complex and multiple exchanges were unproblematic, given a shared cultural substructure and derived from centuries of cultural interaction. In recent times, however, the purging of Malay culture of things deemed "Indic" or "Indian," coupled with the discourses of racial exclusivity and privilege, has disaggregated these intertwined and intimate exchanges, upsetting the more fluid and protean boundaries between Indians and Malays that had once existed (106).

Nowadays, as his informants put it, "Muslims won't come" to Tamil feasts and celebrations and typically won't include Tamils or other non-Muslims among the guests at theirs: "Malays are growing . . . fanatical because of the government's Islamization efforts. . . . Islamization has made them more narrow and afraid to mix. They (Malays) will ask me when they come to the house, 'have you cut the chicken in a *halal* way' . . . . I'm fed up and won't invite them anymore" (139, 212–13).

Pain and hurt associated with the withdrawal of reciprocity and hospitality that Malays used to extend to Tamils are clearly evident in these kinds of remarks. So too is the pain and hurt that Tamils (and other non-Muslims) experience owing to Malays' heightened concerns with *halal* food and ethnic and religious purity. This is partly because the greatly enhanced concerns at issue necessarily entail increased fear and anxiety on the part of Malays that non-Muslims, perhaps especially Hindu plantation workers and urban squatters who engage in religious practices that ordinary Malays (to say nothing of their more reform-oriented co-religionists) have sought to eradicate from their own practices, are sources of grave pollution.

By way of brief summary and elaboration, the *sharia* courts are seen by Indians and other non-Muslims as juggernauts in the struggle to enhance the "bureaucratization of ethnic privilege" (Willford 2015, 18); expand the "racialized state" (17); provide legitimization to the state-sanctioned destruction of Hindu temples and surrounding communities that is carried out in the name of Islamically inflected urban renewal and modernization (Baxstrom 2008); and otherwise advance the march of Islamization and the instantiation of Malay supremacy with which it is closely linked.

Readers might plausibly suggest that these summary comments and some of the non-Muslim discontent outlined in previous pages point to a number of ethno-racial, religious, political, and historical dynamics over which the nation's *sharia* courts have no control and in which they are not involved, either directly or indirectly, in any case. The federal-level JAKIM, for example, which is usefully viewed as both the premier "brand steward" (Klein 2009, 23) and "brand evangelist" with regard to the increasingly monolithic variant of Islam that authorities seek to promote and instantiate throughout the nation, appears to bear primary responsibility for many errant "vice raids" and other excesses that are commonly laid at the feet of the *sharia* courts and/or the JKSM, the regulatory body that oversees the courts. This is despite the fact that JAKIM's operations and personnel, like those of other religious bureaucracies (JAWI, JAIS) that have drawn negative publicity for similar reasons, are largely independent of both the courts and the JKSM, and vice versa (even though both are housed in the Prime Minister's Department). Such a suggestion is certainly reasonable from the perspective of one who parses distinctions and conflicts among state bureaucracies, contrasts and cleavages within juridical fields, and differences between institutional arrangements within these fields and the sometimes diffuse cultural dynamics that help animate and sustain them. It is nonetheless largely irrelevant to the issues at hand, insofar as most people don't make and have no reason to ponder these kinds of distinctions. (Academics and bureaucratic elites are the main exceptions that prove the rule.) As Nonini (1998) put it on the basis of his extensive research among the nation's largest non-Muslim community, Chinese Malaysians not only regard Islamic courthouses as state spaces and thoroughly "Malay"; they also "associate them with police powers that are capricious and dangerous to them, and thus do their best in everyday life to avoid them" (446–47).[15] The more general theme is twofold: the nation's *sharia* courts have long been key players in constituting and policing ethnic, religious, other boundaries and the differential distribution of rights and privileges across them (Peletz 2002). In light of current dynamics and the ways things appear to be heading, no amount of rebranding is likely to dislodge that reality or the ways in which non-Muslims experience, understand, or represent its myriad entailments.

Are Women Getting (More) Justice?

Ethnographic, Historical, and Comparative Perspectives

> *[A] history of family law, written from an anthropological perspective, is a history of narrative strategies engaged in by the state to influence the life course of its nationals. These maneuvers ultimately aim to fix the meaning of kin relations essential to the constitution of citizens as subjects, meaning that the citizens themselves should preferably desire to structure their lives according to the official rules. . . . In this attempt at nation-building—to define, regularize, institutionalize, and normalize the domestic practices of the self—the state codifies and legalizes the desires for specific kinds of relations and specific kinds of selves.*
>
> —JOHN BORNEMAN (1992)

Family law ostensibly grounded in religion comprises an important and deeply contested domain of legal practice in much of the world, including India, South Africa, Israel, Egypt, and Lebanon, to mention just a handful of well-studied examples. Why is this realm of religiously-inflected law frequently represented by Western scholars, local activists, journalists, novelists, and the international human-rights community as deeply conservative and unfriendly to women, if not backward-looking and anachronistic? One set of reasons is that it was historically segregated from other areas of law and otherwise "traditionalized" by moderniz- ing elites (Halley and Rittich 2010, 771–72); it is commonly the sole remnant of an historically male-dominated religious community's "collective right to religious liberty and . . . their sovereignty over a domain in which they are understood to have jurisdiction" (Mahmood 2012, 56). Another set of reasons, especially germane to Islamic family law, has to do with the thrust of recent academic scholarship. This scholarship tends to highlight three themes: the resonance between the current instantiations of the relevant laws and normativities and their classical antecedents; the incommensurabilities that distinguish their core elements from key ("liberal") features of the more encompassing secular legal regimes in which they are typically embedded; and the need to bring about feminist-oriented or other reform. Scholarship driven by the latter concerns (advocacy, activism, reform) commonly underscores the other themes mentioned here. And it often involves largely synchronic perspectives, a focus on women as distinct from the more encompassing domain of gender, and a kind of (broadly construed) strategic essentialism that emphasizes dynamics of kinship, marriage, gender, and sexuality in terms of the proverbial glass that is half-empty rather than half-full.[1]

One goal of this chapter is to complicate this imagery by describing and analyzing a relatively "female-friendly" pattern of historical shifts in Islamic family law in Malaysia since the late 1970s. A second, related goal is suggested by the epigraph, drawn from John Borneman's research on kinship, family law, and belonging in Berlin shortly before the reunification of the city in 1990. This goal involves illustrating how states endeavor to define, codify, and normalize particular kinds of relations and particular kinds of selves that political and religious elites see as essential to the constitution of citizens as subjects. I focus partly on women's prerogatives to obtain divorce/annulment without their husbands' consent. The more encompassing dynamic under study is the role played by *sharia* courts, which are integral features of the state apparatus that I foreground in this chapter, in the cultural politics of marriage, and in gender pluralism as a whole. More specifically, I describe and analyze how Malaysian women have fared in *sharia* courts since my earlier research in the 1970s and 1980s, and problematize various tensions and oppositions between Islamic law and women's rights that have been the subject of considerable scholarly debate in recent decades. My research reveals that due partly to initiatives undertaken by progressive NGOs, women receive more timely and flexible responses to their legal claims than in times past (the 1970s–1980s and previously),[2] and that the courts are less indulgent and more punitive when husbands transgress *sharia* family law. In addition, women nowadays have much greater access to information bearing on their legal options and rights with respect to marriage and divorce, and can rather easily enmesh themselves in networks of support to help them negotiate marriage, its dissolution, and its aftermath. I am not suggesting that women and men come to or experience marriage, divorce, or the *sharia* judiciary on an equal footing; clearly they do not. But this situation is changing in ways favorable to women as long as they conform to increasingly salient and restrictive codes of obedience and heteronormativity.

I have organized my comments into four sections. The first deals with termination of marriage via *fasakh* (judicial rescission/voiding of the marriage contract, or annulment), a key site in the struggle for justice and equality in gender relations within the family and beyond. This section begins with an ethnographic vignette in the form of a transcript of a *fasakh* hearing I sat in on in 2012 and continues with brief comments on selected aspects of the case. It then delves deeper into the labyrinth of *fasakh* legalities by considering both the formal expansion of grounds for *fasakh* effected by Islamic family law reforms of 1983–91 and ensuing, informal shifts further broadening the basis for this type of judicial relief. This material provides crucial context for—and a partial answer to—the question about whether women are getting (more) justice, the focus of the second section of the chapter. Here I addresses themes outlined in the previous paragraph and related matters such as gender patterns in harsh sentencing and dynamics of heteronormativity and pluralism. The third section of the chapter presents comparative-historical perspectives from Egypt and other parts of the Muslim world that have liberalized one or another aspect of Islamic family law in recent decades in accordance with a diffuse but nonetheless discernible shift toward companionate marriage. The Egyptian case is selected for relatively extended comparative treatment both because of Egypt's cultural and political centrality in the Middle East and the Muslim world generally (it is also, not coincidentally, the largest Arab-majority nation as well as home to Al-Azhar University, the most esteemed institution of higher education in the Muslim world), and because of the wealth of high-quality scholarship on issues that are relevant to this chapter and the book as a whole.[3] Of primary concern here is whether developments of the sort seen in Egypt and certain other countries might be on the near horizon in Malaysia, and why this may—or may not—be so. The conclusion offers summary comments and brief discussion of some of the chapter's comparative and theoretical implications.

TERMINATION OF MARRIAGE VIA *FASAKH*

Fasakh is currently the chief if not sole option available to a Malay or other Muslim woman in Malaysia who seeks to dissolve her marriage without her husband's consent or cooperation.[4] (A Muslim man, on the other hand, may divorce his wife at will, on any grounds, without her consent, as we have seen.) This situation contrasts with the options available to Muslim women in some Muslim-majority nations (discussed shortly) that have made explicit provision for women to opt out of marital unions that do not live up to the ideals of companionate marriage.

The following hearing, which was the final session in a *fasakh* case, affords us a useful entrée into some of the ways those at the helm of the *sharia* judiciary are endeavoring to make the courts friendlier to women, even as they hold firm to the "maintenance-obedience paradigm" that undergirds Islamic and state discourses on kinship, gender, and citizenship. *Fasakh*, as I emphasize at various points in this chapter, is a critically important site in the struggle for justice and equality within the family and beyond.

CASE 6

A Woman Seeking a Fasakh *Divorce (Annulment)*
in a Hearing Set Aside for the Judge to Deliver His Verdict

This brief hearing, which occurred in Kuala Lumpur in July 2012, followed a number of earlier sessions devoted to resolving the marital problems that the female plaintiff, who was probably in her thirties, had brought to the court's attention. She sought to address the problems not by petitioning authorities to force her husband to pay the back maintenance (*nafkah*) he owed her or to properly fulfill his other obligations as a husband, the path usually chosen by female plaintiffs. Rather, the resolution she pursued involved requesting that the court annul the marriage so that she would be rid of her delinquent spouse and able to move on with her life.

The case is of interest partly for reasons noted earlier. In Malaysia, as in most of the rest of the Muslim world, *fasakh* is the primary if not sole option available to a woman seeking to terminate her marriage without her husband's consent or cooperation (Raihanah Abdullah 1997). This situation is unlike Egypt, discussed later in this chapter, and a few other Muslim-majority settings (e.g., Pakistan) where a woman may avail herself of unilateral "divorce by redemption" (*khul*) so long as she repays the dower (*mahr*) the husband provided or pledged to deliver at the time of wedding (or subsequently), renounces certain financial claims, and agrees to other stipulations (Sonneveld 2012). It also differs from Indonesia, where in recent years Islamic courts have effectively legalized unilateral no-fault divorce initiated by women or men (Huis 2015).

Fasakh requires that a woman seeking divorce/annulment present evidence of serious wrongdoing or physical or mental defect on her husband's part, and that she convince the judge that the husband's shortcomings would cause her serious harm (*mudarat*) should the marriage continue. Neither of these requirements exists in Egypt or Indonesia. This is to say that Egypt's innovative but controversial "*khul* laws," which date from 2000, along with their previously noted Indonesian counterparts, are among the most "women-friendly" divorce laws in the Muslim world, though recent developments in Iranian and Moroccan family courts are also highly significant (Osanloo 2009; Carlisle 2013; see also n3). Malaysia has yet to and may never adopt any such laws, but the expansion of grounds for *fasakh* and their more generous interpretation since the early 1980s suggest a liberalization of grounds for female-initiated divorce/annulment. We see evidence of these developments in this case.

The hearing involved the plaintiff (P) and three men: her lawyer (PL), the judge (J), and the registrar (R). The plaintiff's husband (the defendant) was not present, had not attended previous sessions devoted to this case (despite court orders that he do so), and had not hired counsel to represent him. The registrar initiated the hearing, which had been set aside for the judge's decision, by reading out the case number and the names of the plaintiff and the defendant. The plaintiff's lawyer then rose from his chair and addressed the judge, requesting his verdict concerning his client's petition.

PL: I request the decision of the court, Your Honor.

J: Various notices and summonses have been issued to the defendant, but he has failed to attend all hearings related to the case. The plaintiff has requested *fasakh* based on six grounds: (1) The defendant hurt/injured (*menyakiti*) the plaintiff; (2) The defendant neglected his duty to provide *nafkah* for more than three months; (3) The defendant did not provide the plaintiff with *nafkah batin* (sexual companionship) for more than a year; (4) The defendant disposed of the plaintiff's properties; (5) *Shiqaq* (a state of conjugal disharmony/dissension) has occurred more than once; and (6) . . . [Inaudible]. There are also oral statements [supporting the plaintiff's contentions] from three witnesses.

After close examination, there is evidence of grounds for *fasakh* along with consistent statements made by the aforementioned witnesses . . . . The court orders the plaintiff to swear before the court makes its decision. Are you willing to recite an oath involving potential retribution from Allah (*sumpah laknat Allah*) in the court?

By this time, perhaps prior to the J's opening remarks, the P had taken her place in the witness box.

P: Yes, Your Honor.

J: You realize that if you make any false statements, you will incur the wrath of Allah?

P: Yes, Your Honor.

She proceeded to read the *sumpah* from the laminated sheet the R handed her.

P: By Allah, by Allah, by Allah . . . In the name of Allah, I . . . [name and IC number] swear that . . . [defendant's name and IC number] . . . left me for three months without providing *nafkah* and I have never been convicted of *nusyuz* [disobedience]. If I lie in this court, I will incur the wrath of Allah.

J: The court decision, *Bismillah [il-rahman il-rahim]*. The court is satisfied with the statements and evidence collected. The court decides that: (1) The defendant is convicted of failing to perform his duties (*tanggungjawab*) as a husband; (2) The court annuls (*fasakhkan*) the marriage between the defendant and plaintiff; (3) The marriage certificate is rendered invalid from this day onward; and (4) This annulment is to be registered with the Department of Islamic Religion.

Initial Comment on the Judge's Narrative

Three features of this exchange merit note. First, in rendering his verdict, the judge cited a single generic transgression on the part of the defendant—failing to perform his duties as a husband—rather than the broader range of legally salient shortcomings outlined in the plaintiff's petition. When delivering his verdict, moreover, the judge did not specify which particular negligence he had in mind—the failure to provide financial support or the dereliction with respect to sexual companionship. Presumably he had in mind the former, since that is the one the wife swore to under oath and it is most likely what the witnesses corroborated.

Second, the judge mentioned, without elaboration or clarification, that a state of conjugal disharmony/dissension was one of the grounds for the plaintiff's petition, using the technical Arabic term *shiqaq* rather than one or another Malay expression that was commonly invoked in judicial narratives and ordinary Malay discourse in times past. The designation *shiqaq* was almost certainly included in the wife's petition at the behest of her lawyer. The term is not widely known among the lay public, and is relatively rarely invoked in courtroom settings, though recent years have seen its increased salience there and a growing technical literature on the subject produced by students and scholars of Islamic law and jurisprudence who have graduated from Islamic institutions of higher education in Malaysia (see, e.g., Norzulaili Mohd Ghazali and Wan Abdul Fattah Wan Ismail 2007). In the latter dynamics we thus see another example of the ways that lawyers and those training them are influencing the discourses and practices of the *sharia* courts, in this instance by encouraging the use of technical Arabic and specifically Islamic terms in lieu of their more conventional vernacular counterparts.

According to some interpretations of classical texts, *shiqaq* presupposes *nusyuz* on the part of both husband and wife (Norzulaili Mohd Ghazali and Wan Abdul Fattah Wan Ismail 2007, 26–27). In this view, for a state of *shiqaq* to exist, both husband and wife must behave egotistically, must refuse to accommodate one another, must be unwilling to admit their faults, or must treat one another with cruelty. The idea that husbands, not simply wives, may be guilty of *nusyuz* is congruent with certain passages in the Quran, which contains five separate references to *nusyuz*, at least one of which (Surah An-Nisa [4:128]) makes clear that husbands may commit *nusyuz*. It is nonetheless largely out of keeping with the dominant view espoused by the Islamic courts and the Department of *Syariah* Judiciary, particularly but not only on its websites, that only women may be guilty of *nusyuz*.

Note in any event that the plaintiff swore under oath that she had never been convicted of *nusyuz*, and that the judge accepted her statement at face value, rather than proceeding as if she bore the burden of proving her innocence with respect to *nusyuz*. The verb she used ("convicted") leaves open the possibility that she did in fact engage in behavior that might be construed as *nusyuz* by her husband (or the judge) but was never convicted of this offense. Since her husband failed to appear for any of the hearings and had no counsel to represent him, she did not have to speak to this possibility.

This is revealing, partly because husbands' lawyers increasingly endeavor to undercut current and former wives' claims against their clients by counter-charging the women with *nusyuz* or threatening to do so. My interviews with court officials indicate that such endeavors usually fall on judges' deaf ears due to lack of evidence, as mentioned earlier. But they can have a chilling effect on women's commitments to pursuing their cases in court through to their completion or bringing the cases to court in the first place.

Third, the judge cited the plaintiff's claim that the defendant had unlawfully disposed of her property, which, along with "making her life miserable," falls under the category of "cruelty" in the relevant enactment (discussed below). This raises questions concerning the grounds for *fasakh,* the ways they have expanded in recent decades, how this expansion has resulted in greater congruence between the *sharia* courts and their civil counterparts, and some of the contexts in which women are getting more justice.

Deeper into the Labyrinth

The basis for a woman obtaining *fasakh* is fairly consistent from state to state, as is the technical language of the relevant enactments. In Kuala Lumpur, as in all state jurisdictions, there are twelve specific grounds for *fasakh*. The enactment in effect in Kuala Lumpur at the time of the hearing in question, which I have edited for readability, establishes the bases for *fasakh* as follows:

1. That the whereabouts of the husband have not been known for more than one year;
2. that he has neglected or failed to provide for her maintenance for three months;
3. that he has been sentenced to imprisonment for three years or more;
4. that he has failed to perform, without reasonable cause, his marital obligations [with respect to sexual companionship] for one year;
5. that he was impotent at the time of the marriage and remains so and the wife was unaware [of this] at the time of the marriage;
6. that he has been insane for two years or is suffering from leprosy or vitiligo or a communicable venereal disease;
7. that the wife, having been given in marriage by her . . . [guardian] before she attained . . . [maturity], repudiated the marriage before attaining the age of eighteen, the marriage not having been consummated;
8. that the husband treats her with cruelty, that is to say, *inter alia,* (i) habitually assaults her or makes her life miserable by cruelty of conduct; (ii) associates with women or men of evil repute; (iii) attempts to force her to lead an immoral life; (iv) disposes of her property or prevents her from exercising her legal rights over it; (v) obstructs her observance of her religious obligations or practice; or (vi) if he has more than one wife, does not treat her equitably in accordance with the requirements of *Hukum Syarak;*

9. that even after four months the marriage has not been consummated owing to the willful refusal of the husband to consummate it;

10. that she did not consent to the marriage or her consent was not valid, whether in consequence of distress, mistake, unsoundness of mind, or any other circumstance recognized by *Hukum Syarak;*

11. that at the time of the marriage she, though capable of giving consent, was a mentally disturbed person within the meaning of the . . . Mental Health Act 2001 (Act 615); or

12. any other ground recognized as valid for dissolution of marriage or *fasakh* under *Hukum Syarak.*[5]

This enactment delineates twelve different grounds for a woman to obtain *fasakh*, but some of them, like item 8, bearing on cruelty, contain multiple provisions, such that the list of grounds for *fasakh* is closer to twenty. The term "inter alia" in item 8 is significant, making clear that the items listed there are not meant to be exhaustive. Similarly, item 12, "any other ground recognized as valid for dissolution of marriage or *fasakh* under *Hukum Syarak*," leaves open the possibility for plaintiffs, lawyers, judges, women's rights groups, and others to argue that *fasakh* may and should be granted for reasons not specifically delineated in the enactment. One example would be *shiqaq*, or, in the common-law language that is relevant in the country's civil courts, "irretrievable breakdown" of marriage. Neither of these terms, to be clear, appears anywhere in the language of the enactment.

Most of the major changes in *fasakh* provisions in the last sixty to seventy years occurred with the 1983–91 reforms, which replaced the laws previously in force. The earlier enactments, dating mainly from the 1950s and 1960s, typically contained about half as many grounds for *fasakh*, focusing chiefly on the husband being impotent, insane, afflicted with a communicable disease, or on his absence for a period of three or more months, his imprisonment, failure to provide *nafkah*, etc. (Ahmad Ibrahim 1965 [1975]). The principal expansion of provisions that took place with the 1983–91 enactments involved the inclusion of: (1) item 8, bearing on cruelty, which, importantly, includes the term "inter alia" at the end of the first line; and (2) item 12, concerning "any other ground recognized as valid for . . . *fasakh* under *Hukum Syarak.*"

This expansion and liberalization of the grounds for *fasakh* has been interpreted by scholars such as Donald Horowitz (1994) as evidence of the convergence, at the level of substantive as distinct from procedural law, of *sharia* and British common law.[6] Horowitz's argument is not that the Islamic concept of *shiqaq* was borrowed or derived from British law, or invented in response to British or other Western-origin pressures or incentives. He is well aware that the notion of *shiqaq* is enshrined in foundational Islamic texts such as the Quran and *hadith*. Rather, his point is that in Malaysia, *shiqaq* has been accorded increased salience in recent decades due largely to British-origin common-law sensibilities that bestow legitimacy on "irretrievable breakdown of marriage" as a basis for non-Muslim divorce. The larger dynamic has to do with the politics of the juridical field. Many innovations and reforms in the *sharia* judiciary are motivated by concerns to be "as modern as" yet ethically superior to—hence both the same and different from—the civil judiciary, which is simultaneously the *sharia* judiciary's primary patron and main competitor.

The judge's ruling in the case at hand cited the husband's failure to perform his *duties* as a husband, rather than the wife's *right* to claim *shiqaq*. But the inclusion of *shiqaq* as a basis for *fasakh* in the wife's petition is telling. Perhaps more germane is that the judge reiterated it as he was about to render his verdict; he did so, moreover, without any balking or dressing down of the wife's lawyer, as commonly occurs when a judge feels that a litigant's counsel is off base, out of order, or ill-prepared. This suggests some degree of normalization of *shiqaq* as grounds for *fasakh*.

Interview material, court documents, and other data (addressed shortly) suggest that *shiqaq* or the emotional or mental suffering associated with it is listed by women and accepted by judges as grounds for *fasakh* more frequently now than at the time of Horowitz's research, the early 1990s. They also indicate that *fasakh* suits account for notably larger percentages of the *sharia* courts' caseloads than in decades past and are almost always decided in women's favor (see also Hirsch 1998, 127–29; Rosen 2018, chapter 2). This is important insofar as the period since the early 1990s could have seen a reversal of the trend identified by Horowitz.

To get a quick sense of why I contend that *fasakh* claims comprise appreciably larger percentages of *sharia* courts' casework than in previous decades, we might briefly consider comparative-historical perspectives from the town of Rembau in the state of Negeri Sembilan. During 1987–88, only 9 percent (3/33) of the civil cases I observed involved *fasakh* claims (Peletz 2002, 156).[7] The relevant figure for newly registered civil cases in Rembau some twenty-five years later (2012) is 16.2 percent (37/228), nearly double what it was earlier.

Statewide data for Negeri Sembilan for 1998–2002 yield a different set of perspectives on the prevalence of *fasakh*. But they also make clear that *fasakh* suits have become exceedingly common, accounting for 25.8 percent of claims bearing on divorce/annulment, and fully 41.2 percent of all petitions for divorce/annulment brought by women (International Islamic University of Malaysia 2005, 74–76). Especially when viewed alongside earlier data from Rembau and elsewhere, this material provides further corroboration of the point that the period since the late 1980s has seen sharp increases in both the frequency and the overall numbers of *fasakh* cases.

Some of the factors contributing to the increase were clarified in an interview I conducted in July 2012 with one of my most knowledgeable interlocutors, Haji Musa, a former high-court judge on the *sharia* bench who was then a senior official in the JKSM. As Haji Musa phrased it, *sharia* judges have become "a bit more flexible" in adjudicating cases involving *fasakh* when a woman's petition is not based on any of the specific grounds delineated in the relevant enactment(s). In this regard, *sharia* judges are friendlier to women (my expression, not Haji Musa's). This is also to say that with respect to the termination of marriage via *fasakh,* women have an easier time getting justice—put differently, are getting more justice—than in decades past.

According to Haji Musa, this development has come about partly because judges exercise *ijtihad* (innovative legal interpretation of—or on the basis of—sacred texts; judicial creativity) in ascertaining whether a woman has experienced harm (*mudarat*) in her marriage. Haji Musa went on to say that in recent years judges have broadened the notion of harm to include a wife's emotional and mental suffering, though, significantly, there has been no corresponding shift in statutory law.

Before elaborating on his views, I should point out that the concept of harm (to women) has been elevated to a status it did not enjoy during my research in the 1970s and 1980s. This is partly a response to pressures from NGOs and civil society (considered below) and partly a function of the *sharia* judiciary's adoption of sensibilities and norms enshrined in local common-law, though the more encompassing dynamic is the intensified transnational circulation during this period of various kinds of "rights-talk" (see also Osanloo 2009). During my earlier research, the central issues for judges in *fasakh* cases involved ascertaining whether or not the specific statutory conditions for *fasakh* had been met. During the period 2011–14, by contrast, the forms that women were required to complete as part of their *fasakh* petitions foregrounded the concept of harm by subsuming all specific offenses committed by husbands under the umbrella rubric of "incidents or things that have caused harm" (*perkara-perkara yang telah memberi kemudharatan*). The relevant forms asked for three examples of such harm, though some women provided many more. Commonly cited examples included "no mutual understanding" (*tiada persefahaman*) or variations on the general theme, such as "mental and emotional suffering/torture" (*penderitaan/penderaan mental dan emosi*), "emotional stress" (*tekanan emosi*), and "we always quarrel" (*selalu gaduh*). Also conspicuously present were more conventional arguments for *fasakh*, such as a husband who "has not come home for a year and a half," "has not provided financial support or sexual companionship," "does drugs," "is in and out of jail," and "hits me."[8]

To clarify what he meant when he told me that emotional and mental suffering currently constitutes acceptable grounds for *fasakh* and that today's judges are more accommodating than their predecessors, Haji Musa offered the following example.

> [Suppose] a man marries a rich woman and cannot afford to provide her with the luxury she enjoyed before their marriage. If the wife experiences emotional or

mental suffering on account of this situation, she can petition for *fasakh* on the basis of that suffering. The judge can then effect an annulment. In earlier times, it was more difficult to accept emotional or mental suffering [as grounds for *fasakh*]. But things have become a bit more flexible . . . Nowadays it is easier to annul marriages.

The scenario Haji Musa provided off the top of his head is revealing, suggesting that the "fit" between husbands and wives has grown much more complex and fraught. The increased complexity and potential for stress and anxiety is a feature of the synergy created by a number of socioeconomic and cultural-political dynamics. They include the emergence of a new Malay middle class; the development of massive socioeconomic disparities among Malays; and the fact that Malay women situated at the top of the social-class hierarchy often experience difficulty finding suitable husbands, especially if the women have earned advanced degrees. Germane as well is the increased salience of companionate marriage, defined both "as a marital ideal in which emotional closeness is understood to be . . . one of the primary measures of success in marriage" and "a form of kinship in which the conjugal partnership is privileged over other family ties" (Wardlow and Hirsch 2006, 4). All such changes have gone hand in hand with the decline of arranged marriage, the erosion of extended kin bonds, and the reconfiguration of myriad other features of kinship and affinity. Many of these transformations reflect state-sponsored social engineering aimed at creating a new Malay middle class from the ranks of the once largely agrarian and relatively impoverished Malay populace (Peletz 1988, 1996, 2002).

The idea that it is easier to annul a marriage these days as compared with decades past is, in any event, a thoroughly relative point. One would be hard pressed to argue that a woman seeking an annulment currently has an easy go of it. I should remind the reader, though, that the *fasakh* petition discussed earlier was adjudicated in the plaintiff's favor, as were fully 95 percent (296/310) of *fasakh* cases heard in Kuala Lumpur during 2014–15.[9] More broadly, the fact that judges are nowadays more obliging in terminating marriage via *fasakh* is of great importance in the Malaysian context, where, as we have seen, Muslim women's options to extricate themselves from loveless or otherwise untenable unions, especially without the consent or cooperation of their husbands, are highly restricted.

Before turning to the more general question as to whether Muslim women in Malaysia are getting (more) justice from the nation's *sharia* courts, we might briefly consider perspectives from neighboring Indonesia, the largest Muslim-majority country in the world. Muslims in both Malaysia and Indonesia are overwhelming Sunni, adhering to the Shafi'i legal tradition, but in Indonesia marriage and divorce procedures, including the cultural logic of judicial process, have followed a different developmental trajectory than in Malaysia. Most relevant for us is that Indonesian women enjoy more freedom to extricate themselves from untenable marriages, albeit not through an expansion of the grounds for *fasakh*, as has occurred in Malaysia, or a liberalization of *khul* procedures, as we see in Egypt. The historical and other factors that account for this divergence need not concern us (see Bowen 2003; Feener and Cammack 2007; Nurlaewati 2010; Feener 2013; Nasir 2013; Huis 2015). I am more interested in drawing attention to some of the contrasts at issue, though two similarities also merit quick note: in both nations Islamic courts deal mostly with issues of marriage and divorce, and in both contexts the vast majority of plaintiffs are women.

Stijn Van Huis's (2015) study, *Islamic Courts and Women's Divorce Rights in Indonesia,* provides deeply nuanced and exquisitely detailed descriptions and analyses of Indonesia's Islamic judiciary and is especially useful here (see also Nasir 2013). Huis focuses on two courts, one in Cianjur, a town located in the West Javanese district of the same name, the other in the town of Bulukumba, which is also the name of the surrounding district, in South Sulawesi. One of his more significant findings is that in both towns the majority of women's petitions for divorce specify as grounds for marital dissolution that there is "no longer any common understanding [or agreement or harmony]" between them and their husbands, that a state of "continuous strife" or *shiqaq* exists, or, more simply, as judges tend to rephrase things, that the marriage is "broken" (*pecah*) insofar as the "peace, love, and compassion" (*sakinah, mawaddah, warahmah*) that is supposed to characterize marital relations no longer exists and perhaps never did (149–50, 205–6, 234–38). Of at least comparable importance is that in most cases judges accept women's claims that are based on these kinds of arguments, commonly taking a woman's petition on these grounds as sufficient evidence that the marriage has indeed failed or collapsed, and not requiring any further proof that such breakdown has occurred. Put differently, if a woman is determined to end a marriage, the judge will honor that request, even if the husband remains committed to maintaining the union and does not consent to its termination (239). One result is that "no-fault divorce" now obtains throughout Indonesia. An important caveat here is that this situation obtains less in doctrinal or explicitly codified (positive-law) legal terms than in the judicial practices of both the lower courts that hear the majority of cases and in the Supreme Court, which in a number of landmark decisions has upheld lower courts' positions on what amounts to no-fault divorce (241–43). This is one reason why Huis concurs with a Bulukumba judge who, in his disapproval of these trends, argues that Indonesia's Islamic courts "have been turned into [little more than] divorce registration offices" (243).

Two other important points bear on *nusyuz*: (1) In Indonesia, men, not just women, are sometimes charged with and found guilty of *nusyuz*—a sharp contrast with Malaysia; and (2) as in Malaysia, despite the common belief (or claim) on the part of men that their wives are guilty of *nusyuz*, women are rarely convicted of this offense (Huis 2015, 158, 244, 247, 252, 261, 272). This is partly because the grounds for finding women guilty of *nusyuz* have been narrowed in recent years, although this narrowing, like the de facto emergence of no-fault divorce, has occurred at the level of judicial practice and has not entailed a corresponding shift in formal legal doctrine.

In light of the above, it is worth remembering that Malaysian political and religious elites often pride themselves on having encouraged a moderate and progressive Islam that is in the vanguard of modernizing developments both in the Muslim world and the West. It may seem surprising, in other words, that they have not followed Egypt's or Indonesia's leads by making statutory or *de facto* provision for other forms of marital dissolution initiated by women that do not require a husband's consent or cooperation. The implementation of such provisions in Malaysia could go a long way toward improving the lives of Muslim women, as suggested by data from Indonesia, Egypt, and Malaysia alike (Nurlaewati 2010; Sonneveld 2012; Huis 2015). But as material from these and other settings also makes clear, such reforms can result in backlash from men and conservative sectors of Muslim civil society, and can thus be costly and dangerous for the ruling elites involved in pursuing them (see, e.g., Sonneveld and Lindbekk 2015; see also Hirsch 1998).[10] A more general point here is that until such time as Egyptian- or Indonesian-style initiatives bearing on female-initiated divorce are implemented in Malaysia, and it is possible they never will be, debates concerning the expansion, contraction, and interpretation of the grounds for *fasakh* will continue to be central to the struggle for gender justice and equality within the family and beyond.

ARE WOMEN GETTING (MORE) JUSTICE?

The material on *fasakh* I have presented provides valuable context for addressing—and partially answers, in the affirmative—a critically important question: Are Malay and other Muslim women in Malaysia able to get more justice from the *sharia* courts than was the case during my research in the late 1970s and 1980s?

To begin to address the issues, one needs to distinguish the (*sharia*) laws from the (*sharia*) courts. The latter institutions do not make the laws. Their mandate is, rather, to enforce them. This of course requires the interpretation of law, though the interpretive dimension of *sharia* judicial practice, the realm of *fiqh*, is often played down by political and religious elites spanning the "religious/secular" divide. This is done in the interest of stressing the uniformity of *sharia*, its unchallengeable nature as God's will, and, by implication, the uncontestable because ostensibly divine nature of state initiatives and arrangements cast in Islamic discourse or with reference to key symbols of Islam.

That said, if the laws are skewed in favor of men, then, all things being equal, court practices will be as well. There is no question that as far as legal texts (both classically Islamic and modern Islamic family law enactments) are concerned, men have more legal privileges and prerogatives than women. This skewing is evident in litigant practices and in judicial engagement with them; it was quite apparent during my earlier fieldwork and remains so. Hence the question I focus on here, clearly a relative one, is whether today's women are in a better position to receive justice than their counterparts in earlier decades (i.e., the 1970s–1980s and previously; see n2). I hasten to add that I am not interested in engaging abstract notions of justice or developing a one-size-fits-all concept of justice that could perhaps be utilized across the Muslim world or further afield. For present purposes, justice for women in Malaysia's *sharia* courts may be narrowly defined as timely, reasonable, and otherwise equitable responses to the claims they register with court authorities. A more expansive conceptualization of justice for women, such as the one deployed here, also takes into account the spiritual, textual, social, and material resources and networks available to them to address their marriage- and divorce-related (and other) grievances in the courts and in society at large. Additionally, it involves consideration of gender patterns in harsh sentencing, a topic of considerable scholarly and media attention in recent years.

The short, partial answer to the question is fivefold. First, women's legal petitions are dealt with by the courts in a more timely and substantive fashion than in the past. Second, compared to the previous decades under consideration here, the courts are more likely to impose punitive sanctions on men who contravene *sharia* family-law enactments. A third, more general point, also related to sentencing, is that most harsh punishments are meted out to men, not women. Fourth, women currently have at their disposal much more information concerning their formal legal entitlements and obligations with regard to conjugal ties and their dissolution, and can rather easily tap into densely configured networks of support to aid them in negotiating marriage, the shoals of divorce/annulment, and the precarities that may ensue. The fifth component of the answer is that, despite these generally encouraging developments, women and men do not experience marriage, divorce, or the *sharia* court system on a level playing field. This too is changing in ways beneficial to women, however, albeit primarily for those who heed increasingly pronounced and restrictive expectations regarding obedience and heteronormativity. I will address these and related issues one at a time, beginning with the expansion of resources and networks, proceeding with matters of timeliness and punitiveness, and turning finally to themes bearing on obedience, heteronormativity, and pluralism. I should note that I consider some topics very briefly (especially if they are taken up elsewhere in this or other chapters), others in greater depth.

There Has Been a Proliferation of Institutional Resources and Networks Created for the Benefit of Women (and Children)

This is the most dramatic and unequivocally positive change bearing on women and *sharia* justice that has occurred since the late 1970s. Women are presently able to access a wide variety of women- and family-friendly institutional networks and resources (spiritual, textual, social, and material) that they increasingly draw upon to enhance their understanding of their rights and responsibilities in the context of marriage and its dissolution, their husbands' duties and prerogatives, and how officers of the court manage such matters.

Before delving into specifics bearing on historical change and the emergence of NGOs that helped bring about that change, I should make clear that in the 1970s–1980s the vast majority of these resources and networks did not exist. At that time, elderly village women provided the main forms of assistance and support, commonly serving as sounding boards for younger female relatives experiencing difficulties with husbands or ex-husbands and offering both strategic advice and emotional support (Peletz 1996, 2002). SIS, the progressive Muslim feminist NGO founded in 1988, is the chief exception to my generalization concerning the (relative) absence in the 1980s of resources and networks for women experiencing difficulties in marriage or divorce. SIS also deserves the lion's share of credit both for drawing public attention to the need to develop resources and networks of the sort at issue here, and for providing pressure and templates for the initiation of relevant government programs conducive to enhancing pluralistic sensibilities and dispositions with respect to women.

SIS's internationally well-publicized commitment to advocacy, activism, and reform is noteworthy on other grounds as well. It typically entails a PR and scholarly focus on women as distinct from the more expansive domain of gender; it often involves relatively synchronic analyses, highlighting short-term backlashes and setbacks rather than progress over the long term; and it relies heavily on strategic essentialism of the sort mentioned at the outset of this chapter (see, e.g., Zainah Anwar 2001, 2008; Norani Othman 2005; see also Maznah Mohamad 2010a; Liow 2009, 124–31.) This is one reason why members of the public and international communities of scholars and human rights advocates tend to have rather dim views of Islamic family law and Muslim women's rights in Malaysia.

Another reason has to do with the existence of NGOs at the other end of the (Muslim) civil society spectrum. Consider, for example, the PGSM and groups like the Muslim Brothers, which is apparently composed mainly of current and former *sharia* judges and lawyers (Hoffstaedter 2011, 139–45). NGOs such as these, aided at times by government religious bureaucracies like JAKIM, commonly criticize SIS and file police reports and lawsuits against them on the grounds of their alleged hostility to the *sharia* judiciary and their demeaning of Islam. This too makes for good copy, both nationally and internationally. The more general point here is threefold. Malaysia boasts a vibrant civil society (Weiss 2006; Moustafa 2018); some of its key players advocate tirelessly for the expansion of Muslim women's rights (and pluralism regarding ethno-racial and other diversity), while others are strongly opposed to their efforts; and media coverage of either side conduces toward views of the proverbial glass of women's rights under Islamic family law as half empty rather than half full.

The resources currently available to women take many forms. In terms of print media, they include colorful, easy-to-read (Malay-language) handouts and informational brochures created and distributed by the JKSM. As I observed on many occasions, these are widely available in the waiting rooms and lobbies of *sharia* courthouses, sometimes right below or next to a sign reading *Sila Ambil Satu* (Please Take One). The vast majority of women seeking the *sharia* court's services can read, write, and speak Malay. This material is thus directly and fully accessible to them.

One such brochure I examined concerns husbands' and wives' rights to lodge formal legal claims while they are married. But it focuses almost entirely on the rights of wives (e.g., to receive material support from their husbands for the purpose of maintaining themselves and their children). Another brochure addresses husbands' and wives' rights to lodge formal legal claims after they have divorced, though it too deals mostly with the rights of wives to receive maintenance, a share of conjugal earnings (*harta sepencarian*), custody of children, etc. Yet another brochure delineates the various types of marital dissolution that are available, involving the *talak* repudiation clause, for example, or alternatively, via procedures laid out for *fasakh, tebus talak* (*khuluk*), and *taklik*.

Some courthouses (e.g., Rembau's) also distribute handouts and informational sheets bearing on polygamy (polygyny) that contain discussions of a woman's rights with respect to her husband taking a second wife while he is still married to her. The fact that this material exists and is available to women even in small courthouses such as Rembau's is significant. I never encountered brochures or printed information of this sort in the late 1980s or earlier, despite the fact that men taking second wives without the permission or knowledge of their first wives has long been a serious concern for women.

The focus in these brochures on the rights (*hak*) of wives and women generally is enormously consequential. In the late 1980s and previously, much of the discourse in and outside the courts centered on the duties (*tanggungjawab*) of men as husbands and fathers, and, more specifically, on how they failed to perform them properly, not on wives' or women's rights per se. The cultural elaboration and "thick" institutional backing of the idea that women are rights-bearing, entitled citizens, not simply jural minors yoked to men through ties of marriage and co-parenthood, is a huge step forward for Malay and other Muslim women. This generalization is also relevant to the heightened centrality of rights-talk in other Muslim-majority settings, including Iran's family courts, as Arzoo Osanloo (2009) has incisively documented. The dynamic at issue is, at the same time, a momentous development for those who favor the spread and entrenchment of more inclusive political discourses in the highly contested terrain of citizenship in present-day Malaysia, as discussed in the conclusion to this chapter.

In addition to the brochures and handouts mentioned here, eye-catching posters and banners that publicize the existence of legal and other support services for women and families adorn many public spaces of *sharia* courthouses. Some of them advertise secularly oriented national legal aid bureaus (e.g., Biro Bantuan Guaman). Others celebrate the rollout of new (as of 2010) Transit Services offered by the Family Support Division (Bahagian Sokongan Keluarga) of the Federal Territory *Syariah* Court that include free round-trip transportation to the court from one's home in the Klang Valley (which encompasses Kuala Lumpur) as well as food and lodging, presumably for a day or two.

These initiatives are also widely covered in print media, typically with impressive quantitative information bearing on the numbers of women they have helped since their inception. So too are different types of counseling services and mediation programs geared toward assisting women (and men) experiencing marital difficulties. Much of this information is also available through the Internet, particularly on websites sponsored by the *sharia* judiciary and federal-, state-, and district-level departments of Islamic religion.[11] Suffice it to add that most Malaysians, men and women alike, have ready access to the Internet through their smartphones, iPads, and laptops, or the devices of their relatives.

The Court's Engagements with Women's Claims Are More Timely, Consistent, and Substantive

Comprehensive studies of district- and state-level data bearing on the period 1998–2002 conducted by the International Islamic University of Malaysia with the collaboration of Malaysia's Department of *Syariah* Judiciary indicate that cases initiated by women, like those initiated by men, are generally resolved more quickly than in times past (International Islamic University of Malaysia 2005). There is much regional variation and considerable divergence by type of case, and long delays sometimes still occur. This is due partly to obstructive strategies by husbands and husbands' lawyers. Other contributing factors include one or both litigants failing to appear for their scheduled hearings and incomplete paperwork.

In the state of Selangor between 2005 and 2010, the courts resolved "nearly 80% of [divorce] cases in less than six months" (Siti Zubaidah Ismail et al n.d., 9), a clear improvement over the situation reported for the early 1980s, during which time "a divorce petition . . . [was] normally settled . . . [in] about seven to eight months" (Sharifah Zaleha Syed Hassan 1986, 195). As for *taklik* divorces, which typically take longer than other types of marital dissolution, in Selangor during this period nearly half were resolved in less than six months and two-thirds were resolved in less than twelve months (Siti Zubaidah Ismail et al n.d., 9); the corresponding figure for the 1980s was "seven to fifteen months on the average," at least in the state of Kedah (Sharifah Zaleha Syed Hassan 1993, 81). Another, arguably far more telling, body of data indicates that roughly 60 percent of the cases referred to the *sharia* courts nationwide from 2002 through 2012 were settled via *sulh,* which, as we have seen, typically (but not always) means that they were concluded in less than three months.[12]

These and other relevant figures index an upgrading of the services provided by the courts that is of great import, especially since, as British Prime Minister William Gladstone (1809–98) once famously remarked, "justice delayed is justice denied." Tellingly, Gladstone's observation is commonly invoked verbatim by critics—and supporters—of both the *sharia* judiciary and its civil counterpart, typically in efforts to incite a more substantive "will to improve" (Li 2007) than already exists.

To say that in comparison with previous decades the courts are more timely in responding to women's claims does not necessarily mean that the courts' engagements are more consistent or substantive. These engagements *are* more consistent and substantive, however, as will be readily apparent to readers who compare the material presented here with my findings from the late 1980s (Peletz 2002). This is despite the fact that the dynamics at issue sometimes result in women being encouraged by officials to accept mediated compromises that are not necessarily in their best interests.

The Courts Are Less Tolerant of—and More Punitive toward—Errant Husbands

We have seen that due to changes in Islamic family law implemented during 1983–91, the state has criminalized certain practices of husbands that were merely frowned upon or discouraged in the early 1980s and previously. Such practices include taking a second wife without the court's approval and pronouncing the *talak* without the court's permission. The courts often impose relatively heavy sanctions on men found guilty of these offenses, including fines, non-payment of which can result in jail time. They could be more severe, however, given their commitment to the proposition that harsh punishment serves as deterrence, which is one facet of the punitive turn evident in many realms of law, politics, and culture (chapter 2).

Being more punitive toward men who mistreat women in the context of marriage or subsequent to its dissolution is not the same thing as treating women more equitably. But there is a positive correlation between these two dimensions of judicial practice insofar as the present-day disposition of cases bearing on *nafkah,* for example, is much more likely to involve strict enforcement than in the past (International Islamic University of Malaysia 2007). This is a relative point, and lapses still occur, but the trend toward stricter enforcement is largely beyond dispute.

Most Harsh Punishments Continue to Be Meted Out to Men, Not Women

Discussions of gender justice would be incomplete without brief mention of Western stereotypes bearing on the harsh punishments assumed to be routinely administered to women in the name of Islam in nations such as Pakistan, Afghanistan, and Nigeria (Abu-Lughod 2013). I want to make clear that, with two exceptions, I have never observed a *sharia* judge impose a fine, jail time, or corporal punishment on a female litigant.[13]

There have, however, been a few well-publicized instances, some of which drew exceedingly negative national and international attention from women's groups and human rights advocates (among others), involving *sharia* judges ordering stiff penalties for female defendants prosecuted for consuming alcohol or engaging in other moral breaches. One (in)famous case involved Kartika Seri Dewi Binti Shukarno, known simply as Kartika in the media, a Singaporean national of Malay-Javanese ancestry.[14] In 2008, the thirty-two-year old nurse, model, and mother of two was caught up in a police raid on a nightclub in the state of Pahang and arrested for drinking beer. After being found guilty of consuming alcohol, she was sentenced to pay a fine of RM\$5,000 (around US\$1,400 at the time) or to serve three years in jail, *and* to be flogged with six strokes of a rattan cane. The sentence provoked immediate outcry from national and international NGOs fighting for women and human rights and was eventually commuted by the Sultan of Pahang to three weeks of community service. Around the same time (February 9, 2010), three unmarried women (aged seventeen to twenty-five) were reportedly caned for having sex outside of marriage, but since the caning was done in secret (if it did in fact occur) and was only made public afterwards, it did not provoke the kind of outcry associated with Kartika's initial sentence. One knowledgeable human rights activist told me in the fall of 2013 that she questioned the very existence of this case, suggesting that the entire narrative was manufactured by state authorities to counter the impression, engendered by the (then pending) commutation of Kartika's sentence, that authorities were "soft on (female) crime."[15]

Cases such as these are exceptions that prove the rule, a rule that flies in the face of Western stereotypes implying that in the course of their day-to-day duties, judges in Muslim-majority countries are routinely involved in disciplining women in draconian ways. I have already suggested that it is quite rare in a statistical sense for Malaysia's *sharia* courts to impose corporal punishment or jail sentences on women; fines are also relatively unusual, except in cases of *khalwat* (illicit proximity) and fornication/adultery. By contrast, it is not at all uncommon for *sharia* judges to render decisions against male litigants that include fines and, if they are unable to pay the fines, jail sentences of four to six weeks or more (but not corporal punishment).

Also crucial to underscore is that almost all of the flogging that occurs in Malaysia is ordered by the civil courts, not the *sharia* courts. Such sentences are meted out to men (judged or assumed to be "illegal immigrants" or convicted of serious offenses involving drugs, sexual assault, or other forms of violence), but never to women, since the civil judiciary does not subject women to corporal punishment.[16] This is part of the larger gendered and juridical context we need to bear in mind when assessing cases such as Kartika's. So too is the fact that, nationwide, men comprise roughly 80 percent of defendants in *sharia* civil cases, which are typically initiated by their wives, and more than 64 percent of defendants in *sharia* criminal suits, which are usually initiated and prosecuted by one or another state religious bureaucracy (such as the Department of Islamic Religion).[17] Failure to consider this larger context, because of a focus on women as distinct from the more encompassing domain of gender, for example, can easily give rise to the erroneous impression that the nation's *sharia* courts are increasingly targeting women and subjecting them to harsh, medieval punishment. Statistically speaking, it is far more accurate to say that the *sharia* establishment and other government bureaucracies, "religious" and "secular" alike, are honing in on what they take to be *male* delinquency and criminality.[18] Clearly, however, the larger concern lies with reinscribing and otherwise managing dynamics of kinship, gender, class, race, religion, and citizenship, and both cleansing the nation and fortifying the state.

Of Obedience, Heteronormativity, and Pluralism

My generally affirmative but importantly qualified answer(s) to the question highlighted in the title of this chapter requires additional caveats if we interrogate the idea, increasingly prevalent in official quarters and popular culture, that wives are entitled to material and other support from their husbands only if they are obedient (*taat*). Still further qualification is warranted if we look beyond majoritarian circles and consider the communities of women who transgress heteronormative expectations and ideals. I address these issues one at a time, ranging beyond the courts to convey a sense of how law is lived and what types of cultural-political forces are involved in shaping both present-day socio-legal dynamics and their possible futures.

This term *taat* is commonly understood by Malays to mean obedient and loyal, particularly *in relation to one's husband*. The inverse of *taat* is *nusyuz*, which, as I have mentioned, is usually taken to refer to a wife's disobedience, disloyalty, and overall recalcitrance vis-à-vis her husband. Both concepts are heavily freighted in moral, ethical, and specifically Islamic terms. And both tend to be invoked in relation to patterns of behavior involving women but not men. This is the case even though the Quran makes clear that *nusyuz* can occur on the part of men and women alike, and despite the fact that many of the Islamic family law offenses that men commit entail behavior that fits the definition of *nusyuz* (e.g., failing to support one's wife or children, taking a second wife without the first wife's knowledge).

A central issue here is the maintenance-obedience paradigm enshrined in certain classical Islamic texts. This paradigm has been discussed by Ziba Mir-Hosseini (2016) and other Muslim feminist reformers (Wadud 2008; K. Ali 2006), some of whom were instrumental in the 2009 founding of Musawah (Arabic for "equality"), an international NGO dedicated to obtaining justice for women under Islamic family law. One of their interventions has involved revisiting and evaluating the larger context of Quranic verses cited by conservative Muslim jurists over the centuries to bolster their view of marriage as a strongly patriarchal arrangement akin to a master-slave relationship, or one defined by the transfer through sale of rights over a woman from her father to her husband. They point out that such passages exist alongside others in the Quran that depict marriage as a more symmetrical and equitable partnership in which husband and wife, like men and women generally, have (or should enjoy) more or less equal or complementary rights; and that some of them also promote gender relations characterized by harmony, love, and mercy (see, e.g., Surah An-Nisa [4:128], Surah Ar-Rum [30:21]). A focus on these latter verses yields very different Quranic perspectives on matrimony and gender relations than those enshrined both in classical Islamic legal theory and in colonial-era and postcolonial regimes of Islamic family law.

Interpretations of Islamic law and of the scholarship bearing on these interpretations have long been influenced by the vicissitudes of historical change. A classic example has to do with the practice of slavery. The Quran condones slavery under certain circumstances, but it was formally abolished throughout the Muslim world in the nineteenth and twentieth centuries in keeping with the values and other realities of those times. Mir-Hosseini and other reform-oriented scholars thus argue that it is high time for Muslims to rethink the textual foundations and contemporary legal dynamics of marriage, divorce, and gender.

There is good evidence, as we have seen, that these kinds of arguments have become more mainstream in Malaysia and elsewhere in the Muslim world (Norani Othman 2005; Zainah Anwar 2009; Sonneveld 2012; Huis 2015). Such changes reflect pressures from civil society, including NGOs like SIS and Musawah, efforts on the part of *sharia* judiciaries to adopt key norms of their civil counterparts, and globally widespread discourses emphasizing individual rights. But there are strong countercurrents, backlashes, and orthogonal pressures as well, and the future is by no means settled. This is especially so since there are clear limits to the new kinds of relations and new kinds of selves, to borrow from Borneman's epigraph once again, that political and religious elites shaping *sharia*-court practice and other features of state policy are willing to countenance, let alone nurture.

Some of the countercurrents are exemplified by the formation in Kuala Lumpur in 2011 of the Obedient Wives Club (OWC), an organization of mostly middle-class professional women that is an outgrowth and sister organization of the Polygamy Club (PC) established the previous year. Both of these organizations are closely associated with the business conglomerate Global Ikhwan. This consortium produces *halal* consumer goods in keeping with the vision of Al-Arqam, a Sufi-oriented group whose members seek to emulate the Prophet's lifestyle and to propagate and enrich the faith.[19] In October 2011, the OWC published a highly controversial book with the curious title *Islamic Sex, Fighting Jews to Return Islamic Sex to the World.* The volume was advertised as a manual that would help Muslim women better serve their husbands' sexual needs and simultaneously recuperate Islamic discourses on sex suppressed by a global conspiracy of hostile Jews. Its authors enjoined married women to behave like "first-class whores" in bed so that their husbands would not be tempted to stray and sin. The book drew sharp criticism from women's rights groups, government ministries, and others, many of whom claimed that it objectified and demeaned women, effectively blamed them for their husbands' errant ways, reduced marriage to sex, and was otherwise deeply problematic and offensive (Mackinnon 2011).[20]

Perhaps not surprisingly, two women associated with the OWC, the PC, or both (the memberships of these two groups appear to overlap) spoke ardently in defense of polygynous unions at a conference on polygamy (polygyny) that I attended at the Universiti Kebangsaan Malaysia, in Bangi, Selangor, in August 2011. The purpose of the daylong conference was to mark the release of a long-awaited national study on polygyny conducted by Sisters in Islam and researchers from a number of the nation's top universities. The three-year project yielded extensive quantitative and qualitative data on the economic, psychological, and other consequences for married women (and children) of their husbands' taking a second wife. One altogether unambiguous takeaway was the statistically significant pattern of decline in the living standards of the first wife and her children, a dynamic that can be devastating for many women and children in lower income groups. The two women mentioned earlier stood up during the Q & A period following some of the presentations and proceeded to strongly criticize the study, and, by implication, the conference in its entirety, for being "so negative," and for ignoring the positive features of polygynous marriages, which they proceeded to extol based on their ongoing experience in such unions.

Antipathy to greater marriage equality of the sort at issue here and other forms of backlash are by no means confined to seemingly marginal groups such as the PC or the OWC, or to the more expansive umbrella organizations (Al-Arqam, Global Ikhwan) with which they are associated. They are prevalent as well among Malay men occupying widely varied subject positions and social locations who have political and religious orientations that span the spectrum. In many instances, moreover, these stances are shared by their wives, as is clearly the case with the elite cadre of globe-trotting, PhD-bearing *"sharia* advisors" (see, e.g., Sloane-White 2017, 123–27). Such enmity is also pronounced among conservative *ulama* and *mufti,* and is broadly congruent with the messages conveyed in the nation's Islamic schools and by the main Islamist opposition party, PAS (Kraince 2009). Resistance to the kinds of marriage equality that Mir-Hosseini, Musawah, and Sisters in Islam propose is frequently justified with statements like "that's against Islam." And it is sometimes packaged with overt suspicion and criticism of the

Western foundations and granting agencies that help finance their conferences, publications, and other endeavors, including, most notably, the Konrad Adenauer Foundation and the Rockefeller Foundation. These latter organizations are commonly said to be in league with Zionist and neocolonial forces bent on disparaging if not destroying Islam and subjecting Muslims to colonial-era servitude if not wholesale annihilation.

This brings us back to the theme of heteronormativity that I broached at the beginning of this section. One set of relevant issues has to do with the nature of revisionist accounts of Quranic passages and other foundational texts bearing on gender and sexual normativity that have been proposed by progressive Muslim scholars in recent years. A related concern is whether there might be growing acceptance of such accounts in Malaysia, as is true of the re-readings of sacred texts bearing on gender equality in marriage, despite the opposition to such equality that I have outlined here.

To begin to address these issues we might first consider the Arabic-origin term *liwat,* which is usually rendered into English as "sodomy." This term is enshrined in the lexicon of Malaysia's *sharia* judiciary (and its civil counterpart), as we have seen. But it was not widely known among the Malay-speaking public, or the lay public generally, until the first Anwar affair (1998–2004), which saw then Deputy Prime Minister Anwar charged in the civil courts with various counts of sodomy and corruption, and also entailed the widespread deployment of terms such as *liwat* in mass-mediated accounts that saturated the airwaves and all varieties of local media for nearly a decade. The second Anwar affair (2008–15), which also focused on seemingly trumped up charges of sodomy, helped ensure that that term was both seared into the national imaginary and deeply intertwined with the public's fears of criminality and opposition to established order.

Liwat derives from the Arabic term for the Prophet Lut, whose experiences are recounted in the Quran as well as the Hebrew Bible, where he is known as Lot. Conventional theological and juristic interpretations of the Quranic story of Lut emphasize three points that are salient here: (1) that God punished Lut and his followers for subjecting male guests who were visiting their community to (forcible) anal intercourse; (2) that in legal and ethical terms this particular act (anal intercourse) is more or less equivalent to all other practices entailing same-sex relations, whether or not they involve anal penetration in contrast to other kinds of acts, or males as distinct from females; and (3) that the punishment for all such offenses should be on a par with those meted out for *zina* (heterosexual fornication, adultery), since the latter offense also involves penetration—e.g., one hundred lashes or stoning to death.

For the vast majority of the world's Muslims, the relevant Quranic passages on the subject are largely if not altogether beyond debate (though the appropriateness of the latter sanctions is sometimes contested), and are subsumed under the category of *muhkam* as distinct from *mutashabih*. *Muhkam* is usually translated as "inherently clear," "beyond doubt, and not susceptible to abrogation," hence amenable to "only one clearly definitive interpretation"; *mutashabih*, by contrast, is used to refer to passages and positions in the Quran and the *hadith* that are "ambiguous, susceptible to different interpretations" (Abou El-Fadl 2001, 304–5).

In recent years, however, some progressive Muslim scholars have questioned this conventional wisdom (see, for example, El-Rouayheb 2005; Kugle 2010; see also Najmabadi 2005, 2014). Based on painstaking textual analysis of the Quran and other relevant sources, they usually take as their point of departure Quranic passages bearing on the story of Lut, some of which are (re)interpreted to suggest that God's condemnation and wrath had little if anything to do with acts of same-sex sexuality on the part of Lut's followers, and everything to do with them robbing their visitors, assaulting them (partly by subjecting them to anal rape), and chasing them away. Their sins, in other words, involved being greedy, selfish, inhospitable, and otherwise violating basic ethical norms unrelated to sexuality per se (Kugle 2010). Relevant too is that prior to the late nineteenth century there were no terms in Arabic (or other Middle Eastern languages) for "homosexual," "homosexuality," "lesbianism," etc. Questions have thus been raised about the logic employed by medieval and early modern theologians and jurists who argued that sanctions against male-to-male anal penetration should be extended to same-sex relations that do not involve such penetration. It has also been noted that in the course of his lifetime the Prophet is known to have been relatively nonchalant about the male-bodied individuals he encountered who transgressed majoritarian gender practices (e.g., by dressing as women), even though some *hadith* clearly disparage men who attire themselves in women's clothes.

To date, these interpretations have acquired little if any traction among Malaysia's religious or political elites or the nation's ordinary Muslims.[21] Indeed, recent decades have seen a pronounced constriction of pluralistic sensibilities and dispositions with respect to gender and sexuality alike both among elites and in popular (Malay/Muslim) culture; and this constriction is often justified with reference to Islamic normativity (Peletz 2009). NGOs and networks promoting LGBT rights such as the PT Foundation (formerly known as the Pink Triangle Foundation) and Seksualiti Merdeka (Sexuality Independence) do exist, but like the vibrant communities they represent, they are subject to harassment and are under periodic siege, unless, as in the case of the PT Foundation, they position themselves primarily as organizations that advocate for and provide services to communities at risk for HIV/AIDS, like MSM (men who have sex with men, to use their international public-health language), sex workers, and intravenous drug users. Progressive NGOs like SIS that have been in the trenches fighting for women's rights for decades generally go to some length to avoid taking principled stands on LGBT matters for fear of alienating their target audience and institutional allies, even though a number of SIS leaders are known in NGO circles to be supportive of lesbian and gay rights. Much the same is true of Marina Mahathir, who is a strong supporter of PT and related groups and was once described to me by one of the heads of PT as their "patron saint," "our Lady Diana" (Peletz 2009, 243–44).

It remains to add that "pluralism" is a (very) dirty word in Malaysia, and that this situation did not obtain even a decade or so ago. At present, advocates of pluralism (in Connolly's [2005] sense) are commonly seen by Malay spokesmen as hostile to Islam and Malays alike. The charge that one supports pluralism (or is a pluralist) is frequently hurled at critics of the status quo who, like SIS, draw upon feminist arguments, international human-rights language, and/or discourses of democracy, transparency, accountability, and inclusiveness. Many of these same generalizations pertain to the terms "liberalism" and "secularism." The latter signifiers are often used interchangeably. And they are sometimes employed as shorthand to refer to doctrines or philosophies that allegedly celebrate untrammeled individualism and promote homosexuality, same-sex marriage, and "LGBT," an expression that has become part of the national political lexicon in recent years. These designations are sometimes uttered in the same breath, as in then Prime Minister Najib Razak's (in)famous June 25, 2012 declaration, reiterating earlier pronouncements along the same general lines, that there is no place in Malaysia for "liberalism, pluralism, and Lesbian, Gay, Bisexual, and Transgender (LGBT)." Proclamations such as these were enshrined on the prime minister's website and have become mainstream mantras (Shanon Shah 2018). The situation is reminiscent of neighboring Indonesia, where Islamic authorities coined the acronym "SEPLIS," which is pronounced and spelled almost exactly like the local term for syphilis (*sipilis*), to refer to a "new virus." As expressed in an Indonesian *fatwa* of 2005, the new virus is the conjoined threat of secularism, pluralism, and liberalism.[22]

Where does all this leave the communities of Malay/Muslim women who transgress heteronormative expectations and ideals, and what kinds of relationships do they have with the *sharia* judiciary? Women in the latter communities find the *sharia* judiciary and the religious bureaucracies closely associated with it increasingly unfriendly and threatening. This is due in part to a spate of *sharia* laws passed since the early to mid-1990s that criminalize same-sex relations among women, and in part to state- and national-level *fatwa* and *sharia* enactments that condemn "tomboys" and all transgender practices involving female-bodied individuals (tan beng hui 2012; Pang Khee Teik 2015; Shanon Shah 2018).[23] Clearly, then, there are limits to the "female-friendliness" we see in the *sharia* juridical field, and to the specific kinds of relations and specific kinds of selves that political and religious elites shaping Islamic family law and other state policies are willing to accommodate, let alone promote and nurture. This situation is by no means unique to Malaysia; variations on the theme can be found throughout the world.

SOME COMPARATIVE PERSPECTIVES:
EGYPT AND BEYOND

The ethnographic and historical perspectives I have presented in the proceeding pages of this chapter have focused largely on Malaysia from the late 1970s and 1980s to the present, though I have also included brief material on Indonesia (concerning the emergence there of no-fault divorce) and other Muslim-majority countries. By way of rounding out the picture and furthering the analysis I turn to comparative perspectives drawn from Middle East and North Africa, particularly Egypt, whose innovative but controversial *khul* laws I mentioned in passing. This material, from the Islamic heartlands, provides further illustration of the ways in which Islamic family-law regimes and gender dynamics are changing in ways that are generally favorable to women (Rosen 2018). But this material also makes clear that, as in Malaysia and Indonesia, the changes we see in Egypt have proceeded in fits and starts, have occasioned short-term backlashes and setbacks, and have met with orthogonal and other pressures that threaten to undo them. It also indicates that the changes in question do not necessarily signal enhanced pluralism "across the board," and that pluralism, like citizenship, sovereignty, and justice, is invariably graduated.

Malaysia and Egypt have much in common, though they also differ in critically important ways. Broad similarities include lengthy periods of colonial occupation by the British, formal independence in the 1950s, and subsequent decades of (variably successful) secularly-oriented development. Another significant commonality is that in both Muslim-majority countries heightened piety on the part of Muslims since the 1970s has been a pronounced feature of the national cultural-political landscape, as has the greater salience of Islamic symbols, idioms, and normativities in myriad political institutions and discourses, some of which call for the establishment or further entrenchment of an Islamic state based on *sharia*.

For our purposes, one of the key differences between the two nations is that in Egypt, in contrast to Malaysia and many other regions of the Muslim world, specifically Islamic courts do not exist, having been abolished by President Gamal Abdel Nasser in 1955 as part of his secularly oriented program of modernization. Since that time, matters involving the personal status law of Muslims, including Muslim family law, have been handled by the nation's civil courts, which thus adjudicate both "secular" and "religious" disputes (Sangerman 2005; Sonneveld 2012). In 2004, moreover, separate family courts were established to deal with Islamic family law and the family law of non-Muslims, partly so as to reduce the backlog in non-family law courts, thereby enabling them to devote more of their resources to addressing commercial, trade, and other business-related disputes.

Throughout the judiciary, judges are trained primarily in civil law, though those assigned cases in Islamic family law also have background in Islamic law and *fiqh*.

When dealing with matters involving the latter corpus of law, the sources they tend to cite are, in "order of priority . . . [,]: (1) legislation and judicial practice, (2) the Qur'an; (3), the *sunna* [the sayings and actions/traditions of the Prophet], and (4) the Hanafi school [of Islamic law]" (Sonneveld 2012, 97), which is commonly regarded as the most liberal of the four main schools of Sunni jurisprudence and traditionally tolerant of other religions (An-Na'im 2002, 26). In this respect, they are much like *sharia* judges in Malaysia, except that the latter orient themselves toward the Shafi'i school of Islamic law rather than the Hanafi.

In her study of *khul* divorce in Egypt, Nadia Sonneveld (2012) notes that since the early twentieth century there have been three major phases of reform in Egypt's Islamic family law. Each phase, however much informed by political, religious, and other dynamics within Egypt, was encouraged by transnational developments, particularly United Nations World Conferences on Women (30, 108). These dynamics raised the possibility that international aid packages to Egypt might be reduced or eliminated if its leaders failed to introduce reforms in Islamic family law that offered women more justice and equality in marriage.

Some of the most important reforms, dating from 2000, are known as "the *khul* law(s)." In the Egyptian context, this law allows a woman to unilaterally divorce her husband without the latter's consent—and without documenting faults on his part—so long as she meets certain conditions. The conditions include that she (1) returns (or relinquishes rights to) the dower (*mahr*) that the husband paid (or pledged) at the time of the marriage; (2) agrees to renounce other financial claims (e.g., the three months of spousal support to which she would normally be entitled, assuming she is "without fault"); (3) consents to a three-month waiting period designated for possible reconciliation with her husband; and (4) insists that she hates her husband and fears transgression of Islamic law/normativity should she be forced to remain married to him. (Insistence of such hatred and fear is sufficient; proof is not required.) Egyptian authorities represented this initiative to the public as grounded in *sharia*—as they are inclined to do with all sorts of state laws, regardless of their provenance or correspondence with Islamic sources (Lombardi 2006)—partly because it involved *ijtihad* and continued to draw upon foundational Islamic concepts (such as *khul, mahr,* and a famous *hadith* that recounts the Prophet granting a woman a divorce without inquiring whether she had the consent of her husband (Sonneveld and Lindbekk 2015, 7). But it is out of keeping with all four major schools of Sunni jurisprudence, including the Hanafi school that prevails in Egypt, each of which requires the husband's consent in termination of marriage via *khul* (Sangerman 2005; Sonneveld 2012).

The *khul* initiative met with opposition from various groups, including Islamists and *ulama,* some associated with Al-Azhar, others not, though it remains in place as of this writing and has proven to be a godsend to women desirous of extricating themselves from untenable marriages. Half of all petitions for divorce brought by women in the governate of Cairo during the twelve-month period beginning April 1, 2001, involved *khul* cases (Sonneveld 2012, 199n9), though significantly this period did not see an appreciable increase in the overall number of divorce petitions brought by women. This is to say that, at least in the Cairo region, the new *khul* provisions did not so much contribute to an increase in women's petitions for divorce as it enabled women to avoid other expensive and time-consuming legal alternatives (32).

One reason the *khul* law was opposed in some quarters is that it was seen as violating the foundational Quranic concept of *qiwama,* a key feature of the maintenance-obedience paradigm, famously articulated in Surah An-Nisa (4:34) and elsewhere, that is widely interpreted as according husbands (and men in general) a dominant role vis-à-vis their wives (and women as a whole). How can men exercise dominance in marriage, critics argued, if wives are allowed to divorce their husbands without their consent? Surely this would lead to gender reversal, with women free to exercise men's prerogatives in marriage, men assuming the secondary status of women (Sonneveld 2012, chapter 3).

Another, related objection had to do with stereotypical, Islamically informed views of the differences between men and women, which hold that women are less rational and more emotional and id-driven than men (Abu-Lughod 1986; Peletz 1996). According to this view, women will seek *khul* divorces simply because they are desirous of indulging whims associated with their attraction to better-looking and more financially secure men as potential husbands, to replace those to whom they are currently wed, and will thus destroy family units and society alike.

Yet another objection derived from the assumption that the *khul* option would be exercised primarily by wealthy women who could afford both to pay back the dower and to forego the financial rights to which they might otherwise be entitled, and that it would thus do little to ameliorate the plight of the overwhelmingly poor women who find themselves trapped in unworkable marriages. More generally, as commonly occurs with Islamic family law reform in Malaysia and elsewhere in the Muslim world, some critics argued that the reforms were "Made in America [or the West]"; others that they were a cover for conspiracies involving secularization, colonization, and Zionism (Sonneveld 2012, 44–45; see also Fawzy 2004, 67; Johnson 2004, 152). Partly to offset some of these criticisms, the reforms were followed by concessions that included the abolition of measures that had given women the right to travel (e.g., to work) without their husbands' consent, though these measures were introduced at a later date (Sonneveld 2012, 52).

We have seen this same kind of toing and froing (one step forward, two steps backward, or vice versa) in Malaysia. The decades following the marriage reforms of 1983–91 witnessed the passage of a number of enactments that diluted the reforms, and in some respects made them more or less meaningless. These included declaring (*inter alia*) that men's repudiation of their wives outside the court and without the court's permission, like men's contracting of polygynous unions without the court's approval, were potentially valid in religious terms and could, indeed, must, be registered with authorities, even though they violated state law and were therefore subject to punishment. The earlier (1983–91) legislation effectively denied the potential religious validity of all such practices on men's part and formally prohibited their registration, much like authorities in newly independent Tunisia did in 1956 when they banned polygyny outright and simultaneously prohibited the formal registration and de facto recognition of all polygynous unions. Because Tunisian officials and their successors, unlike their Malaysian counterparts, have continued to maintain this position through to the present (An-Na'im 2002:101; Mashhour 2005; Zeghal 2013), brief comments on Tunisia may be useful here.

When Tunisian President Habib Bourguiba outlawed polygyny in 1956 he drew on Maliki and Hanafi drafts of Islamic family law, arguing that that the Quranic ideal is clearly monogamy insofar as men are not able to live up to Quranic provisions specifying that they are only entitled to take a second (or third or fourth) wife if they are able to treat all wives equally. Amira Mashhour (2005) explains that "In Islamic law, actions that are permitted but are not mandatory or recommended can be regulated or restricted for the sake of public welfare. As polygamy was permitted but neither mandatory nor recommended, it could be regulated or even prohibited by the state." Not surprisingly, Tunisian *ulama* issued a *fatwa* denouncing the innovation, but "public reaction . . . was muted" (585). Mashhour's more general observations merit quoting at length.

> The experiences of Tunisia in the field of personal status offers a progressive model based on a liberal interpretation of Islamic texts. The importance of the Tunisian model stems from the fact that the Personal Status Code in Tunisia is based on Islamic law and the spirit of the Quran and Sunna regarding gender equality. In addition, Tunisia emphasizes its identity as an Islamic state and the fact that religion is a very important source of the Tunisian tradition, unlike Turkey where the personal status law is a completely secular positive one. Therefore, it could be argued that, although Bourgaiba [sic] was accused of being secular from Tunisian Islamic groups and other Muslim scholars, all of his justifications were based on Islamic norms, the Maliki law, and the principle of public welfare (587).

The Tunisian and Egyptian material that I have discussed here raises a number of important questions. Most are beyond the scope of the present discussion but a few of them, focusing especially on Egypt, are nonetheless worth posing. Have innovative legal initiatives that allow Egyptian women to unilaterally divorce their husbands without their husbands' consent made possible new kinds of dialogues between husbands and wives and perhaps contributed to the partial democratization both of marriage ties and of kinship and gender relations as a whole? Sonneveld (2012, 7, passim) presents compelling evidence that judges and mediators allow for husband-wife dialogue that doesn't often occur in spouses' daily lives, but there is much more to be done on this important topic. More generally, are such initiatives contributing to the emergence of new legal and religious sensibilities in Egypt? And how have political, religious, and other developments since the fall of President Mubarak in February 2011 informed the discourses and operations of the courts when they deal with Islamic law as well as family law and other issues involving non-Muslims?

It is perhaps too soon to definitively answer many of these questions. Supporters of Egypt's 2000 reforms are nonetheless worried that Egyptian leaders may be inclined to overturn the relevant legislation should they feel a need to ally themselves more closely with conservative *ulama* and Islamists and otherwise shore up or burnish their Islamic credentials. There is also widespread concern that while recent laws informing marital relations among Muslims have become somewhat more egalitarian, the past few years have seen a deterioration of relations between Muslims and non-Muslims, especially the Coptic Christian minority, which has fared poorly in Egypt in the past decade or so, particularly since 2011 (Heo 2013; Mahmood 2015). Recent years have also witnessed an increased stigmatization and criminalization of transgender practices and same-sex relations (see, e.g., Walsh 2017). Here too the comparison with Malaysia is telling. Such a comparison reveals a nexus of dynamics that Aihwa Ong (1999) subsumes under the rubric of graduated sovereignty, which involves "the state mak[ing] different kinds of biopolitical investments in different subject populations," sometimes privileging one gender or community defined in terms of ethnicity, religion, or social class over others (217). Progressive developments in Malaysia's *sharia* judiciary with respect to (Malay/Muslim) women—including the introduction of *sulh* sessions and the liberalization of grounds for *fasakh*—have gone hand in hand both with a punitive turn in the juridical field as a whole and with acute polarization among the nation's main ethnic and religious groups. Clear evidence of the latter trends appear in stepped-up efforts to stigmatize and criminalize not only interfaith marriage, apostasy, and Shia teachings, but also the use by non-Muslims of terms, such as "Allah," that are seen as "belonging to" Muslims, as well as all varieties of non-heteronormative practices and identities.

Among the more interesting aspects of Egypt's *khul* law are the expansive and lively debates that have occurred on the subject. These debates have involved members of parliament and other government officials, NGOs, women's groups, media outlets of myriad stripes, and Islamists and *ulama,* some associated with Al-Azhar, others not. Much of the discussion and disputation has taken place in the realm of popular culture—in films, serialized television shows, music, cartoons in mainstream (and other) print media, the blogosphere and other realms of the online world (Sonnefeld 2012). The widely ramifying debates have continued in the period since Mubarak's resignation in 2011, moreover, and have come to include new actors, such as groups of divorced fathers advocating a "Restoration of Manhood." Among these new organizations are groups like "The Movement for Saving the Egyptian Family," "The Movement of the Revolution of Men," "Egypt First," and "The Network of Men Harmed by the Personal Status Laws" (Sonneveld and Lindbekk 2015, 10; see also Schielke 2015), many of which share the same general concerns (the restoration or revitalization of "traditional" family values) as Malaysia's Muslim Brothers and organizations such as the OWC and the PC.

The scope, force, and passion of the debates that have taken place in Egypt are largely unlike anything we have seen in Malaysia on topics related to Islamic family law or Islam more broadly. The paradoxes and ironies are striking insofar as Egypt under the Mubarak regime (1981–2011) was widely regarded as far more repressive and authoritarian than Malaysia at the time. Put differently, in the ostensibly less repressive and less authoritarian context of Malaysia, the political culture and authoritarian populism fostered by (mostly Malay) political and religious elites have strongly discouraged wide-ranging debate and the vibrant civil society that is evident in Egypt.

These and other differences aside, there is a striking similarity between Egypt and Malaysia. In both cases, critics of government policy walk a thin, ever-shifting line, the crossing of which may result in the mobilization against them of state resources including both secular statutes bearing on national security and state versions of *hisba* provisions that "enjoin good and forbid wrong" (Lombardi 2006; Agrama 2012). Mobilization of secular laws and attendant resources to police religious boundaries, including those associated with Islamic family law, may seem anomalous, but as Deniz Kandiyoti (1991) made clear in an important essay some years ago, political and administrative maneuverings bearing on Islamic family law often have more to do with state formation than anything else (see also Brown 1997). John Borneman (1992), writing about state policy and modes of belonging in the two Berlins shortly before the dismantling of the Wall in 1989, made a series of analogous points about state-defined realms of family law in the passage that serves as an epigraph to this chapter, though he focused on strategies keyed to nation-building rather than state formation per se.

In Malaysia, one of the groups that has suffered most due to its detractors invoking *hisba*-like laws is Sisters in Islam. I mentioned earlier that Islamist NGOs including associations of *sharia* lawyers (such as the PGSM) routinely lodge police reports against SIS, commonly doing so on the grounds that their public statements and advocacy efforts insult, defame, or demean Islam or its principal guardians, the sultans and the king. In some cases the charges contained in the police reports also claim, reminiscent of what we have seen in Egypt, that SIS activities aimed at the reform of Islamic family law are heavily funded by Western governments and the foundations linked to them (which is, in fact, true); and that they are ultimately part of secular/liberal neocolonial conspiracies, Zionist plots, or both (which seems rather farfetched).

Most of these reports do not result in the filing of formal court charges against SIS—charges that are, in any event, typically aired in the nation's civil courts rather than in their *sharia* counterparts. But they are annoying, disconcerting, and frightening, carrying as they do the threat of steep fines and prolonged incarceration. They also consume a good deal of SIS's energy and resources, requiring that their principal spokespersons and lawyers present police and other officials with reams of detailed evidence to prove that they have operated within the bounds of Malaysian law.

Conservative Muslim civil society groups are by no means alone in leveling these kinds of charges against groups like SIS. Government bureaucracies such as the Home Ministry and JAKIM, both of which, like the *sharia* judiciary, are under the direct control of the Prime Minister's Department, have sometimes taken the lead in charging SIS with serious crimes and have otherwise endeavored to limit their influence. One example is the attempt, beginning in 2008, to ban the SIS book *Muslim Women and the Challenge of Islamic Extremism*, which was edited by Norani Othman (2005) and funded by the Rockefeller Foundation. The original title of the volume, *Muslim Women and the Challenge of Political Islam*, had to be scrapped to pass muster with government censors. The censors were apparently uncomfortable with a potential critique of political Islam, variants of which the state both endorses and embodies. But they had no strong objection to a title suggesting that the book delineated the challenges and threats posed by Islamic *extremism*, which state actors routinely denounce, despite charges from various quarters that state policies encourage if not directly sponsor such extremism. To date, these efforts, including those aimed at belatedly banning the 2005 book, have been largely unsuccessful, thanks in part to the civil-court judges who have heard the charges and dismissed them as groundless. (Government prosecutors in the aforementioned case failed to show that the book had caused any harm in the years it had circulated widely.) But such efforts do have a chilling effect on individuals' and groups' willingness to engage in the kinds of expansive debates associated with the introduction and implementation of *khul* laws in Egypt.

A further point of contrast with Egypt has to do with the ways in which the timing of Egyptian reforms in Islamic family law was keyed to stepped-up pressure from Western governments and the foundations and agencies that are strongly committed to the furtherance of their policies: the World Bank, the International Monetary Fund, the Asian Development Bank, etc. The waves of reform in Islamic family law that occurred in Egypt followed directly on the heels of United Nations Conferences on Women, as noted earlier. These conferences highlighted and criticized gender inequalities in the realm of Egyptian (and other Middle Eastern and North African) Islamic family law, simultaneously raising the specter of reduced aid from Western nations, especially the United States, if Egypt failed to remedy some of the problems. Foreign aid from the United States in particular, which has averaged more than US$2 billion annually since 1979, and is earmarked mostly for the military, which has received a whopping US$1.3 billion annually since 1987 (Sharp 2018, 23–24), is simply too important to jeopardize. Hence ruling elites have encouraged Islamic family law reforms, even when they have alienated some of their supporters, including members of the Islamic religious establishment. A broadly similar dynamic helps explain why in 1979 Egyptian rulers established a Supreme Constitutional Court with the power to overrule them, as Tamir Moustafa (2007) has shown.

United Nations Conferences on Women did not have the same impact in Malaysia. They did not, in other words, give rise to or help usher in Egyptian-style reforms—perhaps partly because their spokespersons did not target Malaysia to the same degree as they did Egypt (and other countries in the Middle East and North Africa). Compared to Egypt, moreover, Malaysia is far less dependent on Western, and especially U.S., foreign aid, which has been quite paltry in recent decades, averaging less than US$11 million annually since 2001[24]—and thus has far less to fear from Western threats of reduced aid for economic development and support of the military. Malaysia's economic development, moreover, is highly impressive (however uneven), and has been for decades, unlike Egypt's. And Malaysia's military plays a relatively low-key role in affairs of state and public life. This too involves a striking contrast to Egypt, where the military looms large in state affairs, public life, and the national imaginary. Since the mid-twentieth century Egypt has seen a number of military coups and attempted coups—and the assassination of a sitting president—and has been ruled by a military strongman (President El-Sisi) since the army ousted democratically elected President Morsi in July 2013, whose brief tenure in office followed years of military dictatorship under Mubarak. Malaysia, by contrast, has never experienced a coup or an assassination of a sitting head of state; was governed by the same multiparty coalition dominated by a single party (UMNO) from its independence in 1957 all the way through mid-2018; and with a few key exceptions (e.g., the 1948–60 communist insurgency, known as "The Emergency") has never seen the military deployed to maintain order. All of this is to say that Malaysia's national leaders have enjoyed relative stability since the nation's independence and compared to their Egyptian counterparts do not need to worry as much about the military, the support they give to and receive from it, and the external sources of its funding that help guarantee the continued functioning of the state apparatus.

Another piece of the puzzle as to why Egyptian-style liberalization of Islamic family law (in the form of the 2000 *khul* law) has not occurred in Malaysia is that Western calls for the reform of Malaysian legal institutions have focused less on the need to "save Muslim women" (Abu-Lughod 2013) and thus reform Islamic

family law, than on corruption and inefficiency in the civil judiciary, its manipulation by the executive branch, and its illiberal turn, especially during Prime Minister Mahathir's first stint in office (1981–2003). *New York Times* columnist Nicholas
Kristof and Somali-born émigré Ayaan Hirsi Ali, for example, have written quite a
bit about "the plight of Muslim women" in newspaper columns and novels that
have circulated widely in the West (much of this, I hasten to add, is quite problematic). But they have tended to focus on Muslim women in the Middle East, North
Africa, Pakistan, and Afghanistan. Malaysia (like Indonesia) is rarely mentioned
in the same breath as these other areas and is thus largely off the radar of Westerners and UN Conferences on Women when they engage issues of gender and Islam.

Western media coverage of Malaysia over the past few decades has tended to
focus instead on the heavy-handedness of Prime Minister Mahathir, who sacked a
number of Supreme-Court Judges, including the Chief Justice, in 1987–88, appears
to have orchestrated the first Anwar affair, and otherwise waged what many consider to be all all-out war on the judiciary's relative independence during the
twenty-two years of his first tenure in office. Things did not improve after Mahathir
passed the baton to his successor Abdullah Badawi (r. 2003–09). Indeed, by many
criteria they got worse, especially in the period that Najib Tun Razak served as
prime minister (2009–18). Najib oversaw stepped-up repression and has been
embroiled for some time now in a multibillion dollar scandal that has resulted in
more than a half-dozen countries launching criminal investigations into his (and
his family's) financial dealings and foreign holdings. (He is currently on trial.) In
recent years, Western media coverage of Malaysia has concentrated on scandals
such as these, on Najib's close relationship with U.S. presidents Barack Obama and
Donald Trump (who has famously referred to Najib as "my favorite prime minister" [Lander 2017]), and on the U.S. State Department's highly controversial 2015
upgrading of Malaysia's status with respect to human trafficking, to facilitate passage of the Trans-Pacific Partnership Agreement.

For reasons such as these, the possibility of further (Egyptian-style) reforms in
Malaysian Islamic family law seems increasingly remote, at least in the short term.
This seems especially true in light of two additional sets of dynamics. First, the
long-dominant ruling coalition, the Barisan Nasional, lost much support not only
among Chinese and Indians but also among Malays, as evidenced by (inter alia)
the outcomes of the 2008, 2013, and 2018 general elections, the last of which saw
the coalition's ousting from office. Because of its declining popularity in recent
years and fears that its uninterrupted dominance since 1957 might come to an
ignoble end, which did in fact just happen, the Malay/Muslim mainstay of the
coalition (UMNO) increasingly endeavored to win over rural Malay voters in Kelantan, Terengganu, and other areas that have embraced PAS/opposition calls for
the introduction of *hudud* laws. UMNO has not (yet) formally endorsed *hudud*
laws, but it has backed away from the strongly worded aversion to *hudud* it once

widely articulated, and has adopted a more conciliatory, arguably *hudud*-friendly stance. In the Malaysian context and most others *hudud* laws are notoriously unfriendly to women in general and to the expansion of women's legal prerogatives in particular, including especially those bearing on marriage and divorce.

The second dynamic that is relevant here involves the emergence in the past two decades of a powerful new elite and the likelihood that their views on gender and equality within the family and in society at large will further reinforce conservative and punitive trends. I refer to the hundreds of PhD-bearing, globetrotting "*sharia* advisors" who sit on the boards of the nation's premier banking and financial institutions and are centrally involved in formulating *sharia*-compliance policies for the workplace and the overall operations and goals of myriad industries and institutions, including government ministries. Patricia Sloane-White's (2017) fascinating and nuanced ethnography of this powerful, overwhelmingly male group makes clear that its members are deeply conservative with respect to kinship and gender roles and—no small matter—that the same is true of both their female colleagues and their wives (see especially chapter 5). The men and women who move in these elite circles seek "more Islam," including the implementation of *hudud* laws, in all realms of public and private life. Their strategies to achieve these goals involve the development of banking and business models, including extensive HR protocols, whose material and spiritual benefits will ultimately "trickle down" to the masses, including non-Muslims, rather than legislative or political efforts per se. Members of this new elite warmly embrace the maintenance-obedience paradigm that is enshrined in (some) classical Islamic texts and in the nation's Islamic family law, and do so in largely unqualified terms; and they appear altogether unreceptive if not overtly hostile to the kinds of changes advocated by Sisters in Islam and liked-minded reformers. In an environment such as this, it would be foolhardy for Malay political leaders to come out in support of the introduction of Egyptian-style *khul* laws or broadly similar changes like those that have occurred in Tunisia or Indonesia. Indeed, such support might play badly in the Malay hinterlands and risks alienating and jeopardizing ties to the elites who are best positioned to help situate Malaysia at the center of global Islamic banking and finance, and who are in any event exceedingly well placed to facilitate the enrichment of the economist-technocrats presiding over Malay political parties and other ruling bureaucracies.

But things are not all cut and dried. We have also seen that the *sharia* judiciary has been increasingly receptive to calls to expand women's legal prerogatives, with regard to *fasakh*, for example. It is reasonable to expect to see further movement in this general direction in the decades to come, especially in light of the contours and dynamics of the more encompassing juridical field and the fact that civil judiciary provides the gold standard for many of the (more liberal) provisions bearing on divorce initiated by women. Much may well depend on the role played in the years ahead by *sharia* lawyers. I refer less to the ways that they have sidelined their clients (and judges) in formal hearings (a key concern of chapter 4) than to the increasingly important political role they play in NGOs and as lobbyists and members of Islamist pressure groups in the juridical field and beyond.

CONCLUSION

This chapter has provided ethnographic, historical, and comparative perspectives on a domain of family law ostensibly grounded in religion that is heavily informed by the ways the secular constitution enshrines its encompassment within a juridical field dominated by common law and the civil judiciary, its principal patron, chief competitor, and the source of many of its gold standards. This domain straddles and blurs the categories and identities of "religious" and "secular" as well as "*sharia*" and "common law." Their deep entanglement precludes definitively distinguishing them from one another either empirically or analytically (Asad 2003; Sullivan et al 2011); for as Anna Tsing (2015) has put it, "Entanglement bursts categories and upends identities" (137). I have also documented some of the ways Malaysia's Islamic courts are involved in defining, codifying, and normalizing specific kinds of relations and specific kinds of selves that political and religious elites spanning the secular/religious divide see as essential to the constitution of citizens as subjects. The liberalization of the grounds for *fasakh* mandated by the Islamic family law reforms of 1983–91 was amplified by shifts, in practice rather than doctrine, that occurred subsequently, further augmenting women's abilities to obtain this kind of judicial relief. The cultural and legal buttressing of companionate marriage and the expanded grounds for annulment this entailed suggest that women are currently getting more justice from the *sharia* courts than women in the 1970s and 1980s (and previously).

More broadly, I have drawn upon ethnographic and historical methodologies conducive to describing and analyzing the routine, gendered practices of litigants and officials in *sharia* courts since the 1970s–1980s. The perspectives I offer differ in substantive ways from those based on largely synchronic approaches that focus on women as distinct from the more expansive domain of gender, many of which rely overly much on mass-mediated accounts of cases, like Kartika's, that are statistically highly atypical. The methodologies I utilize reveal that women's legal claims are handled more expeditiously than in times past, and that the courts are more inclined to punish men who violate *sharia* family law. We also saw that due to recent court, state, and civil-society initiatives, women nowadays have appreciably greater access to information and other resources concerning their legal rights within and beyond marriage and can rather easily draw upon networks of support to help them negotiate conjugal ties, their dissolution, and the uncertainties and precarities that may follow.

The fact that these networks and resources and the myriad brochures and web-sites advertising them highlight the rights of wives, mothers, and women generally is of considerable consequence. In the late 1980s and previously, the relevant dis-course in and outside the courts tended to revolve around the (poorly performed) duties of husbands and fathers rather than the rights of wives or women. The cul-tural elaboration and institutional bolstering of the notion that women are enti-tled, rights-bearing citizens, as distinct from mere jural minors tethered to men through ties of marriage or other modalities of relatedness, is also of great import insofar as it might be scaled up to other power-laden arenas. It is, put differently, a highly significant development for those who support the diffusion and entrench-ment of more inclusive political discourses keyed to citizenship, sovereignty, and the contours of possible Malaysian futures. This is particularly true inasmuch as variations of the maintenance-obedience paradigm have informed how ruling political parties approach the allocation of state resources. Ethnic and religious groups, political blocs, NGOs, and others who toe the party line are likely to ben-efit from the parceling-out of such resources, including formal legal protection and other perks. Those who do not, and are thus by definition disobedient if not treasonous, are more likely to find themselves at the end of the queue, if not alto-gether excluded from consideration of state maintenance and protection, or worse (Whiting 2017). The expanded jurisdiction and greater power of the (*sharia*) courts, hence the (secular) state, does in any event bring danger as well, even to pious, law-abiding middle-class Malay/Muslim women, who sometimes worry that their religious-study sessions could be construed as unauthorized public gath-erings and thus result in their arrest and incarceration (Frisk 2009, 21–22, 68; see also Merry 1990). Another downside of these and attendant developments is that within courtrooms (as distinct from *sulh* chambers), women's voices tend to be silenced or at least ventriloquized by lawyers who increasingly monopolize dis-course and practice alike. This is part of the price women pay for the profession-alization and bureaucratization of justice.

It bears reiterating that the broadly encouraging findings outlined in this chap-ter are not meant to imply that women and men experience married life, its formal undoing, or the *sharia* juridical field as social equals; they do not, as we have seen. We have also seen that this situation is changing in ways generally beneficial to women, as long as they adhere to strictures of obedience and heteronormativity that are increasingly pronounced and inflexible. The latter caveat points to one of the ways that pluralism in any given field or case is not simply present or absent, but is graduated, much like zones of sovereignty, citizenship, and justice (Peletz 2009). All of this is to say, as well, that the domain of religiously-inflected family law examined in this chapter and elsewhere in this book is indeed unabashedly partial and deeply contested, but is also far more dynamic, reform-oriented, and otherwise this-worldly than the relevant scholarship and media representations might lead us to assume.

Many of these latter generalizations also pertain to Egypt, Indonesia, and other parts of the Muslim world, as is clear from the comparative material presented in this chapter. The heightened valorization of companionate marriage that is apparent in Malaysia's expansion of grounds for *fasakh* (and in other developments in that nation's *sharia* juridical field), for instance, is evident as well both in Egypt's more liberal *khul* laws and in Indonesia's de facto embrace of no-fault divorce. These are but three examples from across the Muslim world of the different ways in which *sharia* judges and the political and religious elites overseeing their practices have engaged increasingly global trends associated with the rise of new forms of kinship and marriage and the attendant idea that women are rights-bearing citizen-subjects. These developments benefit women insofar as they make it easier for them to extricate themselves from abusive or otherwise untenable unions and to pursue other kinds of claims. In all three cases the architects of the changes in question have drawn on classical *sharia* resources to achieve their goals, much as Tunisian authorities did when they banned polygyny in 1956, though some of their critics have argued that such changes do not comport with *sharia* since they upend more or less pan-Islamic understandings of gender along with notions of *qiwama* (undergirding the maintenance-obedience paradigm) that are grounded in foundational texts such as the Quran.

One set of concerns in the final section of the chapter involved charting some of the global dynamics that led to the Egyptian reforms, considering whether Egyptian-style (or related) changes in Islamic family law might be on the horizon in Malaysia in the near future, and exploring why this may—or may not—be so. Understanding these global dynamics entailed consideration of United Nations Conferences on Women, foreign aid packages from the United States geared toward propping up unpopular regimes in volatile regions of the world that contain strategic resources seen as vital to the interests of the United States and its continued status as a global hegemon, and the relative importance of the military both in domestic affairs, state formation, and national imaginaries. The fact that such variables have informed shifting patterns of Islamic family law is compelling evidence that our analyses, even or especially of matters in private/domestic domains, need to be attuned to the play of forces within expansively construed juridical fields and the ever more expansive transnational/geopolitical fields and relations of power in which such fields are situated. My tentative conclusion, in any event, is that we may not witness Egyptian- (or Indonesian-) style reforms in Malaysia in the near future (the coming decade or so), even though the period since the 1970s–1980s has seen a clear (though by no means unilinear or uniform) trend in the general direction of liberalizing Islamic family law. The long-term prognosis, on the other hand, is more encouraging, based as it partly is on the overall trajectory of change since the 1970s and 1980s, though we will undoubtedly continue to see backlashes, short-term reversals, and orthogonal developments that may complicate and obscure both the directionalities of change and our understandings of them.

Conclusion

In these final remarks I summarize themes addressed in the preceding pages and provide brief comments on some of their comparative and theoretical implications. I have pursued five overarching goals: First, to delineate the empirical complexities of Malaysia's *sharia* judiciary (including its canonical and newly invented Islamic components as well as its civil-law procedures, Japanese audit regimes, and corporate rebranding) and the heterogenous if not mutually contradictory directions in which it is moving. Second, to problematize the trope of Islamization as a gloss for the directions and other entailments of these movements. Third, to illustrate that this judiciary is profitably viewed as a global assemblage. Fourth, to document and analyze the ways in which the punitive and pastoral modalities of governance associated with this assemblage are entangled and how they differentially impact men and women. And fifth, to demonstrate the value of historicized inquiries grounded in ethnographic practice informed by engagement with the scholarly literature on Muslim cultures and politics and the work of Foucault, Bourdieu, and assemblage theorists.

In this book I have argued that Malaysia's *sharia* judiciary is usefully regarded as a global assemblage insofar as the transformations it has undergone in recent decades have been forged in relationship with a multiplicity of global discourses, practices, incentives, and constraints, widely disparate in origin, often keyed to analytically distinct processes of bureaucratization, rationalization, and neoliberal corporatization. Some of these changes involve what is commonly referred to as "Islamization," but most do not. Processes of Islamization and *sharia*tization, moreover, are not monolithic or seamless; nor are they all-consuming, like a steadily advancing lava flow or a cataclysmic earthquake or tsunami. Their dynamics and overall vicissitudes vary from one case to the next and across the terrain of any particular case. This is partly to say that legal (and other) assemblages have their own unique, sometimes mutually contradictory, logics and enjoy a variable measure of semi-autonomy, even when they are encompassed within states characterized by top-heavy executive branches that routinely engage in lawfare.

There is an elementary but nonetheless important point I should perhaps emphasize here about assemblage theory, or "assemblage thinking," as some prefer, especially for the benefit of those who are unfamiliar with the scope of its application: its purview is quite extensive, and ranges far beyond late-modern Islamic judiciaries. I underscore the theme partly because some readers may understandably regard the latter judiciaries as highly distinctive (if not exceedingly unusual) in terms of their remarkably diverse components and the expansive range of forces that help shape them and give them meaning, and may thus feel that they are amenable to certain kinds of analysis that have otherwise limited applicability. Thus I add that iterations of assemblage thinking—there are many; it is not a single "it entity"—have been usefully deployed to help make sense of dynamics in Western juridical fields (Strathern 2000, 2005; Latour 2010), an issue to which I return momentarily, and scores of other phenomena. The latter phenomena include medieval, national, and global configurations of territory, authority and rights; audit regimes of assorted stripes; the entanglements of science, commerce, and politics in genomics research; transnational commodity chains; the pastoral care and bio-political control of refugees; and the co-imbrication of gender, sexuality, race, class, and national belonging/exclusion in post-9/11 America (Rabinow 1999; Ong 2003; Ong and Collier 2005; Puar 2007; Sassen 2008; Tsing 2015).

Readers acquainted with Bruno Latour's *The Making of Law: An Ethnography of the Conseil d'État* (2010), which focuses on the daily, routine processes of decision-making in the production of the ostensibly homogenous and seamless realm of French administrative law, will appreciate some of the aforementioned points. Based on his extensive ethnographic research in the formal chambers, corridors, and back-room contexts of this supreme court, and on his careful study of relevant archival material, Latour offers a number of incisive observations bearing on the literal making of law, the "laboratory life of law," that are informed by the variant of assemblage theory he has developed (sometimes referred to as Actor-Network Theory); I quote him at length.

> What is involved [in the making of law] is not exactly a process of reasoning, in which a flow of homogenous ideas are linked together more or less logically, nor is it an ordered body of texts, which it would be sufficient to stitch together in order to generate another document. Nor is it about the [sometimes] hesitant process of 'applying' a standard text to some fact, as if one were trying to identify the category 'duck' using an atlas of the birds of France to make sense of a fleeting vision of a feathered object skimming over a pond .... In legal reasoning, everything counts

. . . . [including] interests, and passions, . . . [and] the irresistible force of prejudice, or at least of presuppositions . . . . [T]he quality of the judgment does not depend either on total independence regarding the social and political context and relations of power, or on the strict application of forms, . . . but rather on the *breadth of the disjointed elements* which they managed to retain after [occasionally] having extensively and decently 'hesitated.' What is crucial is the *mode of attachment,* the knot with which the judges tied together, on the one hand, a President, a skeptical opinion, an efficient administration, a powerful State, a free economy and, on the other, the immense body of precedents of the Council, not forgetting the litigants, who can make the Republic tremble, without the help of a lawyer, through the simple mean[s] of a letter on blank paper (140–41, 168; emphases added).

Latour continues:

Law is not made "of law" any more than a gas pipe is made *of* gas or science *of* science. On the contrary, it is by means of steel, pipes, regulators, meters, inspectors, and control rooms that gas ends up flowing uninterruptedly across Europe; and yet it is well and truly gas that circulates, and not the land, nor steel. Yes, law is indeed autonomous compared to the social, for it is one of the means for producing the social defined as association, for arranging and contextualizing it. [But no], there is no domain, no territory that belongs to law. Notwithstanding the claims of jurists served by the sociologists of systems, it does not form a sphere; *without the rest holding it, law would be nothing. Yet it holds everything, in its own way* (264; emphases added).

Many of Latour's observations bearing on the production of French administrative law are germane to the making of law in the Muslim world, though things are arguably more complicated in the latter context insofar as the dynamics there tend to be entwined with processes involving the florescence of religion in public and private spheres (i.e., desecularization, Islamization), ostensibly unlike the overarching situation in formally secular France. I argued, however, that terms such as "desecularization" and "Islamization" are floating, open-ended signifiers, and that since the 1970s Islamization in particular has become a gatekeeping concept. Like their conceptual siblings—Islamic fundamentalism, political Islam, Islamism—such concepts "define the quintessential and dominant questions of interest in the region" (Appadurai 1986, 357) and, in doing so, inhibit awareness and theorization of the phenomena to which they are purportedly relevant: social, cultural, and political dynamics among contemporary Muslims. Recent developments in Tunisia, Egypt, Libya, Syria, and Yemen—to say nothing of post-9/11 dynamics in Afghanistan and Iraq—make it clear that we do not get very far by shoehorning our observations and analyses into problematic binaries such as secularization vs. desecularization/Islamization, or alternatively, "good Muslims" vs. "bad Muslims," or "good Islam" vs. "bad Islam" (Eickelman and Piscatori 1996; Mamdani 2004; Shryock 2010; Abu-Lughod 2013). More broadly, if other recent critical studies are anything to go by (e.g., Schielke 2015; Hoesterey 2016; cf. Soares and Osella 2009), it is increasingly apparent that there is "too much Islam" both in the anthropology of the Muslim world and in the ways that world is understood in Western media and popular culture.

JURIDICAL FIELDS, LEGAL LIBERALISM, AND "EXTREMISM"

One of this book's more general and abstract contentions, inspired partly by Bourdieu, has to do with an important range of the discourses, practices, self-representations, and congeries of symbols manifested in juridical fields, and with what might be termed their "adversarial" qualities in light of the ways they are sometimes pressed into service against rivals or opponents, if not consciously designed by well positioned elites with such challenges in mind. The contention is that the discourses, practices, and other phenomena at issue here are fruitfully considered in relation to struggles, negotiations, and compromises, at once political and pragmatic, involving disparate and potentially irreconcilable social forces (of diverse provenance), interest groups and their agents and allies, and the ethics, social imaginaries, and claims emanating from them. Formulations along these lines provide vital correctives to Foucault's tendency toward overarching generalization, elision, and silence with regard to both the distinctive constellations of forces conducing towards specific instantiations of governmentality and their empirical, socially-engineered "achievements." A converse contention is that Bourdieu's work on the patterned regularities of juridical fields and their internal cleavages, contested logics, and fraught, porous borders has more analytic value if we think beyond and against it (Wacquant 1992, xiv). One way to do this is to augment Bourdieuean perspectives both by historically informed Foucauldian concerns with governance and by substantive engagement with the scope, force, and content of religious sensibilities, dispositions, and commitments, which both theorists tend to gloss over when dealing with law, related phenomena, and a good deal else.

These formulations are clearly relevant to late-modern Malaysia, as we have seen, even though "The notion of field does not provide ready-made answers to all possible queries" (Bourdieu, in Bourdieu and Wacquant 1992, 110). They also afford valuable optics through which to view what has been occurring since early 2011 in in the streets, mosques, barracks, and high-level political corridors of Egypt. During this time, Egyptians have sought to negotiate their post-Mubarak/post-Morsi constitutional charters in light of innumerable debates bearing on the desirability and feasibility of further revising them. In the process they have also endeavored to negotiate the continual but oftentimes opaque and indeterminate (re)drawing of lines defining and distinguishing the realms of law, politics, and religion—and the domains of the secular and the sacred—through which the state enacts its legitimacy and dominion, ostensibly to guarantee public order, morality, and national security (Agrama 2012, 224–35; Wickham 2013).

Formulations such as these in conjunction with the other frames developed in this book are germane to many parts of the world, Muslim and non-Muslim alike. One reason for this, as Jean and John Comaroff have argued in a number of important works (2006, 2009, 2016), is that the dynamics of neoliberal globalization have encouraged growing numbers of individuals, communities, corporations, and states to turn to legal discourse and courts of law to instantiate and solidify their identities (both old and new), to redefine and otherwise manage their relationships, and to safeguard the prerogatives, material interests, and ethical imperatives bound up with them.

It is important to appreciate that these developments, though exceedingly widespread, are not universal in the sense of comprising a monolithic, indivisible, or invariant "cultural(-political) package." We see this in the ways that Thais in the rapidly globalizing Chiangmai province of northern Thailand interpret and respond to personal injury associated with automobile and motorcycle accidents, occupational hazards, sports mishaps, and the like. David and Jaruwan Engel's (2010) longitudinal study bearing on the period 1965–2000 indicates that Thais residing in Chiangmai, who are mostly Theravada Buddhist, increasingly deal with personal injury by eschewing both customary and formal legal redress. They are ever more inclined to turn instead to informally negotiated remedies focusing on harmony, reconciliation, and forgiveness, which are seen as grounded in "[p]iety, compassion, generosity, and selflessness" and thus likely to enhance one's store of karma (139). To put some of this differently, and more generally, "The [increased salience of the] law of karma has come to be positioned in opposition to the law of courts and lawyers" (90).

The northern Thai case may be an exception that proves the (global) rule; alternatively, it may point to the heterogeneity of global currents with respect to legal discourse and courts of law that is sometimes obscured when we identify dominant national and transnational trends. It should be noted in any event that Engel and Engel deal more or less exclusively with personal injury (tort law) and that, as such, the data and arguments they marshal, while significant, have no necessary bearing on Comaroff and Comaroff's more expansive claims, which share deep resonance with the material presented in this book. These claims concern the rise of lawfare, the judicialization of politics and religion, and the increasingly global circulation of "rights-talk" and legally-inflected discourses and practices driven by a will to improve that Comaroff and Comaroff (2016) characterize as part and parcel of "the fetishism of legalities." To wit, that "the rule of law and constitutionalism have become a dominant global discourse, to the extent that even in the most remote reaches of the planet, people have learned, through a populist pedagogy of rights, to see themselves as *homo juralis*—and to address their identities, interests, and injuries by recourse to the legal" (139). More cross-cultural and historical research on these topics is clearly warranted. Especially welcome would be additional research in diverse Buddhist and Hindu contexts in which notions of karma and rebirth loom large and may possibly discourage engagement with formal legal institutions—as in different ways do Southern Baptist sensibilities in the American South (Greenhouse 1997)—particularly those institutions that are seen as both favoring wealthy and powerful individuals and being largely unreceptive to the claims of ordinary people.

The larger issue bears on globalization and what Engel and Engel (2010) refer to as "legal liberalism," defined as including "some commitment to rule of law practices and institutions, individual rights, free markets, and democratic government" (3). In their view, "the decline of law [in the context of globalization] . . . demands our attention, and its absence from everyday life may be the hallmark of our age" (161).

Muslim-majority nations such as Malaysia and perhaps most of the rest of the world, if Comaroff and Comaroff's position is accepted, provide weighty counterexamples to the case of northern Thailand. The Muslim-majority examples (Eickelman and Piscatori 1996; Hefner 2011b, 2016b) are all the more instructive in light of widespread Western views, both scholarly and popular, as to the incommensurabilities between legal liberalism and *sharia*. This book has shown that *sharia* courts in Malaysia do evince "some commitment to rule of law practices and institutions [and] individual rights"; and that they are expanding women's legal privileges and prerogatives (partly as an endorsement of companionate marriage and a greater concern to punish errant husbands), albeit with qualification, and in fits and starts. These same courts are exceedingly friendly to capitalist markets and attendant institutions. Indeed, the *sharia* courts are heavily informed by capitalist market sensibilities in a number of areas: their day-to-day operations, their understandings of "best practices," their embrace of international standards of operation and audit, and the exceedingly high-tech and otherwise market-savvy rebranding campaigns that draw upon the collective wisdom and corporate sartorial styles of captains of global industry.

As for democratic governance, the dynamics are rather more complex. But on balance they too point to a general commitment to legal liberalism, despite their inclusion of certain types of "extremism" addressed below. Recall that those in the employ of the *sharia* courts are not in the business of making policy on formal governance and must of necessity take most of their cues from and implement policy measures originating in the Prime Minister's Department and the nation's executive branch generally. Important to bear in mind too is that throughout Malaysia's postcolonial history, the increasingly powerful and ever-more top-heavy executive branch has posed a much greater obstacle to democratic governance, and to transparency, accountability and due process, than the *sharia* courts or Islam per se (Peletz 2002, 2009). The more general and more significant point is that, notwithstanding the latter dynamic—and in sharp contrast to what we have recently seen in various quarters of the Muslim world (e.g., Afghanistan, Iraq, Syria, Egypt, Sudan, Libya, Nigeria, Algeria, Tunisia, and Mali)—the vast majority of the struggles that are currently being waged in Malaysia over Islam and other key symbols and institutional resources are taking place in relatively democratic and largely peaceful ways. For the most part, they have not involved disappearances, torture, assassinations, suicide or other bombings, large-scale uprisings, coup d'état, or vigilante campaigns of stoning, amputation, and maiming. More specifically, these struggles are occurring through elections that are oftentimes (but not always) relatively free and fair; constitutional amendments and other legislation; court battles (some of which clearly involve lawfare); weekly seminars and educational outreach; legitimate lobbying, PR blitzes, and merchandising efforts (many of which involve sophisticated corporate rebranding); and letters to the editors of local newspapers. Other fora involve electronic media, including of course the largely ungovernable Internet, and a myriad of academic and non-academic seminars and town-hall meetings, some of which are designed to make provision for disparate voices and variously defined subalterns.

The fourteenth general election of May 9, 2018, provides a case in point. This election saw the long-dominant ruling party (UMNO) and its multiparty coalition (the National Front, formerly the National Alliance) ousted from the corridors of power, where they had been comfortably ensconced ever since formal independence from the British in 1957. Prime Minister Najib's electoral loss was followed by his arrest on charges of corruption, abuse of power, breach of trust, money-laundering, and the like associated with (among other egregious crimes) his apparent embezzlement of the equivalent of hundreds of millions if not billions of dollars of assets from Malaysia's sovereign wealth fund (1MDB). But neither his or UMNO's (or the coalition's) supporters, nor their detractors, took to the streets in violent protests or clashes, and there were no suicide or other bombings, assassinations, widespread arrests, or disappearances. Instead, the nation rallied around its "new" leader, the ninety-two-year-old Mahathir, who served as prime minister from 1981–2003 and had pledged in his campaign that he would arrange his long-time adversary's (Anwar Ibrahim's) release from prison on seemingly bogus charges of sodomy and would work with him in the months and years ahead both to bring Najib to justice and to reinvigorate the economy. Malaysians I spoke with in and around Kuala Lumpur in July 2018 seemed content to let the trials run their course, though most of them also felt that Najib is guilty of massive corruption and other criminality, and if found guilty as charged, should be sent to prison, perhaps for the remainder of his life, and stripped of all illicitly acquired assets. Significantly, I encountered no other talk of payback, judicial or otherwise.

It is nonetheless true that state-sponsored Islamization is by some criteria more "extreme" in Malaysia than in Saudi Arabia, Iran, Pakistan, and Sudan, to take a handful of relatively well-studied examples. I invoke the term "extreme" not to describe the state's imposition of *hudud* laws or its support of public executions or the obligatory seclusion of women; there is none of this in Malaysia. (Nor do I deploy the term with reference to the few hundred Malaysian jihadists who have reportedly joined the ranks of ISIS or similar organizations in recent years.) Rather, I use "extreme"—common synonyms for which include "remarkable," "extraordinary," "exceptional," and "radical"—in a threefold sense, all attesting to the strengths and accomplishments, some of them decidedly illiberal, of the nation's corporate bureaucracies. First, agents of the state and of other institutions of bureaucratized governmentality have gone to great lengths to regulate and homogenize Islamic sensibilities and dispositions and the discourses and practices associated with them; a key feature of this strategy is the highly coordinated stigmatization—if not overt, explicit criminalization—of heterodoxy, non-conformity, and the like. (Recall that "Malaysia has one of the most tightly regulated religious spheres in the world" [Moustafa 2018, 4].) Second, and ironically, these same agents have drawn upon an extremely diverse array of sources (Islamic tradition, both real and imagined; British-origin colonial- and postcolonial common law; Japanese management and auditing regimes; ISO protocols; and the world of neoliberal/global corporate capitalism) to conjure, solidify, and police this homogeneity. The third aspect of the "extremism" has to do with the fact that from a historical and cross-cultural perspective, efforts to effect the homogeneity at issue have been remarkably successful.[1]

Indeed, by certain measures, legal and other developments associated with *sharia* in Malaysia might be said to be moving in the opposite direction to those in Saudi Arabia, widely regarded by outside observers as far more homogenous, intolerant, and repressive than Malaysia and forever committed to staying the course. Saudi Arabia has recently witnessed a relative flowering, in legal, political, religious, and lay circles, of pluralistic sentiments and dispositions concerning beliefs and practices long considered heretical by Saudi authorities, such as those of Shias and Sufis. The landmark religious edict of 2017 that authorized women to drive beginning in mid-2018 is relevant here. So, too, is the astonishing emergence in recent years of new forms of ("friend") marriage such as *sadiq*, which was "developed for young people not [financially] established enough for conventional marriage, . . . allow[ing] them to meet for sexual relations from time to time without establishing a home together" (Vogel 2011, 85). These developments are especially worthy of note since there is nothing comparable on the horizon in Malaysia, where religious authorities invest ever greater resources in policing the boundaries of conventional (Muslim) marriage and carefully regulating all varieties of sexual relations and bodily comportment. Frank Vogel's incisive research indicates that "Saudis appear to feel, both individually and civilly, a new sense of power and initiative to treat directly with the meanings and legitimacies of shari'a" and to do so "without waiting for or depending on the state or even establishment scholars" (60). Dynamics such as these incline him and others (Okruhlik 2005; Hefner 2011a, 28–29) to a guarded optimism concerning the development of new subjectivities in the Saudi context and perhaps "the emergence, even, of a Habermasian-type 'public sphere'" (Vogel 2011, 88).

It may seem anomalous in light of Malaysia's tremendous economic successes and its burgeoning and increasingly well-educated Malay middle classes that there has been relatively little opposition, ambivalence, or publicly elaborated alternatives vis-à-vis state-sponsored Islamization, at least among Malays (but see Peletz 1997, 2002; Zainah Anwar 2001; Farish Noor 2005; Weiss 2006; Lee 2010). The anomalies are less striking when one considers that ever since the Melaka Sultanate (1400–1511), Malays have tended to view the state as the protector of their interests, priorities, and ethical wellsprings, including, most notably, (Malayan) Islam, in the face of real and imagined threats from rival groups of Muslims as well as Chinese, Indians, and other non-Muslims (Muzaffar 1979). Another, related issue is that Malay criticism of those who cast themselves as stewards of the nation's Islamic resources and identity is often construed by fellow Malays as "letting down the (ethnic/racial/religious) side." This is a grave ethical breach akin to the offense of treason (*derhaka*), which has long been linked in Malay mythology with both incest and cannibalism, the most heinous crimes imaginable. Dynamics such as these need to be considered alongside the fact that many Malays have recently attained middle-class status and are understandably reluctant to jeopardize all that they have gained by rallying against the very state whose policies and corporate bureaucracies have helped them garner their new class standings. These realities help explain why Malay opposition to the bureaucratically-driven homogenization entailed in state-sponsored Islamization—and to the kinds of excesses commonly associated with top-heavy executive branches—is less pronounced than one might expect, though it certainly exists. More generally, the constellation of variables outlined here makes Malaysia somewhat unique relative to other Muslim-majority nations, but not at all unusual in a theme-and-variation sense.

A few remarks involving comparisons with the West are also warranted lest we lose sight of far-reaching transnational dynamics and mistakenly assume that Malaysia or the Muslim world generally—or the West—constitute exceptions to pervasive global trends. Neoliberal doctrines, projects, and techniques of governance, it is clear, are increasingly global (and nearly universal) phenomena, however much they vary from one national (or sub-national) context to the next and across the terrain of any particular case. Their many entailments tend to include a surge in punitiveness, though the latter surge is also empirically variable in terms of scope, force, etc. Thus Malaysia's punitive turn, though striking from an historical point of view, pales in comparison to that of the United States, which is situated at the extreme end of the spectrum, as we have seen. The Malaysian example also seems less pronounced than what has been described for the United Kingdom and

France (Wacquant 2009); it might be said to lie, like Indonesia, somewhere along the continuum between these latter cases and those of Canada, Scandanavia, and Italy, which, at least in the early years of the new millennium, had not experienced a rising tide of punitiveness (Pratt et al 2005; Muehlebach 2012). The strong correlation at issue is not amenable to simple "cause and effect" types of explanations. It is better understood in terms of elective affinities and "enabling and constraining conditions" (Lancaster 2011, 224), much like the pastoral dimensions of modern governance that help legitimize statecraft, particularly in the eyes of the potential beneficiaries of one or another variant of pastoral care.

Going forward, key challenges lie in identifying and helping to create the specific conditions for the possibility of scaling up the pastoral and pluralistic dimensions of assemblages of governance, which in the Malaysian context include the female-friendly sensibilities and dispositions associated with *sulh* sessions and expanded grounds for *fasakh*. Recent efforts on the part of Malaysian NGOs and other members of civil society to engage these and similar challenges do in any event make hope practical. This is one reason it is important that anthropologists and others document such efforts, even or especially when their descriptions and analyses do not focus on the anthropology of the good.

Also conducive to hopefulness and thus vital to underscore is a set of facts commonly papered over by brand stewards and others in Malaysia and beyond who seek to market norms and forms of authority and governance as "natural," God-given, and immutable, as distinct from contingent, fragile, and susceptible to both challenge and subversion. First, "consumers are fickle and brands come and go," as James Hoesterey (2016, 17) has shown in his study of the meteoric rise and precipitous fall from grace of an Indonesian televangelist cum entrepreneur (Aa Gym) and the crisis of religious authority and brand integrity that ensued. And second, assemblages are always in the making, their mutual influences never fully settled, an observation that leads Anna Tsing (2015) to remark that "assemblages are defined by the strength of what they gather as much as their always-possible dissipation" (43). The "always-possible dissipation" component of this remark is relevant to the transnational commodity chains involved in the harvesting, transporting, and marketing of highly sought matsutake mushrooms and other landscape-based assemblages that are the focus of Tsing's fascinating work. But it doesn't adequately distinguish overarching form, scope, force, and content, and for these and other reasons would seem to overstate the case for assemblages of the sort examined in this book. It does in any event raise questions about the limits of the assemblage analogy.

Just as scholars have at times been too quick to see evidence of Islamization—and of the rise of political Islam, Islamism, post-Islamism, and the like—amidst the transformations presently occurring in the Muslim world, there are analogous dangers in usages of terms like assemblage that are overly facile or literal. The concept of assemblage has been utilized by anthropologists, geographers, and others since the late 1990s in lieu of notions such as system, structure, totality, and essence. The latter notions undergirded a good deal of descriptive and analytic work in the social sciences and humanities through the mid-to-late twentieth century and were often intended or taken to imply degrees of regularity, fixity, coherence, stability, and finality. I would caution that we need to avoid throwing the baby out with the bathwater by placing too much emphasis on disorder, uncertainty, congeries of contingencies, "the ephemeral, the emergent, the evanescent, the decentered and the heterogeneous" (Marcus and Saka 2006, 101)—and assemblages' "always possible dissipation." The risk in according too much significance to these latter phenomena is that in doing so, we give short shrift to the noncontingent, to structured and systematic imperatives and constraints that are reproduced over time—such as continuities in gender, power, prestige, and lawfare addressed toward the beginning of chapter 1 and elsewhere—and to generalization and explanation. "If pushed too far, if insisted on too literally—if it becomes anything more than an allusion—assemblage rapidly becomes a dead metaphor in one's work. . . . rigidifying into the thingness of final or stable states that besets the working terms of classical social theory" (Marcus and Saka 2006, 106; J. L. Comaroff 2010, 528–29).

A good way to guard against these dangers is to ground our descriptions and analyses in historicized inquiries that are closely attentive to detail and careful generalization and are based on the kind of deep hanging out that has long been the hallmark of the ethnographic enterprise. Clearly, however, no combination of extant methodologies or conceptual or analytic terminologies can fully resolve all dilemmas associated with the ways we understand, negotiate, and characterize the complexities we encounter in the field. This is at once one of the more formidable if not unsettling challenges of fieldwork and a chief source of its enduring fascination.

NOTES

INTRODUCTION

1. In this formulation, the term "Islamic" refers to symbols, norms, discursive traditions, and related phenomena that derive from or are otherwise associated with sacred texts such as the Quran and *hadith,* are commonly held to be broadly congruent or ultimately compatible with the legal and/or non-legal discourses linked with such texts, or both. Both popular and elite assessments of the congruence and compatibility at issue vary widely across time and space, and are characterized by ambiguities, ambivalences, paradoxes, and contradictions, as Shahab Ahmed has shown in his masterful *What Is Islam?* (2016). Analogous situations obtain within other religious communities as well.

2. There is, however, a rich tradition of scholarship on new media in the Muslim world; see, e.g., Eickelman and Anderson 2003; Hirschkind 2009; Schulz 2012.

3. Standard and Poor's Global, Inc., "Islamic Finance Outlook, 2018 edition," page 4. Accessed September 10, 2018. https://www.spratings.com/documents/20184/4521646 /Islamic+Finance+2018+Digital-1.pdf/cf025a76-0a23-46d6-9528-cecde80e84c8.

4. For additional discussion of methodology, see Peletz 1988, 1996, 2002.

5. As will be clear in due course, I take pluralism to involve conditions or settings in which diversity is accorded legitimacy (Connolly 2005). I use the term "gender pluralism" as a gloss to refer to pluralism with respect to both gender and sexuality (see Peletz 2009; see also Rubin 1984).

CHAPTER ONE. *SHARIA* JUDICIARY AS GLOBAL ASSEMBLAGE

A number of people kindly provided comments on earlier formulations of material presented in this chapter: Janice Boddy, Mark Cammack, John Comaroff, Vincent Cornell, Kim Dovey, Bruce Knauft, Robert Hefner, Jim Hoesterey, Michael Lambek, Andrew

Shryock, Fatima Siddiqi, Winnifred Sullivan, tan beng hui, Steve Tipton, Amanda Whiting, and anonymous reviewers for *Comparative Studies in Society and History*. I presented some of the material at the Association for Asian Studies annual meeting (2011), the Koninklijk Instituut voor Taal-, Land- en Volkenkunde (KITLV) (2011), New York University (2011), the University of Victoria (2011), the European Academy, Berlin (2012), the Rockefeller Foundation's Bellagio Center (2012), the University of Malaya (2012), and the Free University Amsterdam (2013). An early version of the chapter was published in *Comparative Studies in Society and History* 55, no. 3 (2013); an abridged version of that essay appeared in *A Companion to the Anthropology of Religion,* edited by Janice Boddy and Michael Lambek (New York: Wiley-Blackwell, 2013). The second epigraph for this chapter, from Dezalay and Garth, *Global Prescriptions: The Production, Exportation, and Importation of a New Legal Orthodoxy* ©2002 University of Michigan Press, is reprinted with permission. (All other epigraphs in the book are utilized in accordance with fair use provisions.)

Epigraphs: Latour 2005, 77; Dezalay and Garth 2002, 308.

1. By way of brief elaboration: "Malaysia's economy grew at an average annual rate of almost 6.5 percent from 1961 to 2011" (Felker 2015, 133), the nation is on track to attain "fully developed" economic status within the next few years, and its population is roughly 75 percent urban (according to 2016 data), almost double the figure for the late 1970s (https://tradingeconomics.com/malaysia/urban-population-percent-of-total-wb-data.html). Data on literacy and education help round out the ("development-miracle") picture: The literacy rate for individuals in the 15–24 age group is over 98 percent as of 2016 (https://data.unicef.org/country/mys/), and roughly 44 percent of college-age individuals are enrolled in tertiary educational institutions, women comprising over 59 percent of those enrolled (https://tradingeconomics.com/malaysia/school-enrollment-tertiary-percent-gross-wb-data.html, https://data.unicef.org/country/mys/). GDP per capita, moreover, exceeded US$9,500 in 2016 (https://data.worldbank.org/indicator/NY.GDP.PCAP.CD?locations=MY). These are stunning achievements in a region that includes Myanmar, Laos, Cambodia, Vietnam, Indonesia, and East Timor, though they fall short of those boasted by neighboring Singapore; they also mask broad ethnic, social-class, and other disparities (Jomo Kwame Sundaram and Wee Chong Hui 2014).

2. *http://worldpopulationreview.com/countries/malaysia-population/*, last accessed April 25, 2019.

3. https://www.worldatlas.com/articles/ethnic-groups-of-malaysia.html, last accessed April 25, 2019.

4. The fact that the nation's secular courts are generally referred to as civil courts even though they handle both civil *and* criminal offenses may be confusing to the uninitiated reader. Further confusion may arise from the fact that infractions handled by the *sharia* court system are classified as either civil cases (*kes mal*) or criminal cases (*kes jenayah*). This is to say that both the civil and the *sharia* judiciaries make use of the civil/criminal distinction in the infractions subject to their jurisdictions. The meanings of subsequent references to civil and criminal offenses will be clear from the context of the discussion.

5. Malaysia's *sharia* courts also deal with matters of inheritance that are subject to Islamic law. These matters are usually subsumed under the rubric of *faraid* (which refers to obligatory ritual duties as well as Quranic stipulations concerning the allocation of shares in inheritance), and are administratively distinguished from both civil and criminal suits. I

observed only a few of these cases in my research in 2010–13 and 2018, largely because they typically comprise a negligible percentage of the cases on courts' dockets; hence I do not discuss them here. I have described and analyzed aspects of both "customary" and Islamic inheritance (and property relations generally) in considerable detail in earlier publications (e.g., Peletz 1988, 1996, 2002).

6. The temporal changes with respect to any particular state, i.e., the rise in the percentage for Negeri Sembilan and the declines in the percentages for Selangor and Kedah, may reflect coding procedures as much as anything else and/or the fact that the samples from the 1980s and 1990s were quite small, in some instances limited to those cases involving proceedings that the anthropologist(s) actually observed.

7. In the Malaysian context, the concept of *Islam Hadhari,* usually translated as "civilizational Islam," is widely associated with Abdullah Ahmad Badawi, Malaysia's fifth prime minister (r. 2003–09), who developed and branded the concept in a number of speeches and position papers and sought to implement many of its basic features (Abdullah Ahmad Badawi 2006). Abdullah's popularity declined rather precipitously during his last years in office, as did the general currency of the branded expression *Islam Hadhari,* except in certain think tanks, research centers, NGOs, and the publications linked with them. More important for our purposes is that the overall vision entailed in *Islam Hadhari* was shared by Abdullah's predecessor, Mahathir Mohamad, and also resonates deeply with the approach to Islam adopted by Abdullah's successor, Najib Tun Razak. Although they have branded themselves in different ways—Mahathir: Vision 2020; Abdullah: *Islam Hadhari;* Najib: 1Malaysia—all three prime ministers have advocated what Robert Hefner (2011a) refers to as a broadly "ethicalized" Islam, as distinct from the more "*sharia*-minded" (Hodgson 1974) platform articulated by the Islamist opposition party, PAS.

8. Catherine Eu, former Executive Director of the Malaysian Bar Council, personal communication, Kuala Lumpur, September 9, 2013.

9. For additional information on Islam and Islamization in Malaysia, see Nagata 1984; Muzaffar 1987; Hussin Mutalib 1993; Peletz 1997, 2002, 2005, 2013; Zainah Anwar 2001; Farish Noor 2005; Fischer 2008; Norani Othman et al 2008; Liow 2009; Lee 2010; tan beng hui 2012; Müller 2014; I. Hussin 2016; Daniels 2017; Mohamed Nawab Mohamed Osman 2017; Sloane-White 2017; Ahmad Fauzi Abdul Hamid 2018; and Moustafa 2018.

10. These are among the government agencies promoting Islamization (Liow 2009; tan beng hui 2012).

11. The chief exceptions include Horowitz 1994; Whiting 2008; and Maznah Mohamad 2010b.

12. Malay *adat* ("custom," "customary law") specifies a more "wife-friendly" distribution of "conjugal acquisitions" (*harta sepencarian*) following a divorce than does Islamic law. The more liberal division at divorce of conjugal acquisitions that one sees in Malaysia's Islamic courts in recent decades builds on *adat,* but this situation exists largely because the relevant features of *adat* resonate with and have been implicitly authorized by common-law sensibilities. Horowitz (1994, 566) notes that *adat* "has been embellished and expanded through common law adjudication and . . . adoption of . . . secular statute[s], whose roots are neither in *adat* nor Islam. The main source of the change, in other words, is the adjacent English legal system," which regulates marriage and divorce among non-Muslims and aims to accord non-Muslim women some measure of equality vis-à-vis men.

246 NOTES TO CHAPTERS ONE AND TWO

13. In some instances, appeals to common-law sensibilities are implicit or indirect, as in the December 18, 1998 letter to the prime minister signed by Sisters in Islam and other women's groups that "Muslim women of this country must also benefit from the growing sphere of rights . . . accorded to their non-Muslim sisters" (cited in Kamali 2000, 119). The rights of non-Muslim women in Malaysia are governed by common law, hence the standard invoked here is clearly the latter body of law.

14. The passage quoted is from then Prime Minister Mahathir's foreword to *E-Government in Malaysia* (Muhammad Rais Abdul Karim and Nazariah Mohd Khalid 2003).

15. The tallies of "hits" posted on the webpages of the E-*Syariah* Portal and the sites to which they are linked indicate that these websites are widely visited by the public. But I do not know of any reliable data indicating how dependable they are, e.g., when potential litigants endeavor to use them to download forms. Anecdotal evidence suggests that they are often inoperable.

16. The passages from Horowitz pertain to legal developments in Malaya during the colonial period, but they are in keeping with his overall argument about late twentieth century developments in Malaysian law.

17. These claims are contested. According to some scholars, "Sayyid Qutb's epistemological critique of the West in *Ma'alim fi al-Tariq* [Milestones or Signposts on the Path] (1964) inspired the educational experiment known as the 'Islamization of Knowledge,'" though the founder of the movement was Ismail al-Faruqi. In this account, Al-Attas was neither the primary inspiration for—nor the founder of—the movement, though he was its main theorist (Cornell 2014, 143); see especially his *Prolegomena to the Metaphysics of Islam: An Exposition of the Fundamental Elements of the Worldview of Islam* (1995) (Cornell 2014, 149n47).

18. Malaysia's longest serving Prime Minister (Mahathir Mohamad), for example, who was responsible for many of the cultural-political and other changes that are commonly subsumed under the gloss of Islamization, devotes a chapter to "Islam and Islamisation" in his widely read memoirs, *A Doctor in the House: The Memoirs of Tun Dr. Mahathir Mohamad* (2011), which were published in English and Malay, thus assuring that they attracted a broad readership. The term also crops up in many of his speeches and in those of his subordinates as well as his successors.

19. For critical reviews of many such usages, see Volpi 2010 and Ahmed 2016.

CHAPTER TWO. A TALE OF TWO COURTS

Some of the material in this chapter was presented at Leiden University (2011), Boston University (2013), the University of Toronto (2013), the Academy of Islamic Studies at the University of Malaya (2013), the International Institute of Advanced Islamic Studies (Malaysia) (2013), New York University (2013), and Emory University (2016). The feedback I received in those settings, especially from Samera Esmeir, Michael Gilsenan, Christine Harrington, Robert W. Hefner, Mark Massoud, and Brinkley Messick, helped me refine my arguments and was much appreciated. The same is true of written comments provided by Angelique Haugerud, Jim Hoesterey, Bruce Knauft, and anonymous reviewers for *American Ethnologist*. An early, much abridged version of the chapter was published in *American Ethnologist* 44, no. 1 (2015); parts of the chapter were included in my essay "Syariah, Inc," which

appeared in *Sharia Law and Modern Muslim Ethics,* edited by Robert W. Hefner (Bloomington: Indiana University Press), 2016.

Epigraphs: Foucault 1980, 14; Tsing 2015, 111.

1. Most of the information in this paragraph and the next derives from the brochure on
professional programs distributed by Harun M. Hashim Law Center, IIUM, obtained by the
author in July 2012.

2. Islamic religious affairs are, in theory, overseen by state- rather than federal-level
authorities (a legacy of the colonial era), even though federal religious bureaucracies have
increasingly encroached on their state-level counterparts; consequently, *sharia* regulations
vary somewhat from state to state. That said, most of the patterns described in this book are
more or less "pan-Malaysian."

3. See also the extensive Malay-language literature on Islamic law and *sharia* courts in
Malaysia that includes Ahmad Hidayat Buang (2007) and a number of important works
cited there.

4. This amendment specifies that civil courts have no jurisdiction over matters within
the purview of Islamic courts, thus largely eliminating civil-court reviews of Islamic-court
rulings and setting the stage, as far as many Malaysians and outside observers are concerned, for Islamic sensibilities to trump the Constitution.

5. I began working with Ikmal in 2011 while he was studying at my home institution.
Partly because his (handwritten, then typed) transcripts of hearings that we both attended
were exquisitely detailed and in many instances more complete and nuanced than mine
(which were also handwritten, then typed), I put great store in the accuracy of the (condensed) transcript presented here. Ikmal and I also later consulted extensively about the
details of this case and his transcript, and I sat in on a number of hearings in the same
court—with the same judge, the same prosecutors, and the same bailiffs—the following
year (2013). I selected this hearing (rather than one at which I was present) for extended
treatment here because it provides a more succinct illustration of the range of dynamics
evident in today's *sharia* courts than any other case (civil or criminal) that I observed in
Rembau or elsewhere in Malaysia in 2010–13 or 2018.

6. Malaysia boasts "one of the highest Internet penetration rates [both] globally" and
among Muslim-majority countries (Moustafa 2018, 94).

7. The term Foucault uses in the passage at issue is "responsibilization."

8. For some reaction to his position, see *The Star* 2013b.

9. For these statistics see the JKSM Files (2011–18).

10. Section 377, which is often taken by outside observers as a sign of Oriental Despot-
ism and Islamic sexual repression, is of British colonial, not Islamic origin; this is why the
terminology of Section 377 has long been virtually identical across a number of former British colonies, including Malaysia, Singapore, Myanmar, India, and Pakistan.

11. Some of these latter cases are discussed by Whiting 2008; Harding 2012; and Moustafa 2018.

12. According to some sources, beginning in June 2012 RELA members were no longer
authorized to conduct raids on their own (Nadaraj 2013).

13. See World Prison Brief: Malaysia, http://www.prisonstudies.org/country/malaysia).

14. These figures are from 2018; see World Prison Brief, *https://www.prisonstudies.org
/sites/default/files/resources/downloads/wppl_12.pdf*, last accessed August 21, 2019.

CHAPTER THREE. WHAT ARE *SUHL* SESSIONS?

An early, much abridged version of this chapter was presented at the Workshop on Islamic Law and Society that was held at the Hagop Kevorkian Center for Near Eastern Studies at New York University in 2015. I am indebted to Morgan Clarke, Michael Gilsenan, Iza Hussin, Brinkley Messick, and Tamir Moustafa for their comments on that material.

Epigraphs: Syed Khalid Rashid 2008, 10; Walid Iqbal 2001, 1045.

1. Whether Malaysia's *sharia* judges do in fact have the freedom or opportunity to exercise *ijtihad* is another matter. Some *sharia* judges and others I have interviewed claim that they do, citing as evidence how they handle a "triple *talak*," which involves a husband pronouncing the standardized divorce formula ("I divorce you") three times in a single utterance; for example, "I divorce you, I divorce you, I divorce you." According to locally dominant interpretations of the Shafi'i conventions that prevail in Malaysia, this should normally be handled as an irrevocable divorce since it includes three distinct repudiations. But certain of the nation's *sharia* judges feel that it is sometimes (usually?) more appropriate to follow jurists from Maliki or other (non-Shafi'i) legal schools who treat a triple *talak* as a single repudiation because it occurs in the context of a single utterance. This means that it can be revoked so that the couple can reconcile and resume married life without the wife having to marry another man in the meantime, consummate the marriage, and then divorce him in order to remarry her first husband. More generally, in these accounts, the local adoption of traditions from non-Shafi'i legal schools is an example of *ijtihad*. However, some knowledgeable Malay scholars specializing in the theory and practice of Islamic law in Malaysia who I've interviewed reject this claim, insisting that at present the nation's *sharia* judges have little if any opportunity to exercise *ijtihad*. I am inclined toward the latter view, especially since the handling of a triple *talak* was the only example ever provided me in support of the position that Malaysia's *sharia* judges engage in *ijtihad*.

2. Personal communication (email correspondence), February 27, 2015.

3. Sa'odah apparently sent out 250 questionnaires, 128 of which (51.2 percent of the total) were returned to her. 28 of those returned may have been incomplete, hence the N of 100 referenced in the text above.

4. A number of scholars have examined these cases; for a concise overview, see Moustafa 2018.

5. The household survey I conducted in the village of Bogang in 1979–80 revealed that 66 percent of all completed marriages in which women had been involved had ended in divorce; the corresponding figure for men was 73 percent (Peletz 1988, 237, 250–59). Similar patterns were reported by scholars working in other regions of the Malay Peninsula at the time. The Malay divorce rate appeared to decline in most areas of the country through the mid-1990s, but the years since the mid- to late-1990s have seen a reversal of that trend, with some accounts suggesting a doubling of the annual rate (measured as the number of registered divorces in relation to the number of registered divorces each year) during the period 1995–2010 (Dommaraju and Jones 2011, 735; Siti Farhanah binti Md Sam and Puzziawati Ab Ghani n.d., 5).

6. Anwar served more than six years in prison (1998–2004) before being released at the behest of Prime Minister Abdullah Badawi (r. 2003–09); his unsuccessful appeal of his second conviction (associated with "the second Anwar affair," which began in 2008) resulted in

another five-year sentence, which he began serving in 2015. Anwar was freed from prison in May 2018, following the general elections that saw his long-time nemesis (Prime Minister Mahathir Mohamad; r. 1981–2013) returned to power as prime minister, with Anwar's wife (Dr. Wan Azizah Wan Ismail) serving as deputy prime minister. Ironically, one of Mahathir's campaign promises was that he would seek Anwar's release from prison and would essentially serve as caretaker until Anwar sought election as prime minister.

7. My discussion of this case incorporates material adapted from Peletz 2009, 187–88.

CHAPTER FOUR. DISCOURSE, PRACTICE, AND REBRANDING IN KUALA LUMPUR'S *SHARIA* COURTHOUSE

I presented some of the material in this chapter at the Workshop on Islamic Law and Society that was held at the Hagop Kevorkian Center for Near Eastern Studies at New York University in 2016. For their helpful comments, I wish to thank Hussein Agrama, Morgan Clarke, Michael Gilsenan, Mark Massoud, and Brinkley Messick. Thanks also to Maria Carrion, Kim Collins, and Ross King for clarification of architectural matters, and to Andrew Willford, who read the penultimate draft of the chapter and provided valuable feedback.

Epigraph: Bourdieu 2014, 174.

1. "Greater Kuala Lumpur," a designation that is sometimes used more or less synonymously with the term "Klang Valley," is home to more than 7.2 million people according to data from 2016 (http://worldpopulationreview.com/world-cities/kuala-lumpur-population; https://www.dosm.gov.my/v1/index.php?r=column/cone&menu_id=bjRlZXVGdnBue DJKY1BPWEFPRlhIdzo9).

2. The term "Indo-Saracenic" designates a stylistically hybrid type of architecture invented by the British in India in the late nineteenth century and subsequently introduced in various other British colonies including the Federated Malay States. It combines features of Mughal and other Indian architecture with elements drawn from nineteenth- and early twentieth-century British building styles, particularly Neo-Classical, Victorian, and Gothic Revival (Zain Abdullah 2014). Indo-Saracenic is sometimes referred to as the "Raj style," "Hindu-Gothic," "Neo-Mughal," or simply "Mahometan" (King 2008, 183). The expression "Late Modern Indo-Saracenic Revival" refers to variants of the (revived) style that were developed in the late twentieth century and the early years of the new millennium.

3. Ross King, personal communication (email correspondence), November 2, 2012.

4. For a discussion of issues related to *aurat* in this *hadith*, see Mahmood 2005, 106–7.

5. The contrast at issue derives from Clifford Geertz's (1966 [1973]) discussion of religious symbols. Geertz emphasizes the dual role of such symbols as both representing (providing "models of") reality and serving as guides or programs that direct or inform social activity, thereby shaping reality (and providing "models for" it).

6. Some recently designed courtrooms in Australia, by contrast, have sought to minimize the power differential that exists between judges and the state on the one hand, and court users, especially litigants, on the other, or at least the ways these differentials are experienced (Mulcahy 2011). The Australian movement toward inclusion and democratization is in many ways diametrically opposed to current architectural and attendant developments in Malaysia.

7. Black business suits do of course come in many styles, and there are undoubtedly hierarchies of preference and prestige that are calibrated in terms of brand names, provenance of materials and manufacture, details of tailoring, overall pricing, and the like. Unfortunately, I do not have any information of this topic.

8. This case dragged on for a number of years and continued to be litigated through the latter part of 2018, providing paparazzi and media outlets with salacious grist for their mills. This is partly because of the former husband's reputation in some quarters as a "playboy tycoon," a reputation fueled by revelations that he secretly married two other women (one Australian, the other Russian) while he was wed to Shahnaz.

9. Around 50–60 percent of the nation's (roughly three thousand) *syariah* lawyers also practice in the civil courts, according to Tuan Musa Awang, president of the PGSM, who kindly provided these figures to my research assistant, Mr. Hariz Shah, via Whatsapp, on July 26, 2018 and October 2, 2018.

10. Amanda Whiting has been tracking relevant developments for a number of years now and sees no evidence of an "Islamist capture" of the Bar Council or the juridical field as a whole (personal communication [email correspondence], June 27, 2018).

11. This definition derives from Wikipedia (https://en.wikipedia.org/wiki/Rebranding).

12. Foreign investment in Malaysia has skyrocketed since the early 1990s, despite periodic downturns (associated with the Asian financial Crisis, for example [see https://www.indexmundi.com/facts/malaysia/foreign-direct-investment]), but the available data do not indicate whether actual or potential investors' perceptions of the *sharia* courts or the more encompassing juridical field may have influenced their decisions to invest in—or steer clear of—Malaysia.

13. This highly fraught controversy, also known as the *Catholic Herald* case, centered on whether Malaysian Catholics could continue to use the word "Allah" as a translation of the words "God" and "Lord" in their Malay-language newspapers (such as the *Herald*) and other publications, especially those distributed among Malay-speaking Christians residing in the states of Sabah and Sarawak. The controversy began in 2007 when the Home Ministry banned the Catholic Church from using the word "Allah" in its publications. The Catholic Church took the matter to court and received a High Court ruling in its favor in 2010, much to the chagrin of Muslims who saw the decision as an infringement on Islam and a thinly veiled attempt to "confuse Muslims" and encourage their conversion to Christianity. Subsequent months saw mass demonstrations and the firebombing of churches and other buildings, including three mosques. The High Court's decision was overturned by the Federal Court in 2015 (Maznah Mohamad 2010a, 521–23; Moustafa 2018, 150).

14. Moorthy Maniam (1969–2005), mentioned briefly in chapter 3, was an Indian Malaysian, born and raised Hindu, who rose to the ranks of corporal in the Malaysian army and was among the first group of Malaysians to climb Mount Everest (1997). He quickly became a national hero but suffered serious injuries from a fall shortly after his return to Malaysia, from which he never recovered. A deeply fraught controversy erupted after his death when authorities claimed, based on questionable evidence, that he had converted to Islam shortly before dying and that he should therefore be buried in a Muslim cemetery in accordance with Islamic rites. His wife, supported by many others, challenged this claim in the courts, seeking to obtain her deceased husband's body and perform appropriate Hindu rites, but the hospital refused to release it in accordance with a *sharia*-court ruling upholding his (deeply

contested) conversion to Islam. The wide-scale protests that ensued, some of which were of international in scope (involving officials in India, for example), centered partly on Moorthy's Muslim burial being yet another example of Malaysian authorities' violation of non-Muslims' human rights. For additional details on the case, see Moustafa 2018, 99–102.

15. This means, among other things, that Chinese Malaysians are highly unlikely to visit the museum in Kuala Lumpur's *sharia* courthouse, and that the revisionist histories enshrined in its displays are entirely lost on them.

CHAPTER FIVE. ARE WOMEN GETTING (MORE) JUSTICE?

Some of the material in this chapter was presented at the Workshop on Courts, Religion, and Politics in Contemporary Muslim States, Simon Fraser University, Vancouver (2016); the Law and Society Association Annual Meetings, Mexico City (2017); the Max Planck Institute for Social Anthropology, Halle (Saale) (2017); and the Department of Anthropology at the University of Colorado, Boulder (2018). For helpful suggestions and other feedback, I am grateful to Carla Jones, Monika Lindbekk, Tamir Moustafa, Dominik Müller, Arzoo Osanloo, Jeffrey Sachs, Patricia Sloane-White, Nadia Sonneveld, and Amanda Whiting, as well as anonymous reviewers and editors for *Law and Society Review*. An abridged version of the chapter appeared in *Law and Society Review* 52, no. 3, 2018.

Epigraph: Borneman 1992, 75.

1. See Abu-Lughod 2013 for a discussion of this literature and a delineation of productive tensions within the scholarship produced by reform-minded feminist activists and human-rights advocates writing about family law and related matters in the Muslim world; for alternative perspectives, see Zainah Anwar 2009 and Mir-Hosseini et al 2015.

2. It is important to emphasize that my frame of comparison takes as its point of departure the 1970s–1980s and previously, *before* the introduction of the Islamic Family Law Enactments of 1983–84 (the state-specific implementation of which occurred during 1983–91), rather than the 1990s or the early years of the new millennium. I utilize this optic because I am interested in long-term change and because I conducted my original fieldwork in Rembau in 1978–80 and began doing research on Rembau's Islamic court in 1987–88 when the new enactments had *not yet* been implemented. Some of the reforms contained in the Islamic Family Law Enactments implemented in the period 1983–91, hereafter usually referred to as the "Islamic family law reforms of 1983–1991," were diluted by amendments passed in the 1990s and early 2000s. This situation has led some scholars to suggest that "Polygamy and divorce have been made easier for men" (Norani Othman et al 2005, 91). These contentions are true if one is comparing the original wording of the Islamic family law reforms of 1983–91 with their subsequent dilution or the situation at present. But, importantly, these contentions do not hold up if one is viewing the relevant dynamics from the longer-term historical perspective adopted here.

3. The comparative focus on Egypt is not meant to suggest that developments in its Islamic family law over the past few decades are the most far reaching, "female friendly," or progressive in the Muslim world. Had I chosen a comparative case with these concerns foremost in mind, I probably would have selected Morocco.

4. Limitations of space preclude substantive discussion of *taklik* divorce (aspects of which were addressed in chapter 4); this usually involves a woman convincing a judge that

her husband has violated written provisions of the marriage contact. In practice, a *taklik* divorce often requires the husband's cooperation, though not necessarily his formal consent to the termination of the union. In many jurisdictions *taklik* is quite rare (International Islamic University of Malaysia 2005; Nik Noriani Nik Badli Shah 2008).

5. From *Islamic Family Law (Federal Territories) Act 1984 (Act 303)* (As at 10th March 2012), 41–43.

6. Most of the convergence over the years has involved procedural rather than substantive law.

7. Corresponding figures for the towns of Kempas, Selangor and Kota Jati, Kedah during the same general period (1990–91) were even lower, 1.5 percent (2/132) and 3.3 percent (5/151), respectively (Sharifah Zaleha Syed Hassan and Cederroth 1997, 74–75).

8. These generalizations concerning commonly cited examples of marital harm are based partly on my research assistant's perusal of a batch of *fasakh* files (apparently bearing on some twenty-five or thirty cases) from Rembau for the years 2011–14 that court staff randomly selected and shared with him, coupled with the material from seventeen files that he was able to photograph and forward to me for further scrutiny. (There were probably around 140 *fasakh* cases heard in Rembau during the period in question.) More recent data underpinning these generalizations derive from my study of around three dozen *fasakh* files that Rembau's *sharia* judge kindly shared with me and allowed me to photocopy in July 2018. These files involved all of the *fasakh* suits resolved during the period 2015–17 that included the judge's written summaries and decisions.

9. JKSM Files (2014–15).

10. One manifestation of such backlash in Malaysia culminated in legislation introduced in 2005. The legislation allows *men* to terminate their marriages via *fasakh*, which in the Malaysian setting and in canonical Islamic texts has generally been construed as a prerogative available only to women. In accordance with this legislation, men may now seek exemption from having to pay the roughly three months of spousal support (*nafkah edah*) they would normally be expected to provide their wives if they divorced them by pronouncing the *talak* clause. (There are hardly any cases of male-initiated *fasakh* on record, largely because it is much easier and usually less costly in all senses of the term for a man to pronounce the *talak* than to subject himself and his wife to *fasakh* proceedings.) Another manifestation of backlash involves the dilution in the 1990s and 2000s of the Islamic family law reforms' (1983–91) restrictions on polygyny and on men's divorcing their wives without court permission (Nik Noriani Nik Badli Shah 2008, Maznah Mohamad 2010a).

11. See, e.g., http://www.esyariah.gov.my.

12. "60% *Kes Berjaya Deselesaikan Menerusi Sulh di Mahkamah Syariah*," JKSM Webarchives, 2012.

13. One exception was a 2011 case in Kuala Lumpur involving a woman who entered into a polygynous union without the court's permission. The judge fined her RM$500 (around US$150), which, if not paid, could have resulted in her serving five days in jail. (The husband was sentenced to a fine of RM$700 or ten days in jail.) The other exception, from 2010, also in Kuala Lumpur, involved an "unauthorized marriage" where both husband and wife were sentenced to fines of RM$800 or eight months in jail.

14. For the official account of the case, see "Pendakwa Syarie *lwn.* Kartika Seri Dewi Binti Shukarno," *Jurnal Hukum* 30, no. 2 (2010): 269–85.

15. A recent instance of women being caned by a *sharia* court occurred on September 3, 2018; in that case, two women, aged 22 and 32, were convicted by the *Syariah* High Court of Terengganu of *musahaqah* ("sexual relations between women") and were subsequently sentenced to fines of RM$3,300 and six strokes of a rattan cane. For additional details and reactions, see *The Star Online* 2018.

16. The exception involves capital punishment (hanging), which authorities may impose on men and women alike if they are convicted of crimes such as murder, drug trafficking, or terrorism. Precise information on capital punishment in Malaysia is difficult to come by, but it appears that men account for almost all (perhaps more than 95 percent) of those sentenced to death and executed by the state in recent years (Piotrowski 2018). More generally, there were apparently 1,279 inmates on death row in Malaysia as of December 2018, 932 of whom were convicted of drug offenses and 317 of murder. Foreign nationals are disproportionately represented in these figures, comprising roughly 44 percent of those on death row; see http://www.deathpenaltyworldwide.org/country-search-post.cfm?country =malaysia.

17. JKSM Files (2007–13).

18. Unfortunately, the JKSM does not maintain databases relevant to sentencing; hence one cannot readily compare patterns of sanctions imposed on female and male defendants for the same category of offense in order to assess possible gender bias in this sphere of judicial practice. Importantly, however, perusal of *sharia* law journals such as *Jurnal Hukum* suggests that sentences for crimes like *khalwat* (illicit proximity), which typically involve both a male and a female defendant arrested and charged at the same time, and commonly tried in linked hearings (though technically as two separate cases), tend to be identical for both partners. (But see tan beng hui 1999 for a discussion of sentencing [and media] biases against female-bodied [as distinct from male-bodied] individuals involved in transgender practices and same-sex relations.) The sentences can conceivably include fines, or jail time if the fines cannot be paid, as well as flogging. But, in practice, restitution almost always occurs through the payment of fines, with no jail time or corporal punishment. The same is true for other criminal offenses that involve heterosexual couples, such as fornication /adultery.

19. Al-Arqam was outlawed by the government as "deviationist" in 1994. But Arqam disciples continue to exist under the umbrella of Global Ikhwan.

20. Shortly after its release the book was banned in Malaysia, Singapore, and Indonesia. But the group, which apparently has chapters operating in Malaysia, Singapore, Indonesia, Australia, Jordan, Kazakhstan, and elsewhere, continues to exist, and claimed some three thousand members in 2014.

21. I might add that these interpretations have sparked considerable controversy among scholars of Islam; see, for example, AbuSulayman and Anjum 2017.

22. For contemporary perspectives on the larger context, see Lindsey 2018; see also Ricklefs 2012.

23. Importantly, these individuals do not usually have direct experience of the *sharia* judiciary (but see tan beng hui 1999 and n15, above). As noted earlier, they are typically dealt with by the police "extra-judicially": harassed, sometimes detained and abused, and then released without formal charges. The same is true of their male-bodied (Malay/Muslim) counterparts, though the latter individuals are more likely to be hauled before the *sharia*

courts than (Malay/Muslim) women involved in same-sex relations or transgender practices, partly because they are more visible.

24. See https://explorer.usaid.gov/cd/MYS.

CONCLUSION

1. These are of course relative points, and I am not suggesting utter uniformity in experiences, understandings or representations of Islamic ethics, law, or ritual; there is still a great deal of variation in these realms, though decidedly less than in earlier decades (Peletz 1996, 1997, 2002, 2005, 2009). One is reminded of M. C. Ricklefs's (2012) historical study of neighboring Java, which shows that the highly syncretic variant of rural Javanese Islam that Geertz (1960) subsumed under the rubric of *abangan,* subsequently referred to by Javanese and others as *kejawen,* has all but disappeared. Ricklefs also demonstrates that there are few if any cultural, political, or other impediments to processes of Islamization, however regionally variable and otherwise uneven, that proceeded apace in the second half of the twentieth century and that have been especially pronounced since the fall of President Suharto in 1998 and the onset of the *reformasi* era that followed (see also Bruinessen 2013).

BIBLIOGRAPHY

OFFICIAL DOCUMENTS AND RECORDS CONSULTED

Data dan Maklumat Kekeluargaan/Sosial Masyarakat Islam di Malaysia [*Data and Information about Muslim Families and Communities in Malaysia*]. 2011. Putrajaya: JAKIM.

Jabatan Kehakiman Syariah Malaysia [Malaysian Department of *Syariah* Judiciary] Files, 2005–2018. Putrajaya: JKSM.

Laporan Statistik Kes Mal Dan Jenayah, Tahun 2005–2010, Mahkamah Syariah Seluruh Malaysia [*Statistical Report Concerning Civil and Criminal Cases in Syariah Courts in Malaysia, 2005–2010*]. n.d. (2011). Putrajaya: JKSM.

Mahkamah Rendah Syariah Daerah Rembau (*Syariah* Lower Court, District of Rembau) Files, 2011–2017. Rembau.

Mahkamah Syariah Wilayah Persekutuan [Federal Territory *Syariah* Court] Files, 2011–2013. Kuala Lumpur: MSWP.

Manual Kerja Sulh [*Sulh Work Manual*]. 2003. Putrajaya: JKSM.

Panduan Amalan 5S Sektor Awam [*5S Practice Guide(book) for the Civil Service*]. 2010. Putrajaya: MAMPU.

Pejabat Kadi Daerah Rembau [Kadi's Office, District of Rembau] Files, 1963–1988. Rembau.

"Pendakwa Syarie *lwn.* Kartika Seri Dewi Binti Shukarno" ["*Syarie* Prosecutor vs. Kartika Seri Dewi Binti Shukarno"]. 2010. *Jurnal Hukum* 30, no. 2: 269–85.

BOOKS, ARTICLES, AND THESES

Abdullah Ahmad Badawi. 2006. *Islam Hadhari: A Model Approach for Development and Progress*. Petaling Jaya: MPH Publishing.

Abou El Fadl, Khaled. 2001. *Speaking in God's Name: Islamic Law, Authority and Women*. Oxford: Oneworld.

Abu-Lughod, Lila. 1986. *Veiled Sentiments: Honor and Poetry in a Bedouin Society.* Berkeley: University of California Press.

———. 2013. *Do Muslim Women Need Saving?* Cambridge, MA: Harvard University Press.

AbuSulayman, AbdulHamid A., and Ovamir Anjum, eds. 2017. "Islam and Homosexuality." Special issue, *American Journal of Islamic Social Science* 34, no. 3 (Summer).

Afsaruddin, Asma. 1999. *Hermeneutics and Honor: Negotiating Female "Public" Space in Islamic/ate Societies.* Cambridge, MA: Harvard Middle Eastern Monographs No. 32, Harvard Center for Middle Eastern Studies, Harvard University Press.

Agrama, Hussein. 2012. *Questioning Secularism: Islam, Sovereignty, and the Rule of Law in Modern Egypt.* Chicago: University of Chicago Press.

Ahmad Fauzi Abdul Hamid. 2018. "Shifting Trends of Islamism and Islamist Practice in Malaysia, 1957–2017." *Southeast Asian Studies* 7, no. 3: 363–90.

Ahmad Hidayat Buang. 2007. "Islamic Contracts in a Secular Court Setting? Lessons From Malaysia." *Arab Law Quarterly* 21: 317–40.

Ahmad Ibrahim. 1965 [1975]. *Islamic Law in Malaya.* Kuala Lumpur: Malaysian Sociological Research Institute.

Ahmad, Imtiaz, and Helmut Reifeld, eds. 2004. *Lived Islam in South Asia: Adaptation, Accommodation, and Conflict.* Delhi: Social Sciences Press.

Ahmed, Shahab. 2016. *What is Islam? The Importance of Being Islamic.* Princeton, NJ: Princeton University Press, 2016.

Al-Attas, Syed Muhammad Naquib. 1969. *Preliminary Statement on a General Theory of the Islamization of the Malay-Indonesian Archipelago.* Kuala Lumpur: Dewan Bahasa dan Pustaka.

———. 1978. *Islam and Secularism.* Kuala Lumpur: Muslim Youth Movement of Malaysia (ABIM).

———. 1995. *Prolegomena to the Metaphysics of Islam: An Exposition of the Fundamental Elements of the Worldview of Islam.* Kuala Lumpur: ISTAC.

al-Shirbini [al-Imam Shams al-Din Muhammad ibn Ahmad al-Khatib al-Shirbini]. n. d. (2014). *Mughni al-Muhtaj ila Ma'rifat Ma'ani alfaz al-Minhaj* [*The Enrichment of the One in Need of Knowledge of the Meanings of the Words of the Minhaj*]. 5th ed. Beirut: Dar al-Maarifah.

al-Zuhayli, Wahbah Mustafa. 1997. *al-Fiqh al Islami wa Adillataha* [*Islamic Jurisprudence and Its Proofs*], 8 vols. Damascus: Dar Al-Fikr.

Alexander, Michelle. 2010 [2012]. *The New Jim Crow: Mass Incarceration in the Age of Color-blindness.* Rev. ed. New York: New Press.

Ali, Kecia. 2006. *Sexual Ethics and Islam: Feminist Reflections on Qur'an, Hadith, and Juris-prudence.* Oxford: Oneworld.

Ali, Muhammad Mumtaz. 2010. *The History and Philosophy of Islamization of Knowledge: A Preliminary Study of Pioneers' Thought.* Kuala Lumpur: International Islamic University of Malaysia.

Andaya, Barbara and Leonard Andaya. 2001. *A History of Malaysia,* 2nd ed. Honolulu: University of Hawai'i Press.

An-Na'im, Abdullahi Ahmed. 1999. "The Cultural Mediation of Human Rights: The Al-Arqam Case in Malaysia." In *The East Asian Challenge for Human Rights,* edited by Joanne R. Bauer and Daniel A. Bell. New York: Cambridge University Press.

———. 2008. *Islam and the Secular State: Negotiating the Future of Shariʿa.* Cambridge, MA: Harvard University Press.

———, ed. 2002. *Islamic Family Law in a Changing World: A Global Resource Book.* London: Zed.

Anderson, Ben, Matthew Kearnes, Colin McFarlane, and Dan Swanton. 2012. "On Assemblages and Geography." *Dialogues in Human Geography* 2, no. 2: 171–89.

Appadurai, Arjun. 1986. "Theory in Anthropology: Center and Periphery." *Comparative Studies in Society and History* 28, no. 2: 356–61.

Asad, Talal. 1986. "The Idea of an Anthropology of Islam." Occasional Paper Series. Washington, D.C.: Center for Contemporary Arab Studies, Georgetown University.

———. 1993. *Genealogies of Religion.* Baltimore, MD: Johns Hopkins University Press.

———. 2003. *Formations of the Secular: Christianity, Islam, Modernity.* Stanford, CA: Stanford University Press.

Babayan, Kathryn, and Afsaneh Najmabadi, eds. 2008. *Islamicate Sexualities: Translations Across Temporal Geographies of Desire.* Harvard Middle Eastern Monographs 39. Cambridge, MA: Harvard University Press.

Banks, David. 1983. *Malay Kinship.* Philadelphia: ISHI.

Barnes, J. A. 1994. *A Pack of Lies: Towards a Sociology of Lying.* Cambridge: Cambridge University Press.

Baxstrom, Richard. 2008. *Houses in Motion: The Experience of Place and the Problem of Belief in Urban Malaysia.* Stanford, CA: Stanford University Press.

Borneman, John. 1992. *Belonging in the Two Berlins: Kin, State, Nation.* Cambridge: Cambridge University Press.

Borneo Post Online. 2013. "JKSM Golf Tourney This Sunday." September 6, 2013.

Bourdieu, Pierre. 1977. *Outline of a Theory of Practice.* Cambridge: Cambridge University Press.

———. 1987. "The Force of Law: Toward a Sociology of the Juridical Field." *The Hastings Law Journal* 38: 814–53.

———. 2014. *On the State: Lectures at the College de France, 1989–1992.* Edited by Patrick Champagne, Remi Lenoir, Franck Poupeau, and Marie-Christine Riviere. Malden, MA: Polity.

———, and Loïc J. D. Wacquant. 1992. *An Invitation to Reflexive Sociology.* Chicago: University of Chicago Press.

Bowen, John R. 2003. *Islam, Law, and Equality in Indonesia: An Anthropology of Public Reasoning.* Cambridge: Cambridge University Press.

———. 2012. *A New Anthropology of Islam.* Cambridge: Cambridge University Press.

Brown, Nathan J. 1997. *The Rule of Law in the Arab World: Courts in Egypt and the Gulf.* Cambridge: Cambridge University Press.

Broyde, Michael J. 2017. *Sharia Tribunals, Rabbinical Courts, and Christian Panels: Religious Arbitration in America and the West.* New York: Oxford University Press.

Bruinessen, Martin van. 2013. "Introduction: Contemporary Developments in Indonesian Islam and the 'Conservative Turn' of the Early Twenty-First Century." In *Contemporary Developments in Indonesian Islam,* edited by Martin van Bruinessen. Singapore: Institute of Southeast Asian Studies.

Bunnell, Timothy. 2004. *Malaysia, Modernity, and the Multimedia Super Corridor: A Critical Geography of Intelligent Landscapes.* Abingdon, OX: RoutledgeCurzon.

Cannell, Fanella. 2010. "The Anthropology of Secularism." *Annual Review of Anthropology* 39: 85–100.

Carlisle, Jessica. 2013. "Moroccan Divorce Law, Family Court Judges, and Spouses' Claims: Who Pays the Cost When a Marriage is Over?" In *Feminist Activism, Women's Rights, and Legal Reform,* edited by Mulki Al-Sharmani. London: Zed.

Casanova, Jose. 1994. *Public Religions in the Modern World.* Chicago: University of Chicago Press.

Clarke, Morgan. 2012. "The Judge as Tragic Hero: Judicial Ethics in Lebanon's Shari'a Courts." *American Ethnologist* 39, no. 1: 106–21.

Clifford, James. 1986. "Introduction: Partial Truths." In *Writing Culture: The Poetics and Politics of Culture,* edited by James Clifford and George Marcus. Berkeley: University of California Press.

Cohen, Jean. 1995. "Interpreting the Notion of Civil Society." In *Toward a Global Civil Society,* edited by Michael Walzer. Providence, RI: Berghahn.

Collier, Stephen J., and Aihwa Ong. 2005. "Global Assemblages, Anthropological Problems." In *Global Assemblages: Technology, Politics, and Ethics as Anthropological Problems,* edited by Aihwa Ong and Stephen J. Collier. Malden, MA: Blackwell.

Comaroff, Jean, and John L. Comaroff. 2000. "Millennial Capitalism: First Thoughts on a Second Coming," in "Millenial Capitalism and the Culture of Neoliberalism," special issue, *Public Culture* 12, no. 2: 291–343.

———. 2016. *The Truth About Crime: Sovereignty, Knowledge, Social Order.* Chicago: University of Chicago Press.

———, eds. 2006. *Law and Disorder in the Postcolony.* Chicago: University of Chicago Press.

Comaroff, John L. 2009. "Reflections on the Rise of Legal Theology: Law and Religion in the 21st Century." *Social Analysis* 53, no. 1: 193–216.

———. 2010. "The End of Anthropology, Again: On the Future of an In/Discipline." *American Anthropologist* 112, no. 4: 524–38.

Comaroff, John L., and Jean Comaroff. 2006. "Law and Order in the Postcolony: An Introduction." In *Law and Disorder in the Postcolony,* edited by Jean Comaroff and John L. Comaroff. Chicago: University of Chicago Press.

———. 2009. *Ethnicity Inc.* Chicago: University of Chicago Press.

Conley, John, and William O'Barr. 1998. *Just Words: Law, Language, and Power.* Chicago: University of Chicago Press.

Connolly, William. 2005. *Pluralism.* Durham, NC: Duke University Press.

Cornell, Vincent J. 2014. "Islam." In *The Crisis of the Holy: Challenges and Transformations in World Religions,* edited by Alon Goishen-Gottsetein. Lanham, MD: Lexington.

Daniels, Timothy. 2017. *Living Sharia: Law and Practice in Malaysia.* Seattle: University of Washington Press.

Deeb, Lara. 2006. *An Enchanted Modern: Gender and Public Piety in Shi'i Lebanon.* Princeton, NJ: Princeton University Press.

DeLanda, Manuel. 2006. *A New Philosophy of Society: Assemblage Theory and Social Complexity.* London: Continuum.

Deleuze, Gilles, and Felix Guattari. 1987. *A Thousand Plateaus: Capitalism and Schizophrenia.* Minneapolis: University of Minnesota Press.

Dezalay, Yves, and Bryant Garth. 2002. *The Internationalization of Palace Wars: Lawyers, Economists, and the Contest to Transform Latin America*. Chicago: University of Chicago Press.

———. 2010. *Asian Legal Revivals: Lawyers in the Shadow of Empire*. Chicago: University of Chicago Press.

Dezalay, Yves, and Mikael Madsen. 2012. "The Force of Law and Lawyers: Pierre Bourdieu and the Reflexive Sociology of Law." *Annual Review of Law and Social Science* 8: 433–52.

Dolan, Sean. 2019. *Halal Things: Ontology and Ethics in the Malaysian Halal Ecosystem*. PhD diss., Emory University.

Dommaraju, Premchang, and Gavin Jones. 2011. "Divorce Trends in Asia." *Asian Journal of Social Science* 39: 725–50.

Douglas, Mary. 1970. *Natural Symbols: Explorations in Cosmology*. New York: Pantheon.

Dovey, Kim. 2010. *Becoming Places: Urbanism/Architecture/Identity/Power*. London: Routledge.

Dupret, Baudouin. 2007. "What is Islamic Law? A Praxiological Answer and an Egyptian Case Study." *Theory, Culture, and Society* 24, no. 2: 79–100.

———, Barbara Drieskens, and Annelies Moors, eds. 2008. *Narratives of Truth in Islamic Law*. London: I. B. Taurus.

Durkheim, Emile. 1893 [1964]. *The Division of Labor in Society*. New York: Free Press.

Eickelman, Dale, and James Piscatori. 1996. *Muslim Politics*. Princeton, NJ: Princeton University Press.

Eickelman, Dale, and Jon Anderson, eds. 2003. *New Media in the Muslim World: The Emerging Public Sphere*, 2nd ed. Bloomington: Indiana University Press.

El-Rouayheb, Khaled. 2005. *Before Homosexuality in the Arab-Islamic World, 1500–1800*. Chicago: University of Chicago Press.

Emon, Anver. 2016. "Shari'a and the Rule of Law." In *Shari'a Law and Modern Muslim Ethics*, edited by Robert W. Hefner. Bloomington: Indiana University Press.

Engel, David, and Jaruwan Engel. 2010. *Tort, Custom, and Karma: Globalization and Legal Consciousness in Thailand*. Stanford, CA: Stanford University Press.

Fardon, Richard. 1990. "Localizing Strategies." In *Localizing Strategies: Regional Traditions of Ethnographic Writing*, edited by Richard Fardon. Edinburgh: Scottish Academic Press.

Farish Noor. 2005. *From Majapahit to Putrajaya: Searching for Another Malaysia*. Kuala Lumpur: Silverfish Books.

———. 2006. "Malaysia's Secular Vision vs. 'Writing on the Wall.'" *International Herald Tribune*, August 28.

Fawzy, Essam. 2004. "Muslim Personal Status Law in Egypt: The Current Situation and Possibilities of Reform Through Internal Initiatives." In *Women's Rights and Islamic Family Law: Perspectives on Reform*, edited by Lynn Welchman. London: Zed.

Fealy, Greg. 2005. "Islamization and Politics in Southeast Asia: The Contrasting Cases of Malaysia and Indonesia." In *Islam in World Politics*, edited by Nelly Lahoud and Anthony Johns. London: Routledge.

Feener, R. Michael. 2013. *Shari'a and Social Engineering: The Implementation of Islamic Law in Contemporary Aceh, Indonesia*. Oxford: Oxford University Press.

———, and Mark Cammack, eds. 2007. *Islamic Law in Contemporary Indonesia: Ideas and Institutions*. Cambridge, MA: Islamic Legal Studies Program, Harvard Law School, Harvard University Press.

Felker, Greg. 2015. "Malaysia's Development Strategies: Governing Distribution-Through-Growth." In *Routledge Handbook of Contemporary Malaysia*, edited by Meredith L. Weiss. New York: Routledge.

Ferguson, James. 2009. "The Uses of Neoliberalism." *Antipode* 41, no. S1: 166–84.

Fernando, Joseph. 2006. "The Position of Islam in the Constitution of Malaysia." *Journal of Southeast Asian Studies* 37: 249–66.

Fineman, Martha A. 1991. *The Illusion of Equality: The Rhetoric and Reality of Divorce Reform*. Chicago: University of Chicago Press.

Fischer, Johan. 2008. *Proper Islamic Consumption: Shopping Among the Malays in Modern Malaysia*. Copenhagen: NIAS Press.

———. 2016. *Islam, Standards, and Science: In Global Halal Zones*. New York: Routledge.

Foucault, Michel. 1977. *Discipline and Punish: The Birth of the Prison*. New York: Vintage.

———. 1979 [2000]. "'Omnes et Singulatim': Toward a Critique of Political Reason." In *Power, Essential Works of Foucault 1954–1984*, edited by James D. Faubion. New York: New Press.

———. 1980. *Power/Knowledge: Selected Interviews and Other Writings, 1972–1977*. New York: Pantheon.

———. 1991. "Governmentality." In *The Foucault Effect: Studies in Governmentality*, edited by Graham Burchell, Colin Gordon, and Peter Miller. Chicago: University of Chicago Press.

———. 2003. *Abnormal: Lectures at the College de France, 1974–1975*. New York: Picador.

———. 2007. *Security, Territory, Population: Lectures at the College de France 1977–1978*. New York: Palgrave Macmillan.

Frederick, William H. 1997. "The Appearance of Revolution: Cloth, Uniform, and the Pemuda Style in East Java, 1945–1979." In *Outward Appearances: Dressing Society and State in Indonesia*, edited by Henk Schulte Nordholt. Leiden: KITLV.

Frisk, Sylva. 2009. *Submitting to God: Women and Islam in Urban Malaysia*. Copenhagen: NIAS Press.

Garland, David. 2001. *The Culture of Control: Crime and Social Order in Contemporary Society*. Chicago: University of Chicago Press.

Geertz, Clifford. 1960. *The Religion of Java*. Chicago: University of Chicago Press.

———. 1964 [1973]. "'Internal Conversion' in Contemporary Bali." In *The Interpretation of Cultures*. New York: Basic Books.

———. 1966 [1973]. "Religion as a Cultural System." In *The Interpretation of Cultures*. New York: Basic Books.

———. 1983. *Local Knowledge: Further Essays in Interpretive Anthropology*. New York: Basic Books.

Goh, Lisa. 2013. "Rela Earns Well-Deserved Boost." *Sunday Star*, September 29.

Gomez, Edmund Terence. 2009. "The Rise and Fall of Capital: Corporate Malaysia in Historical Perspective." *Journal of Contemporary Asia* 39, no. 3: 345–81.

———, and Jomo K.S. 1997. *Malaysia's Political Economy: Politics, Patronage, and Profits*. Cambridge: Cambridge University Press.

Goodman, Jane, and Paul Silverstein, eds. 2009. *Bourdieu in Algeria: Colonial Politics, Ethnographic Practice, Theoretical Developments*. Lincoln: University of Nebraska Press.

Greenhouse, Carol. 1997. "Interpreting American Litigiousness." In *History and Power in the Study of Law: New Directions in Legal Anthropology.* June Starr and Jane F. Collier, eds. Ithaca, NY: Cornell University Press.

Grillo, Trina. 1991. "The Mediation Alternative: Process Dangers for Women." *The Yale Law Journal* 100, no. 6: 1545–1610.

Gullick, J. M. 1958. *Indigenous Political Systems of Western Malaya.* London: Athlone Press.

Gupta, Akhil. 2012. *Red Tape: Bureaucracy, Structural Violence, and Poverty in India.* Durham, NC: Duke University Press.

Hajah Noresah bt. Baharom, ed. 2015. *Kamus Dewan [Institute of Language and Literature Dictionary]*, 4th ed. Kuala Lumpur: Dewan Pustaka dan Bahasa.

Hallaq, Wael. 2009. *Shari'a: Theory, Practice, Transformations.* Cambridge: Cambridge University Press.

———. 2013. *The Impossible State: Islam, Politics, and Modernity's Moral Predicament.* New York: Columbia University Press.

Halley, Janet, and Kerry Rittich. 2010. "Critical Directions in Comparative Family Law: Genealogies and Contemporary Studies of Family Law Exceptionalism." *American Journal of Comparative Law* 58: 753–75.

Hamayotsu, Kikue. 2002. "Islam and Nation Building in Southeast Asia: Malaysia and Indonesia in Comparative Perspective." *Pacific Affairs* 75, no. 3: 353–75.

Harding, Andrew. 1996. *Law, Government, and the Constitution in Malaysia.* Petaling Jaya: LexisNexis.

———. 2012. *The Constitution of Malaysia: A Contextual Analysis.* Oxford: Hart Publishing.

Harvey, David. 1990. *The Condition of Postmodernity: An Enquiry into the Origins of Culture Change.* Malden, MA: Blackwell.

Harvey, John. 1995. *Men in Black.* Chicago: University of Chicago Press.

Hefner, Robert W. 2011a. "Introduction: Shari'a Politics—Law and Society in the Modern Muslim World." In *Shari'a Politics: Islamic Law and Society in the Modern World,* edited by Robert W. Hefner. Bloomington: Indiana University Press.

———, ed. 2011b. *Shari'a Politics: Islamic Law and Society in the Modern World.* Bloomington: Indiana University Press.

———. 2016a. "Shari'a Law and the Quest for a Modern Muslim Ethics." In *Sharia Law and Modern Muslim Ethics,* edited by Robert W. Hefner. Bloomington: Indiana University Press.

———, ed. 2016b. *Shari'a Law and Modern Muslim Ethics.* Bloomington: Indiana University Press.

Hilley, John. 2001. *Mahathirism, Hegemony, and the New Oppositon.* London: Zed.

Heo, Angie. 2013. "The Bodily Threat of Miracles: Security, Sacramentality, and the Egyptian Politics of Public Order." *American Ethnologist* 40, no. 1: 149–64.

Hirsch, Susan. 1998. *Pronouncing and Persevering: Gender and the Discourses of Disputing in an African Islamic Court.* Chicago: University of Chicago Press.

Hirschkind, Charles. 2009. *The Ethical Soundscape: Cassette-Sermons and Islamic Counter-Publics.* New York: Columbia University Press.

Hodgson, Marshall. 1974–1977. *The Venture of Islam: Conscience and History in a World Civilization,* 3 vols. Chicago: University of Chicago Press.

Hoek, Janet, and Philip Gendall. 2002. "Ambush Marketing: More Than Just a Commercial Irritant?" *Entertainment Law* 1, no. 2: 72–91.

Hoesterey, James. 2016. *Rebranding Islam: Piety, Prosperity, and a Self-Help Guru.* Stanford, CA: Stanford University Press.

Hoffstaedter, Gerhardt. 2011. *Modern Muslim Identities: Negotiating Religion and Ethnicity in Malaysia.* Copenhagen: NIAS Press.

Hooker, M. B. 1999. "Qadi Jurisdiction in Contemporary Malaysia and Singapore." In *Public Law in Contemporary Malaysia,* edited by Wu Min Aun. Petaling Jaya: Longman.

Horowitz, Donald. 1994. "The Qur'an and the Common Law: Islamic Law Reform and the Theory of Legal Change." *The American Journal of Comparative Law* 2: 233–93 and 3: 543–80.

Huis, Stijn van. 2015. *Islamic Courts and Women's Divorce Rights in Indonesia: The Cases of Cianjur and Bulukumba.* Leiden: E. M. Meijers Research Institute and Graduate School of Leiden University.

Hussin, Iza. 2016. *The Politics of Islamic Law: Local Elites, Colonial Authority, and the Making of the Muslim State.* Chicago: University of Chicago Press.

Hussin Mutalib. 1993. *Islam in Malaysia: From Revivalism to Islamic State?* Singapore: Singapore University Press.

International Islamic University of Malaysia (IIUM). 2005. *Kajian Tempoh Penyelesaian Kes-Kes Pembubaran Perkahwinan di Mahkamah Syariah Seluruh Malaysia (1998–2002)* [*A Study of the Time Involved in Resolving Marital Dissolution Cases in Syariah Courts in Malaysia (1998–2002)*]. Kuala Lumpur: IIUM Entrepreneurship & Consultancies Sdn. Bhd. Dengan Kerjasama Jabatan Kehakiman Syariah Malaysia.

———. 2007. *Kajian Perlaksanaan dan Penguatkuasaan Perintah Nafkah di Mahkamah Syariah Seluruh Malaysia (2001–2005)* [*A Study of the Implementation and Enforcement of Maintenance Orders in Syariah Courts in Malaysia (2001–2005)*]. Kuala Lumpur: IIUM Entrepreneurship & Consultancies Sdn. Bhd. Dengan Kerjasama Jabatan Kehakiman Syariah Malaysia.

Iqbal, Walid. 2001. "Courts, Lawyering, and ADR: Glimpses into the Islamic Tradition." *Fordham Urban Law Journal* 28: 1035–45.

Jewell, Elizabeth, and Frank Abate, eds. 2001. *The New Oxford American Dictionary.* Oxford: Oxford University Press.

Johnson, Penny. 2004. "Agents for Reform: The Women's Movement, Social Politics, and Family Law Reform." In *Women's Rights and Islamic Family Law: Perspectives on Reform,* edited by Lynn Welchman. London: Zed.

Jomo K. S., ed. 1995. *Privatizing Malaysia: Rents, Rhetoric, Realities.* Boulder, CO: Westview Press.

Jomo Kwame Sundaram and Wee Chong Hui. 2014. *Malaysia @50: Economic Development, Distribution, Disparities.* Petaling Jaya: Strategic Information and Research Development Centre.

Jones, Carla. 2010. "Materializing Piety: Gendered Anxieties About Faithful Consumption in Contemporary Urban Indonesia." *American Ethnologist* 37, no. 4: 617–637.

Jones, Leroy, and Fadil Azim Abbas. 1994. "Sports Toto Malaysia." In *Welfare Consequences of Selling Public Enterprises: An Empirical Analysis,* edited by Ahmed Galal, Leroy Jones, Pankaj Tandon, and Ingo Vogelsang. New York: Oxford University Press.

Juergensmeyer, Mark. 2003. *Terror in the Mind of God: The Global Rise of Religious Violence,* 3rd ed. Berkeley: University of California Press.

Just, Peter. 2001. *Dou Donggo Justice: Conflict and Morality in an Indonesian Society*. Lanham, MD: Rowman and Littlefield.

Kafka, Franz. 1925. *The Trial*. New York: Penguin/Random House.

Kamali, Mohammad Hashim. 1991. *Principles of Islamic Jurisprudence*. Cambridge: Islamic Texts Society.

———. 2000. *Islamic Law in Malaysia: Issues and Developments*. Kuala Lumpur: Ilmiah Publishers.

Kandiyoti, Deniz. 1991. "Introduction." In *Women, Islam, and the State*, edited by Deniz Kandiyoti. Hong Kong: Temple University Press.

Kepel, Gilles. 2002. *Jihad: The Trail of Political Islam*. Cambridge, MA: Harvard University Press.

Kessler, Clive. 2008. "Islam, the State and Desecularization in Malaysia: The Islamist Trajectory During the Badawi Years." In *Sharing the Nation: Faith, Difference, Power, and the State 50 Years after Merdeka*, edited by Norani Othman, Mavis Puthucheary, and Clive Kessler. Petaling Jaya: Strategic Information and Development Research Centre.

King, Ross. 2008. *Kuala Lumpur and Putrajaya: Negotiating Urban Space in Malaysia*. Singapore: National University of Singapore Press.

Klein, Naomi. 2009. *No Logo*. 10th Anniversary Edition. New York: Picador.

Kloos, David. 2018. *Becoming Better Muslims: Religious Authority and Ethical Improvement in Aceh, Indonesia*. Princeton, NJ: Princeton University Press.

Kraince, Richard. 2009. "Reforming Islamic Education in Malaysia: Doctrine or Dialogue?" In *Making Modern Muslims: The Politics of Islamic Education in Southeast Asia*, edited by Robert W. Hefner. Honolulu: University of Hawai'i Press.

Kugle, Scott Siraj al-Haqq. 2010. *Homosexuality in Islam: Critical Reflections on Gay, Lesbian, and Transgender Muslims*. Oxford: Oneworld.

Lambek, Michael. 2010. "Introduction." In *Ordinary Ethics: Anthropology, Language, and Action*, edited by Michael Lambek. New York: Fordham University Press.

Lancaster, Roger. 2011. *Sex Panic and the Punitive State*. Berkeley: University of California Press.

Lander, Mark. 2017. "Trump Welcomes Najib Razak, the Malaysian Leader, as President, and Owner of a Fine Hotel." *New York Times*, September 12.

Latour, Bruno. 2005. *Reassembling the Social: An Introduction to Actor-Network-Theory*. Oxford: Oxford University Press.

———. 2010. *The Making of Law: An Ethnography of the Conseil D'État*. Cambridge: Polity Press.

Lee, Julian. 2010. *Islamization and Activism in Malaysia*. Singapore: Institute of Southeast Asian Studies.

Lévi-Strauss, Claude. 1962. *Totemism*. Boston: Beacon Press.

———. 1966. *The Savage Mind*. Chicago: University of Chicago Press.

Li, Tania M. 2007. *The Will to Improve: Governmentality, Development, and the Practice of Politics*. Durham, NC: Duke University Press.

Lianos, Michalis, with Mary Douglas. 2000. "Dangerization and the End of Deviance: The Institutional Environment." In *Criminology and Social Theory*, edited by David Garland and Richard Sparks. New York: Oxford University Press.

Lim, P. G. 2008. "The Growth and Use of Mediation Throughout the World: Recent Developments in Mediation/Conciliation Among Common Law and Non-Common Law Jurisdictions in Asia." *The Malayan Law Journal* 4: 105–12.

Lindsey, Tim. 2018. "Jokowi's Deputy Pick Confirms Rise of Conservative Islam in Indonesia," *Pearls and Irritations,* August 17. https://johnmenadue.com/tim-lindsey-jokowis-deputy-pick-confirms-rise-of-conservative-islam-in-indonesia.

Liow, Joseph. 2009. *Piety and Politics: Islamism in Contemporary Malaysia.* Oxford: Oxford University Press.

Lombardi, Clark B. 2006. *State Law as Islamic Law in Modern Egypt: The Incorporation of the Shari'a into Egyptian Constitutional Law.* Leiden: Brill.

Long, Nicholas. 2013. *Being Malay in Indonesia: Histories, Hopes, and Citizenship in the Riau Archipelago.* Singapore: National University of Singapore.

Luhrmann, Tanya M. 2012. *When God Talks Back: Understanding the American Evangelical Relationship with God.* New York: Knopf.

Lurie, Allison. 1981. *The Language of Clothes.* New York: Vintage/Random House.

Mackinnon, Ian. 2011. "Explicit Islamic Sex Manual Encourages Group Sex." *The Telegraph,* October 14.

Mahathir Mohamad. 2011. *A Doctor in the House: The Memoirs of Tun Dr. Mahathir Mohamad.* Kuala Lumpur: MPH Publishers.

Mahmood, Saba. 2005. *The Politics of Piety: The Islamic Revival and the Feminist Subject.* Princeton, NJ: Princeton University Press.

———. 2012. "Sectarian Conflict and Family Law in Contemporary Egypt." *American Ethnologist* 39, no. 1: 54–62.

Makdisi, George. 1985–1986. "The Guilds of Law in Medieval Legal History: An Inquiry Into the Origins of the Inns of Court." *Cleveland State Law Review* 34, no. 3: 3–18.

Makdisi, John. 1999. "The Islamic Origins of the Common Law." *North Carolina Law Review* 77: 1635–1739.

Mamdani, Mahmood. 2004. *Good Muslim, Bad Muslim: America, the Cold War, and the Roots of Terror.* New York: Pantheon.

Marcus, George, and Erkan Saka. 2006. "Assemblage." *Theory, Culture, and Society* 23, no. 2–3: 101–106.

Marsden, Magnus. 2005. *Living Islam: Muslim Religious Experience in Pakistan's North-West Frontier.* Cambridge: Cambridge University Press.

Mashhour, Amira. 2005. "Islamic Law and Gender Equality—Could There Be a Common Ground? A Study of Divorce and Polygamy in Sharia Law and Contemporary Legislation in Tunisia and Egypt." *Human Rights Quarterly* 27: 562–97.

Massoud, Mark Fathi. 2013. *Law's Fragile State: Colonial, Authoritarian, and Humanitarian Legacies in Sudan.* New York: Cambridge University Press.

Maznah Mohamad. 2010a. "Making Majority, Undoing Family: Law, Religion, and the Islamization of the State in Malaysia." *Economy and Society* 39: 360–84.

———. 2010b. "The Ascendance of Bureaucratic Islam and the Secularization of the Sharia in Malaysia." *Pacific Affairs* 83, no. 3: 505–24.

Mazzarella, William. 2003. *Shoveling Smoke: Advertising and Globalization in Contemporary India.* Durham, NC: Duke University Press.

————. 2006. "Internet X-Ray: E-Governance, Transparency, and the Politics of Immediation in India." *Public Culture* 18, no. 3: 473–505.

Merry, Sally E. 1990. *Getting Justice and Getting Even: Legal Consciousness Among Working Class Americans.* Chicago: University of Chicago Press.

Messick, Brinkley. 1992. *The Calligraphic State: Textual Domination and History in a Muslim Society.* Berkeley: University of California Press.

Milner, Anthony. 1983. "Islam and the Muslim State." In *Islam in South-East Asia,* edited by M. B. Hooker. Leiden: E. J. Brill.

Mir-Hosseini, Ziba. 2000. *Marriage on Trial: Islamic Family Law in Iran and Morocco.* Rev. ed. London: I. B. Taurus.

————. 2016. "Moral Contestations and Patriarchal Ethics: Women Challenging the Justice of Muslim Family Laws." In *Shari'a Law and Modern Muslim Ethics,* edited by Robert W. Hefner. Bloomington: Indiana University Press.

————, Mulki Al-Sharmani, and Jana Rumminger, eds. 2015. *Men in Charge? Rethinking Authority in Muslim Legal Tradition.* London: Oneworld.

Mohamad Tajuddin Mohamad Rasdi. 2005. *Malaysian Architecture: Crisis Within.* Kuala Lumpur: Utusan Publications and Distributors Sdn. Bhd.

————. 2010. *Rethinking Islamic Architecture.* Petaling Jaya: Strategic Information and Research Development Centre.

Mohamed Nawab Mohamed Osman. 2017. "The Islamic Conservative Turn in Malaysia: Impact and Future Trajectories." *Contemporary Islam* 11: 1–20.

Mohd Faizal Musa and tan beng hui. 2017. "State-Backed Discrimination Against Shia Muslims in Malaysia." *Critical Asian Studies* 49, no. 3: 308–29.

Moore, Sally Falk. 1978. *Law as Process: An Anthropological Approach.* London: Routledge and Kegan Paul.

Moustafa, Tamir. 2007. *The Struggle for Constitutional Power: Law, Politics, and Economic Development in Egypt.* Cambridge: Cambridge University Press.

————. 2018. *Constituting Religion: Islam, Liberal Rights, and the Malaysian State.* Cambridge: Cambridge University Press.

Muehlebach, Andrea. 2012. *The Moral Neoliberal: Welfare and Citizenship in Italy.* Chicago: University of Chicago Press.

Muhammad Rais Abdul Karim and Nazariah Mohd Khalid. 2003. *E-Government in Malaysia.* Kuala Lumpur: Pelanduk Publications.

Mulcahy, Linda. 2011. *Legal Architecture: Justice, Due Process, and the Place of Law.* New York: Routledge.

Müller, Dominik M. 2014. *Islam, Politics and Youth in Malaysia: The Pop-Islamist Reinvention of PAS.* New York: Routledge.

Muzaffar, Chandra. 1979. *Protector?* Penang: Aliran.

————. 1987. *Islamic Resurgence in Malaysia.* Kuala Lumpur: Fajar Bakti.

Muzellec, Laurent, and Mary Lambkin. 2006. "Corporate Rebranding: Destroying, Transferring, or Creating Brand Equity?" *European Journal of Marketing* 40, no. 7/8: 803–24.

Nadaraj, Vanitha. 2013. "Reinventing RELA: Malaysia's Volunteer Cops Moving with the Times." *The Establishment Post,* November 27.

Nader, Laura. 2002. *The Life of the Law: Anthropological Projects*. Berkeley: University of California Press.

Nagarajan, S. 2008. "Indians in Malaysia: Towards Vision 2020." In *Rising India and Indian Communities in East Asia,* edited by K. Kesavapany, A. Mani, and P. Ramasamy. Singapore: Institute of Southeast Asian Studies.

Nagata, Judith. 1984. *The Reflowering of Malaysian Islam: Modern Religious Radicals and Their Roots*. Vancouver: University of British Columbia Press.

Najibah M. Zin. 2012. "The Training, Appointment, and Supervision of Islamic Judges in Malaysia," in "Islamic Law and Islamic Legal Professionals in Southeast Asia," special issue, *Pacific Rim Law and Policy Journal* 21, no. 1: 115–31.

Najmabadi, Afsaneh. 2005. *Women with Moustaches, Men Without Beards: Gender and Sexual Anxieties of Iranian Modernity*. Berkeley: University of California Press.

———. 2014. *Professing Selves: Transsexuality and Same-Sex Desire in Contemporary Iran*. Durham, NC: Duke University Press.

Nasir, Mohamad Abdun. 2013. *Islamic Law and Social Change: The Religious Court and the Dissolution of Marriage Among Muslims in Lombok, Indonesia*. PhD diss., Emory University.

Newfield, Christopher. 2007. "Corporation." In *Keywords for American Cultural Studies,* edited by Bruce Burgett and Glenn Hendler. New York: New York University Press.

Ng Cheng Yee. 2010. "Don't Sideline Women Judges, Syariah Court Told." *The Star,* July 16.

Nik Noriani Nik Badli Shah. 2008. "Legislative Provisions and Judicial Mechanisms for the Enforcement and Termination of the Islamic Marriage Contract in Malaysia." In *The Islamic Marriage Contract: Case Studies in Islamic Family Law,* edited by Asifa Quraishi and Frank Vogel. Cambridge, MA: Islamic Legal Studies Program, Harvard Law School, Harvard University Press.

Nonini, Donald. 1998. "Chinese Society, Coffee-Shop Talk, Possessing Gods: The Politics of Public Space Among Diasporic Chinese in Malaysia." *Positions* 6, no. 2: 439–73.

———. 2015. *"Getting By": Class and State Formation among Chinese in Malaysia*. Ithaca, NY: Cornell University Press.

Noraini Mohd Noor, Jamil Farooqui, Ahmad Abd. Al-Rahim Nasr, Hazizan Bin Md. Noon, and Shukran Abdul Rahman. 2005. *Sexual Identity: Effeminacy Among University Students*. Kuala Lumpur: International Islamic University Malaysia.

Norani Othman. 2008. "Religion, Citizen Rights and Gender Justice: Women, Islamization and the Shari'a in Malaysia Since the 1980s." In *Sharing the Nation: Faith, Difference, Power and the State 50 Years After Merdeka,* edited by Norani Othman et al. Petaling Jaya: Strategic Information and Research Development Centre.

———, ed. 2005. *Muslim Women and the Challenge of Islamic Extremism*. Kuala Lumpur: Sisters in Islam.

———, Zainah Anwar, and Zaitun Mohamed Kasim. 2005. "Malaysia: Islamization, Muslim Politics, and State Authoritarianism." In *Muslim Women and the Challenge of Islamic Extremism,* edited by Norani Othman. Kuala Lumpur: Sisters in Islam.

———, Mavis Puthucheary, and Clive Kessler, eds. 2008. *Sharing the Nation: Faith, Difference, Power and the State 50 Years After Merdeka*. Petaling Jaya: Strategic Information and Research Development Centre.

Norzulaili Mohd Ghazali and Wan Abdul Fattah Wan Ismail. 2007. *Nusyuz, Shiqaq, dan Hakam Menurut Al-Quran, Sunah, dan Undang-Undang Keluarga* Islam [Spousal Disobedience, Conjugal Dissension, and Mediation According to the Quran, the Actions and Sayings of the Prophet, and Islamic Family Law]. Nilai, Negeri Sembilan: Universiti Islam Malaysia.

Nurlaewati, Euis. 2010. *Modernization, Tradition, and Identity: The Kompilasi Hukum Islam and Legal Practice in Indonesian Religious Courts.* Amsterdam: Amsterdam University Press.

Okruhlik, Gwenn. 2005. "Empowering Civility Through Nationalism: Reformist Islam and Belonging in Saudi Arabia." In *Remaking Muslim Politics: Pluralism, Contestation, Democratization,* edited by Robert W. Hefner. Princeton, NJ: Princeton University Press.

Ong, Aihwa. 1987. *Spirits of Resistance and Capitalist Discipline: Factory Women in Malaysia.* Albany, NY: SUNY Press.

———. 1999. *Flexible Citizenship: The Cultural Logics of Transnationalism.* Durham, NC: Duke University Press.

———. 2003. *Buddha is Hiding: Refugees, Citizenship, the New America.* Berkeley: University of California Press.

———. 2006. *Neoliberalism as Exception: Mutations in Citizenship and Sovereignty.* Durham, NC: Duke University Press.

———, and Stephen J. Collier, eds. 2005. *Global Assemblages: Technology, Politics, and Ethics as Anthropological Problems.* Williston, VT: Blackwell.

Ortner, Sherry. 1973. "On Key Symbols." *American Anthropologist* 75, no. 5: 1338–46.

———. 2016. "Dark Anthropology and Its Others: Theory Since the Eighties." *Hau: Journal of Ethnographic Theory* 6, no. 1: 47–73.

Osanloo, Arzoo. 2009. *The Politics of Women's Rights in Iran.* Princeton, NJ: Princeton University Press.

Osella, Filippo, and Benjamin Soares, eds. 2010. *Islam, Politics, Anthropology.* Malden, MA: Wiley-Blackwell.

Osman Bakar. 2008. "Malaysian Islam in the Twenty-First Century: The Promise of a Democratic Transformation?" In *Asian Islam in the 21st Century,* edited by John Esposito, John Voll, and Osman Bakar. Oxford: Oxford University Press.

Otto, Jan Michiel, ed. 2010. *Sharia Incorporated: A Comparative Overview of the Legal Systems of Twelve Muslim Countries in Past and Present.* Leiden: Leiden University Press.

Pang Khee Teik. 2015. "Sexual Citizenship in Conflict." In *Routledge Handbook of Contemporary Malaysia,* edited by Meredith Weiss. New York: Routledge.

Peletz, Michael G. 1988. *A Share of the Harvest: Kinship, Property, and Social History Among the Malays of Rembau.* Berkeley: University of California Press.

———. 1996. *Reason and Passion: Representations of Gender in a Malay Society.* Berkeley: University of California Press.

———. 1997. "'Ordinary Muslims' and Muslim Resurgents in Contemporary Malaysia: Notes on an Ambivalent Relationship." In *Islam in an Era of Nation States: Politics and Religious Renewal in Muslim Southeast Asia,* edited by Robert W. Hefner. Honolulu: University of Hawai'i Press.

———. 2002. *Islamic Modern: Religious Courts and Cultural Politics in Malaysia.* Princeton, NJ: Princeton University Press.

———. 2005. "Islam and the Cultural Politics of Legitimacy: Malaysia in the Aftermath of September 11." In *Remaking Muslim Politics: Pluralism, Contestation, Democratization,* edited by Robert W. Hefner. Princeton, NJ: Princeton University Press.

———. 2009. *Gender Pluralism: Southeast Asia Since Early Modern Times.* New York: Routledge.

———. 2013. "Malaysia's *Syariah* Judiciary as Global Assemblage: Islamization, Corporatization, and Other Transformations in Context." *Comparative Studies in Society and History* 55, no. 3: 603–33.

———. 2015. "A Tale of Two Courts: Judicial Transformation and the Rise of a Corporate Islamic Governmentality in Malaysia." *American Ethnologist* 44: 144–60.

———. 2016. "Syariah, Inc.: Continuities, Transformations, and Cultural Politics in Malaysia's Islamic Judiciary." In *Shari'a Law and Modern Muslim Ethics,* edited by Robert W. Hefner. Bloomington: Indiana University Press.

———. 2018. "Are Women Getting (More) Justice? Malaysia's *Sharia* Judiciary in Ethnographic and Historical Perspective." *Law and Society Review* 52, no. 3: 652–84.

Pew Research Center. 2018. *Global Uptick in Government Restrictions on Religion in 2016.* https://www.pewforum.org/2018/06/21/global-uptick-in-government-restrictions-on-religion-in-2016.

Piotrowski, Daniel. 2018. "Exclusive—Confessions of a Mass Executioner: Notorious Malaysian Hangman Who Has Killed 130 Criminals Reveals Australian Grandmother Caught Smuggling Meth Will Be Given Just One Day's Notice Before She Is Put to Death." *Daily Mail,* June 1.

Powell, Richard, and Azirah Hashim. 2011. "Language Disadvantage in Malaysian Litigation and Arbitration." *World Englishes* 39, no. 1: 92–105.

Pratt, John, David Brown, Mark Brown, Simon Hallsworth, and Wayne Morrison, eds. 2005. *The New Punitiveness: Trends, Theories, Perspectives.* Portland, OR: Willan.

Puar, Jasbir. 2007. *Terrorist Assemblages: Homonationalism in Queer Times.* Durham, NC: Duke University Press.

Rabinow, Paul. 1999. *French DNA: Trouble in Purgatory.* Chicago: University of Chicago Press.

Raihanah Abdullah. 1997. "Reasons to Dissolve a Marriage Through *Fasakh.*" *Syariah Journal* 5, no. 1: 1–13.

Ramizah Wan Muhammad. 2008a. "The Theory and Practice of Sulh (Mediation) in the Malaysian Shariah Courts." *IIUM Law Journal* 16, no. 1: 33–50.

———. 2008b. "Women Judges in Islam and the Application in the Malaysian Shariah Court." *Shariah Law Reports* 3: 26–36.

Reid, Anthony. 1988. *Southeast Asia in the Age of Commerce, 1450–1680. Vol. 1: The Land Below the Winds.* New Haven, CT: Yale University Press.

———. 1993. *Southeast Asia in the Age of Commerce, 1450–1680. Vol. 2: Expansion and Crisis.* New Haven, CT: Yale University Press.

Ricklefs, M. C. 2012. *Islamisation and Its Opponents in Java, c. 1930 to the Present.* Singapore: National University of Singapore Press.

Rittich, Kerry. 2000–2001. "Who's Afraid of *The Critique of Adjudication?*: Tracing the Discourse of Law in Development." *Cardozo Law Review* 22: 929–45.

Robbins, Joel. 2013. "Beyond the Suffering Subject: Toward an Anthropology of the Good." *Journal of the Royal Anthropological Institute* (N.S.) 19: 447–62.

Rodinson, Maxime. 1988. *Europe and the Mystique of Islam.* New York: I. B. Tauris.

Roff, William. 1967. *The Origins of Malay Nationalism.* Kuala Lumpur: University of Malaya Press.

Rosen, Lawrence. 1989. *The Anthropology of Justice: Law as Culture in Islamic Society.* Cambridge: Cambridge University Press.

———. 2018. *Islam and the Rule of Justice: Image and Reality in Muslim Law and Culture.* Chicago: University of Chicago Press.

Roslina Mohamad. 2010. "Syariah Breakthrough." *The Star,* July 5.

Rubin, Gayle. 1984. "Thinking Sex: Notes for a Radical Theory of the Politics of Sexuality." In *Pleasure and Danger: Exploring Female Sexuality,* edited by C. Vance. New York: Routledge and Kegan Paul.

Rudnyckyj, Daromir. 2010. *Spiritual Economies: Islam, Globalization, and the Afterlife of Development.* Ithaca, NY: Cornell University Press.

Ruskola, Teemu. 2013. *Legal Orientalism: China, the United States, and Modern Law.* Cambridge, MA: Harvard University Press.

Salim, Arskal. 2008. *Challenging the Secular State: The Islamization of Law in Modern Indonesia.* Honolulu: University of Hawai'i Press.

Sa'odah binti Ahmad. 2010. *The Effectiveness of Mediation and Sulh in Resolving Family Disputes: A Study of Parties' Satisfaction with Sulh in the State of Selangor.* PhD diss., International Islamic University of Malaysia.

Sangerman, Diane. 2005. "Rewriting Divorce in Egypt: Reclaiming Islam, Legal Activism, and Coalition Politics." In *Remaking Muslim Politics: Pluralism, Contestation, Democratization,* edited by Robert W. Hefner. Princeton, NJ: Princeton University Press.

Sassen, Saskia. 2008. *Territory, Authority, Rights: From Medieval to Global Assemblages,* updated edition. Princeton, NJ: Princeton University Press.

Schielke, Samuli. 2015. *Egypt in the Future Tense: Hope, Frustration, and Ambivalence Before and After 2011.* Bloomington: Indiana University Press.

Schmitz, Jason. 2005. "Ambush Marketing: The Off-Field Competition at the Olympic Games." *Northwestern Journal of Technology and Intellectual Property* 3, no. 2: 203–8.

Schulte Nordholt, Henk. 1997. "Introduction." In *Outward Appearances: Dressing Society and State in Indonesia,* edited by Henk Schulte Nordholt. Leiden: KITLV.

Schulz, Dorothea. 2012. *Muslims and New Media in West Africa: Pathways to God.* Bloomington: Indiana University Press.

Scott, James C. 1985. *Weapons of the Weak: Everyday Forms of Peasant Resistance.* New Haven, CT: Yale University Press.

———. 1990. *Domination and the Arts of Resistance: Hidden Transcripts.* New Haven, CT: Yale University Press.

———. 1998. *Seeing Like a State: How Certain Schemes to Improve the Human Condition Have Failed.* New Haven, CT: Yale University Press.

Sekimoto, Teruo. 1997. "Uniforms and Concrete Walls: Dressing the Village Under the New Order in the 1970s and 1980s." In *Outward Appearances: Dressing Society and State in Indonesia,* edited by Henk Schulte Nordholt. Leiden: KITLV.

Shaikh, Farzana. 2007. "The Shariatization of Pakistani Nationalism." Occasional Paper No. 29, School of Social Science, Institute for Advanced Study (IAS). Princeton, NJ: IAS.

Shamsul A. B. 2001. "Shadow of Afghan War." *Economic and Political Weekly*, December 22, 4708–09.

Shanon Shah. 2018. *The Making of a Gay Muslim: Religion, Sexuality, and Identity in Malaysia and Britain*. London: Palgrave-Macmillan.

Sharifah Zaleha Syed Hassan. 1986. "Women, Divorce, and Islam in Kedah." *Sojourn* 1:183–98.

———. 1989. "Versions of Eternal Truth: Ulama and Religious Dissenters in Kedah Malay Society." *Contributions to Southeast Asian Ethnography* 8: 43–69.

———. 1993. "Settling Marital Disputes in a *Syariah* Court in Malaysia." *Jurnal Antropologi dan Sosiologi* 20: 73–90.

———, and Sven Cederroth. 1997. *Managing Marital Disputes in Malaysia: Islamic Mediators and Conflict Resolution in the Syariah Courts*. Richmond, Surrey: Curzon Press.

Sharp, Jeremy M. 2018. "Egypt: Background and U.S. Relations." Washington, D.C.: Congressional Research Service.

Shryock, Andrew, ed. 2010. *Islamophobia/Islamophilia: Beyond the Politics of Enemy and Friend*. Bloomington: Indiana University Press.

Siti Farhanah binti Md Sam and Puzziawati Ab Ghani. n.d. "Determinants of Divorce Among Women in Malaysia." Unpublished ms.

Siti Zubaidah Ismail, Ilhaamie Abdul Ghani Azmi, and Zulfikri Yasoa. n.d. "Justice Delayed is Justice Denied? Delays in Disposing Divorce Cases in Malaysian Shariah Court." Unpublished ms.

Sloane-White, Patricia. 2017. *Corporate Islam: Sharia and the Modern Workplace*. Cambridge: Cambridge University Press.

Smith-Hefner, Nancy. 2007. "Javanese Women and the Veil in Post-Soeharto-Indonesia." *Journal of Asian Studies* 66: 389–420.

Soares, Benjamin, and Filippo Osella. 2009. "Islam, Politics, Anthropology." *Journal of the Royal Anthropological Institute* (N.S.) 15, S1: S1-S23.

Sonneveld, Nadia. 2012. *Khul Divorce in Egypt: Public Debates, Judicial Practices, and Everyday Life*. Cairo: American University in Cairo Press.

———, and Monika Lindbekk. 2015. "A Revolution in Muslim Family Law? Egypt's Pre- and Post-Revolutionary Period (2011–2013) Compared." *New Middle Eastern Studies* 5: 1–19.

The Star. 2006. "Mediation Reduces Backlog." December 28.

———. 2013a. "Nik Aziz Denies He Wants *Ulama* to be PAS Deputy Prime Minister." September 12.

———. 2013b. "Zahid Defends Statement on Shooting Suspected Criminals." October 10.

The Star Online. 2012. "Ex-Wife Wants Taib's Son to Pay RM121 mil in Maintenance." December 20.

———. 2018. "Duo in Lesbian Sex Case Whipped Six Times at Terengganu Syariah High Court." September 4.

Starrett, Gregory. 2010. "The Varieties of Secular Experience." *Comparative Studies in Society and History* 52, no. 3: 626–51.

Strathern, Marilyn. 2005. *Kinship, Law, and the Unexpected: Relatives Are Always a Surprise*. Cambridge: Cambridge University Press.

———, ed. 2000. *Audit Cultures: Anthropological Studies in Accountability, Ethics, and the Academy*. London: Routledge.

Sullivan, Winnifred F. 2005. *The Impossibility of Religious Freedom*. Princeton, NJ: Princeton University Press.

———, Robert Yelle, and Mateo Taussig-Rubbo, eds. 2011. *After Secular Law*. Stanford. CA: Stanford University Press.

Sunday Star. 2010. "First Syariah Women Judges." July 4.

———. 2013a. "*Rakan* Cop to Get Year-End Facelift." September 22.

———. 2013b."1,500 Syiah Practitioners Identified Across the Country." December 15.

Syed Ahmad Syed Hussein et al., trans. 1994. *Fiqh dan Perundangan Islam* [Islamic Jurisprudence and Interpretation]. Translation of Wahba Mustafa al-Zuhayli's *al-Fiqh al Islami wa Adillataha*. Kuala Lumpur: Dewan Bahasa dan Pustaka.

Syed Azhar and Qishin Tariq. 2013. "'Keep Aurat Covered' Zone: Male Civil Servants at Kelantan Govt Complex Now Included in Circular." *The Star*, October 3.

Syed Khalid Rashid. 2008. "Peculiarities and Religious Underlining of ADR in Islamic Law." Paper presented at Conference on Mediation in the Asia Pacific: Constraints and Challenges. IIUM, Kuala Lumpur, June 16–18.

Tan, Jeff. 2007. *Privatization in Malaysia: Regulation, Rent-Seeking, and Policy Failure*. London: Routledge.

tan beng hui. 1999. "Women's Sexuality and the Discourse on Asian Values." In *Female Desires: Same-Sex Relations and Transgender Practices Across Cultures*, edited by Evelyn Blackwood and Saskia Wieringa. New York: Columbia University Press.

———. 2012. *Sexuality, Islam, and Politics in Malaysia: A Study on the Shifting Strategies of Regulation*. PhD diss., National University of Singapore.

Taylor, Jean Gelman. 1997. "Costume and Gender in Colonial Java, 1800–1940." In *Outward Appearances: Dressing Society and State in Indonesia*, edited by Henk Schulte Nordholt. Leiden: KITLV.

Temporal, Paul. 2011. *Islamic Branding and Marketing: Creating a Global Islamic Business*. Singapore: John Wiley and Sons (Asia) Pte. Ltd.

Terdiman, Richard. 1987. "Translator's Introduction" [to Pierre Bourdieu's "The Force of Law"]. *The Hastings Law Journal* 38: 805–13.

Thoreau, Henry David. 1854 [1997]. *Walden; or, Life in the Woods, with an Introduction and Annotations by Bill McKibben*. Boston: Beacon.

Tsing, Anna. 2015. *The Mushroom at the End of the World: On the Possibility of Life in Capitalist Ruins*. Princeton, NJ: Princeton University Press.

Tucker, Judith. 2008. *Women, Family, and Gender in Islamic Law*. Cambridge: Cambridge University Press.

Utusan [Malaysia] Online. 2011. "Mahkamah Syariah KL di Bangunan Baru." October 27.

Veblen, Thorstein. 1899. *The Theory of the Leisure Class: An Economic Study of Institutions*. New York: Macmillan.

Vogel, Frank. 2011. "Saudi Arabia: Public, Civil, and Individual Shari'a in Law and Politics." In *Shari'a Politics: Islamic Law and Society in the Modern World*, edited by Robert W. Hefner. Bloomington: Indiana University Press.

Volpi, Frederik. 2010. *Political Islam Observed*. Oxford: Oxford University Press.

Wacquant, Loïc J.D. 1992. "Preface." In *An Invitation to Reflexive Sociology*, by Pierre Bourdieu and Loïc J. D. Wacquant. Chicago: University of Chicago Press.

———. 2009. *Punishing the Poor: The Neoliberal Government of Social Insecurity.* Durham, NC: Duke University Press.

Wadud, Amina. 2008. *Inside the Gender Jihad: Women's Reform in Islam.* Oxford: Oneworld.

Walsh, Declan. 2017. "Egyptian Concertgoers Wave a Flag, and Land in Jail for Promoting Homosexuality." *New York Times,* September 27.

Wan Mohd. Nor Wan Daud. 1998. *The Educational Philosophy and Practice of Syed Mohammad Naquib Al-Attas: An Exposition of the Original Concept of Islamization.* Kuala Lumpur: ISTAC.

Wardlow, Holly, and Jennifer Hirsch. 2006. "Introduction." In *Modern Loves: The Anthropology of Romantic Courtship and Companionate Marriage,* edited by Jennifer Hirsch and Holly Wardlow. Ann Arbor: University of Michigan Press.

Weber, Max. 1925 [1968]. *Economy and Society: An Outline of Interpretive Sociology* (2 vols.), edited by Guenther Roth and Claus Wittich. Berkeley: University of California Press.

Weiss, Meredith. 2006. *Protest and Possibilities: Civil Society and Coalitions for Political Change in Malaysia.* Stanford, CA: Stanford University Press.

Welsh, Bridget. 2008. "New Identities, New Politics: Malaysia's Muslim Professionals." *National Bureau of Asian Research* 18, no. 3: 35–51.

———. 2013. "Abdullah Badawi's Quiet Revolution in Political Institutions." In *Awakening: The Abdullah Badawi Years in Malaysia,* edited by Bridget Welsh and James Chin. Petaling Jaya: Strategic Information and Development Centre.

Whiting, Amanda. 2008. "Descularizing Malaysian Law?" In *Examining Practice, Interrogating Theory: Comparative Legal Studies in Asia,* edited by Penelope (Pip) Nicholson and Sarah Biddulph. Leiden: Martinus Nijhoff.

———. 2010. "Secularism, the Islamic State and the Malaysian Legal Profession." *Asian Journal of Comparative Law* 5, no. 1, Article 10: 1–34.

———. 2011. "Political Struggles and Practical Ethics: A History of Malaysian Lawyers and Lawyering." Paper presented at the Workshop on Law and Society in Malaysia: Pluralism, Islam, and Development. Victoria, British Columbia, July 14–17.

———. 2012. "The Training, Appointment, and Supervision of Islamic Lawyers in the Federal Territories of Malaysia," in "Islamic Law and Islamic Legal Professionals in Southeast Asia," special issue, *Pacific Rim Law and Policy Journal* 21, no. 1: 133–61.

———. 2017. "Rebooting the Emergency: Najib's Law 'Reform' and the Normalisation of Crisis." In *Illusions of Democracy: Malaysian Politics and People,* vol. 2, edited by Sophie Lemière Kuala Lumpur: SIRD.

Wickham, Carrie. 2013. *The Muslim Brotherhood: Evolution of an Islamist Movement.* Princeton, NJ: Princeton University Press.

Willford, Andrew. 2006. *Cage of Freedom: Tamil Identity and the Ethnic Fetish in Malaysia.* Ann Arbor, MI: University of Michigan Press.

———. 2014. *Tamils and the Haunting of Justice: History and Recognition in Malaysia's Plantations.* Honolulu: University of Hawai'i Press.

Williams, Raymond. 1982. "The Politics of Nuclear Disarmament." In *Exterminism and Cold War,* edited by the *New Left Review.* London: Verso.

Yeang, Ken. 1992. *The Architecture of Malaysia.* Amsterdam/Kuala Lumpur: Pepin Press.

Yegar, Moshe. 1979. *Islam and Islamic Institutions in British Malaya, 1874–1941: Policies and Implementation.* Jerusalem: Magnes Press.

Zain Abdullah. 2014. "The Influence of Islamic Architecture on Colonial Buildings in Malaysia." https://tinyurl.com/IslamicArchMalay.

Zainah Anwar. 2001. "What Islam, Whose Islam? Sisters in Islam and the Struggle for Women's Rights." In *The Politics of Multiculturalism: Pluralism and Citizenship in Malaysia, Singapore, and Indonesia,* edited by Robert W. Hefner. Honolulu: University of Hawai'i Press.

———. 2008. "Advocacy for Reform in Islamic Family Law: The Experience of Sisters in Islam." In *The Islamic Marriage Contract: Case Studies in Islamic Family Law,* edited by Asifa Quraishi and Frank Vogel. Cambridge, MA: Islamic Legal Studies Program, Harvard Law School, Harvard University Press.

———, ed. 2009. *Wanted: Equality and Justice in the Muslim Family.* Petaling Jaya: Musawah/Sisters in Islam.

Zaman, Muhammad Qasim. 2016. "Islamic Modernism, Ethics, and Shari'a in Pakistan." In *Shar'ia Law and Modern Muslim Ethics,* edited by Robert W. Hefner. Bloomington: Indiana University Press.

Zeghal, Malika. 2013. "The Implicit Sharia: Established Religion and Varieties of Secularism in Tunisia." In *Varieties of Religious Establishment,* edited by Winnifred Fallers Sullivan and Lori G. Beaman. New York: Routledge.

Zuern, John. 2010. "Mind Your Own Business: Cisco Systems in the Power/Knowledge Network." In *Cultural Critique and the Global Corporation,* edited by Purnima Bose and Laura Lyons. Bloomington: Indiana University Press.

SELECTED STATUTES CITED

Administration of Islamic Law (Federal Territories) Act 1993 (Act 505) and Rules
Islamic Family Law (Federal Territories) Act 1984 (Act 303)
Islamic Family Law (Negeri Sembilan) Enactment 2003
Syariah Court Civil Procedure (Federal Territories) Act 1998 (Act 585) and Rules
Syariah Court Evidence (Federal Territories) Act 1997 [Act 561]
Syariah Criminal (Negeri Sembilan) Enactment 1992
Syariah Criminal Offenses (Federal Territories) Act 1997 [Act 559]
Syariah Criminal Procedure (Federal Territories) Act 1997 [Act 560]

INDEX

Founded in 1893,
UNIVERSITY OF CALIFORNIA PRESS
publishes bold, progressive books and journals
on topics in the arts, humanities, social sciences,
and natural sciences—with a focus on social
justice issues—that inspire thought and action
among readers worldwide.

The UC PRESS FOUNDATION
raises funds to uphold the press's vital role
as an independent, nonprofit publisher, and
receives philanthropic support from a wide
range of individuals and institutions—and from
committed readers like you. To learn more, visit
ucpress.edu/supportus.

www.ingramcontent.com/pod-product-compliance
Lightning Source LLC
Chambersburg PA
CBHW020502270326
41926CB00008B/705